Communists in Harlem during the Depression

Communists in Harlem during the Depression

MARK NAISON

GROVE PRESS, INC. / NEW YORK

Copyright © 1983 by the Board of Trustees of the University of Illinois
Reprinted by arrangement with the University of Illinois Press

First Evergreen Edition 1984
First Printing 1984
ISBN: 0-394-62301-0
Library of Congress Catalog Card Number: 84-48112

Library of Congress Cataloging in Publication Data

Naison, Mark, 1946–
   Communists in Harlem during the depression.

   Reprint. Originally published: Urbana: University of Illinois
Press, c1983. (Blacks in the New World)
   Bibliography: p.
   Includes index.

   1. Communist Party of the United States of America –
History.   2. Communism – New York (N.Y.) – History.   3.
Depressions – 1929–United States.   4. Harlem (New York,
N.Y.) – History.   I. Title.   II. Series: Blacks in the New
World.

JK2391.C53N56 1984   324.273′75′09   84-48112
ISBN 0-394-62301-0 (soft)

Printed in the United States of America

GROVE PRESS, INC. / 196 West Houston Street, New York, N.Y. 10014

To Elizabeth Phillips and Nettie Zachary

Contents

PART THREE

Acknowledgments

This book has been a long time coming. Begun in the late '60s, it has gone through many stages as the political climate—and my life—have changed. In my evolution from student activist to college professor, this book has been the one thread of continuity. In working on it, I kept touch with a precious legacy of my '60s experience—a belief that racial barriers can be overcome, and that people of different racial backgrounds can live and work in friendship and solidarity. To some, this viewpoint may be utopian, but my research on Communist racial policies in the '30s continually reaffirmed my sense that "the impossible is possible" and helped keep my idealism alive in a time of conservative ascendancy and "declining expectations."

This book has benefited from the generous help and inspiration of people of different generations and political backgrounds. My first debt is to Nettie Zachary, my partner and friend during the tumultuous years of the late '60s and early '70s. In forging a friendship with her, I learned first hand how much racial prejudice shaped the outlook and political behavior of most Americans, and also how much people could change if they had the will and courage to do so.

My next debt is to Paul Buhle, my editor at *Radical America,* who encouraged me to keep working on this subject when I had little patience for scholarship, and who kept my confidence up by publishing everything I sent him, no matter how bad. Through the years, he's been my biggest cheerleader and most astute critic. If I've become a serious historian, it's in large part due to his influence.

Thanks is also due to many veterans of the 1930s Communist Party, who opened their lives and archives to me because they believed that I would give them an opportunity to speak about a part of their lives that had been consistently misrepresented and distorted. Abner Berry, Theodore Bassett, and Harry Haywood, in particular, gave unstintingly of their time, but this book could also not have been written without the help of Sam Coleman, William Patterson, Herbert Aptheker, Louise

Thompson, Abe Shtob, Alice Citron, Audley Moore, James Allen, James Jackson, George Charney, Morris Schappes, Edith Segal, Solomon Harper, Max Gordon, Richard Moore, William Weinstone, Jibby Needleman, and Howard Johnson.

I was also fortunate enough to have excellent and supportive mentors at Columbia Graduate School, where this project began as a dissertation. James Shenton, Nathan Huggins, and Eric Foner gave freely of their time and energy to impart greater clarity to my writing and thinking, and provided needed emotional support when I was making the transition from "the movement" back to academia.

I also benefited from the generosity and critical intelligence of many scholars working in black history and the history of American radicalism. Mark Solomon gave me access to his dissertation, helped me locate interview subjects and documentary sources, and provided trenchant criticism of my writings. Ernie Allen read through my work on the early '20s and helped me understand the complex interplay between the Garvey movement and the first generation of black Communists. Eric Perkins helped me understand the strength of black nationalism and the role of communal institutions and kinship networks in shaping black political behavior. Ken Waltzer gave me insight into the role of ethnic considerations in shaping third-party activity in New York City. Max Gordon helped refine my analysis of the relationship between left-wing trade unions and the black community. And Eugene Genovese, Herbert Gutman, Jim O'Brien, and Molly Nolan read through the manuscript in its dissertation form and gave me excellent suggestions about what was needed to make it a strong book.

Officials at Fordham University, where I have taught for the last twelve years, have given this project their enthusiastic support. Without the faculty fellowship, and the two leaves of absence they granted me, I would never have been able to complete my research. My chairman and friend, Claude Mangum, consistently encouraged me in my scholarly aspirations even when the pressures of running a black studies department were most intense, and offered helpful criticism of my manuscript at its various stages of development.

A grant from the American Council of Learned Societies helped this project along at a critical point.

I was also fortunate enough to have extraordinarily energetic and demanding guidance from August Meier, the Vince Lombardi of editors. Augie drove me mercilessly, forcing me to consult sources I would have never looked at, to clarify inconsistencies I would have overlooked, and to make analytical leaps I would have otherwise avoided. Augie believed in me enough to push me to my limits.

To my wife, Elizabeth Phillips, no thanks are fully adequate. A brilliant editor, an astute critic, and a supportive political comrade, Liz read through every phase of this work from the dissertation on ard helped improve its clarity, consistency, and political impact. Her encouragement kept me going when I was ready to throw in the towel, and her firm but loving influence invested our household with a sense of shared purpose that made this work more meaningful.

To my children, Sara and Eric Naison-Phillips, thanks is due for their patience, good humor, and joie de vivre, which were sorely tested during this project. Sara's reflections on the impact of scholarship on family life serve as the last word on the subject: "Daddy, I don't want you to write another book."

Introduction

SINCE THE LATE 1930s, the encounter between blacks and the Communist Party has been an important theme in American intellectual life. Richard Wright and Ralph Ellison, perhaps the greatest black literary figures of the mid-twentieth century, both made this a major subject in their novels, and Wright's autobiographical essay on why he left the Communist Party has become a landmark statement of anti-Stalinist liberalism. Harold Cruse's *Crisis of the Negro Intellectual* (1967), a work which had a profound influence on black and white intellectuals in the late '60s, used the history of Communist involvement among blacks to argue that blacks must remain organizationally independent of the left and pursue nationalist strategies oriented to the permanence of ethnic power struggles in the American nation.[1]

These works, written by former Communists or Party allies, have until recently set the tone for most historical writing on the Party's role in Black America. Though the logic of their writing was hardly conservative —indeed, Wright and Cruse represented an important ideological influence on black artists and campus activists during the height of the '60s protests—it tended to reinforce a tendency, quite powerful during the Cold War years, to view Communist activity largely through the dynamics of manipulation, disillusionment, and betrayal. Wilson Record's two books, *The Negro and the Communist Party* (1951) and *Race and Radicalism: The NAACP and the Communist Party in Conflict* (1964) exemplify this approach. Based almost exclusively on articles by Communist leaders and officials of black organizations with which they competed, the books view the Party as the arm of an international conspiracy, an alien tendency within black protest which used the legitimate grievances of blacks as a "front for the expansion of world communism." In Record's analysis, blacks involved with the Party were either naive idealists deceived by the Party's rhetoric, or cynical servants of Soviet power, since the movement they were part of had no indigenous roots.[2]

However, in the last ten years, a new historiographical image of the black-Communist encounter has begun to appear. Scholars of the civil rights generation, interested in tracing black activism to its roots in the '30s and '40s have come to question whether the term "manipulation" adequately describes Communist involvement in black issues. Dan Carter's book on the Scottsboro case and Charles Martin's book on the Angelo Herndon case persuasively challenged the dominant view (expressed by Record and others) that Communist defense strategy in these cases jeopardized the lives of the defendants and raised huge sums of money for other Party activities.[3] Nell Painter's oral history of Hosea Hudson, a Birmingham Communist organizer, brilliantly demonstrated how the Party, in the early '30s, instilled confidence and imparted leadership skills to a small number of radical southern blacks "who did not find political sufficiency in church and lodge."[4]

In addition, several scholars examining the evolution of black activism in the Depression concluded that black Communists, from the mid-'30s on, were swimming in the same ideological current as many non-Communist black intellectuals, and were presenting the "Communist message" in a highly Americanized idiom. Not only did Communists participate centrally in a nationwide upsurge of black protest, but they helped contribute to a new appreciation by blacks of the power of organized labor and prodded white liberals and radicals to emphasize civil rights issues more than they had in the past.[5] "On balance," Harvard Sitkoff concluded, summarizing much of this recent work, "the positive effects of the Left's involvement in racial matters outweighed the negative. . . . The Left publicized the evils of racism and the benefits of integration to a far greater extent than any other white organization. . . . It sparked and financed civil rights groups whose radicalism made the established Negro organizations more militant in their tactics and yet more respectable to the American mainstream."[6]

However, if the work of recent scholars has given us a more balanced picture of the Party's impact on black life, it has not come fully to grips with some important questions that Wright, Ellison, and Cruse raised. With the exception of Painter, whose work focused on a somewhat idiosyncratic locale where the Party was all-black, scholars have focused more on the practical impact of the Party's activity rather than the personal experience of black Party members or the evolution of Party racial policies. Yet it was discontent with the inner workings of the Party—its pattern of decision making, its language and ideology, and above all its interracialism—which commanded the attention of its most eloquent black critics. Because of its links to an international revolutionary movement and efforts to encourage integration within its entire sphere of influence, the Party represented something decisively new in Afro-American life. Blacks who came in contact with it faced important questions regarding the role of revolution and reform, nationalism and integration, protest and legal action, in the struggle for black equality.

To illuminate their dilemma, we need historical writing which meticulously examines the Party's work in specific black communities, and which treats the evolution of Party theory, the practical impact of its organizing, and the personal experience of its members with equal seriousness. In the pages that follow, I will try to meet this need by giving a detailed portrait of Communist activity in Harlem from 1928 to 1941. Focusing on the most dynamic period in Party history, I will analyze how the Party emerged from obscurity to become an important influence in Harlem life, explore its changing relationships with black organizations, and assess the Party's impact on the diverse group of blacks who passed through its ranks or competed with it for leadership. Concerned with the political history of the Party, particularly the role of the Soviet Union in shaping Party policy, I will also show how the social and cultural atmosphere of Harlem gave a distinctive cast to Party activity, creating problems and opportunities which Party "theory" did not always anticipate.

Harlem represents an ideal setting for an in-depth study of Party "Negro work." The largest black community in the nation and an intellectual and cultural center of international importance, Harlem was chosen by the Party as the "concentration point" of its strategy to win influence in Black America. From the early '30s on, the Party made a practice of sending talented black organizers all over the country into Harlem, convinced that the Party's progress in that community would be crucial to its overall success. Alternately competing and cooperating with major black organizations—the National Association for the Advancement of Colored People, the Urban League, the Garveyite organizations, and the black church—the Party acquired an impressive sphere of influence. At its high point, in 1938, the Harlem CP had close to a thousand black members and activated many thousands more through its work in trade unions, WPA workers groups, the Workers Alliance, tenants unions, legal defense organizations, and cultural groups. No socialist organization before or since has touched the life of an Afro-American community so profoundly.

In addition, a history of the Harlem Communist Party offers a vantage point on a neglected period of Harlem's history, one of equal significance to the "Harlem Renaissance." During the Depression, Harlem experienced an unprecedented explosion of protest activity, some of it under Party auspices, much of it independent of Party influence. Mass marches for Scottsboro, "Don't Buy Where You Can't Work" campaigns, rent strikes, relief bureau sit-ins, unionization drives, rallies against discrimination in education and cutbacks in the WPA—all became *common* features of Harlem's political landscape, led by ministers and politicians as well as nationalists and Party militants. How these activities spread from the "radical fringe"—particularly the Communist left—into the mainstream of community activity is an important story and one for which considerable documentary evidence exists. Because the Harlem CP was so strong and competed so openly for leadership with other organizations, a record of its activities can be found not only in the black and Party press, but in the records of government commissions, and the manuscript collections of important black organizations—especially the Universal Negro Improvement Association, the NAACP, and the Negro Labor Committee.

Finally, the Harlem experience gives the historian an opportunity to examine the tension between "nationalism" and "integration" which pervaded the Party during its first twenty years. Drawing its most talented early recruits from Harlem nationalist circles, the Harlem CP gradually evolved toward a policy which insisted on complete integration of blacks and whites in every aspect of Party life. Ironically, the full implementation of interracialism in Harlem coincided with the theoretical affirmation of the existence of a "Black Belt Nation" in the South. But this nationalist impulse remained largely confined to theory. From 1929 on, being a black Communist in Harlem meant meeting, studying, protesting, and socializing with whites. For blacks and whites in the Party—and for non-Communists who came in contact with it—this constituted a new experience, one which evoked tension, confusion, curiosity, and excitement. Fortunately, Harlem newspapers and the Party press contained a rather extensive commentary on race relations in the Harlem CP. With the help of in-depth interviews with former Party organizers, it is possible to provide a fairly detailed and nuanced analysis of how the Party functioned as an interracial organization in Harlem, and how this affected its reception by different segments of the black community.

In deference to the complexity of the task I am attempting, the book will be divided into three parts. Part One will recount the Harlem Party's growth from its formation in the early '20s to the founding of the National Negro Congress in 1936. This section will be chronological, examining how the Party recruited its first black cadre and gradually grew from a marginal and isolated sect to a powerful community organization. The role of the Soviet Union in shaping Party "Negro work" will be emphasized, as will the efforts of black Communists to transform the Party from an organization dominated by the problems and perspectives of foreign-born members to a force capable of making a major impact on American race relations. This section will also assess leadership conflicts in the CP, and the Party's efforts to "prove itself" to a skeptical community through protests against racist practices and efforts to ease the impact of Depression conditions. It will conclude by examining the convergence in ideology and strategy between the Party and major black organizations in the course of the Scottsboro campaign, the 125th Street boycott movement, and the controversies surrounding the Harlem Riot of 1935.

Part Two will deal with the Harlem Party during the Popular Front, the high point of its influence. Here I will shift from a chronological to a thematic organization, a step made necessary by the sheer volume of Party activity and the reorientation of Party structure and goals that took place during the period. Inspired by Comintern directives to promote "unity against fascism," the Harlem CP underwent an Americanization process designed to improve its ties with black organizations and increase its influence in every sphere of Harlem life. Chapters in this section will examine Communist electoral strategy, particularly its efforts to elect third-party candidates, its economic organizing, and its initiatives in the cultural arena. Introductory and concluding chapters will focus on the inner life of the Party, particularly its efforts to increase membership recruitment and reduce membership turnover, and examine the impact of interracialism on its cadre and rank and file. The Party's success in acquiring a following among black intellectuals and developing broad protest coalitions will be weighed against its failure to generate a loyal following at the polls or a stable membership among working-class blacks.

Part Three will deal with the partial disintegration of the Party's power base in the period between the signing of the Nazi-Soviet Pact and the American entry into World War II. The efforts of Harlem CP leaders to hold their organization together in the face of a disastrous "international line" will be explored, as will the gradual collapse of many united-front relationships the Party had developed. Continued sources of Party strength – in trade union movements, and in cultural and intellectual activities – will be explored, but the big story is the emergence of a protest leadership in Harlem independent of Communist influence, capable of upholding the banner of mass militancy without any formal ties to the Communist left. By the end of 1941, Communists in Harlem were still influential, but they were most definitely on the defensive and had lost much of their moral credibility.

If the author tells this story well, the reader should come away with an understanding of both the impact of Party organizing in Harlem, and the experience of blacks who tried to make the Party serve their needs. For many Harlemites who came of age in the Depression, especially those of an activist bent, the Party helped to define a generational experience.

Whether they joined it or fought it, learned from it or measured themselves against it, the Party left an important mark on their lives. Yet this involvement often evoked profoundly ambivalent feelings. Through an irony of history, the elan of the Harlem Party derived from the example of the Soviet Revolution and the interaction of blacks and whites within Party ranks. Both of these features were new to Harlemites and subjected the Party to pressures that made its actions difficult to predict. But at the same time, the chemistry of Party growth released an energy and a creative spirit that proved attractive, even intoxicating, to some blacks and whites who were in it. For those who found sustenance in the Party's utopian visions, whether of socialism, interracialism, or antifascist unity, repudiating the Party, even for the most sensible reasons, often involved a genuine sense of loss. Richard Wright's vision of Party life as *tragic,* while overdramatic, contains a strong element of truth. The story of the Party in Harlem is in some measure the story of the rise and fall of a dream of human betterment. To scrutinize the dream, while respecting the dreamer, is the historian's special challenge.

NOTES

1. Ellison treats this encounter in *Invisible Man* (New York: Random House, 1952); Wright in *Native Son* (New York: Harper & Brothers, 1940), *The Outsider* (New York: Harper & Brothers, 1953), and *Uncle Tom's Children* (New York: Harper & Brothers, 1938). Wright's autobiographical essay on why he left the Communist Party was published in *Atlantic Monthly,* 174 (Aug., 1944), and subsequently reprinted in Richard Crossman, ed., *The God That Failed* (New York: Harper & Brothers, 1949). It was recently reissued in a more complete form, under the title *American Hunger* (New York: Harper and Row, 1977). See also Harold Cruse, *Crisis of the Negro Intellectual* (New York: William Morrow, 1967).

2. Wilson Record, *The Negro and the Communist Party* (Chapel Hill: University of North Carolina Press, 1951), and *Race and Radicalism: The NAACP and the Communist Party in Conflict* (Ithaca, N.Y.: Cornell University Press, 1964); Harold Cruse's influence on black and white intellectuals in the '60s is treated in Christopher Lasch, *The Agony of the American Left* (New York: Vintage Books, 1969), pp. 117–69; and in articles by Ernest Allen, William Eric Perkins, and Arthur Paris in a special issue of the *Journal of Ethnic Studies,* 5 (Summer, 1977), 1–68.

3. Dan Carter, *Scottsboro, A Tragedy of the American South* (Baton Rouge: Louisiana State University Press, 1969, paperback edition), and Charles H. Martin, *The Angelo Herndon Case and Southern Justice* (Baton Rouge: Louisiana State University Press, 1976).

4. Nell Irvin Painter, *The Narrative of Hosea Hudson: His Life as a Negro Communist in the South* (Cambridge: Harvard University Press, 1979), p. 15.

5. Raymond Wolters, *Negroes and the Great Depression* (Westport: Greenwood Press, 1971); Lawrence S. Wittner, "The National Negro Congress: A Reassessment," *American Quarterly,* 22 (Winter, 1970); August Meier and Elliot Rudwick, "The Origins of Nonviolent Direct Action in Afro-American Protest: A Note on Historical Discontinuities," in *Beyond the Color Line: Explorations in the Black Experience* (Urbana: University of Illinois Press, 1976), p. 314.

6. Harvard Sitkoff, *New Deal For Blacks, The Emergence of Civil Rights as a National Issue: The Depression Decade* (New York: Oxford University Press, 1978), p. 140.

PART ONE

1

The Roots of Party Growth in Harlem

For MOST OF THE 1920s, the Communist Party repre-
sented a marginal phenomenon in Harlem's political life. Until the very
end of the decade, its initial black cadre, drawn from the Socialist Party
and the African Blood Brotherhood, failed to attract black members or
organize effective protests around racial and economic issues. Attracted
to Communism by the "enlightened attitude of the Russian Bolsheviks
toward national minorities," these Harlem Communists found that Party
membership isolated them from the main currents of political and social
activism in Harlem. Most Harlem organizations, from the NAACP
through Garvey's Universal Negro Improvement Association (UNIA), regarded capitalism as a fact of life, if not a positive good. Convinced that
revolution on the Bolshevik model was impossible — or undesirable — in
the United States, they viewed the white working class, the ally Communists urged blacks to embrace, largely as an enemy and a competitor.[1]
Communists proved unable to influence black organizations or form viable organizations of their own, and as late as 1929, "one could almost
count the Negro [Communist] membership on the fingers of one's hand."[2]
Few would then have predicted the Party's emergence as a major force in
Harlem's political life.

Nevertheless, the roots of future Communist growth in Harlem can be
observed within this period of stagnation and isolation for the black left.
Although the number of black Communists in Harlem remained small, it
included people of ability and substance, whose intellectual and political
commitments enabled them to persist in a political course even when it
yielded few tangible results. Cyril Briggs and Richard B. Moore, two of
the first blacks to join the Party, were leading figures in the upsurge of
radical protest that swept through Harlem during and after World War I.
They joined the Party only after several years of independent efforts to
combine militant nationalism with support for the international working-
class movement. Both were strong "race men" who joined the American
Party largely because of the Communist International's commitment to

supporting "racial and national movements against imperialism." Frustrated in their efforts to maintain a mass following among blacks, they concentrated their energies on transforming the American Communist Party—an organization composed almost exclusively of white immigrants —into a phalanx capable of smashing through the barriers that subordinated blacks. By the end of the decade, this inner party struggle had, with Soviet help, elevated the organization of blacks into a matter of top political priority and transformed a previously apathetic white membership into a force willing to bring the Party's message to black communities. Communist activity in Harlem began to assume a new visibility, as black and white Communists organized tenants committees, election rallies, and demonstrations against police violence, displaying a combativeness toward government authority rarely seen before in Harlem.[3]

In the early 1920s, affiliating with the Communist Party represented a difficult choice for black intellectuals, a leap of faith that seemed to go against the direction of black political life. Prior to World War I, Harlem, like the rest of Black America, had no tradition of mass socialist activism. A handful of black intellectuals, including W. E. B. Du Bois, had ties to the Socialist Party, but the mass of Harlemites, overwhelmingly recent migrants from the South and the Caribbean, had no exposure to Socialist organizations and were predisposed to look skeptically on doctrines of class solidarity. In a country where many trade unions drew the color line and white workers participated in lynch mobs and race riots, Socialists had to take a strong stand against jim crow to be creditable among blacks, and the prewar Socialist Party had refused to do this.[4]

During World War I, a number of black intellectuals, inspired by accelerating radical protest in the United States and abroad, began to articulate socialist positions, and, for the first time, the Socialist Party in New York strongly encouraged this development. In 1917, a Florida-born City College student named A. Philip Randolph founded a Socialist political club in Harlem and helped amass a sizable black vote for Socialist mayoralty candidate Morris Hillquit. In subsequent years, several black magazines arose in Harlem with a socialist or quasi-socialist editorial policy —the *Messenger,* the *Emancipator,* and the *Crusader.* But the shocks of the postwar era—the Red Scare, the Palmer Raids, and the split in the Socialist Party—undermined this incipient socialist subculture before it could strike deep political roots. Harlem's working class, largely unorganized at the workplace, had never been drawn into socialist activism. By the early 1920s, when the battle lines in the socialist movement had been drawn over support of the Bolshevik Revolution, neither the "left wing" nor the "right wing" of Harlem socialism had a large following who shared their beliefs.[5]

As a result, Communism followed a very different trajectory in Harlem than it did in ethnic communities—Finnish, Jewish, Slavic, German—where it could draw upon a longstanding socialist tradition. In those communities, especially ones inhabited by Russian immigrants, thousands of left-wing Socialist Party members joined the Communist Party en masse, bringing with them an entire network of organizations and institutions. Such a development could not occur in Harlem: there were socialist intellectuals, but no socialist subculture that permeated daily life; no fraternal orders, trade unions, or cultural organizations with a distinctly socialist cast. In addition, the gut-level loyalties that attracted Russian Jews to Communism, rooted in the participation of friends or relatives in the Russian Revolution and steps taken by the Soviets to end discrimination against their countrymen, had no analogue in Harlem.[6]

The first known Communists in Harlem—Otto Huiswoud, Cyril Briggs, Richard Moore, Grace Campbell, and Lovett Fort-Whiteman—all came into the movement at least a year after the split in the Socialist Party in 1919 and were recruited by white Communist leaders (if available evidence can be trusted) largely because of the prodding of Soviet officials.[7] Nevertheless, Party recruitment in Harlem did follow some clear patterns. Of the five earliest Harlem Communists, four were of West Indian ancestry (only Fort-Whiteman was American born). As in white neighborhoods, the foreign born seemed to respond disproportionately to the Communist message. Secondly, most were intellectuals; Briggs was an editor, Campbell a schoolteacher, Moore a professional lecturer, Fort-Whiteman an actor and critic, Huiswoud a union printer. Thirdly, the Party seemed to attract blacks who possessed a strong nationalist orientation. Of the five early Harlem Communists, all but Huiswoud were recruited out of the African Blood Brotherhood, a "secret revolutionary order" founded in 1919 which emphasized self-defense, race pride, and self-determination for blacks in countries where they were the majority. It was the anticolonialism of the Bolshevik Revolution which commanded their attention, not the organizational accomplishments of American Communists.[8]

The intersection of nationalism and socialism in the Party's growth in Harlem is epitomized by the career of Cyril Briggs, the most influential of the early Harlem Communists. Born on the island of Nevis, Briggs had served as an editor of the *Amsterdam News* until 1917, when his antiwar stand led to his dismissal from the paper. In 1918, he founded a magazine called the *Crusader*, "dedicated . . . to a renaissance of Negro power and culture throughout the world," and in 1919 he founded the "African Blood Brotherhood for African Liberation and Redemption."[9] A tall, impressive-looking man who could almost pass for white, Briggs struggled with a speech impediment that made it difficult for him to speak in public. But his physical courage, the power and fluidity of his prose, and his willingness to sacrifice gain for political principle made him a formidable figure. By the time he joined the Communist Party, Briggs had developed a small but loyal coterie of supporters in Harlem's West Indian community and a readership for the *Crusader* in several American cities and West Indian islands.[10]

The early issues of the *Crusader* reveal Briggs as a militant nationalist, strikingly similar in his thinking to Marcus Garvey. From 1918 through the beginning of 1920, Briggs's editorials consistently presented African liberation—and sometimes African emigration—as the only hope for blacks in the Western Hemisphere. Strongly anticapitalist and sympathetic to organized labor, Briggs nevertheless expressed extreme skepticism that blacks could ever achieve full equality in the United States and live in harmony with their white neighbors.[11] "The ultimate, equitable, peaceful solution of this country's race problem," he wrote, "is by all signs . . . a chimera and an idle dream. . . . Thus it is Glory and Necessity both that call us to the mother land to work out a proud and glorious future for the African race."[12]

By the end of 1919, however, a new element began to creep into Briggs's writing. Excited by the antiimperialist orientation of the Bolshevik Revolution and by some examples of antiracist activity by American radical groups (he mentioned an IWW strike in Bogalusa, Louisiana, as evidence of new possibilities), Briggs began to call on blacks to form "alliances with the liberal and radical forces of the country—of the world." Still convinced that "internal peace is impossible until the African question is settled right," Briggs cautiously began to express optimism that multiracial egalitarian societies could be created if capitalism was overthrown.[13] By the end of 1921, Briggs was no longer advocating African emigration; rather, he was presenting racial progress in the United States and African liberation as mutually complementary, and suggesting that Afro-Americans could best work for the latter objective in the United States. "Just as the Negro in the United States," he wrote, "can never hope to win equal rights with his white neighbors until Africa is liberated and a strong Negro state (or states) created on that continent, so too we can never liberate Africa until the American Section of the Negro Race is made strong enough to play the part for a free Africa that the Irish in America now play for a free Ireland. Every Negro in the United States should use his vote, and use it fearlessly and intelligently, to strengthen the radical movement, and thus create a deeper schism within the white race in America. . . ."[14]

Briggs's "tilt" toward the left, which preceded his membership in the

Communist Party by more than a year, coincided with the formation of the African Blood Brotherhood. Because of limited documentary evidence, what this organization actually *did* remains something of a mystery. Founded in the pages of the *Crusader,* requiring "no dues, fees, or assessments," it may have been little more than a discussion group, with its 3,000 claimed "members" existing largely on paper. But though one can find no clear evidence of an organizing strategy, or program of action, it did attract some black radicals, in Harlem and elsewhere, who shared Briggs's belief in armed self-defense, African liberation, and an alliance with labor and the left.[15] Perhaps the most important of these was Richard B. Moore, who was to become Briggs's closest collaborator for the next fifteen years. Born on Barbados, Moore excelled where his colleague faltered—as a public speaker. A ramrod-straight man with a light complexion, immaculately though not expensively dressed, Moore was one of Harlem's great orators, a person who combined logic and erudition with a taste for invective. A bibliophile and a student of black history, he assumed an air of great ferocity in political debate, an activity which he excelled in from a soapbox or a lectern. Like Briggs, he seemed most at home in a stance of uncompromising militancy, arousing blacks to a defense of their dignity. Agitators par excellence, the two men had little taste for the back slapping, maneuvering, and bureaucratic details involved in building organizations, but they had the capacity to inspire loyalty and admiration in those who shared their vision.[16]

For Briggs and Moore, perhaps the central political preoccupation of their lives, and one which significantly shaped their future involvement with Communism, was their ambivalent attitude toward Harlem's great nationalist movement—the Universal Negro Improvement Association of Marcus Garvey. Initially, they had watched the UNIA's growth with considerable enthusiasm; not only did they share Garvey's emphasis on race pride and African redemption, but they had personal and political ties with important members of Garvey's entourage. The first editor of Garvey's *Negro World,* the West Indian businessman W. A. Domingo, was a member of the Socialist Party and a personal friend of Briggs, and Richard Moore worked with Garvey's associate John E. Bruce as American agent for Duse Mohammed's London-based *African Times and Orient Review.*[17] However, in the summer of 1919, Garvey caused consternation among left-wing Harlem nationalists when he forced Domingo to resign from his editorship of the *Negro World.* Coming at a time when federal authorities were beginning to raid socialist organizations, and when a New York state legislative committee had begun to probe "bolshevist" influence among blacks, Domingo's ouster may have represented an effort by Garvey to protect his organization from the antiradical hysteria that was sweeping through the United States. From this point on, the UNIA leader began to distance himself organizationally and ideologically from the American left, even though he retained his favorable attitude toward the Soviet Revolution.[18]

Garvey's actions, coming at a time when his mass following was growing rapidly, troubled Briggs greatly. Possibly jealous of Garvey's success, and convinced that support of the left was essential to black advancement, Briggs simultaneously tried to forge an alliance between the UNIA and the African Blood Brotherhood, and to expose irregularities in Garvey's business practices. These efforts, conducted *prior* to Briggs's recruitment to the CP, increased tension between the two leaders, but did not lead to a formal break.[19] In the summer of 1921, however, when Briggs was either a CP member or about to become one, Briggs's efforts to create a leftist presence at Garvey's "Convention of the Negro Peoples of the World" received a stinging rebuke. Although Garvey allowed Rose Pastor Stokes, a white Communist leader (and Briggs's main contact with the CP leadership), to address his convention on the significance of the Bolshevik Revolution, his supporters tabled resolutions asking the convention to endorse the African Blood Brotherhood program and refused to seat ABB delegates. From this point on, relations between Garvey and Briggs deteriorated sharply. Stung by *Crusader* editorials criticizing Garvey's tactics at the convention, Garvey accused Briggs of being a "white man passing as a Negro," and the infuriated Briggs sued him for libel.[20]

Throughout the rest of the decade, this personal dispute assumed an increasingly ideological cast. While Briggs devoted an increasing part of his energies to trying to recruit black members for the Communist Party (Moore, Campbell, and Fort-Whiteman followed him in from the ABB), Garvey took positions on racial and economic issues that seemed to align him with the most conservative forces in the United States. Expressing contempt for black organizations that emphasized civil rights and social equality, Garvey held a meeting with the leader of the Ku Klux Klan and began to openly express skepticism that blacks could escape second-class citizenship in the United States. In addition, Garvey's pronouncements for an American audience assumed an increasingly procapitalist cast. Arguing that "Capitalism is necessary to the progress of the world," he warned his followers against "the present brand of Communism, or Workers Partisanship as taught in America, and to be careful of the traps and pitfalls of white trade unionism." Finally, Garvey's rhetoric increasingly emphasized the theme of racial purity. Calling on blacks to reject intermarriage and social equality, he declared himself in favor of a "pure black race just as self-respecting whites are in favor of pure white race," and attacked black leaders of mixed ancestry as "mongrels" and "miscegenationists."[21]

These arguments profoundly disturbed Briggs and his black Communist colleagues. Convinced that Garveyism represented a positive phenomenon, a sign of the radicalization of the black masses, they feared that Garvey's conservative preachments would isolate them from the UNIA rank and file, whom they viewed as potential recruits for the Communist Party. Throughout the mid '20s, they tried, with the encouragement of the Communist Party's top leadership, to push the Garvey movement to the left; alternately criticizing its policies and programs, offering it cooperation on limited objectives, and trying to mobilize the UNIA rank and file against Garvey. But at a time when American capitalism seemed triumphant and the left was on the defensive, none of these tactics succeeded, Garvey shrewdly concluded that the American Communists he dealt with, whether black or white, lacked the political muscle to make their attacks or their overtures meaningful and he had little difficulty getting this position accepted by the UNIA rank and file. In 1924, at the UNIA's International Convention, Garvey gracefully derailed an attempt by the white Communist Robert Minor to create an alliance between the UNIA and the Party on the question of fighting discrimination in trade unions and declaring war on the Ku Klux Klan. When Communists distributed handbills attacking the Klan and submitted a resolution to that effect on the floor of the convention, Garvey spoke against the resolution as an "act of political suicide" and submitted a much milder one in its place, which the delegates approved.[22]

Their failure to influence the Garvey movement represented only one dimension of the political difficulties Harlem Communists experienced in the early '20s. Virtually the entire black community felt the effects of the conservative political current that swept through the United States and of the prosperity that followed the postwar recession. Radical and activist black organizations suffered rapid losses in membership. The NAACP, the largest black protest organization in the United States, declined from 90,000 members in 1919 to 20,000 in 1929.[23] Socialist Party vote totals in Harlem, almost 25 percent of those cast in the 1917 mayoralty race, dwindled to a trickle, and in 1923 A. Philip Randolph and Chandler Owen disbanded the Harlem Socialist political club that they had founded during the war. The *Messenger* magazine, once the *bête noire* of government investigators, pushed its socialist views to the background, increasing its cultural offerings dramatically and printing glowing portraits of black businessmen as a way of attracting advertising. Among Harlem intellectuals, developments in the left and organized labor seemed far less important and exciting than the flowering of the black arts, the growth of black business and the emergence of Harlem as an entertainment center that attracted international attention.[24]

Radicals like Briggs and Moore, who refused to adapt to the new polit-

ical climate, found themselves leaders without a constituency. In the early
'20s, the African Blood Brotherhood fell apart. The *Crusader* folded and
membership in the Brotherhood fell to the point where the organization
was kept alive only by an infusion of new members from the Communist
Party (an ironic twist, since Party leaders who had recruited Briggs hoped
that the Brotherhood would be a conduit for blacks into the Party, not
vice versa!).[25] Briggs and Moore, who had wanted to function as both
Communists and black nationalists, now found that the nationalist organization they had created could not function on an independent basis.
Worse yet, no other nationalist organization represented a viable alternative, since Garveyism had entered a conservative phase. To play their
chosen role as advocates of revolutionary upheaval among blacks, Briggs
and Moore now *needed* the Communist Party, both for financial and political support. This dependence, they would soon discover, would draw
them into an interracial political milieu vastly different from the one with
which they were familiar.

The incorporation of black Communists into an interracial setting took
place rather gradually. For at least three years after they joined the Communist Party (until 1925) Briggs and Moore conducted most of their work
in Harlem in an all-black setting. In addition to their work within the
African Blood Brotherhood, Briggs ran a news service with Party funds
that sent news releases to black newspapers throughout the country, and
Moore helped organize a Harlem Educational Forum in cooperation with
W. A. Domingo and Hubert Harrison, a West Indian socialist-nationalist
known for his prowess as a street speaker and pamphleteer.[26] They had
little contact with rank-and-file Communists in the white neighborhoods
of Harlem, concentrated east of Fifth Avenue and south of 125th Street.
The vast majority of these were non-English-speaking immigrants—Finns,
Estonians, Italians, Swedes, Germans, and Jews—who had neither the
ability, nor the desire, to interact with their black neighbors. The structure of the Party, inherited from the Socialist Party, legitimized this pattern of ethnic separation. Foreign-language federations, each with their
own newspapers, meeting halls, and social clubs, served as the Party's
major governing units, incorporating almost 95 percent of the Party's
membership as of 1922.[27]

The pressure to break down these ethnic divisions, like the pressure to
organize blacks at all, came from the top leadership of the American
Party, and it was at this level, rather than the neighborhoods, that the
bulk of interracial contact occurred. From the time they were recruited,
the tiny group of Harlem Communists were drawn into the task of developing a new theoretical approach to the "Negro Question," and of creating strategies to attract blacks into the Party. Despite the indifference of
rank-and-file Communists to the entire question, some leaders of the

Party saw the need to move beyond the "color blind" Marxism of the Socialist Party and to define racial persecution "as a matter of tremendous importance . . . (for) the class struggle." A few American-born Party leaders, notably Robert Minor, William Foster, and Bill Dunne, provided enthusiastic support for this new theoretical stance, and the English-speaking Party press began publishing regular features on economic and political trends in the black community.[28]

However, the most consistent pressure to force the U.S. Party to emphasize black issues came from the Communist International, which was thoroughly dominated by Soviet Party leaders. The success of the Soviet Revolution had in large part been due to the support of minorities in the Russian Empire, and the Soviets translated this strategic formula directly to the United States, where blacks represented the largest and most victimized minority group. Soviet leaders welcomed black American visitors with open arms and milked them for every drop of information concerning the conditions of blacks in their country and the racial policies of the American Party. Complaints about white chauvinism in the American Party, even when registered by non-Communists, evoked a sympathetic response, and resulted in stinging reprimands to American Party leaders. In addition, the Comintern encouraged black American Communists to come to the Soviet Union for intensive ideological training, where they were exposed to a multiracial milieu unlike any they had seen before. Afro-Americans at Soviet schools mingled with Africans, Asians, and non-European Soviet nationals, as well as Communists of European descent, in a setting where their blackness elicited approval rather than contempt. The more talented of these students found themselves serving on Comintern committees, developing new theoretical positions on the Negro question, and addressing gatherings of representatives of the international Communist movement.[29]

These experiences had a profound effect on black Communists, even those who never went abroad. The absence of prejudice in Soviet society, at least in places where visitors went, seemed to suggest that racism could dissolve under revolutionary conditions and multiracial organizations could flourish in the Communist movement. If the Soviet Party could overcome age-old divisions in the Russian Empire, might not it be possible for the American Party, ethnically fragmented though it was, to ultimately transcend American prejudices and fight aggressively for black concerns? Isolated in their own communities, surrounded by white comrades who spoke twenty languages, black Communists looked to the Soviet Union as the one force on the horizon resisting the convervatism of the age.

Given these perspectives, it is not surprising that black Communists supported the "bolshevization" of the American Party that began, under

Comintern direction, in 1925. This program, designed to consolidate the U.S. Party into a centralized body on the Soviet model, stripped the foreign-language federations of their power and required their members to join street units where they lived, or shop units where they worked. An Americanization program accompanied this reorganization: Party members had to learn the English language and work cooperatively with members of other nationalities. Though these measures ultimately helped the Party move out of the immigrant ghettoes, they made it far more hierarchical and gave the Central Committee and the Comintern virtually unlimited control over the political lives of the membership. Thousands of rank-and-file Communists, reluctant to undergo forced Americanization and jealous of the autonomy of their ethnic organizations, left the Party in dismay. Others departed because they rejected the Comintern's authority to remold a member Party without its membership's consent.[30]

To my knowledge, no blacks stood among the departing group (evidence on the composition of the Party in Harlem is lacking for this period). Certainly, none of the key black cadre left. From their point of view, any program which increased Soviet control of the Party seemed *positive,* since the Soviets had been the strongest force in the movement pressing for recruitment of black members and emphasis on black issues. In addition, they felt very little attachment to the foreign-language federations, which seemed like centers of ethnic exclusiveness, and at times, of outright racism. In an organization where support for black activities tended to flow from the top down, blacks found little reason to defend the principle of rank-and-file control, and aligned themselves with the centralizers in the Party leadership.[31]

Bolshevization marked an important change in the lives of Harlem Communists. Under the new system of Party organization, they found themselves in much closer contact with rank-and-file white Communists in their geographical area. Party leaders in New York consolidated all Party activities, from Yorkville to Washington Heights, into a multinational "Harlem Section" that functioned under a consolidated administration. Within this structure, black Communists, like all other Party members, were required to join street units in their neighborhoods or shop units where they worked. Following the logic of bolshevization, which defined ethnic solidarity among Communists as an obstacle to Party unity, Party leaders encouraged, and later required, these units to be interracial.[32]

For Briggs and Moore, bolshevization meant movement into new political terrain. Hitherto, they had functioned as the "left wing" of the nationalist movement in Harlem, meeting regularly with Party leaders, but conducting their political work within all-black organizations like the African Blood Brotherhood. But in the reorganized Party, they emerged publicly as spokesmen for an interracial movement and conducted their political work in daily contact with whites. This shift created tensions. Briggs and Moore were race conscious and sensitive to insults, ready to reprimand any white person who displayed signs of chauvinism or paternalism. Since Party whites were by no means free of such sentiments, the two leaders frequently found themselves at odds with their white comrades over social niceties as well as theoretical and organizational difficulties. In addition, bolshevization presented Briggs and Moore with a difficult, perhaps impossible theoretical problem: how to reconcile the interracialism of the Party with their oft-expressed commitment to black unity and solidarity.[33]

Despite these difficulties, Briggs and Moore felt the advantages of reorganization outweighed the drawbacks. Within a newly centralized, interracial Party, black leaders could mobilize the entire movement behind the struggle for Negro rights rather than only the miniscule black membership. They would have to fight for such an orientation against significant white resistance, but they felt confident that the Comintern would support them in such a struggle. Fired with enthusiasm for the Soviet Revolution, they looked forward to increasing Comintern pressure to bring the Negro question to the fore in the American Party and to promote black comrades to high Party positions. In this expectation, they were not to be disappointed.[34]

Within the next few years, black Communists, preoccupied with inner-Party tasks, registered few gains in mass activity. Their one major effort to assume leadership in the black community, the organization of an American Negro Labor Congress in the fall of 1925, only dramatized their extreme isolation from the mainstream of Black America. Designed, under Comintern direction, as a "united front" of black organizations and trade unions to eliminate discrimination in organized labor, the congress carried with it a whole panoply of demands, ranging from "the complete abolition of discrimination against the Negro people as a whole," to "the liberation of Haiti, Santo Domingo, the Virgin Islands, Puerto Rico . . . and all victims of American and European imperialism."[35] The revolutionary rhetoric of its program guaranteed the enmity of the AFL and the small segment of the black community that expressed prolabor views. AFL President William Green warned unions who participated that they would lose their charters, and the most important group of trade unionists in Harlem, led by A. Philip Randolph, boycotted its founding convention. Black observers at the convention who sympathized with the congress's goals found the behavior of some of its organizers extraordinarily bizarre. Lovett Fort-Whiteman, the congress's national organizer, fresh from a sojourn in the Soviet Union, made it clear that Communists tended to dominate the organization and reinforced this message by his choice of costume—a Russian rabochka—and of entertainment—a Russian ballet! While *any* effort to encourage trade unionism among blacks had rough sledding in the mid-'20s—including A. Philip Randolph's Trade Union Committee for Organizing Negro Workers—the ANLC's approach had something to offend virtually everyone in the black community. Subsidized by Party funds, it became little more than a forum for the Communist position on the "Negro question," which it expressed through its newspaper, the *Negro Champion,* edited by Richard Moore.[36]

In the three years following the ANLC convention, Harlem Communists did little to recover from this fiasco. Working-class Harlemites remained immune to their appeals, and Communist strike-support activities, whether in behalf of motion picture operators at the Lafayette Theatre, or left-wing workers in the garment industry, attracted little attention in the community.[37]

But among a small section of Harlem's intellectuals, the Party's views received a respectful hearing. Although most black intellectuals viewed Communists as hopelessly out of joint with the major events of the era—the growth of race awareness and the flowering of the black arts—some listened carefully to the Party's claim that the Soviet Union had abolished race discrimination and that Communism would bring race equality and self-determination of nations. In the West Indian community, the Party's "internationalism" seemed to have particular resonance. Throughout the '20s Briggs and Moore continued to present the Party's view through the Harlem Educational Forum, which they ran cooperatively with the West Indian intellectuals W. A. Domingo, Hubert Harrison (until his death), and Rev. Ethelred Brown, a Unitarian minister who espoused socialist beliefs.[38]

The Party attracted several key black recruits during this era, all from middle-class backgrounds: George Padmore, a Trinidad-born student leader and journalist; Solomon Harper, an embittered black engineer and inventor, and William Patterson, a California-educated lawyer poised on the edge of a career in Harlem politics. Padmore's influence was to come largely in the international domain—first as a director of Negro Work for the Red International of Trade Unions, later as a critic of Comintern colonial policy—but Patterson and Harper did much of their organizing in Harlem and deserve brief portraits.[39]

Solomon Harper represented a classic case of the "outsider" sometimes attracted to radical movements. The creator of numerous patented inventions, ranging from the aerial torpedo to railway switching and signalling devices, Harper was deeply scarred by his inability to get remunerated for his inventions or to get the academic or professional position that he believed his talents merited. Despite numerous awards and honors, including designation by the NAACP magazine *Crisis* as one of its "Men of the Month" in 1915, Harper lived from pillar to post, taking odd jobs, sleeping in rented rooms, borrowing lab space for his scientific work. When the Harlem CP recruited Harper in the mid-'20s, it acquired a bona fide eccentric, a person without family ties, roots, or a stable profession, but it also got an utterly selfless, dedicated worker. For the next twenty years, Harper would be the Harlem CP's "Jimmy Higgins," speaking for the party at countless street meetings, experiencing beatings and arrests at Party demonstrations, staffing the Party office at all hours of the day and night. A gentle individual, totally devoid of political ambitions, Harper never sought Party leadership and avoided factional conflicts. For him, the Party was a home, a family, and a voice of protest against the racism of a society which seemed to have no place for a man of his talents.[40]

William Patterson, by contrast, was a person who seemed destined for a comfortable life as a member of Harlem's professional strata. A graduate of the University of California law school, Patterson came to Harlem after a trip to Europe (which he financed by working as a seaman) and quickly established himself as one of Harlem's most promising young lawyers. Ensconced in a rooming house on "Strivers Row," a two-block area of elegant brownstones designed by Stanford White, Patterson became close friends with Paul Robeson and Eslanda Goode (a young chemist later to become Robeson's wife) and joined a circle of upwardly mobile young artists and professionals. The law firm he helped to found, Dyett, Hall and Patterson, began acquiring a substantial share of Harlem's legal work, and became a center of discussion and political debate for Harlem's "young men on the make."[41]

But Patterson felt dissatisfied with the direction his life was taking. Exposed to radical politics in California and London, anxious to use his talents to challenge racial barriers, Patterson now spent most of his time representing black landlords or arranging political "protection" for successful black businesses. Patterson's contact with Richard Moore, who attended some of the "bull sessions" at Patterson's office, increased his restlessness. Engaging Patterson in long discussions about history and politics, Moore persuaded Patterson that neither machine politics nor the law could effectively improve the status of black Americans or empower American workers. Through Moore's influence, Patterson began meeting regularly with Harlem Communists and joined the campaign to free Sacco and Vanzetti, Italian-American anarchists accused of armed robbery and murder. Patterson's experiences in this campaign, which included a clubbing by police at a Boston demonstration and close association with prominent intellectuals identified with the left, led him to join the Communist Party. He was the first *American-born* black of real stature in Harlem to take such a step. In 1927, with Moore's encouragement, he was sent to the Soviet Union for training, a common step for blacks identified as future leaders of the U.S. Party.[42]

The role of Soviet influence in maintaining the morale of black Communists during this era cannot be overestimated. In the late '20s, a steady stream of black Party members went to the Soviet Union for training, and with few exceptions, they returned with their faith affirmed. Carefully insulated from the poverty and cruelty of Soviet life, they were treated as celebrities by Soviet leaders and given political and intellectual responsibilities almost unimaginable in the United States. Some, like Patterson, married Soviet women during their tenure there, and all found freedom from the phobia about "social equality" that made Afro-Americans feel like pariahs in the presence of whites of the opposite sex. In some cases, these experiences blunted their critical faculties. Many black Communists came to see the world entirely through the theoretical categories offered by their Soviet teachers, and to become ardent defenders of any and all policies of the Soviet ruling group. But if their contact with the international movement made them dogmatic and sectarian, it also kept alive a sense of optimism that blacks could, through revolutionary agitation, emancipate themselves from poverty and discrimination. Whether attending a Comintern-sponsored Conference Against Imperialism, as Richard Moore did in 1927, or studying at the "University of the Toilers of the East," black Communists imbibed a sense of the power of the international movement that made their weakness in American life seem easier to bear.[43]

In 1928, with bolshevization nearly completed, Harlem Communists began to break out of their isolation. In February of that year, Richard Moore attended a meeting called in Harlem by the white leader of a tenants organization in Washington Heights who was seeking black support for a protest against the impending expiration of the city's Emergency Rent Law. Invited to the rostrum to speak, Moore so impressed the audience with his oratory that they agreed to form a Harlem Tenants League and elected him president. Shortly thereafter, other black Communists—George Padmore, Solomon Harper, Grace Campbell, and Edward Welsh—joined the league and began mobilizing Harlem tenants to fight individual landlords and to attend meetings of the Board of Aldermen where the Rent Law was being discussed.[44]

Later that year, Communists organized an election campaign in Harlem designed to dramatize the Party's commitment to total racial equality. Party presidential candidate William Foster, who had been arrested in Wilmington, Delaware, for advocating "social equality," made several appearances in Harlem, and leading black and white Communists appeared regularly in Harlem at street meetings and indoor rallies. The campaign, which ran Richard Moore for Congress and Edward Welsh for State Assembly, attracted almost no support outside the Party's ranks — Moore got only 296 votes in a multiracial district. But it demonstrated that Party leaders had come to see championship of Negro rights as an essential component of the Party's program and were ready to dramatize that message in all of its activities.[45]

Simultaneous events in the Soviet Union gave a powerful, if indirect stimulus to the Party's activities in black communities. Faced with a crisis in agricultural production, the dominant wing of the Soviet leadership, led by Stalin, decided to embark on a rapid program of industrialization, accompanied by collectivization of agriculture and an attack on the middle peasantry. The most powerful opposition to these policies came from Bukharin, the highest official of the Comintern, and Stalin decided to vanquish him on his own home ground. Beginning in December, 1927, Stalin prepared the way for a dramatic reorientation of the world Communist movement aimed at reinforcing his domestic policies and his claim to sole leadership of the Soviet state. Lining up allies within every Communist Party, Stalin asserted that the era of capitalist stabilization had come to an end and a "new revolutionary upsurge" was close at hand. Communist parties, Stalin demanded, had to break with reformist allies, begin openly revolutionary agitation, and mobilize their members to defend the Soviet Union from attack. Although he could offer no concrete evidence that capitalism had entered a period of crisis, Stalin fought to have this position adopted as the line of all Communist parties, choosing the Sixth World Congress of the Comintern as the place to achieve this objective.[46]

The Negro question in the United States became one key proving ground for Stalin's new policy. Shortly before the Sixth World Congress, Soviet nationality experts, with the help of a midwestern black Communist named Harry Haywood (who had participated briefly in the African Blood Brotherhood), drafted a resolution which argued that blacks in the United States were an oppressed nation which had the right of self-determination in those parts of the South where they formed a majority of the population. No such proposal had ever been put forth by the African Blood Brotherhood or black members of the Communist Party (the *Crusader* always spoke of Africa and the West Indies when it called for self-government for Negroes), and Haywood apparently had to be convinced of the resolution's merits by his Soviet colleagues. But he joined with them in bringing the resolution up for discussion at the Comintern's Negro Commission, and sought to have it approved as official Comintern policy.[47]

Significantly, the black Communists on the Negro Commission, who included Otto Hall, Haywood's gifted but troubled older brother (he suffered from a brain disease which limited his capacity for "prolonged concentration"); James Ford, a former postal worker from Chicago being groomed for Party leadership, and Harold Williams, a West Indian seaman from Harlem (a recent Party recruit), all initially objected to the resolution. None of these individuals had a strong background in nationalist movements (Hall and Haywood had joined the CP first—in Chicago— and were then assigned by it to the African Blood Brotherhood), and they regarded black Americans as a racial minority rather than an oppressed nation. But since other parts of the resolution emphasized key points of concern to them—the struggle for "social and political equality" in the United States, and the struggle against "white chauvinism" in the American Party—they expressed their opposition cautiously while they sniffed the political winds. When it became clear that the resolution had the backing of Stalin's faction and that it would pass the congress overwhelmingly, they decided to drop their objections and try to work within its framework.[48]

On the face of it, the behavior of black Communists at the congress looks like a simple case of opportunism, obeisance to Soviet authority at the expense of political principle. But if the Comintern had handed them an albatross ("self-determination in the Black Belt" would be a singularly poor mobilizing device in the North or the South), it had also placed a powerful weapon in their hands. By defining blacks as an oppressed nation, even in this bizarre fashion, the Comintern had, within the Leninist lexicon of values, endowed the black struggle with unprecedented dignity and importance. Dissatisfied with their position in the U.S. Party, black Communists could, and would, use this to their advantage.

The formal resolution that passed the congress, dated October 26, 1928, dramatically changed the whole climate in the U.S. Party within which black issues were considered. Defined as a nation with the right of "self-determination," blacks now represented an important ally of the proletariat, whose support had to be carefully cultivated if the revolutionary movements were to succeed. Blacks in the rural South, the resolution argued, had the potential to become a "revolutionary force . . . able to participate in the joint struggle with all other workers against capitalist exploitation." Communists had to consider work in the South, which they had previously avoided, as one of their major tasks, and "begin to organize the black agrarian population to struggle for control of the land and against . . . lynching, Jim Crowism, and segregation."[49]

In defining self-determination, the resolution contained ambiguities: it did not specify whether the Black Belt should become an independent nation or a self-governing region within the United States. But on the importance of Negro work as a whole, the resolution spoke with unmistakable clarity. The entire American Party had to "consider the struggle on behalf of the Negro masses . . . as one of its major tasks." To implement this objective, the "Party must take up the task of training a cadre of Negro comrades as leaders . . . and make every effort to draw Negro proletarians into active and leading work in the Party." But Negro work was not to be confined to blacks. "White comrades must be specially trained for work among the Negroes," and "the Negro problem must be part and parcel of all and every campaign conducted by the Party." In the past, the resolution asserted, the Party had been hampered in its Negro work by "white chauvinism" within its ranks, "manifested . . . even in open antagonism . . . to Negro comrades." This had to be countered by a "thorough educational campaign . . . within the Party . . . to stamp out all forms of antagonism, or even indifference among our white comrades toward the Negro work."[50]

This resolution had an immediate impact upon the U.S. Party. Although the slogan of self-determination provoked some opposition and much confusion, the resolution contained a clear moral imperative to place Negro work in the forefront of Party activity, and the top leadership of the Party hastened to comply. The Party's Sixth National Convention, meeting in March, 1929, elected five black Communists to the Party's Central Committee, including Harlemites Cyril Briggs, Otto Huiswoud, and Edward Welsh; established Negro work committees within the Party districts; and appointed Cyril Briggs as director of the "Negro Department" of the Party's Central Committee. Harold Williams, recently returned from the Soviet Union, was appointed section organizer of the Harlem section, and director of Negro work for the New York district.[51]

Black Communists took advantage of their new powers to push for a broad-based educational campaign to make rank-and-file Communists aware of the importance of Negro work. Briggs and Moore, who stayed home during the World Congress, became enthusiastic supporters of the Comintern resolution, seizing upon it as an affirmation of their nationalist views, an alternative to Garveyism, and a source of political leverage over their white comrades. On Briggs's initiative, the Party declared May 10 to 20, 1929, to be "National Negro Week," a time for sponsoring meetings honoring black revolutionary heroes, for discussing the Negro question in Party units, and for demonstrating against jim crow theatres and restaurants. At the same time, Party publications began printing articles analyzing employment patterns, class divisions, and political and ideological trends in black communities, as well as evaluations of the Party's progress in implementing the Comintern resolution.[52]

In Harlem, organizers could now count on far more support from the Party apparatus, and this had an immediate effect on the Party's work in the Harlem Tenants League. In April, 1929, the *Daily Worker* published an eight-part feature on housing conditions in Harlem designed to coincide with a campaign by the league to protest the expiration of the second phase of the Emergency Rent Laws, covering apartments of less than ten dollars a room. Written by a white former college instructor named Sol Auerbach, who later rose to prominence for his writings on black history under the name of James Allen, the series emphasized the role of black churches and real estate companies in the maintenance of high rents and slum conditions in Harlem. A major target for Tenants League organizing was a row of tenements on 135th Street owned by St. Philip's Episcopal Church, one of the wealthiest and most prestigious churches in Harlem, and the *Worker* devoted two whole articles to the role of the church as a real estate operator. Dubbing the St. Philip's buildings "Rats and Cats Row," Auerbach attacked the black church as an ally of the "capitalist" and the "politician" in the exploitation of black tenants: "The pulpit from which the Rev'd Bishop talks is nothing but a money box in which is collected the coins, sweated out and lived by the tenants on Rats and Cats Row."[53]

The emphasis of this series on black landlords, who controlled slightly more than a third of Harlem real estate, represented a new element in the Party's Negro work inspired by the Comintern Congress, a comprehensive declaration of war on the black middle class. The new line of the Comintern, calling for a repudiation by Communists of all forms of reformism, sparked a mechanical reinterpretation of class relations in Black America whereby black business and professional people became "parasites" on the backs of black workers, and black betterment organizations (e.g. the NAACP, the Urban League, and the Garvey movement) simple "tools" of white capitalists. Defining "revolution" as the only way out, Communists began to use all of their activities in black communities, especially efforts to improve economic conditions, as platforms from which to discredit established black leaders.[54]

With its tone set by the *Daily Worker* series, the Tenants League campaign became a strange mixture of practical protest tactics and ideological warfare. League organizers, headed by Richard Moore and Grace Campbell, developed committees in individual buildings to press for repairs and lower rents, sponsored demonstrations at the Board of Aldermen to demand extension of rent control, held regular indoor meetings at the 135th Street Public Library, and organized a march through Harlem to protest high rents. But at the same time, they launched an attack on virtually every leadership group in Harlem and invoked an image of an exploited and impoverished Harlem community that diverged markedly from the one stressed by most black spokesmen.[55] Throughout the 1920s, most black intellectuals took an optimistic view of the settlement and growth of Harlem and devoted little attention to "tenements, crime, vice and poverty." The transformation of a community with beautiful churches, wide streets, luxury buildings, good shopping, and good transportation into the "greatest black city in the world" seemed to represent the very apogee of black accomplishment in the twentieth century, and the black real estate operators who engineered this development were regarded as heroes by the black press.[56]

In challenging the heroic image of the black landlord, Harlem Communists took issue with the pervasive tendency of the black press—and many ordinary Harlem citizens—to define the accomplishments of Harlem's middle class as "manifestations of universal Afro-American progress."[57] With the Tenants League as their platform, they argued that the black middle class—whether landlords, editors, businessmen, or ministers—profited at the *expense* of black workers; that they had a direct financial interest in the maintenance of segregation.[58] "The capitalist caste system," Richard Moore wrote, "which segregates Negro workers into Jim Crow districts makes these doubly exploited black workers the special prey of rent gougers. Black and white landlords and real estate agents take advantage of this segregation to squeeze the last nickel out of the Negro working class who are penned into the 'black ghetto.' Rents in Negro Harlem are already often double and sometimes triple those in other sections of the city."[59]

This concentration on the black middle class as the "enemy," as we have seen, owed much to the new line of the Comintern. But in the context of the tenants movement, it had an element of political logic. Black tenants *did* pay more for their housing than did whites of comparable incomes; Harlem housing *was* deteriorating rapidly, and the problems of Harlem's poor were not receiving much attention in the black or white press. As crude as Communist polemics were, as insensitive to the pride blacks took in their churches and institutions, they touched a raw nerve among some segments of the community's population.[60]

In addition, the tactics Communists used in the tenants movement represented a departure from those commonly employed by black leaders. Throughout the 1920s, Harlem political leaders, even those renowned for their militancy, rarely employed strategies of confrontation and mass protest to achieve their goals. A. Philip Randolph, one of the strongest advocates of strikes and boycotts, lacked the mass support to employ them in his work with the Pullman Porters,[61] and Marcus Garvey, though willing to use violence against black opponents, carefully avoided tactics that could lead to confrontations with government authority. Thus when dealing with the problem of high rents, negotiating, lobbying, and litigation represented the chosen methods of most black leaders and when the Emergency Rent Laws expired, they responded in these terms. On June 6, 1929, Democratic and Republican district leaders sponsored a meeting at Abyssinian Baptist Church to demonstrate community support for rent control, and to encourage tenants to deal with housing problems through their local political organizations. Communists, who held a street rally outside the Church, described its proceedings contemptuously: "Negro landlords were praised as the 'best people,' and the cheated and oppressed tenants . . . of Harlem were invited to call at the offices of various aldermen to get their doses of honeyed promises in return for voting."[62]

In mid-June, the Tenants League revealed its own tactical preferences by calling for a Harlem-wide rent strike to protest a new round of rent increases. The response to this appeal exceeded that aroused by any previous Party activity. Tenant League membership rose to over five hundred and the league had to call for Communist volunteers from other parts of the city to help staff its offices. Black landlords remained a special target of the league's propaganda and activities, although white landlords were also struck. League spokesmen claimed to have organized strikes in twenty-eight buildings owned by the black millionaire Watt Terry and singled out St. Philip's Church and the black realty firm of Nail and Parker for special attack. For the first time in their history, Harlem Communists had found a practical issue which could gain them an audience, and were making their presence felt on the streets of Harlem.[63]

In July, 1929, Communists initiated a municipal election campaign in Harlem that offered an even more dramatic display of combativeness. Nominating Richard Moore for Congress and Otto Hall for city comptroller, the Party organized regular street meetings in Harlem, with and without permits, "to test the right of the Communist Party . . . to conduct open air meetings." As police broke up meeting after meeting and arrested its participants, the New York District leadership flooded Harlem with a continuous stream of white speakers and bystanders to reinforce their black cadre. For a month or so, most Harlemites kept aloof from the combat. But in early September, during an incident in which thirteen people were arrested and several shots were fired, Party members noticed a change in the local crowds; for the first time, Harlemites had rallied to their defense: "Fifteen Negro workers filled out applications to join the Communist Party when many of our comrades were being clubbed. . . . the Negro workers rallied to the defense of the arrested comrades and expressed strong indignation at the police brutality." In subsequent meetings, crowds of up to two thousand heard the Communist speakers and "booed and hissed" when they were arrested. Top Party leaders, encouraged by this display of sympathy (which probably had more to do with resentment towards the police than admiration for the Party's program) sent their most prominent spokesmen to the rallies, regarding the campaign as a key test of the Party's willingness to bring its message to a black constituency.[64]

This upsurge of Party activity received only limited notice in the Harlem press. Election coverage in local newspapers emphasized Hubert Delany's campaign for Congress on the Republican ticket and efforts to elect Harlem's first black district leader. In a period when third parties had little impact locally or nationally and when Harlemites were gaining influence within the Republican and Democratic parties, Communists were not taken seriously as an electoral force and their conflicts with the police and the content of their platform received scant attention. The *New York Age,* in a rare editorial on the subject, expressed confidence that Harlemites would steer clear of the "Reds": "Concerted efforts to convert Harlem Negroes into adherents of the Communist Party have met with but little success. A few dissatisfied thinkers like the candidate for Congress who was arrested espouse the cause with fanatical enthusiasm. . . . but whether it makes converts is doubtful." The *Age's* views were quite representative. Until the onset of the Depression, most black intellectuals remained confident that blacks would seek change through electoral politics, education, and "race enterprise" and would avoid extremist movements.[65]

Even before the Depression, however, Harlem Communists felt optimistic about their future in the community. The activities of the Harlem Tenants League, and the response to the election rallies, had demonstrated that some Harlemites were dissatisfied with conditions in the "Mecca of the World of Negroes." Black Communists viewed the romantic image of Harlem as a myth fostered by politicians and businessmen who sought to profit from segregation. Black workers knew this, Otto Hall claimed, and would come into the Communist Party when approached in the proper way: "Harlem, in New York, is described as a 'Negro Garden of Eden' by the reactionary parties, the republicans, democrats, and socialists, but the Negro workers know better who are forced by the Jim Crow laws to reside in this overcrowded ghetto, paying 50 percent more rent for dirty, stuffy quarters than white residents, suffering from the regime of brutal police terror, suffering a higher death rate and a tremendous rate of child mortality."[66] Although Hall vastly overestimated popular discontent in Harlem, his analysis of social conditions possessed considerable accuracy. "The most profound change that Harlem experienced in the 1920s," Gilbert Osofsky wrote, "was its emergence as a slum. Largely within the space of a single decade, Harlem was transformed from a potentially ideal community into a neighborhood with manifold social and economic problems called 'deplorable,' 'unspeakable,' and 'incredible.'"[67]

But the Party had problems of its own in building a mass movement to correct these conditions and in winning leadership of Harlem's working class. Although the Party had a core of talented black organizers and had built up its black membership beyond the point "where it could be counted on the fingers of one's hand," it had great difficulty persuading blacks that the Party represented a viable alternative to the NAACP, the Garvey movement, the Democratic and Republican clubs, or the self-help and betterment organizations to which they gave their loyalty. Using language and symbols appropriated from the Bolsheviks, attacking deeply rooted black institutions with reckless abandon, Communists erected formidable cultural barriers between themselves and Harlem's people. Moreover, the interracialism Communists preached contradicted Harlemites' personal experience with nonelite whites. So long as white workers, organized and unorganized, displayed little interest in fighting discrimination or uniting with blacks around day-to-day problems, Party rhetoric about class struggle, revolution, and black-white unity possessed little appeal.[68]

In addition, the Party's ties to the Soviet Union, so responsible for its decision to organize blacks, had the power to disrupt that work with telling effect. During the fall of 1929, factional conflicts with roots in international Communist politics severely disrupted the one mass organization Harlem Communists had built: the Harlem Tenants League. When a group of American Party leaders resisted the Comintern's formula for dissolving factions in the American Party, Comintern leaders expelled them even though they represented a majority at the Party's last convention. When this group, which included Party chairman Jay Lovestone and Harlem activist Edward Welsh, tried to rally the American Party to appeal the Comintern's decision, the Comintern ordered the American Party to drive them out of all organizations in which the Party had influence. This conflict raised havoc within the Harlem Tenants League. Edward Welsh sat on the executive board of the league and had the respect of many people in the organization. When league President Richard Moore, dutifully following Comintern orders, tried to drive Welsh out of the league on the grounds that he was a "Lovestoneite agent" (a charge that must have mystified people unfamiliar with Comintern politics), many tenants, including Party member Grace Campbell, rose to Welsh's defense. At succeeding meetings, this inner-Party controversy, which had no clear class or ethnic component (Afro-Americans and West Indians were on both sides of the conflict), dominated discussion as both the Party and the Lovestone group packed the league with their supporters. By the end of October, 1929, the organization had split into two groups, each calling itself the Harlem Tenants League, while the majority of tenants had become inactive.[69]

This factional conflict, though it seriously weakened the Tenants League, failed to destroy the morale or optimism of the Harlem section's leadership. The vast majority of American Communists rallied behind the Comintern's order and repudiated their elected leaders with a vehemence that reflected their extraordinary deference to Soviet power. Top-level black Communists, steeped in an ethos of "bolshevik discipline," seemed to draw energy from the purge. Although a few black Communists stood with Lovestone in resisting the reorganization of the Party, the majority of the Harlem section's black leaders — Cyril Briggs, Richard Moore, Solomon Harper, Harold Williams, and George Padmore — remained committed to the Comintern line and attacked the "renegade degeneracy of Lovestone group" as vehemently as their white comrades. Sustained by the Soviet example during their years of isolation, they were not about to abandon it when their work was making headway. Confident of the Comintern's leadership in the struggle for Negro liberation, they pressed forward with the election campaign, with tenants work, and with protest meetings against lynching and colonial oppression.[70]

When the Depression struck, therefore, the Communist Party in Harlem had considerable political momentum and organizational experience to call upon in the crisis. Its small black cadre (consisting of no more than fifteen people), although reduced by the expulsion of the Lovestone group, included people who had been active in Harlem since the early '20s and possessed ability as writers, orators, and community organizers. In their years in the Communist movement, they had waged a successful struggle to make Negro work a central task in the Party and to promote black comrades to important Party posts. They now knew that the entire Party would be mobilized behind their efforts to build a political base in the community. Equally important, the last year and a half of organizing had convinced them that "the Negro masses can be drawn into revolutionary struggle when the Party intensifies its activity among them in their everyday struggles." In the tenants movement and the election campaign, they had perceived a "growing discontent among the Negro masses with the conditions under which they lived" and a growing dissatisfaction with the image of community progress presented by Harlem's traditional leaders — ministers, editors, politicians, and businessmen. Armed with an array of protest tactics black organizations rarely employed, they hoped to turn that discontent to the Party's advantage.[71]

NOTES

1. Theodore Draper, *American Communism and Soviet Russia* (New York: Viking Press, 1960), p. 322; Carl Offord, "An Account of the African Blood Brotherhood," in the Federal Writers Project Papers, Reel 13, Schomburg Collection, New York City; Theodore Vincent, *Black Power and the Garvey Movement* (Berkeley: Ramparts Press, 1971), p. 79.

2. Cyril Briggs, "Our Negro Work," *Communist*, 8 (Sept., 1929), 494.

3. *Negro Champion*, Jan. 9, 1929; Richard B. Moore, "The Critics and Oppo-

nents of Marcus Garvey," in John Henrik Clarke, ed., _Marcus Garvey and the Vision of Africa_ (New York: Vintage Books, 1974), p. 213; Theodore Kornweibel, Jr., _No Crystal Stair: Black Life and the Messenger, 1917-1928_ (Westport: Greenwood Press, 1976); Offord, "An Account of the African Blood Brotherhood."

4. Sally Miller, "The Socialist Party and the Negro, 1901-1920," _Journal of Negro History,_ 56 (July, 1971), 220-25; R. Laurence Moore, "Flawed Fraternity: American Socialist Response to the Negro, 1901-1912," _Historian,_ 32 (Nov., 1969), 1-18; Kornweibel, _No Crystal Stair,_ pp. 226-27; Elliott M. Rudwick, _W. E. B. Du Bois, Propagandist of the Negro Protest_ (New York: rev. ed. Atheneum, 1968), pp. 158-59; Sterling D. Spero and Abram L. Harris, _The Black Worker_ (1931; rpt. New York: Atheneum, 1968), pp. 403-6.

5. _Ibid.,_ pp. 411-12; Miller, "The Socialist Party and the Negro," 227-28; Kornweibel, _No Crystal Stair,_ pp. 30-34, 222-28; Jervis Anderson, _A. Philip Randolph: A Biographical Portrait_ (New York: Harcourt, Brace, Jovanovich, 1973), pp. 61-62, 94-98.

6. Nathan Glazer, _The Social Basis of American Communism_ (New York: Harcourt, Brace, and World, 1961), pp. 34-53; Arthur Leibman, _Jews and the Left_ (New York: John Wiley and Sons, 1978), pp. 3-28, 206-18; Carole Poole, "German American Socialist Culture," Paul Buhle, "Yiddish Socialism: The Early Years," Sirkka Tuomi Lee, "The Finns," Joseph Stipanovich, "South Slav Socialists," Peggy Dennis, "A Reminiscence," in _Cultural Correspondence,_ 6 (Spring, 1978, Special issue on the Origins of Left Culture in the United States), 13-31, 41-49, 56-60, 84-86.

7. Draper, _American Communism and Soviet Russia,_ pp. 320-21, 325-26; Harry Haywood, _Black Bolshevik: Autobiography of an Afro-American Communist_ (Chicago: Liberator Press, 1978), pp. 122-23.

8. _Ibid.,_ pp. 124-25,144; William L. Patterson, _The Man Who Cried Genocide_ (New York: International Publishers, 1971), p. 81; Tony Martin, _Race First: The Ideological and Organizational Struggles of Marcus Garvey and the Universal Negro Improvement Association_ (Westport: Greenwood Press, 1976), p. 238.

9. Draper, _American Communism and Soviet Russia,_ pp. 322-23; _Crusader,_ 1 (Nov., 1918), 3; _ibid.,_ 2 (Oct., 1919), 27.

10. Haywood, _Black Bolshevik,_ p. 126; interview with Richard B. Moore, Nov. 14, 1973; inverview with Harry Haywood, May 15, 1973

11. For examples of nationalist and emigrationist views in Briggs's journalism, see _Crusader,_ 1 (Nov., 1918), 5; _ibid.,_ 1 (Apr., 1919), 9; _ibid.,_ 1 (Aug., 1919), 4; _ibid.,_ 2 (Sept., 1919), 12. For examples of his prolabor orientation, see _ibid.,_ 1 (Nov., 1919), 6; and _ibid.,_ 1 (June, 1919), 7.

12. _Ibid.,_ 1 (Apr. 1919), 8.

13. Briggs's growing commitment to seeking alliances with the left may be seen in _ibid.,_ 2 (Dec., 1919), 9; _ibid.,_ 2 (Jan., 1920), 5, 6, 8; _ibid.,_ 2 (Feb., 1920), 5. His tentative acceptance of the _possibility_ of viable multiracial societies may be seen in _ibid.,_ 4 (Apr., 1921), 8.

14. _Ibid.,_ 5 (Nov., 1921), 15.

15. Martin and Draper both repeat Briggs's estimate of 3,000 members (see _Race First,_ pp. 237-38, and _American Communism and Soviet Russia,_ p. 325) but neither provides evidence of concrete activity by any of the brotherhood

"posts." The *Crusader* speaks of the brotherhood in such vague terms as to cast doubt that it functioned as an organization in most of the places it claimed members. See *Crusader,* 1 (Oct., 1919), 27; *ibid.,* 2 (Feb., 1920), 29; *ibid.,* 4 (Feb., 1921), 2. Perhaps future scholarship will reveal that the organization had a substantial political base; for the moment, I have my doubts.

16. Interview with George Charney, Nov. 7, 1973; interview with Abner Berry, July 29, 1974; interview with William Weinstone, July 2, 1974.

17. Vincent, *Black Power and the Garvey Movement,* pp. 74–75; Robert Minor, "The American Negro Labor Congress," unpublished typescript, Robert Minor Papers, Columbia University, Box 12; *Crusader,* (June, 1919), 4–5.

18. Martin, *Race First,* p. 236; Ernest Allen, "'Class First' Versus 'Race First': Black Radical Opposition to Marcus Garvey, 1919–192]," unpublished paper, 31–33.

19. *Ibid.,* pp. 35–37; *Crusader,* 2 (Dec., 1919), 9, 32; *ibid.,* 2 (Apr., 1920), 5–6; *ibid.,* 4 (Feb., 1921), 2, 4, 9.

20. *Ibid.,* 5 (Nov., 1921), 5, 8–9, 11–3; Martin, *Race First,* pp. 239–41; Draper, *American Communism and Soviet Russia,* pp. 324, 507; Vincent, *Black Power and the Garvey Movement,* pp. 81–82.

21. Amy Jacques Garvey, ed., *The Philosophy and Opinions of Marcus Garvey* (1925; rpt. London: Frank Cass, 1967) I, p. 29, II, pp. 57–58, 69, 71–72; Moore, "The Critics and Opponents of Marcus Garvey," pp. 225–28; Kornweibel, *No Crystal Stair,* pp. 155–58.

22. Martin, *Race First,* pp. 245–52; Draper, *American Communism and Soviet Russia,* p. 330; Amy Jacques Garvey, *Garvey and Garveyism* (London: Collier-MacMillan, 1970), pp. 145–46.

23. Sitkoff, *New Deal for Blacks,* p. 25.

24. Anderson, *A. Philip Randolph,* pp. 138–47; Kornweibel, *No Crystal Stair,* pp. 51–52, 209–12.

25. Haywood, *Black Bolshevik,* pp. 125–31; Draper, *American Communism and Soviet Russia,* p. 326.

26. *Negro Champion,* Oct. 27, 1928; *Daily Worker,* Mar. 9, 1929.

27. Draper, *American Communism and Soviet Russia,* pp. 17–27, 324; interview with Abe Shtob, Sept. 28, 1976. Draper points out that in 1922, in the newly unified Communist Party, "the English speaking share hovered at around 5 percent, with another 45 percent capable of using English as a second language."

28. Haywood, *Black Bolshevik,* pp. 138–39, 351–52; Minor, "The American Negro Labor Congress"; Draper, *American Communism and Soviet Russia,* pp. 330–31.

29. *Ibid.,* p. 354; Claude McKay, *A Long Way From Home* (1937; rpt. New York: Harcourt, Brace, and World, 1970), p. 180; Claude McKay, "Speech to the Fourth Congress of the Third Communist International, Moscow," in Wayne F. Cooper, ed., *The Passion of Claude McKay* (New York: Schocken Books, 1973), p. 93; *New York Herald Tribune,* June 29, 1937; Haywood, *Black Bolshevik,* pp. 148–65.

30. Leibman, *Jews and the Left,* pp. 492–97; Draper, *American Communism and Soviet Russia,* pp. 153–63; Glazer, *The Social Basis of American Communism,* pp. 46–53. In the newly bolshevized Party, there were four basic levels of

organization: on top, the Central Committee, the Party's highest body; under that the district committees, each administering a large area (New York City was within District 2); under those, the section committees (Harlem was within Section 4); and under those the street units, shop units, and party fractions within mass organizations. Each of the districts, sections, and units had an organizer and an organization secretary, who served as the major administrative officers.

31. Haywood, *Black Bolshevik*, pp. 140–41.

32. In *Negro Champion,* Mar. 23, 1929, Otto Huiswoud, then the director of Negro work for the Central Committee, boasted that by 1929, "there was not a single special Negro unit in the Party," and that the Negro and white members were "members together of the same units."

33. Interview with Richard B. Moore, Nov. 14, 1973.

34. Draper, *American Communism and Soviet Russia,* pp. 224–25. Draper describes the perspective of black Communists in the following manner: "More than any other segment of the American Party, most Negro Communists maintained a dual existence; they were Negroes first, Communists second. American Negro Communists . . . harbored deep resentments against the whole dominant white American Communist world. The Russian Communists stood outside this disturbing American world, and black Communists could more easily accept them as supreme arbiters over it."

35. Minor, "The American Negro Labor Congress."

36. Briggs, "Our Negro Work," 496–97; *New York Times,* Jan. 17, 1926; Draper, *American Communism and Soviet Russia,* pp. 330–32; Haywood, *Black Bolshevik,* pp. 143–47; Kornweibel, *No Crystal Stair,* pp. 195–99.

37. *Negro Champion,* Oct. 27, 1928; Harold Cruse, *Crisis of the Negro Intellectual* (New York: William Morrow, 1967), pp. 73–80.

38. *Negro Champion,* Oct. 27, 1938; Patterson, *The Man Who Cried Genocide,* pp. 75–81.

39. On Padmore's early involvement in the Party, see James R. Hooker, *Black Revolutionary: George Padmore's Path from Communism to Pan-Africanism* (New York: Praeger, 1970), pp. 6–10.

40. Interview with Abner Berry, Nov. 20, 1973; George Charney, *A Long Journey* (New York: Quadrangle, 1968), pp. 101–2. On Harper's experience as an inventor, see *Negro World,* Oct. 30, 1931; *New York Amsterdam News,* Jan. 10, 1942); Solomon Harper, "For Immediate Release," Jan. 5, 1960, and Oct. 22, 1969, in Schomburg Collection Vertical File, "Inventors and Inventions."

41. Patterson, *The Man Who Cried Genocide,* pp. 28–69; interview with Louise Thompson, Sept. 14, 1977.

42. Patterson, *The Man Who Cried Genocide,* pp. 73–99; interview with William Patterson, Sept. 20, 1971.

43. Patterson's and Haywood's autobiographies provide revealing glimpses of the life of black students in the Soviet Union. Patterson, *The Man Who Cried Genocide,* pp. 100–112; Haywood, *Black Bolshevik,* pp. 148–215.

44. *New York Amsterdam News,* Jan. 9, 1930; interview with Richard B. Moore, Nov. 14, 1973.

45. *Negro Champion,* Oct. 27, 1928, Nov. 3, 1928, Nov. 17, 1928; *Daily Worker,* Nov. 7, 1928.

46. Fernando Claudin, *The Communist Movement: From Comintern to Cominform* (Hammondsworth, England: Penguin Books, 1975), pp. 88–90; Bert Cochran, *Labor and Communism: The Conflict that Shaped American Unions* (Princeton: Princeton University Press, 1977), pp. 43–44.

47. Interview with Harry Haywood, May 15, 1973; Haywood, *Black Bolshevik,* pp. 218–35; Draper, *American Communism and Soviet Russia,* pp. 342–46. Haywood has insisted, in both his autobiography, and in his interview with me, that he had to be convinced of the validity of the self-determination thesis by Soviet colleagues. I tend to agree. My reading of the *Crusader,* and of the Party press in the '20s, had revealed nothing remotely resembling a proposal for a black nation in the South.

48. Draper, *American Communism and Soviet Russia,* pp. 347–53; Haywood, *Black Bolshevik,* pp. 259–69. On Hall's talents and problems, see *Black Bolshevik,* pp. 25–29.

49. "Resolution of the Communist International," Oct. 26, 1928, in *The Communist Position on the Negro Question* (New York: Workers Library Publishers, 1934), pp. 57–58.

50. *Ibid.,* pp. 60–63.

51. *Daily Worker,* Feb. 13, 1929; Haywood, *Black Bolshevik,* pp. 291–92, 317–18.

52. *Daily Worker,* Apr. 25, 1929, June 8, 1929.

53. *Ibid.,* Mar. 9, 1929, Apr. 15, 1929, Apr. 16, 1929.

54. Mark I. Solomon, "Red and Black: Negroes and Communism, 1929–1932," (Ph.D. dissertation, Harvard University, 1972), pp. 264–72, 291–309.

55. *Daily Worker,* May 27, 1929, June 3, 1929.

56. Nathan Huggins, *Harlem Renaissance* (New York: Oxford University Press, 1971), p. 4; Kornweibel, *No Crystal Stair,* p. 105; James Weldon Johnson, *Black Manhattan* (1930; rpt. New York: Atheneum, 1973), pp. 154–55; *Interstate Tatler,* Mar. 29, 1929.

57. David Levering Lewis, *When Harlem Was in Vogue* (New York: Knopf, 1981), pp. 108–13; Kornweibel, *No Crystal Stair,* pp. 24–25, 205. The quote is from Lewis, p. 109.

58. *Daily Worker,* May 9, 1929, May 28, 1929, June 3, 1929; *Negro Champion,* May 25, 1929.

59. *Daily Worker,* Apr. 15, 1929.

60. Gilbert Osofsky, *Harlem, The Making of a Ghetto* (New York: Harper and Row, 1968), pp. 136–43.

61. On Randolph's tactics as a leader of the Pullman Porters Union in the '20s, see William H. Harris, *Keeping the Faith: A. Philip Randolph, Milton P. Webster, and the Brotherhood of Sleeping Car Porters* (Urbana: University of Illinois Press, 1977), pp. 111–16, and Anderson, *A. Philip Randolph,* pp. 191–203.

62. *Daily Worker,* June 8, 1929.

63. *New York Amsterdam News,* June 5, 1929; *Daily Worker,* June 12, 1929, June 25, 1929, July 1, 1929, July 2, 1929, July 4, 1929; *Revolutionary Age,* Nov. 1, 1929. John Nail was the son-in-law of James Weldon Johnson, executive director of the NAACP.

64. *New York Amsterdam News,* July 17, 1929, Aug. 14, 1929, Sept. 18, 1929;

Daily Worker, Aug. 5, 1929, Aug. 14, 1929, Aug. 19, 1929, Sept. 6, 1929, Sept. 14, 1929, Sept. 16, 1929. The indented quote is from *Daily Worker,* Sept. 7, 1929.

65. Osofsky, *Harlem, The Making of a Ghetto,* pp. 173–77; *Negro World,* Nov. 2, 1929; *New York Amsterdam News,* Oct. 30, 1929, *New York Age,* Aug. 3, 1929. The extended quote is from the *New York Age,* Sept. 21, 1929.

66. *Daily Worker,* Nov. 2, 1929.

67. Osofsky, *Harlem, The Making of a Ghetto,* p. 90.

68. Briggs, "Our Negro Work," 494; Spero and Harris, *The Black Worker,* p. 413.

69. *Daily Worker,* Sept. 11, 1929, Oct. 30, 1929; *Revolutionary Age,* Nov. 1, 1929; *New York Amsterdam News,* Jan. 8, 1930; interview with Richard B. Moore, Nov. 14, 1973; Draper, *American Communism and Soviet Russia,* pp. 405–91. The main issue that split the CPUSA was the relationship of the Comintern to the American Party. The group that became the Communist Party Opposition (pejoratively called the "Lovestoneites"), did not believe that the Comintern had the right to depose a majority faction in the American Party and replace it with a minority, or to shape the American Party according to its own specifications. On the Negro question, some differences ultimately emerged between the opposition group and the Party, but these had not been primary when the split first occurred. The opposition group rejected the new Comintern line on "self determination in the Black Belt." But differences over self-determination did not explain why people chose one faction over the other. Many Communists who had initially opposed self-determination (e.g., James Ford and Otto Huiswoud) accepted the Comintern's right to shape Party policy, endorsed the new line in deference to Comintern discipline, and became bitter opponents of the "Lovestone deviation."

70. *Daily Worker,* Oct. 30, 1929. The black members who aligned with the Lovestone group were Edward Welsh, Grace Campbell, Rothschild Francis, and C. B. Jenkins.

71. *Daily Worker,* Sept. 7, 1929, Sept. 14, 1929, Nov. 1, 1929.

2

The Onset of the Depression—
The Party Takes the Offensive

FOR VIRTUALLY EVERYONE in Harlem, the Great
Depression was a traumatic experience. The economic crisis had the same
general impact as in the rest of America—massive unemployment, evictions, bank failures, loss of family savings, loss of businesses—but in
every instance it was far more serious. Throughout most of the Depression, the unemployment rate for Harlem blacks hovered between one-
and-a-half and three times that of the whites in New York City, and the
social dislocations imposed by joblessness were proportionately more severe. In addition, Harlem's emergent business elite, based primarily in
real estate and personal service, lost much of its foothold in the local
economy that had made its members "race heroes" and leaders in community affairs. An Urban League spokesman estimated that the percentage of Harlem real estate owned or managed by blacks had slid from 35
percent in 1929 to 5 percent in 1935, and a census study published the latter year showed an 8 percent decline in black-owned retail units after the
Depression struck.[1]

These economic setbacks struck at the roots of Harlem's political and
intellectual life, and opened the way for new modes of thinking and action. As the impact of the Depression became visible, Harlem's churchmen, editors, politicians, and social-service leaders made an energetic effort to help the community through an intensification of relief measures
that had worked in the past: charity drives in collaboration with white
business leaders, "race loyalty" campaigns to encourage support of black
business, and efforts to persuade white businesses in Harlem to employ
black salespeople.[2] But while these self-help efforts had some positive
effects—Harlem's churches were serving several thousand free meals a
week by the winter of 1930–31—they barely touched the need for jobs,
food, or shelter by the tens of thousands of unemployed Harlemites. The
displaced and demoralized people, of all social classes, represented a
large potential constituency for Communist-led activity, if the Party were

able to provide more effective means of solving Depression problems than other Harlem organizations. After years of isolation and marginal appeal, Harlem Communists had an opportunity to prove that militant action and an alliance with the white working class were the best ways to fight racial discrimination and solve Harlem's economic problems.

However, Communists faced severe obstacles in trying to enroll Harlem's population into protest actions under its leadership. Most Harlemites lacked exposure to the confrontation tactics Communists espoused, either in their neighborhood organizations—which preferred legalistic measures—or in their activities at the workplace. In 1930, nearly 55 percent of Harlem's employed population worked in the service sector: as domestics, porters, elevator operators, waiters, bootblacks, laundry workers, janitors, and the like. Not only were such occupations demoralizing, but they were characterized by a paternalistic ethos that drove workers to personalize resentments, making collective action difficult. In addition, blacks in transportation and manufacturing (composing 10 and 20 percent of Harlem's workforce, respectively) were concentrated in the least skilled and secure occupations, while blacks were barred almost completely from white-collar jobs in finance, communications, insurance and the retail trades. This job profile, compounded by labor union discrimination, isolated black workers from the rest of the labor force and strongly retarded their unionization. In 1928, when blacks composed approximately 12 percent of Manhattan's population, they represented only 3.8 percent of its union members. When the Depression struck, very few Harlemites had experience in industrial conflict, or for that matter in any form of mass protest that challenged governmental authority.[3]

In addition, much of Harlem's working class still bore the mark of the rural southern world from which they came: a world in which kinship networks, the church, and individual white protectors represented the sole buffers against the unchecked power of employers and white supremacist organizations. In 1930, only 21.2 percent of Manhattan's black population was born in that borough; 49 percent were born in southern states, with Virginia, the Carolinas, and Georgia contributing the largest number.[4] Migrating from regions in which government was in the hands of hostile forces, many Harlemites looked to personal solutions to help them through crises, turning to family members and neighbors to provide them with aid, or if that failed, to their minister or the local ward boss. Within this framework, Harlemites displayed considerable ingenuity; rent parties, doubling up of families, and taking in boarders all proliferated during the Depression years, serving as something of a cushion against the worst of the conditions.[5]

But even when these methods failed—or extracted too great a price in privacy or family stability—working-class Harlemites often turned to religious groups, rather than radical politics, as an outlet for their discontent. During the Depression, an enormous variety of religious organizations proliferated among Harlem's poor, ranging from storefront churches, to evangelical movements led by charismatic preachers, to self-contained "new religions" with their own theology and set of rituals. The largest of these, the Father Divine movement, enrolled thousands of members in Harlem alone and spawned a host of businesses that provided jobs for its members, along with a program of cheap meals for needy Harlem residents. Some of these movements incorporated strong political statements into their theology, others remained largely otherworldly, but they offered people with an essentially religious world view a way of focusing their energies, maintaining their self-respect, and meeting some of their immediate economic needs. To the poorest segments of Harlem's population, among whom an African-derived folk culture still held considerable sway and to whom the spirit-world seemed palpable and alive, these movements provided an opportunity for self-expression and a sense of security that secular radicalism and the institutional black church had difficulty matching.[6]

Before the Depression wrought its damage, the atmosphere of Harlem's poorest blocks seemed virtually immune to Communist agitation. In the midst of hawkers selling sweet potatoes, ribs, and other southern delicacies, Harlemites of the older generation practiced a casual neighborliness reminiscent of small-town life, while their children learned to cope with the perils and pleasures of the city streets. The courtly manners of the old folks, the laughter of the children, the sweet talk of the hustlers, the banter of teenage stickball players, and the purposeful movements of working men and women provided an almost impenetrable background to the speeches of Communist soapboxers, filled with images of "class struggle" and "revolution." Until their lives fell apart under the weight of the economic disaster, poorer Harlemites tended to shut out the Communist message — a message lacking the humor, imaginative power, and personalization of great events that they valued in the spoken word.

Nevertheless, a sizable minority of Harlem's population, though suspicious of Communist intentions, carefully scrutinized what Communists said. Harlem's working class contained a small but influential group of skilled and sophisticated men and women who had been exposed to radical ideologies and who were resolutely secular in their approach to politics. Longshoremen and seamen, printers and apparel workers, postmen and musicians, these individuals often had travelled widely (many were veterans) and had been educated far beyond the jobs they actually held. Along with Harlem's intellectuals and small businessmen, they had been the mainstay of the Garvey movement and other militant groups that proliferated after the war, and they relished the street-corner debates that were a feature of Harlem's life. Unlike their poorer and less educated neighbors, they were not as likely to be intimidated by the militancy or intellectualism of Communist speakers or their invocation of history or international events. Having been exposed to a world historical vision in the Garvey movement, or in the orations of great Harlem street speakers like Hubert Harrison, they were prepared to evaluate Communist arguments on their intellectual and political merits. Communists had to win over some of these people to make headway in Harlem, but they could not be organized on rhetoric alone. Deeply cynical of white intentions, they wanted to see concrete evidence that Communist tactics worked, and that white Communists and Party sympathizers would treat them with respect.[7]

Providing such evidence did not prove to be easy. At the time of the stock market crash, Harlem Party leaders, just recovering from the conflict with the "Lovestoneites," were grappling with ways of mobilizing white Communists, located in immigrant sections of Harlem, to do organizing work in black neighborhoods. Many white Communists displayed little enthusiasm for this task and others made black recruits feel unwelcome in Party circles. Late in 1929, black Communist Otto Hall, who had moved into the leadership of the New York District since his return from the Soviet Union, claimed that the Party had lost many black workers "through repeated manifestations of white chauvinism," and warned that the Party would have to "sear out with a red hot iron" all signs of prejudice in its ranks. As evidence, he cited the case of a white Party member who physically attacked a black man for sitting with two white female Communists in the cafeteria of a Party-affiliated fraternal organization. The white member was expelled.[8]

Despite rank-and-file resistance, the Party leadership, prodded by its black cadre, took forceful steps to define the organization of black workers and the defense of black rights as a moral imperative for the Party. In mid-December, 1929, the International Labor Defense, the Party's legal defense organization, made the struggle for Negro rights its central priority and began organizing meetings in black neighborhoods to protest lynching, police brutality, and incidents of racial discrimination. During the same period, Communists organized meetings in Harlem protesting the American occupation of Haiti, held forums on the Gastonia, North Carolina, textile strike publicizing Communist opposition to jim crow, and funded a tabloid called the *Liberator* under the editorship of Cyril Briggs.[9]

These activities, which had little effect on Party recruiting, coincided with a coordinated Communist offensive on the issue of unemployment. In December, 1929, the Party issued a manifesto calling upon Communists to organize employed and unemployed workers into "Councils of the Unemployed" to force federal, state, and city governments to provide direct relief to the unemployed. The Party's general secretary, Earl Browder, accompanied this manifesto with an order to make organization of blacks a top priority, warning that any unemployed movement which did not put black concerns "in the foreground" would be doomed to failure.[10]

The Harlem Party organization enthusiastically implemented this call to organize unemployed black workers. Possessed of capable black leaders and organizers, it could also call on the energies of a growing number of whites assigned to Negro work. Who these individuals were, at this stage in the Party's history, is difficult to determine. Because blacks served as the major Party spokespersons in Harlem, both in large community meetings and in the Party press, the names of white leaders or organizers almost never appear in the public record.[11] But if interviews with Party activists can be trusted, the bulk of whites assigned to work in black neighborhoods were in their teens or early twenties and came either from the two colleges located in the Harlem Section—Columbia and City—or from immigrant neighborhoods surrounding black Harlem (though some were "colonized" in from Brooklyn or the Bronx). Completely unfamiliar with the community and its culture, they were funnelled directly into street organizing—handling out leaflets, canvassing apartment houses, speaking from soapboxes, or organizing spontaneous demonstrations. A good many of them performed their tasks indifferently or poorly, turning off even Harlemites desperate for help. But a few of them proved to be a real asset to the understaffed Harlem leadership. Coming from neighborhoods with a history of militant unionism or support for revolutionary activities in Europe (this was most true of the Jewish, Irish, and Finnish cadre), exposed to strikes and demonstrations since their early teens (many were veterans of Party youth organizations), they helped provide black Party leaders with the critical mass of skilled organizers necessary to persuade unemployed Harlemites to participate in Party sponsored protest actions inside and outside Harlem.[12]

By February, 1930, two months after Browder's directive, the Party had organized an Upper Harlem Council of the Unemployed, which defined, as its first project, the mobilization of blacks for a March 6 demonstration at Union Square marking "International Day of Unemployment." The *Liberator* called upon black workers to "get together with workers of all nationalities and races" and demand "WORK or WAGES": "Fellow Negro workers! Are we going to allow ourselves and our families to starve? Will we allow ourselves to be kicked out into the streets by the greedy landlords. . . . We have only one choice! Fight or starve."[13]

Party activists, following the ultraleft line of the Sixth Comintern Congress, accompanied this campaign with an attack on the credibility of virtually every noncommunist organization active in Harlem. Black International Labor Defense (ILD) organizer Charles Alexander bluntly asserted that "The National Association for the Advancement of Colored People, the National Urban League, and the churches are all agents of the capitalist class in the ranks of the Negro race," and Cyril Briggs charged that black leaders avoided acting against joblessness because of their personal stake in the capitalist system:

> Negro workers! Where are the Negro business and professional class leaders in this terrible crisis. . . . What program against unemployment have the NAACP, the Urban League, the UNIA etc.? What program have Dubois, Fred Moore, A. Philip Randolph, James Johnson, Marcus Garvey, etc.?
> The Negro bourgeoisie does not put up any real fight against Negro oppression for the reason that they have a stake in the system that oppresses us. They are lap dogs at the table of the imperialists, demanding simply increased participation (as landlords, employers, etc.) in the exploitation of the Negro masses.[14]

Despite such attacks on the integrity of black organizations, which exaggerated their subservience to corporate interests, the Party managed to attract a sizable number of blacks to the March 6 demonstrations. With Otto Hall and James Ford, recently returned from the Soviet Union, among the major speakers, and black-white unity among its major slogans, the Union Square rally made blacks feel welcome in New York's first large-scale protest against Depression conditions. A conspicuous part of the huge crowd, blacks played an integral role in the melee that ensued when the protesters tried to march on City Hall.[15] "In numerous instances," the *Liberator* reported, "Negro workers were told by the police to 'get the hell out of here and go back to Harlem where you belong,'" and blacks were represented in the group that tried to defend the demonstration from police attacks. Black and white workers, Cyril Briggs commented proudly, "stood shoulder to shoulder against the brutal attacks of the police," providing "smashing refutation of the lying slanders . . . that Negro workers are too stupid to organize and too cowardly to resist oppression."[16]

Harlem Communists followed this demonstration with an interracial dance at the Rockland Palace Ballroom, a popular Harlem dance hall located on 155th Street, designed to show that the Party's commitment to black-white unity extended to the sphere of personal relations. The program represented a strange pastiche of music, theatre, and politics, featuring music by Duke Ellington, a "black and white" interpretive dance by Allison Burroughs and Edith Segal, speeches by black and white Party leaders, and the singing of the Internationale. The evening ended with a pledge by William Z. Foster, director of trade union work for the CPUSA, to "organize Negro workers side by side with white workers" until the "system of capitalist exploitation was overthrown and a workers' government . . . was introduced throughout the world." An editorial in the *Liberator* boasted with considerable accuracy, that "no such demonstration was ever [before] witnessed in Negro Harlem."[17]

Throughout the spring of 1930, the Harlem Party concentrated its attention on the organization of the unemployed, and protests against lynching. Using street meetings and indoor rallies, the Party tried to make its activities widely known to Harlem's black population. But, it faced important obstacles in trying to do so. Its headquarters, at 306 Lenox Avenue (just north of 125th Street) were located in a predominantly black area adjacent to Harlem's Finnish community, and it held most of its meetings in the Finnish Progressive Hall, on 126th Street between 5th and Lenox, the Harlem Casino, on 116th Street near Lenox, and St. Luke's Hall, on 130th Street near Lenox. Of these, only St. Luke's, located on an all-black block, was a popular gathering place for black organizations. But because of the Party's attacks on the black church, the most important meeting places in Harlem—church meeting rooms and auditoriums—were effectively closed to it. Party street agitation gave it far greater visibility. Party-sponsored meetings on unemployment and lynching ranged from 137th Street and 7th Avenue, north to 144th Street and Lenox Avenue, south to 110th Street and 5th Avenue.[18] In most instances, Party activists faced little difficulty holding such meetings; whites felt safe walking in Harlem at all hours of the day and night, and none regarded street crime as a serious deterrent to political activity.[19] But the most popular speaking corners in Harlem, Lenox Avenue between 133rd and 135th Streets, represented a problem for Party activists; Garvey organizations claimed them as their special "territory" and resented outsiders using this space to denounce Garvey (as Communists were prone to do).[20]

Despite the Party's marginality, Harlem Communists did not tread softly in getting their message across. In both agitation against unemployment and antilynching work, the Party devoted as much attention to attacking other Harlem organizations as to publicizing its own activities. In late March, 1930, Communists disrupted a conference on unemployment sponsored by the leading churches and social organizations of Harlem. Although the conference, chaired by A. Philip Randolph, came up with a number of constructive proposals—among them a five-day week and an eight-hour day, support for black business, and the sponsorship of public works programs to hire the unemployed—black Communists at the conference expressed so much contempt for these proposals that they were ejected from the meeting. In their commentary on the conference,

Party newspapers wrote off the whole enterprise as an "attempt to mislead the Negro jobless," and dismissed the participants as "traitors," "scab herders," and "sky pilots."[21]

Communists assumed a similar stance at an April, 1930, meeting called by the Brotherhood of Sleeping Car Porters to protest the Georgia lynching of a Pullman porter named J. H. Wilkins. Following the strategic guidelines of the Comintern, which defined socialists and reformers as bulwarks of capitalist society, Communists seized upon this incident to organize a "united front from below" with Pullman porters aimed at getting them to repudiate their leaders. When Brotherhood leaders unveiled their plan for nationwide protest meetings and an investigation of the incident, black Communist Herbert Newton arose, attacked them for their timidity, and called for the picketing of Pullman Company offices and a nationwide strike to demand the arrest of the lynchers. In the middle of his speech, police, on the request of the chairman, threw Newton out of the meeting and two Communists present who came to his defense were placed under arrest. One of them, Solomon Harper, received a three-month sentence for his part in the affair, and Communists held street meetings throughout Harlem jointly protesting the "murder of Wilkins" and the "treacherous role of Randolph."[22]

Such disruptive and sectarian tactics, might, in a different time and place, have completely isolated the Party. But in a period of economic collapse, the militancy of the Communists, their willingness to risk arrest to make their demands heard, struck a responsive chord on the streets of Harlem, even though it brought them few new recruits. Despite the strangeness of much Communist rhetoric, the Party was the only group in the community organizing protest marches and street demonstrations in response to economic and racial problems of almost universal concern in Harlem. In July, 1930, Harlem leaders told a Congressional investigating committee that there had been an "increase in sentiment and sympathy among Negroes for the Communist movement" and a growing attendance of blacks at Communist meetings, even though less than fifty Harlemites actually belonged to the "Communist organization."[23]

Most Harlem leaders, at this stage, expressed little concern about the Party's political offensive. The *Amsterdam News* and the *New York Age* assumed a wry and humorous tone when covering Communist activity, arguing that heavy-handed repression by police and public officials gave Communists what little support they had. If employers and public officials dealt fairly with blacks and the working population, they argued, neither Communists nor the Soviet Union would present much of a threat.[24]

However, the Garvey movement newspaper, the *Negro World,* took the Party's offensive in Black America far more seriously. Communists viewed the UNIA rank and file as sincere militants who would make good recruits to the Party if they were separated from "reactionary" leaders, and the Party made special efforts to send the *Negro World* all announcements of Party activities which might attract UNIA members. The *Negro World* published ILD press releases on lynching and antilynching conferences during the spring of 1930, but took umbrage at persistent Communist attacks on Marcus Garvey as a "faker" and "misleader."[25] During April and May, 1930, the paper published a two-part series on "The Negro and Communism" by black Socialist Frank Crosswaith which was highly critical of the Party and the Soviet Union.

Crosswaith, an organizer for the International Ladies Garment Workers Union and head of the Trade Union Committee for Organizing Negro Workers (later renamed the Negro Labor Committee) assailed the lack of democracy in Soviet society and the intolerance Communists displayed toward political opponents. The *Negro World* editor explained that he published the series because he believed that "the Communist movement represents to the Negro in particular and the working class generally a menace," and because he wanted his readers to "be able to more intelligently separate the communist menace from the constructive social, political, and economic movements of our time."[26]

Party conflicts with the Garvey movement were not confined to the newspapers. As Communists took their antilynching campaign and organizing of the unemployed to the streets, they found themselves in direct competition with Garveyite street speakers, who were a fixture of Harlem life. Although the Garvey movement was split into many factions and lacked the concentrated organizational strength it possessed in the early '20s, a number of Garveyite leaders had mass followings and could express with considerable eloquence their version of Garvey's philosophy. One of these leaders, St. William Wellington Wellwood Grant, head of the UNIA's Tiger Division, had a particular distaste for Communists. On the evening of June 28 and 29, his group became involved in altercations with Communists at antilynching meetings the Party sponsored on Lenox Avenue street corners which Garveyites regarded as their territory (130th, 133rd, and 135th Streets). In the second altercation, police intervened, and a black Communist named Alfred Levy died of injuries sustained in the brawl.[27]

Upon hearing of Levy's death, the New York District of the Communist Party called upon black and white Communists from all over the city to attend a funeral demonstration in Levy's honor in Harlem on July 1. The Party's desire to make a show of strength in Harlem was increased by the killing of a Mexican Communist named Gonzalo Gonzales by police in lower Harlem the night before the Levy funeral. Gonzales had been shot while fighting with a policeman who had tried to stop a group of Com-

munists from marching to a protest meeting at the Harlem Casino. When
Party leaders heard about Gonzales's death, they scheduled a funeral demonstration in his honor for July 4 and redoubled their efforts to mobilize the entire district organization of the Party to show its support for
the two fallen comrades.[28]

Both funerals represented impressive displays of Party strength and
pageantry. Over two thousand people attended the Levy funeral, the vast
majority of them white, though a special guard of a hundred blacks was
assigned to protect the funeral parlor. Communists set up a platform
outside the funeral home, where speeches were made honoring Levy's
contribution to the movement and attacking the police and the Garvey
movement. When the speeches ended, the Party members assembled followed the hearse in a funeral procession through the streets of Harlem.[29]
The Gonzales funeral had a similar format and drew an equally large
crowd. "Several thousand communists of every race and color thronged
Lenox Avenue," the *Amsterdam News* reported, and heard Communist
speakers make bitter attacks against capitalism and the police. But the reaction of Harlem residents was rather restrained. "Most of Harlem looked
upon the parade and funeral as part of the holiday demonstration," the
Age commented, "and after the Communist speakers had orated for an
hour . . . everybody went off to lunch or to attend the baseball games."[30]

Following the funerals, Harlem Communists escalated their program
of street meetings on unemployment and lynching while giving even
greater attention than before to the struggle against Garveyism. Communist speakers and writers denounced Garvey and Harlem UNIA leaders
for opposing united action of black and white workers "while at the same
time making friends with the real and only enemy of the Negro people,
the white capitalist class." Such polemics did not improve relations between Communists and Garveyite leaders; at least two Party street meetings that summer were interrupted by open fighting between the two
groups.[31] But the Party fought off the attackers and continued both
meetings, leading it to boast of a growing credibility with Harlem street
crowds. "Many members of the UNIA were present and remained," the
Daily Worker claimed after one of the incidents, "regardless of the attempts of their leaders to break up the meeting."[32]

The growing confidence of Communists in their ability to protect their
public meetings in Harlem stemmed, in part, from their ability to attract
former Garveyites into the Party's orbit. In the summer of 1930, a gruff,
powerfully built ex-Garveyite named Steve Kingston emerged as one of the
Party's major spokesmen in the street wars with Grant, and he was joined
shortly thereafter by Louis Campbell and William Fitzgerald, both of
whom rose to leadership within the Harlem organization. Tough, street-
smart and self-educated, these men provided an important complement

to more theoretically inclined leaders like Briggs and Moore, whose education and manners separated them from the bulk of Harlem's population. From step-ladders and soapboxes, they forcefully projected the Party's image as a "fighting organization" and though they made few recruits, they appear to have neutralized much of the hostility that integrated Party street meetings provoked among Harlemites with nationalist backgrounds.[33]

During the fall of 1930, Communists added to their credibility in Harlem by initiating a strategy to deal with evictions for nonpayment of rent. The Harlem Unemployment Council, which had previously mobilized Harlemites for demonstrations at City Hall, now organized interracial defense squads to return the furniture of evicted tenants to their apartments. Although the tactic did not always succeed in stopping evictions, it attracted broad support—and sometimes participation—from Harlem residents. The *Amsterdam News* described one instance where the landlord tried a second eviction after the "reds" had earlier moved the furniture back. When the city marshals arrived, a crowd of several hundred was gathered at the scene, "carrying banners with the legend 'No Work, No Rent,'" and tried to interfere with the removal of the furnishings. Four Unemployed Council activists, two whites and two blacks, were arrested in the incident and sentenced to ten days in jail. On several other occasions, the Unemployed Council sent large delegations to court with people who had received dispossess notices to try to persuade judges to stop the evictions, and if that failed, to warn them that the evictions would be resisted. In the chaotic atmosphere of the Depression, with court calendars packed with eviction cases and city marshals overextended, these methods kept some unemployed Harlemites in their apartments.[34]

Black Communists also featured prominently in an October 16 demonstration to demand that the Board of Estimate appropriate twenty-five dollars a week for each unemployed person. Maude White, a Soviet-educated black organizer in the Party's Needle Trades Industrial Union, was part of the delegation that marched into the board, and Sam Brown, a leader of the Harlem Unemployed Council, was among the speakers at the accompanying rally in City Hall Plaza. Both were injured in police attacks on the demonstration; Maude White was pushed down a flight of stairs and Sam Brown was badly beaten. But the Board of Estimate appropriated one million dollars to aid the unemployed the day after the demonstration, adding to the esprit de corps of Communists throughout the city. The transformation of the unemployed movement into a practical political instrument brought the Party closer to the day-to-day concerns of the Harlem community and helped it widen its base of support. In mid-December, section organizer Harold Williams reported, the Unemployment Council had made "such great headway" that unemployed black workers were using the headquarters of the Party in Harlem as a social and educational center.[35]

The Party also gained mileage from antilynching agitation, which assumed far greater prominence in its program than it had in the past. Harlem Communists organized forty street meetings against lynching between September 27 and October 2, designated by the Party as National Anti-Lynching Week, and Communists formed a new organization called the League of Struggle for Negro Rights in November, 1930, that made the suppression of lynching the central point in its program. Although this organization represented a thinly disguised vehicle for the Communist program on the Negro question, including its plan for "self-determination in the Black Belt," Communists pulled off a public relations coup by persuading Langston Hughes, perhaps the best known poet of the Harlem Renaissance, to become the organization's president.[36]

Hughes represented the Party's first important convert among Harlem's creative intelligentsia. He was not a Party member when he accepted this post, but he had just ended a long relationship with his patroness, Charlotte Osgood Mason, on a bitter note (she was apparently offended by the appearance of "class struggle" imagery — and militant atheism — in his poetry) and was feeling antagonistic toward the white elite upon whom black writers had been so dependent for financial support. Always drawn aesthetically toward expression of folk themes, Hughes became a "proletarian poet" under the press of Depression conditions, assuming a stance of an advocate for rebellion by the oppressed. Communist leaders, conscious of the prestige Hughes brought to the movement, allowed him to function as a symbolic leader and to devote himself to his writing without political interference. The decision was a shrewd one. Hughes, though drawn to the left by conviction, would have chafed under the rigid discipline demanded of most Party members and would have rejected direct dictation as to the content of his work. By allowing him to function as a "fellow traveller," and publishing and celebrating his work within Party publications in the United States and abroad, Communists improved their standing with black intellectuals of the Renaissance generation, among whom Hughes was a respected figure.[37]

In addition, Hughes's close friend and collaborator, Louise Thompson, a brilliant and vivacious black social worker who shared the same patroness, joined him in establishing ties with the left. Thompson's involvement, first as a "fellow traveller," later as a Party leader, proved to be an enormous asset to the Harlem CP. Though not an artist herself, Thompson knew all of the key figures in the Harlem Renaissance (she was briefly married to novelist Wallace Thurman) and was on first-name terms with black leaders of the Urban League and the NAACP. Her spacious apartment on Convent Avenue, according to Henry Lee Moon, served as one of the meeting places for the "intellectually and artistically inclined black community." Once she became interested in the Communist Party, Thompson used her reputation as a graceful hostess to expose black artists, writers, and theatrical people to leftist causes in a relaxed and low-pressure setting.[38]

Thompson's migration to the left, like that of Hughes, stemmed partially from a "distaste and hatred of white philanthrophy." California-educated, Thompson had taught at Hampton Institute and a black college in Pine Bluff, Arkansas, where she chafed under the arbitrary rule of white trustees, and then came to New York as an Urban League fellow, where she encountered patronizing behavior on the part of many whites who worked in black-advancement organizations. "When I was being interviewed for jobs," she recalled, "people took all kinds of liberties with me, inquiring about the most personal details of my behavior, what I ate, when I went to the bathroom." Thompson discussed these experiences with William Patterson, whom she had sought out in Harlem as a fellow Californian and fellow intellectual (they had briefly known each other on the West Coast). Patterson, a new convert to the CP, described the racial prejudice she experienced as the logical outcome of capitalism, and encouraged her to begin reading Marx and to participate in leftist causes. Although Patterson soon left for the Soviet Union, the seeds he sowed fell on fertile soil. By 1930, Thompson had begun holding discussions in her apartment about the Russian Revolution and the Party's position on the Negro question. For the moment, these "bull sessions" of the Harlem intelligentsia remained worlds apart from the harsh world of Party street organizing, but they gave the Party access to the intimate social networks of Harlem's intellectual elite, which would serve it in good stead when it sought to broaden its political influence.[39]

The political gains registered by the Harlem Party, however limited, brought severe internal tensions in their wake. As larger numbers of blacks began to enter the circle of Party activities, especially on the street level, problems arose as to what blacks and whites in the organization should expect of one another. In some cases, blacks confronted open hostility from white Party members and sympathizers when they participated in social events under Party sponsorship. Three black men attending a dance at the Finnish Workers Club in Harlem, on 126th Street between 5th and Lenox Avenues, were shunted off into a corner and threatened with ejection by a group of white youths at a dance (this incident would soon become the basis for a much publicized "white chauvinism" trial in Harlem). The children of two black Party members attending a Workers International Relief camp were harassed and "called nigger" by other children in spite of the fact that the Party had tried to attract black children to its summer camps. The affair at the summer camp was publicized in the *Negro World* under the heading "Communist Jim Crow" and Party leaders knew that they had to make a determined effort to eliminate open racism from their ranks if they were to have success in recruiting and retaining black members.[40]

However, such open displays of hostility were less common than a more generalized confusion about how far Communists were to go to make blacks feel at home in the movement. Were they obligated to dance with blacks who looked isolated at a social event? Engage them in conversation? Go out with them on a date? Did black members have to pay the same dues as white members? Meet the same standards in performing Party tasks? Be criticized with the same severity for breaches of Party discipline? Such issues, difficult to resolve even with the best of intentions, deeply irritated some rank-and-file white Communists, concentrated in the foreign-language groups, who had only a perfunctory interest in Negro problems. Willing to accept the Party's commitment to formal racial equality, they opposed "bending over backwards" to accommodate black workers, putting forward the position that "all workers should be treated the same."[41]

An incident at the Harlem section headquarters, in December, 1930, dramatized this conflict. A predominantly white Party unit came to the headquarters, located in a black neighborhood, to show a film for fund-raising purposes. A large number of unemployed black people were in the hall at the time, talking and socializing, and the unit organizer insisted that they pay the admission price or leave. When the blacks refused, the unit organizer, "Comrade Gabor," tried to push them out of the hall, and a fistfight almost broke out between the blacks and whites present. When the black section organizer, Harold Williams, criticized the unit for their handling of the incident, he was accused of being a "black chauvinist" and a "Negro terrorist." The unit voted to hold its future affairs at the Italian Workers Club, located in a white neighborhood, rather than in the section headquarters, which was in a black district.[42]

The top leadership of the U.S. Party, located in New York, seized upon this incident as a major offense, almost as serious as the open display of prejudice at the Finnish Workers Club. In the year-and-a-half since the Comintern Resolution, key figures in the Party hierarchy, especially Browder, Foster, and *Daily Worker* editor Clarence Hathaway, had become as passionately committed to antiracist policies as Briggs and Moore and were determined to use Party organs to expose important examples of rank-and-file resistance. In line with this policy, *Daily Worker* writer Vera Saunders severely criticized both the behavior of the white Communists in the incident, and the theoretical justification they offered for their actions. The charge of "black chauvinism" particularly arouse her ire: "Chauvinism is the aggressive attitude and oppression of one nation over another. Can we for one moment seriously entertain the contention that Negroes are aggressively exercising their national rights over the whites? No! What these comrades mean in making the charges of 'black chauvinism' is that these Negroes are race conscious as well as class conscious and this we certainly must commend and not reject." Saunders reaffirmed the leadership's expectation that white Communists take extraordinary measures to win the confidence of blacks who entered Party circles: "We must understand . . . that the Negroes mistrust whites because of ages of oppression and betrayal . . . and that an especial approach is necessary towards them. . . . If a Negro worker goes through Harlem and says that the Communists (who are mostly whites) tried to push him out of their hall, it has much greater political significance than if a white worker were to assert this."[43]

Saunders's argument, which placed the responsibility for easing racial tension in the Party almost entirely upon whites, drew powerfully upon a new—and definitive—resolution on the Negro Question issued by the Executive Committee of the Comintern in October, 1930. Designed to clarify the meaning of "self-determination" in the Black Belt, and the implications of viewing the Negro question "as the question of an oppressed nation," the new document gave the Party much clearer guidelines for work among northern blacks. In the North, the resolution stated, "the broad masses of the Negro population . . . are . . . working for assimilation," and the major focus of the Party's Negro work should be the struggle for equal rights. It was advisable for the Communist Party in the North "to abstain from the establishment of any special Negro organization and in place of this to bring the black and white workers together in common organizations of struggle and joint action." The resolution, despite its theoretical emphasis upon Afro-American nationality, had the practical effect of pushing Communist Negro work in an integrationist direction.[44]

The Comintern's position placed strong pressure on black Communists in the North to conduct their political and social life in an interracial setting, placing Communists at odds with some of the most powerful and progressive impulses in Afro-American life. Since the days of slavery, Afro-Americans had often chosen to organize their religious and cultural affairs in separate organizations, and, while they resented being excluded from the mainstream of American society, they did not, as a group, strive for physical assimilation or complete obliteration of their cultural identity. A voluntary association like the Party stepped into uncharted territory when it sought to push blacks into a completely interracial environment, and it paid a price for this commitment. Its forthright attack on segregation, its insistence on complete equality, and its pioneering efforts to create an interracial social and cultural life appealed to many blacks, but its reluctance to allow blacks to *choose* between interracial and ethnic forms hindered its ability to keep blacks in the Party and opened it up to charges that it limited black self-expression.[45]

Despite the problems posed by this position, the resolution met with no objections from the Party's black cadre, even those with nationalist backgrounds. So great was their faith in the Soviet leadership, so unchallenged its claims to have "eliminated national oppression" that they enthusiastically approved a document calling for the obliteration of racial divisions that had the force of three centuries. But the language of the resolution, filled with indignation against white racial practices, gave a certain substance to this utopian vision. It was the duty of white workers, the resolution declared, to carry on a "relentless struggle against all manifestations of Negrophobia . . . to everywhere make a break in the wall of segregation and Jim Crowism which have been set up by the bourgeois slave market morality." Class-conscious white workers could not merely oppose chauvinism passively, but had to "boldly jump at the throat of the 100 percent bandits who strike a Negro in the face."[46]

With this picturesque phrase, the Comintern endowed the struggle against race prejudice with extraordinary political force. Soon after the resolution was received, the Party initiated a campaign of self-criticism and discussion aimed at mobilizing its membership to destroy white chauvinism "branch and root." Members guilty of chauvinist behavior, wrote black Party leader Ben Amis, would be publicly exposed in the Party press, and placed on trial and "ruthlessly prosecuted" before workers' courts of black and white workers. "Only such methods," Amis concluded, "would win Negro toilers for . . . the Party, thereby closing the gap between our tremendous influence and organizational gains."[47]

Party leaders made the Harlem Section one of the major targets of this campaign. In February, 1931, the New York District Bureau of the Party published a resolution which criticized the Harlem section for failing to eliminate open displays of race prejudice by white Party members and "indifference and passivity in regard to Negroes." It complained of difficulty in mobilizing white Party members for work among blacks, of the failure of white unemployed comrades to participate in the work of the Harlem Unemployed Council, of small attendance by whites at interracial dances, and of attempts to shift responsibility for the carrying out of Negro work to black Communists. To break down this resistance to Party policies, the District Bureau called for a continuous educational campaign in the Party units and mass organizations to demonstrate the importance of Negro work to the revolutionary movement. White workers had to understand that "in spite of their constantly worsening conditions . . . they still occupy a privileged position in relation to the Negro workers," and must take the lead in exposing and eliminating chauvinism in Party activities.

Following the logic of the Comintern resolution, the District Bureau emphasized that it wanted the Harlem Party to be thoroughly interracial, with blacks and whites sharing a common social and cultural life as well as participating in joint struggle. Black Party leaders, it declared, had to "conduct tireless activity among the rank and file Negro comrades against all remnants of distrust, suspiciousness, and supersensitiveness . . . to white revolutionary workers." Tendencies toward racial and ethnic separation had to be combatted and efforts made to insure "the proper attraction of Negroes to all social affairs, dances, concerts, etc." "The greatest degree of fraternization," the Bureau concluded, "the closest association of the white with the Negro comrades in social life inside and outside of the Party is imperative."[48]

The policy the Bureau called for represented something of a landmark in American race relations. Never before had a political movement, socialist or otherwise, tried to create an interracial community that extended into personal sphere, and defined participation in this community as a political duty. Given the cultural barriers between black and white workers, the myths and stereotypes they held of each other, their different tastes in music, food, and dress, the resentments they held stemming from competition for jobs and housing, such an effort could only be awkward and difficult. But Party leaders, with the aid of public rituals, invested the effort with a romantic flavor that had a powerful emotional impact on much of the Party's membership. In February, 1931, the Central Committee announced that August Yokinen, a janitor at the Finnish Workers Club in Harlem, would be publicly tried for white chauvinism at the Harlem Casino, one of the largest meeting halls in Harlem. Yokinen, a Party unit leader in the Club, had justified the hostile reaction that blacks had received at a dance the Club sponsored on the grounds that if "Negroes came into the club . . . they would soon be coming into the bathroom [Finnish baths and sauna] and he for one did not want to bathe with Negroes." Communists gave the event national publicity and tried to attract the broadest possible audience from within the Party and the Harlem community.[49]

The trial itself, orchestrated to the smallest detail, had an air of great drama and seriousness. The Party had distributed thousands of leaflets in Harlem inviting people to attend and its efforts produced a large turnout. "The hall was crowded to the doors long before the proceedings began," the *Times* reported, "Everyone of the 1,000 chairs was occupied and 1,000 more persons stood about."[50]

Seven white Communists and seven black Communists were assigned the role of "jurors," and Alfred Wagenecht, a leader of the unemployed movement, served as presiding judge. Richard B. Moore, the Party's greatest black orator, acted as the defense attorney, and Clarence Hathaway, editor of the *Daily Worker,* served as prosecutor. The two "attorneys" used the trial to make a thorough, and sometimes eloquent, presentation of Party views on the Negro question.[51]

In arguing for Yokinen's expulsion, Hathaway asserted that the Party would never be able to overcome the "suspicions, the doubt, the mistrust, that every Negro worker has of whites so long as incidents such as the Finnish dance are tolerated." Blacks had learned to expect "nothing but broken promises and betrayals," and the Party would be unable to create genuine interracial solidarity in its ranks "unless every member of our Party fulfills *in action* the Communist promise to the Negro masses." Hathaway quoted from the 1930 Comintern Resolution to emphasize that white workers had to prove themselves worthy of the confidence of blacks: "the white workers, every white worker, must unhesitatingly jump at the throat of any person who strikes a Negro in the face, who persecutes a Negro."[52]

Richard Moore agreed with Hathaway's analysis of the implications of Yokinen's "crime," but argued that expulsion was too strong a penalty because the Party had failed to carry out a sufficient educational campaign to root out chauvinist influences. The Party could not free itself of chauvinism, he declared, by "clamoring for Yokinen's expulsion" but "by the manner in which we . . . fight side by side with the doubly oppressed Negro masses against the bosses Jim Crow lynching system, for full equality and self-determination." Since Yokinen had admitted his guilt, Moore added, there was no need to subject him to the ultimate humiliation of expulsion: "We must remember that a verdict of expulsion in disgrace from the Communist Party is considered by a class conscious worker as worse than death at the hands of the bourgeois oppressors. As for myself, I would rather have my head severed from my body by the capitalist lynchers than to be expelled in disgrace from the Communist International." The audience greeted this declaration with a "tremendous cheer."[53]

After Moore's speech, the workers' jury brought back a prepared verdict that represented a compromise between the two positions. They expelled Yokinen from the Party, but gave him an opportunity to win readmission by playing a leading role in the struggle for Negro rights in Harlem. Yokinen gladly agreed to perform these duties, which included organizing meetings at the Finnish Club to explain the trial, fighting for admission of Negroes to the Club, and leading demonstrations against a restaurant in Harlem that refused to serve blacks; but one day after the trial, he was arrested by federal authorities as an undesirable alien and held for deportation.[54]

These events aroused some resentment in sections of Harlem's Finnish community, which felt that Yokinen had been used as a sacrificial lamb, and that the Party was undermining their cultural institutions, but most

Communists regarded the event as an affirmation of a correct policy. Among the younger generation of Party activists, particularly those of Jewish ancestry, the campaign against white chauvinism aroused considerable enthusiasm. To "Americanized" Jewish Communists, who represented an increasing portion of the Party's Jewish membership, the Party's antiracist position represented the American analogue of the bolsheviks war on antisemitism, which they naively believed had "solved" the Jewish question in the U.S.S.R. Convinced that Communism would wipe out "all forms of national oppression," including antisemitism in the United States, they saw the struggle against racial discrimination as the harbinger of a revolution in ethnic relations which would allow them to assimilate into the American nation without feeling defensive about their background.[55]

Not only Jews felt moved by the Party's position: Finnish, Polish, Hungarian, Irish, Italian, and Slavic Communists became passionate exponents of the Party's position on the Negro question. But in New York City, where Jews composed the majority of the Party's membership, the Jewish Communist subculture, with roots in neighborhoods, trade unions, and student organizations, contributed greatly to the group of white organizers that volunteered for work in Harlem and to the crowds that rallied to Party mobilizations around racial issues.[56] So new was the Party's experiment in *racial* integration that the ethnic component of this phenomenon rarely attracted attention: in the early '30s, neither Harlem newspapers nor the Party press spoke of "Jewish predominance" in the Harlem CP, and most Jewish activists in Harlem did not call attention to their ethnic origins (indeed many chose to disguise them).[57] Nevertheless, the Party had begun to generate an interethnic encounter within its ranks of great force and complexity, linking groups which shared a strong consciousness of oppression, but possessed vastly different histories, cultures, and economic profiles. Disguised, for the movement, within the massive Party mobilization against "white chauvinism," this encounter would serve both as an important source of Party energy, and a sign of its marginality and vulnerability within the larger American culture.

The Yokinen trial, and his subsequent arrest, became the focal point of an expanded campaign to bring white Communists to Harlem to register their opposition to racial discrimination and to encourage united action by black and foreign-born workers. Rallies and street meetings were arranged at which Yokinen, after his release on bail, spoke in favor of racial equality and Party leaders appealed to black and white workers to protest his impending deportation. March 28, 1931, was declared a "national day of struggle against lynching and deportations," designed to cement the unity of the working class against black and white leaders who "call upon the workers to fight each other for the few available jobs."[58]

Harlem Communists endowed this activity with special importance because of the growth of support in Harlem for a "Don't Buy Where You
Can't Work Movement," a campaign which the Party perceived as a challenge to its entire strategy in combatting unemployment. In 1929, blacks
in Chicago, using this slogan, had organized a boycott of stores in black
neighborhoods that had refused to hire black salespeople, and had opened
up hundreds of jobs in the process. The tactic had enormous appeal in
Harlem, where blacks could not find employment in most local stores,
and by the spring of 1931, Harlem newspapers were filled with appeals
by ministers, politicians and businessmen to "follow Chicago's example."
The strategies they proposed varied considerably—ranging from legislation prohibiting discrimination by public utilities, to an educational campaign to support black business, to a boycott of Harlem stores which refused to hire black clerks—but they were all based on the concept that
blacks had to unite *across* class lines to protect their interest.[59] Communists interpreted these activities as a direct ideological challenge to the
Party's efforts to unite black and white workers to force the government
to provide work and/or cash relief for the unemployed.[60]

Party leaders were particularly alarmed by the antiforeign rhetoric used
by some advocates of the boycott tactic. The more nationalist groups calling for a boycott, the Harlem Business Men's Club, and the Garveyites,
urged blacks to "PRACTICE and PREACH race loyalty" as a first step
towards winning control of Harlem's economy, and they often directed
their wrath toward immigrant workers who had a large share of the jobs
in Harlem's commercial establishments.[61] "In New York City," Solomon
Harper complained, ". . . meetings are being held in the largest Negro
churches, with membership of thousands; the speakers . . . are making
violent attacks upon the foreign born, thus keeping thousands of Negroes
from uniting with militant white workers for unemployment insurance
and real relief."[62]

In the two months that followed the Yokinen trial, the Party in Harlem
carried on intensive agitation aimed at preventing boycott sentiment
from crystallization into an effective movement. While the Harlem Business Men's Club, the *Negro World,* and a number of church and women's
organizations made plans to sponsor a "race loyalty" parade and a boycott of stores on 125th Street, the Party tried to demonstrate that Harlem's unemployment problem could only be solved by united working-
class action. During March and April, 1931, the Harlem Unemployment
Council organized black and white workers to resist evictions, protested
the quality of food distributed by the Salvation Army in Harlem, pick-
eted the State Employment Service to protest discriminatory job assignments, and participated in hunger marches on the state and city govern-

ments. The March 28 parade in Harlem brought out 1,000 people, mostly white, in a demonstration of black and foreign-born solidarity.[63] Party propagandists accompanied these activities with a bitter attack on boycott supporters, accusing them of trying to undermine working-class unity and the movement for relief and insurance for reasons of personal gain. "The Negro businessmen behind the movement," Cyril Briggs claimed, were attempting to "utilize the misery of the Negro masses" to win a larger share of the black consumer market and advance their personal fortunes.[64]

To the Party's great relief, the advocates of the "Don't Buy Where You Can't Work" campaign were unable to develop an effective political movement in 1931. Factional divisions in the Garvey movement, and vast differences in political viewpoint and style between the street speakers, church leaders, and businessmen who supported the *concept* of a boycott, prevented them from uniting around a single boycott strategy. The "race loyalty" parade organized by the *Negro World* and the Harlem Business Men's Club attracted few participants other than its sponsors, and an attempt by the Harlem Housewives League to picket stores on 125th Street in mid-April had to be dropped because of community indifference.[65]

Nevertheless, the breadth of support for a boycott, aimed at white stores with white employees, made Communists aware of the fragility of their appeals to working-class solidarity. Although the Harlem Unemployed Council claimed 500 black members by late April, 1931, and the antilynching campaign had brought large numbers of blacks into the circle of Communist activities in Harlem, most of those involved were not Party members, and their attachment to the movement was not cemented by ideological commitment or organizational discipline.[66] Distrust of the white working class was a powerful sentiment in Harlem, and the Party knew it would have to "prove to the Negro workers, NOT in WORDS, but in DEEDS, that the white workers will fight for the rights of Negroes."[67]

For the first time in the Party's history, however, its white membership was prepared for such a task. The campaign of internal education that had followed the Comintern and District resolutions, and the drama of the Yokinen trial, had impressed upon white Communists, in no uncertain terms, that it was their duty as Communists "to march at the head of the struggle for Negro rights" and to "leap at the throat" of those who persecuted blacks. The struggle against racial discrimination began to permeate Party activity, from its organizing of the unemployed to its trade union work, to its social and cultural activities, invoking strong moral convictions and a spirit of sacrifice in much of the white membership. The enthusiastic mobilization of the Party for the Levy and Gonzales funerals, the Yokinen trial, the March 28 demonstration, and the role played by Communists in the Harlem Unemployed Council, where arrest and police violence were a routine consequence of the work reflected a growing commitment within the Party to organizing in the black community.[68]

But the real proof of the Party's commitments was yet to come. During late March and early April, 1931, a series of events occurred in Scottsboro, Alabama, that were to accelerate Party Negro work as nothing that occurred before. Nine teenage boys, arrested on a charge of raping two white women in a boxcar on a travelling freight, were sentenced to death after a short trial in a very hostile atmosphere. Upon hearing of the case, the Communist Party dispatched lawyers to Alabama to handle the boys' appeal and launched a worldwide campaign of protest to "stop the legal lynching." In Harlem, this case was to bring the Party into the mainstream of black community life, and give its views a hearing they had never received before.[69]

NOTES

1. New York State Temporary Commission on the Condition of the Colored Urban Population, *Second Report,* Legislative Document No. 69 (Albany, N.Y.: J. B. Lyon, 1939), pp. 33–37; National Urban League, *Annual Report, 1934,* p. 6; E. Franklin Frazier, "Some Effects of the Depression on the Negro in Northern Cities," *Science and Society,* 2 (Fall, 1938), 490–96; *New York Post,* Mar. 21, 1935; U.S. Bureau of the Census, Release No. 45, *Retail Stores and Negro Proprietors, 1929, 1935* (Washington: Government Printing Office, 1935), p. 17; Melville J. Weiss, "Don't Buy Where You Can't Work," (M.A. thesis, Columbia University, 1941), p. 16.

2. *New York Age,* Dec. 13, 1930, Jan. 17, 1931.

3. Charles Lionel Franklin, *The Negro Labor Unionist of New York* (1936; rpt. New York: AMS Press, 1968), pp. 40–44, 159–61; Louise Venable Kennedy, *The Negro Peasant Turns Cityward* (New York: Columbia University Press, 1930), pp. 74–77; Report of the Mayor's Commission on Conditions in Harlem, reprinted in the *New York Amsterdam News,* July 18, 1936, xerox copy in the Schomburg Collection, pp. 7–9.

4. U.S. Bureau of the Census, *Fifteenth Census of the United States, 1930,* Population, vol. II, General Report (Washington: Government Printing Office, 1933), pp. 216–18.

5. *New York Amsterdam News,* Oct. 16, 1937; Frazier, "Some Effects of the Depression on the Negro in Northern Cities," 493–94; Report of the Mayor's Commission on Conditions in Harlem, p. 15.

6. *Ibid.,* p. 16; Roi Ottley, *New World A-Coming* (1943; rpt. New York: Arno, 1968), pp. 82–89; Claude McKay, *Harlem: Negro Metropolis* (1940; rpt. New York: Harcourt, Bracé, Jovanovich, 1968), pp. 32–85; Arthur Huff Fauset, *Black Gods of the Metropolis* (1944; rpt., Philadelphia: University of Pennsylvania Press, 1971), pp. 1–12, 22–67.

7. Franklin, *The Negro Labor Unionist of New York,* pp. 46–57; Theodore

Vincent, *Black Power and the Garvey Movement* (Berkeley: Ramparts Press, 1971), p. 40; Tony Martin, *Race First: The Ideological and Organizational Struggles of Marcus Garvey and the Universal Negro Improvement Association* (Westport: Greenwood Press, 1976), pp. 235–36; Richard B. Moore, "Africa-Conscious Harlem" in John Henrik Clarke, ed., *Harlem U.S.A.* (New York: Collier Books, 1971), pp. 4–43.

8. *Daily Worker,* Nov. 1, 1929, Nov. 4, 1929.

9. *Ibid.,* Nov. 20, 1929, Dec. 26, 1929, Jan. 2, 1930; *Liberator,* Jan. 4, 1930. Gastonia was a textile-mill town in North Carolina, where a Communist-sponsored union led an unsuccessful strike. The Party stunned local people by openly preaching racial equality during the organizing drive and the strike.

10. *Daily Worker,* Dec. 9, 1929, Dec. 30, 1929.

11. A perusal of the Party press, from 1929 to 1932, yields no names of whites who were important Party officials in the Harlem Section (i.e. section organizer, organization secretary, education secretary). Whites occasionally do appear in news articles in the *Daily Worker* as participants in demonstrations in the Harlem section, but few appear with regularity.

12. Interview with Abe Shtob, Sept. 28, 1976; interview with Alice Citron, Aug. 20, 1979; interview with Leon Davis, Nov. 23, 1976; interview with Theodore Bassett, Dec. 15, 1973.

13. *Liberator,* Mar. 1, 1930, Mar. 8, 1930.

14. *Ibid.,* Mar. 1, 1930, Mar. 8, 1930.

15. *New York Times,* Mar. 7, 1930; *New York Amsterdam News,* Mar. 19, 1930; *Liberator,* Mar. 22, 1930.

16. *Liberator,* Mar. 15, 1930.

17. *Ibid.,* Apr. 5, 1930. Edith Segal was the most prominent Communist dance instructor and choreographer from the late '20s through the mid-'50s. Allison Burroughs was the daughter of Williana Burroughs, a black Communist schoolteacher from Queens. They developed their "black and white dance" to dramatize the Party's commitment to interracial solidarity.

18. J. Louis Engdahl, "To All District Organizers of ILD," Jan. 23, 1930, Earl Browder Papers, Syracuse University, Series II, Box 9; *New York Age,* Feb. 22, 1930. For example of Party-sponsored rallies and meetings on these issues, as well as information about their location, see *Liberator,* May 24, 1930; *Negro World,* Apr. 26, 1930; *Daily Worker,* Apr. 18, 1930, July 1, 1930.

19. Interview with Abe Shtob, Sept. 28, 1976; interview with Leon Davis, Nov. 23, 1976; interview with Theodore Basset, Dec. 15, 1973. Every single Communist I interviewed who was active in Harlem emphasized that whites could go anywhere in Harlem, at any hour of the day or night, without meeting hostility or bodily harm.

20. *Daily Worker,* June 30, 1930.

21. *New York Amsterdam News,* Apr. 2, 1930; Harris, *Keeping the Faith,* pp. 164–65; *Daily Worker,* Mar. 31, 1930; *Liberator,* Apr. 5, 1930.

22. *New York Amsterdam News,* Apr. 16, 1930; *Liberator,* Apr. 19, 1930, Apr. 26, 1930; *Negro World,* Apr. 26, 1930; *Keeping the Faith,* pp. 168–69.

23. U.S. Congress, House, Special Committee on Communist Activities in the

United States, *Investigation of Communist Propaganda* (Washington: Government Printing Office, 1930), pp. 243, 248, 253.

24. *New York Amsterdam News,* Jan. 29, 1930, Mar. 26, 1930; *New York Age,* Mar. 15, 1930, June 14, 1930.

25. *Negro World,* Feb. 1, 1930, Feb. 8, 1930, Feb. 15, 1930, Mar. 1, 1930.

26. *Ibid.,* Apr. 19, 1930, May 31, 1930.

27. Interview with Theodore Bassett, Aug. 29, 1974; interview with Richard B. Moore, Nov. 14, 1973; *New York Age,* June 29, 1930; *Daily Worker,* June 30, 1930; Martin, *Race First,* p. 257.

28. *Daily Worker,* June 30, 1930, July 1, 1930.

29. *New York Times,* July 2, 1930; *Daily Worker,* July 1, 1930, July 2, 1930.

30. *New York Amsterdam News,* July 9, 1930; *New York Age,* July 12, 1930.

31. *Daily Worker,* July 30, 1930, Aug. 4, 1930, Aug. 7, 1930.

32. *Ibid.,* July 18, 1930.

33. *Daily Worker,* July 2, 1930; *Liberator,* July 1, 1933; interview with Theodore Bassett, Dec. 15, 1973; interview with Abner Berry, Nov. 20, 1973.

34. *New York Amsterdam News,* Oct. 8, 1930; *Daily Worker,* Dec. 18, 1930; interview with Theodore Bassett, Dec. 15, 1973.

35. *Daily Worker,* Oct. 1, 1930, Oct. 17, 1930; Earl Browder, "Next Tasks of the CPUSA," *Communist,* 9 (Nov.-Dec., 1930), 974.

36. *Daily Worker,* Oct. 1, 1930, Nov. 18, 1930; Jabari Simama, "Black Writers Experience Communism: An Interdisciplinary Study of Imaginative Writers, their Critics, and the CPUSA," (Ph.D. dissertation, Emory University, 1978), p. 118.

37. *Ibid.,* pp. 116–32; Langston Hughes, *Good Morning Revolution; Uncollected Writings of Social Protest,* Faith Berry, ed., (New York: Lawrence Hill, 1973), pp. xi–xx, 9–22; Robert E. Hemenway, *Zora Neale Hurston; A Literary Biography* (Urbana: University of Illinois Press, 1977), pp. 136–47. Hughes claimed the break with his patron came because of a satirical poem he wrote about the opening of the Waldorf Astoria that appeared in the Dec., 1931, *New Masses,* but David Lewis argues persuasively that the break came earlier, possibly as a result of Hughes's cynical poem about Christmas that appeared in the Dec., 1930, *New Masses.* See David Levering Lewis, *When Harlem Was in Vogue* (New York: Knopf, 1981), pp. 257–59.

38. Interview with John Hammond, Sept. 26, 1978; interview with Henry Lee Moon, May 1, 1979; interview with Louise Thompson, Sept. 14, 1977. On Thompson's relations with Hughes, see Lewis, *When Harlem Was in Vogue,* p. 259. On Thompson's relations with NAACP leaders, see L. F. Coles to Walter White, May 13, 1933, NAACP Papers, D 73.

39. Interview with Louise Thompson, Sept. 14, 1977; interview with Theodore Bassett, Nov. 2, 1973.

40. *Daily Worker,* Dec. 10, 1931; *Negro World,* Nov. 22, 1930; *Revolutionary Age,* Jan. 10, 1931.

41. *Daily Worker,* Feb. 26, 1931.

42. *Ibid.,* Feb. 3, 1931.

43. *Ibid.,* Feb. 26, 1931.

44. "Resolution on the Negro Question in the United States, Final Text, Confirmed by the Political Commission of the ECCI," *Communist,* 10 (Feb., 1931), 156–58.

45. C. L. R. James, "Preliminary Notes on the Negro Question," n.d., 1939, unpublished manuscript in possession of author; interview with Abner Berry, Nov. 20, 1973.

46. "Resolution on the Negro Question in the United States, Final Text," 157.

47. *Daily Worker,* Dec. 10, 1930.

48. *Ibid.,* Feb. 19, 1931.

49. *Ibid.,* Feb. 16, 1931, Feb. 24, 1931; Communist Party, U.S.A., *Race Hatred on Trial* (New York: Workers Library Publishers, 1931), p. 9.

50. *New York Times,* Mar. 2, 1931.

51. *Baltimore Afro-American,* Mar. 7, 1931.

52. *Race Hatred on Trial,* pp. 9, 21, 24.

53. *Ibid.,* p. 32; *New York Times,* Mar. 2, 1931.

54. *Ibid.,* Mar. 2, 1931, Mar. 3, 1931.

55. Interview with Abe Shtob, Sept. 28, 1976; interview with Morris Schappes, Aug. 24, 1979; Leibman, *Jews and the Left,* pp. 496–500. Shtob, who was a YCL leader in East Harlem, felt the Yokinen trial was a mistake "because it helped the FBI identify Finnish Communists. . . . There was a reaction against this in the Finnish community, though not enough to destroy the credibility of the movement."

56. Interview with Abe Shtob, Sept. 28, 1976; interview with Alice Citron, Aug. 20, 1979; interview with Morris Schappes, Aug. 24, 1979. Most of the white Communists I interviewed agreed that Jews were disproportionately represented among the white cadre in Harlem, and responded more enthusiastically to the Party position on the Negro question. Shtob recalled that "Jews, as a national group, did respond more quickly on this issue than others, though there were exceptions among the other nationalities."

57. I can recall not one article in the *Negro World,* the *Amsterdam News,* or the *New York Age,* from 1929 to at least 1935, which speaks of the white Communist influx into Harlem as a "Jewish" phenomenon. The only mention I have seen of a black-Jewish encounter within the Party occurred in an article by John Gillard in *Commonweal,* (May 25, 1932), p. 97, and it took the form of a throwaway comment: "the annual May-day demonstrations in which plump Jewesses parade arm in arm with hollow-cheeked Negroes." The lack of documentary evidence about black-Jewish tensions within the party in the early '30s makes it very difficult to discuss the issue in other than a tentative and speculative manner.

58. *Daily Worker,* Mar. 6, 1931, Mar. 15, 1931; *Liberator,* Mar. 14, 1931.

59. For examples of exhortations to start a boycott movement in Harlem, see *Negro World,* Feb. 7, 1931, Mar. 21, 1931, Apr. 25, 1931.

60. Harry Haywood, "The Crisis of the Jim-Crow Nationalism of the Negro Bourgeoisie," *Communist,* 10 (Apr. 1931), 335.

61. *Harlem Business Men's Bulletin,* vol. 1, no. 1 (Mar., 1931), in "Black Newspapers-Sample Issues," Schomburg Collection, New York City.

62. *Daily Worker,* Mar. 17, 1931.

63. *Ibid.,* Mar. 14, 1931, Mar. 20, 1931, Mar. 24, 1931, Mar. 30, 1931, Apr. 7, 1931.

64. *Liberator,* Mar. 28, 1931.

65. *Ibid.,* Apr. 25, 1931; *Negro World,* May 2, 1931.

66. *New York Times,* Apr. 25, 1931. The Unemployed Council organizer who offered the estimate of 500 black members was named Leon Davis, and it was probably the same Leon Davis who helped organize the Pharmacists Union, which later evolved into Local 1199.

67. *Daily Worker,* Mar. 9, 1931.

68. Interview with William Weinstone, July 2, 1974. Mr. Weinstone, a member of the Party's Central Committee during the early 1930s, recalled that the struggle for Negro rights stirred the Party membership "emotionally." Through a process of study and contact with the black population, Weinstone asserted, many white Party members became "passionately involved" in the struggle for racial justice: "injustice makes its appeal to the whole person."

69. Dan T. Carter, *Scottsboro, A Tragedy of the American South* (paperback ed., New York: Oxford University Press, 1971), pp. 11–50; *Daily Worker,* Apr. 10, 1931.

3

They Shall Not Die—
The Impact of the Scottsboro Case
on the Harlem Party

THE CAMPAIGN TO FREE the Scottsboro boys, more than any single event, marked the Communist Party's emergence as a force in Harlem's life. The Party's role in the case, and its conflicts with the NAACP, were front-page news for years, and its protest rallies gave it entry to churches, fraternal organizations, and political clubs that were previously closed to it. From soapboxes, pulpits, and podiums, black and white Communists made the details of the Scottsboro case a part of the daily consciousness of the community until "Scottsboro became synonymous with southern racism repression and injustice."[1] In the process, the Party helped break the political and psychological isolation of Harlemites in a time of terrible adversity. The huge turnout of left-wing whites for Harlem Scottsboro protests showed Harlemites that they had new allies in their struggle against racial injustice and helped convince them that they could fight effectively for their interests in the streets as well as in the courts. Beginning as a struggle led primarily by white radicals, Scottsboro provided the catalyst for passionate protest activity by Harlem's population, both inside and outside the Party's ranks.

The kind of incident that gave rise to the Scottsboro movement, though hardly unique in southern history, was particularly suited to arouse mass indignation. The nine Scottsboro defendants, ages 13 to 21, had not initially been arrested on a charge of rape. The first complaint sworn out against them came from several white boys they had thrown off a freight train they were riding, and local police formulated the rape charge only when they discovered two young white women had been in the same boxcar with some of the black youths. The medical examination of the two young women provided questionable evidence of a "gang rape"; neither woman displayed signs of vaginal injury, and semen samples found inside them were nonmotile and unlikely to have resulted from recent intercourse. But the flimsiness of the state's evidence mattered little in the hysterical atmosphere which the rape charge had created. Soon after the arrest, crowds began to gather outside the jail, and the National Guard had to be called to prevent a lynching. Local officials, and the defendants' white attorney, seemed to be intimidated. Within two weeks of the incident, the defendants had been indicted, tried, and sentenced to death.[2]

From the moment the Scottsboro indictments were handed down, the Communist Party moved to make the Scottsboro case a focus of its antilynching crusade. It dispatched International Labor Defense attorneys to Scottsboro to make contact with the defendants and began organizing protest meetings in their behalf. When news of the death sentences arrived, the Party's Central Committee issued a front-page statement in the *Daily Worker* calling for "mass meetings and militant mass demonstrations" to protest the convictions.[3]

While the Party mobilized for protests against the "Scottsboro legal lynching," ILD attorneys moved to obtain permission of the defendants to handle their appeal. Working through the Chattanooga Negro Ministers Alliance (which did not know they were Communists), they located some of the defendants' parents and persuaded them that the ILD would handle the defense more effectively than the boys' previous lawyer. On April 20, the defendants signed an agreement giving the ILD control of the case.

This action brought the Party into direct conflict with the national leadership of the NAACP. When the case first broke, NAACP executives refrained from commenting on it publicly or making a commitment to the defense. Traditionally circumspect, "the last thing they wanted," in Dan Carter's blunt words, "was to identify the Association with a gang of mass rapists unless they were reasonably certain the boys were innocent or their constitutional rights were abridged." But once the boys were convicted, the NAACP recoiled in horror at the thought of Communists handling their appeal. They sent the defendants' original lawyer to persuade them to break with the ILD and declared that Communists "had no sincere interest in helping these condemned Negroes." But the NAACP made the mistake of ignoring the boys' parents, with whom ILD lawyers had spent a great deal of time. When the defendants signed a statement repudiating their agreement with the ILD, their parents came to them the next day and persuaded them to reverse their decision.

From this point on, Communists defined the struggle against the NAACP as a primary aspect of the Scottsboro movement, almost equal in significance to the "struggle against the lynchers." Early Party statements had criticized the inaction of NAACP officials, but once the battle erupted for control of the defense, the Party accused the NAACP of "every crime short of mayhem." Party leaders viewed Scottsboro as an

excellent platform from which to denounce the timidity of black organizations and to dramatize the effectiveness of Communist tactics of interracial mass protest.[4]

The Party's conflict with the NAACP, though consistent with its
Comintern-inspired "war on Negro reformism," represented a significant
change of emphasis for Party activists. Prior to Scottsboro, Harlem Communists had routinely attacked the NAACP in their speeches and journalism but had not engaged in a systematic effort to disrupt Association
meetings or recruit Association members. Much more concerned with the
activities of the Garvey movement—which they regarded as a direct "competitor" for the loyalty of Harlem's working class—Communists had
given little attention to the NAACP in their day-to-day organizing, and
Association leaders did not regard them as a serious threat: "I would not
call them a counter organization," Walter White told a Congressional investigating committee in June, 1930. "I do not think their purpose is to
oppose us, particularly. . . ."[5]

However, in challenging the NAACP head on, Communists faced a
far more formidable enemy than they confronted in the divided Garvey
legions. The NAACP possessed immense prestige and influence in Harlem.[6] Three of its top national officers, Secretary Walter White, *Crisis*
editor W. E. B. Du Bois, and director of branches Robert Bagnall, lived
in Harlem and knew many of Harlem's ministers, editors, and politicians
on a first-name basis. Their position gave them access to the pages of
Harlem newspapers and to the pulpits of Harlem churches, and they used
their influence to confront local issues as well as civil rights abuses of national significance. But the Association's style of functioning, especially
in Harlem, made it vulnerable to certain aspects of the Party's critique.
Accustomed to working through a network of "influentials"—in city government and the liberal community—and to seeking change through the
courts, the Association had not developed an activist membership in Harlem.[7] Its New York branch (which was located in Harlem), accustomed to
deferring to the national office, had an undistinguished group of leaders,
a small membership, and a poor track record in undertaking independent
projects.[8] As a result, the association's national officers lacked a core
group of committed supporters willing to match the Party in its chosen
arena of propaganda—the streets of Harlem. They would rely instead on
the support of the Harlem press, and their ability to deny Communists
access to the pulpit, to keep Communists safely on the margins of Harlem's life.

The Harlem Party's first protests against the Scottsboro convictions
provided a strong indication that they had seized upon an issue that possessed considerable emotional appeal. On April 24, over seven hundred
people attended a Party-sponsored Scottsboro meeting at St. Luke's Hall,

and a Scottsboro demonstration the next day drew a significantly larger turnout. Five thousand Harlemites jammed Lenox Avenue near 140th Street to hear Communist speakers, and watched a group of 500 Communists, predominately white, march into Lenox Avenue without a permit, precipitating a violent clash with police. Shortly thereafter, Party leaders announced that another protest parade would take place in Harlem on May 16, and that "permit or no permit, the workers will take to the streets to voice their demand for the freeing of the Negro youths."[9]

Within the Harlem community, Party organizers, recognizing Scottsboro's appeal, tentatively began to seek support from black religious and fraternal organizations. Significantly, with a few important exceptions, they contacted organizations which were either not well established, or were outside the NAACP's sphere of influence. Accompanied by Janie Patterson and Ada Wright, mothers of three of the defendants, Party organizers approached leaders of the Seventh Day Adventists (a heavily West Indian congregation), the Theodore Collegiate Society, the Elks, the Odd Fellows, the Jupiter Lodge and the Women's Protective Union to ask them to raise funds for the Scottsboro defense and participate in protest activity. This new ecumenicism even extended to the black press and selected NAACP leaders. Party newspapers gave wide publicity to a letter which NAACP field secretary William Pickens had sent to the *Daily Worker* praising the "promptness with which the white workers have moved toward defending these helpless and innocent boys," and to an article he wrote for the black press expressing similar sentiments (a gesture which infuriated Walter White and members of the NAACP National Board). And Communists praised several black newspapers for their coverage of the April 25 parade and their presentation of the ILD's side of the struggle to represent the defendants, attributing their action to "pressure by the black masses."[10]

This effort to enlist non-Communist black organizations in Scottsboro protests—a clear departure from Party tactics in the unemployed movement—partly reflected the influence of William Patterson, who had recently returned from Russia to become a Party organizer in Harlem, and a national secretary of the ILD. Transformed by his Soviet experience into a committed Communist ideologue, Patterson still possessed the skills and the drive for success that had once marked him as a "young man with a future." Placed in a position of great responsibility by the Party leadership, Patterson did not want his Communist convictions to make him a "marginal man." He had a politician's understanding of black organizations and their leaders, and was willing to work through them to advance the Party's objectives. Through his twin roles as an organizer and legal strategist, Patterson used the Scottsboro issue to project the Communist

Party as a forceful presence in black life, something that mainstream black leaders could not afford to ignore.[11]

The next Scottsboro protest in Harlem, on May 16, demonstrated the Party's new elan and confidence. The march began with a parade of several hundred Communists, predominately white, but drew over three thousand blacks into line as it wound along its route through the streets of Harlem. The march ended at 110th Street and 5th Avenue, where Scottsboro mother Ada Wright praised the ILD for rushing to help the defendants and appealed to "workers of all races to join the . . . defense campaign." Other speakers regaled the crowd, which included Communists of diverse origins, in Finnish, Spanish, and Rumanian. William Patterson hailed the protest as a sign that "Negro workers . . . are no longer willing to go on living in the same old way," and that "white workers are ready and willing to close ranks with them."[12]

Most Harlem newspapers greeted this political offensive with considerable skepticism. "Parades in Harlem, Communistic agitation and wild . . . attacks on the National Association for the Advancement of Colored People will not save the eight boys," the *Amsterdam News* editorialized. "Communists are not really interested in the fate of these Scottsboro Boys," the *Negro World* commented, "otherwise they would not denounce efforts made by others." But another Harlem newspaper, the *New York News,* declared that the "ILD deserves full credit . . . for arousing the nation over the impending doom of the eight boys," and hoped that the "Red organization" would stir the NAACP from its "selfish, social lethargy."[13]

The NAACP met the Party's offensive, legal and political, with a counterattack of its own. Continuing their battle for control over the case, NAACP national officers united their ranks (persuading a repentant Pickens that the ILD tactics jeopardized the defendants' lives) and tried to use their influence with the press and the ministry to deny Communists legitimacy and access to the black public. Not only did association officials write personal letters to black editors who praised the ILD, urging them to reconsider their position, but they tried to prevent Communists from presenting their views from the platforms of important black institutions.[14] In early May, Robert Bagnall persuaded an influential Harlem minister, Rev. A. C. Garner, to cancel an ILD meeting featuring two Scottsboro mothers that William Patterson had set up at his church. A month later, association national officers met with the Interdenominational Preachers Meeting of New York and persuaded them to cosponsor a mass meeting at Harlem's Salem M. E. Church on June 28 to present the NAACP's side of the Scottsboro conflict.[15]

This organizational competition—both for control of the case and for the hearts and minds of the black public—generated an impassioned debate over the appropriate strategy to pursue in civil rights cases in the South. NAACP leaders, spearheaded by Walter White, argued that their aim was to guarantee the boys a "fair trial" in the Alabama courts, which could only be assured if the defense hired local attorneys and avoided actions which antagonized Alabama public opinion. They sharply criticized Communists for organizing demonstrations and sending telegrams to the governor of Alabama demanding the immediate release of the defendants, claiming that such tactics jeopardized the boys' chances of winning their freedom. "Communist involvement in the case," Walter White declared, would only "hamper the proper conduct of the defense."[16]

Communists, in response, argued that the NAACP's reliance on local counsel and nonprovocative tactics was misguided. "There can be no such thing as a 'fair trial' of a Negro boy accused of rape in an Alabama court," a *Liberator* editorial declared. "Anyone who thinks otherwise is a fool. Anyone who says otherwise is trying to deceive." The ILD's strategy was "to give the boys the best available legal defense in the capitalist courts, but at the same time to emphasize . . . that the boys can be saved only by the pressure of millions of workers, colored and white, behind the defense in the courts."[17]

In Harlem, Party activists initiated an intensified program of protests, leading up to a "monster demonstration" on June 27 to demand the release of the Scottsboro boys and to "bring home to the Negro workers of Harlem" the ILD's claim to represent the defendants. Party leaders assigned this protest special significance because it approached the July 10 date of execution set by the Alabama Courts, and preceded an NAACP meeting in Harlem on June 28, at which both Walter White and William Pickens were slated to appear. They called on "working class organizations" from all over the city to make the demonstration "the biggest ever held in Harlem."[18]

In Harlem, the Party's mobilization for the June 27 protest ran into numerous obstacles. Barred, through the NAACP's influence, from the community's largest churches, Communists had difficulty persuading even sympathetic church and fraternal groups to affiliate with Party-dominated defense committees. In addition, the Party's old enemy from the Garvey movement, St. William Grant, continued to present problems for Communist soapboxers. Disturbed by the influx of white organizers and street speakers that Communist Scottsboro protests inspired, Grant organized street meetings of his own to attack the Party's role in the defense. In response, the *Liberator* published an "Open Letter to the Members of the Garvey Organization," which called upon the "rank and file members of the Garvey movement" to break with their leaders and unite with white workers in the June 27 protest "against the Scottsboro legal lynching."[19]

The turnout for this demonstration showed that Harlem Communists had still failed to build a large constituency among blacks. Several thousand people, almost all of them white, marched in the Communist parade and drew an ambivalent response from Harlem crowds. "There were occasional cheers and applause, and once and a while catcalls and jeers," the *Amsterdam News* reported. The marchers invited people on the sidewalks to join them and "an occasional worker fell in along the way, but for the most part, the onlookers were silent, noncommittal." Although the march demonstrated the Party's ability to mobilize whites against racial injustice, it dramatized the Party's failure to make a breach in the web of doubts and suspicions that made most Harlemites keep Communism at arm's length. The *Interstate Tatler* described the march as an "invasion" by the revolutionary workers, a protest many Harlemites were prepared to accept, but not to join.[20]

The NAACP meeting the next day further revealed the Party's weaknesses. Walter White had pulled out the stops to create a large, smooth-running meeting, inviting NAACP branches throughout the metropolitan area to bring their members, and writing to Civil Service Commissioner Ferdinand Morton to arrange police protection (he expected a disruption by Communists and wanted order to be maintained without creating "martyrs").[21] Over 3,000 black people attended the meeting, a far larger number than had attended any of the Communist indoor protests, and heard William Pickens and Walter White declare that Communist activity in behalf of the Scottsboro boys was "harming the case more than helping it." Pickens repudiated his earlier support of the Party's defense activities and denounced its entire strategy in the case. "Everything they have done has antagonized the people and officials of Scottsboro, Alabama," Pickens declared. "They have put the court on the defensive and prejudiced it against . . . the boys."[22]

However, as soon as Pickens concluded his speech, Party activists in the audience pulled a maneuver which put the NAACP leader on the defensive. As Pickens prepared to leave the podium, they rose to demand that Ada Wright, mother of two of the defendants, be given the floor to answer Pickens's charges. The surprised NAACP officials quickly declared the meeting adjourned and rushed up to Mrs. Wright to shake hands with her. But in full view of reporters, Mrs. Wright rejected their handshakes and stalked out of the church, heading directly to an ILD meeting at a nearby hall, where she delivered a speech attacking NAACP officials. She repeated the same speech at a UNIA meeting in Harlem later that day. Once again the Party's close relationship with Scottsboro parents had enabled them to prevent the NAACP from forcing them out of the defense or from discrediting Communist protest strategy.[23]

Following these late-June protest meetings, the momentum in the Scottsboro movement shifted to the legal front. Motions for appeal, filed separately by ILD and NAACP lawyers, automatically postponed the date of execution until the Alabama State Supreme Court reviewed the case. With the threat of execution postponed, Scottsboro protest activities became more difficult to sustain.[24]

However, through the summer and fall of 1931, the Party's bid for leadership in Black America remained a vital subject of discussion in the black press. The Scottsboro demonstrations, and incidents of violence provoked by Communists' activity among black sharecroppers and unemployed people, inspired an impassioned debate as to whether Communists represented a new ally against racism or a group that used blacks as "cannon fodder" to gain publicity for their movement. Writing in the *New Masses,* Eugene Gordon, a black journalist for the *Boston Post,* forcefully expressed the pro-Communist position. Mocking the NAACP's initial hesitancy to support the defendants, which he attributed to its middle-class bias ("It is no longer the National Association for the Advancement of Colored Persons [sic], but the Nicest Association for the Advancement of Certain Persons"), Gordon claimed that militant Communist tactics pointed the way toward an interracial alliance to uproot Jim Crow:

> Negro workers think of the countless times Communists have been beaten insensible for defending...Negro workers.... They see the ILD ... supported by the Communist Party, rushing to the defense of the nine Negro youths at Scottsboro before other Negro organizations in the country condescended to glance superciliously in their direction.... Seeing and hearing all these things, the Negro worker in the United States would be a fool not to recognize the leadership that he has been waiting for since his freedom.[25]

Most Harlem editors took strong issue with Gordon's analysis of Party motives. "As it is the first principle of the Communist faith to make martyrs," the *Age* declared, "it is not likely that they would neglect the chance to make eight in one strike." The *Negro World* accused Gordon of naivete for believing that American Communists are different from other whites. "As far as purely the Negroes' interest [sic] are concerned," the paper declared, there was little to choose between black Communists and "traditional uncle tom leaders."[26]

Nevertheless, these editors seemed concerned that Communist militancy in the face of repression would win it converts in the black community. "Denied an equal opportunity in his struggle for existence," the *Amsterdam News* wrote, "the Negro ... is turning to Communism, even if it means death, which is not so much worse than the burden he carries." Heavy-handed actions of southern authorities, the *Age* warned, were attracting as many Negroes to Communism as "the red agitators themselves," and the *Negro World* complained of Communists "capturing hundreds of Negro workers by promising them Garveyism with a wrapper of red tissue." But such skepticism of Communist intentions did not imply total hostility to Party activities. The *Negro World* asserted that it had "no objection to any Negro flirting with the Communists if he knows how to make use of them to his race's advantage" and offered an ambivalent assessment of white radical support: "Let the liberal minded whites PROVE themselves, but by no means allow them to keep us napping."[27]

This "wait-and-see" attitude toward Party organizing seemed quite representative of popular feeling in Harlem. Throughout the fall of 1931, Communists held regular street meetings and defense conferences on the Scottsboro issue, but failed to attract much support from church and fraternal groups they contacted or from Harlem audiences they spoke to on the streets.[28] NAACP vigilance partly explains this response; in October, 1931, Walter White personally intervened to force cancellation of an ILD meeting at an important Harlem Church—St. Mark's M. E. (Rev. Lorenzo H. King was the pastor).[29] But even outside the association's sphere of influence, Communists registered only minor gains. With the NAACP and the ILD both claiming responsibility for the defense, few Harlemites seemed willing to throw support entirely to the Communists' side.

However, by the end of 1931, Communists' initiatives in the struggle to represent the defendants had begun to dramatically affect its standing in the Harlem community. Between July and December, ILD attorneys had managed to increase the number of defendants committed to them from four to nine. Their success in this venture derived both from the NAACP's failure to develop rapport with the defendants and from the ILD's persistent efforts to win the trust and loyalty of the boys and their parents. While the NAACP tried to persuade a prominent Alabama law firm to assume charge of the case, the ILD sent the parents on speaking tours and showered the defendants with letters, money, and gifts. By mid-August, the ILD's relations with the boys had become so strong that the Alabama lawyers recruited by Walter White withdrew from the case, announcing that Communist propaganda had prejudiced public opinion. White was unable to change their minds, and his strategy of finding the "best local counsel" unceremoniously collapsed.[30]

In a final effort to assure NAACP participation, White persuaded Clarence Darrow and Arthur Garfield Hayes to offer to help argue the case before the Alabama State Supreme Court. ILD attorneys greeted this gesture with extreme skepticism, but felt they could not turn down the services of these two prominent civil liberties attorneys without compromising their credibility among blacks and liberals. They announced that they "welcomed" Darrow's interest, but would continue to exclude the NAACP. When Darrow and Hayes arrived in Alabama, ILD attorneys, with the full backing of the defendants, told the two men that they could participate in the defense only if they repudiated the NAACP and agreed to abide by the decisions of the ILD. Neither Darrow nor Hayes would accept these conditions. After several days of negotiations, they announced their withdrawal from the case, leaving the ILD in undisputed control. On January 4, 1932, the NAACP recognized the *fait accompli* and severed its connection with the Scottsboro defense.[31]

The ILD's actions aroused indignation among black leaders, but an indignation tempered with respect for the Party's position as the leading element in an important civil rights case. Floyd Calvin, a Harlem-based columnist for the *Pittsburgh Courier,* told an embittered Walter White that the Party's actions had put the NAACP at a "terrible disadvantage." "While you were waiting for your friends to defend you," Calvin wrote, "the Communists were dealing you some telling blows, and now all of a sudden you . . . realize just how telling those blows were."[32] The Party's initiatives in this case, at once imaginative, courageous, and ruthlessly sectarian, had placed it in center stage in black life and gave its actions unprecedented political resonance. "Whether the Communist organization will make the saving of the boys' lives its first consideration remains to be seen," the *Amsterdam News* commented. "There is certainly no excuse for not doing so, and their future status among Negroes will be decided by the outcome."[33] As Communists prepared their case for review by the Alabama State Supreme Court, they knew that Scottsboro had emerged as a test both of the value of black-white unity and of the applicability of mass-protest tactics to the struggle against jim crow.

With Scottsboro setting the tone, other aspects of Party organizing in Harlem, most notably its work among the unemployed, displayed greater dynamism and flexibility. During the summer and fall of 1931, the Harlem Unemployment Council began to develop new strategies which tried to incorporate the cooperative traditions of Harlem's population into its program of militant protest. This represented a substantial change for the Harlem Council. During the first year of its existence, Harlem Council leaders, in an effort to distinguish their organization from Harlem's soup kitchens and private charities, had bluntly told the unemployed that the council could not take responsibility for providing them with meals. When rank-and-file council members had tried to collect food, money, or clothing for starving neighbors, or cook communal meals for the unemployed, council leaders had criticized them for "avoiding militant struggle" and failing to shift the responsibility for care of the unemployed to the government. But by the summer of 1931, Harlem Party organizers had come to recognize that such doctrinaire opposition to self-help measures had limited their movement's appeal. "Fear of the self-activity of the masses," they concluded, had isolated the Harlem Council from many "sincere workers" who saw no contradiction between taking a collection for their neighbors and resisting an eviction or marching to City Hall.[34]

The council's new strategy involved three major components: taking up collections on particular blocks to help families who were close to starvation, taking delegations of unemployed people to charitable agencies and sitting in until they received relief, and participating in protest actions at City Hall and the state legislature to demand cash relief for the jobless. The Party's call for a National Hunger March to Washington in December, 1931, gave added focus to these activities. Organizing for the march took the form of public hearings on conditions in Harlem and marches on public and private relief agencies. In several of these actions, the Harlem Council succeeded in getting immediate cash relief for unemployed individuals.[35]

The council's role as an advocate at relief agencies acquired even greater significance following the passage of unemployment relief legislation by the New York State Legislature. In September, 1931, that body appropriated twenty million dollars to provide direct relief for the jobless through a system of home relief bureaus that would be set up throughout the state and financed by matching contributions of the legislature and local governments.[36] These home relief bureaus, which first opened in December, 1931, provided ideal targets for demonstration by local unemployed councils. In Harlem, the home relief sit-in became, with eviction resistance, the core of the council's strategy to meet the day-to-day needs of the unemployed.

While expanding its agitation among the jobless, the Party also registered gains in influence among Harlem's intelligentsia. In December, 1931, Louise Thompson invited a group of acquaintances, including writers, artists, and theatre people, to form a chapter of the Friends of the Soviet Union, an organization designed to "acquaint the American people with developments industrial, political, agricultural and cultural in the USSR." The organizing session, held at her apartment, attracted fifty people, and the group's first public presentation, held at the Elks Hall on 129th Street, drew an audience of over one hundred.[37] Party leaders gave Thompson a free hand in shaping the Harlem group, which emphasized the Soviet Union's achievement in eliminating racial and religious prejudice, and the progress made by nonwhite nationalities under the Soviet regime. Thompson, acutely sensitive to the attitudes of Harlem's elite, avoided Party recruiting at the group's meetings, but through lectures, discussions, and films, Thompson helped encourage an interest in Soviet accomplishments among black intellectuals, as well as a desire to visit the society that Communists claimed as their "motherland."[38]

Thompson's approach proved its value early in 1932 when James Ford returned from a two-year stint in the Soviet Union with a proposal by a Soviet film company to produce a film depicting "the struggle of Negro workers in America," that made use of black actors and screenwriters. Thompson agreed to use her network to recruit for the project, and received an enthusiastic response. The sponsoring committee for the film attracted several prominent non-Communist intellectuals, including actress Rose McLendon and three staffers from the *Amsterdam News,* led by its general manager William H. Davis.[39]

Preparations for the film took place in an atmosphere of naive enthusiasm and good fun. John Hammond, a white music impresario friendly with Louise Thompson, provided funds for transportation, and the prospect of a free trip to the Soviet Union proved as attractive to many of the volunteers as working to produce a film. The delegation chosen to go represented a mixture of unknown and prominent actors and writers: among them, stage performers Rose McLendon and Wayland Rudd; journalists Loren Miller of the *California Eagle* and Theodore Poston and Henry Lee Moon of the *Amsterdam News;* and Langston Hughes. The active Communist sympathizers in the group, led by Hughes and Thompson, were in a distinct minority, and the June, 1932, send-off party for the group had the aura of a Harlem "society event." Some of the people sponsoring the party, such as sports and society columnist Romeo Dougherty, and *Chicago Defender* correspondent Bessye Bearden, had never previously associated with the left: indeed, one year earlier, Bearden had helped NAACP officials to exclude an ILD meeting from a Harlem church and had tried to persuade two Scottsboro mothers to shift their allegiance from the ILD to the NAACP.[40] But the increased visibility of Party activity, and the skillful and persistent organizing of Louise Thompson, had begun to change the Party's "alien" image and make interest in leftist causes almost fashionable among young Harlem intellectuals.

To the consternation of Party leaders, such gains in influence and visibility took place without a dramatic expansion in the Party's black membership. A Party census made in January, 1932, showed only seventy-four black Communists in the New York District, 3.1 percent of the District membership. Even though Harlemites probably composed about two-thirds of this total, this hardly represented an impressive return in membership for the enormous energy Communists expended in conducting activities in Harlem.[41]

The low level of black membership, in a movement of growing dynamism, confused Party strategists. They offered a number of proposals to bolster the Party's effectiveness: an intensified struggle around the "economic demands of Negroes," a "sustained fight against white chauvinism," and a more energetic effort by Party trade unions to organize blacks in the marine industry, the laundries, and the needle trades. But they failed to explore the problem that all organizers in Harlem confronted: that blacks were willing to follow Communist leadership on a specific issue, or participate in a Communist organization, but were reluctant to become Party members or submit to Party discipline. With few exceptions, the Harlemites who joined the Party and stayed in it were people with intellectual and organizational skills who rose to positions of leadership and became Party functionaries. For such individuals, the power they exercised in the movement, the approval their efforts inspired, and the security of a modest salary compensated for the rigors of Party discipline and the tensions generated by working in a predominately white milieu. But without such benefits, Harlemites attracted by Party activities seemed reluctant to join an organization which drew its members into a self-contained network of activities that left little time for previous associations.[42]

So powerful was this resistance to joining the Party, on all levels of the Harlem community, that even the most effective and committed black organizers made concessions to it. Richard Moore, gathering support for the Scottsboro defense, Louis Campbell, organizing the unemployed, and Louise Thompson, leading discussions on Soviet life, all faced a similar dilemma: What do you do with people who respond enthusiastically to your activity, but who you know from experience would have difficulties in the Party? Do you try to recruit them, even though it would make them uncomfortable, or do you concentrate your energies on building the mass movement, recruiting only those individuals who express interest in Party membership? Despite persistent pressures to recruit, all three chose to subordinate Party building to the demands of their practical work, and the Harlem organization bore the mark of their decision. Possessed of a diverse and talented group of black leaders, the Party functioned as a catalyst for popular protests rather than a tightly knit political machine with a disciplined membership.[43]

The Central Committee did not approve of this orientation, but its own promotion policies assured its continuance. Since 1929, the Central Committee, pursuing what it thought was a "class struggle" policy, had insisted on appointing "proletarians" as the section organizers in Harlem, the top administrative post in the local Party. First Harold Williams, a seaman, held this position (through the middle of 1931); then Henry Shepard, a steelworker brought in from Buffalo; then Steve Kingston, a former Garveyite who had worked in a succession of blue-collar jobs.[44] Hard-working, sometimes courageous, these individuals lacked the intellectual breadth and communicative skills of the Party's "middle-class" leaders—Moore, Briggs, Thompson, and Patterson—or the dynamism and charisma of its best street organizers—Campbell and Fitzgerald. The concentration of the Party's talent in second-level leadership positions allowed its single-issue organizing (around Scottsboro and unemployment) to flourish, but hindered its recruiting and membership-training programs—which were the section organizers' responsibility. Real authority in the Harlem Party rested outside the head of the "apparatus," a most unorthodox pattern in a Stalinist organization.

During 1932, Party organizing in Harlem continued to show a pattern of extensive activity, expanding influence, and slow membership growth. With the Scottsboro defense now firmly in Communist hands, protest to free the Scottsboro boys remained at the center of the Party's work. In March, 1932, after the Alabama State Supreme Court upheld the conviction of seven of the nine defendants and set June 24 as the date of execution, the Party began organizing nationwide demonstrations to undergird its legal strategy. Retaining the constitutional attorney Walter Pollak to appeal the case to the U.S. Supreme Court, the Party called for massive demonstrations "in every city, in every town, in every industrial center." Party leaders made Harlem the target for a mobilization of New York's Communists. On April 16, a crowd of two thousand people attended a Scottsboro demonstration there, which included street rallies, a protest march, and a long-distance race. Another protest parade took place on May 7, attracting 1,800 people, 300 of them black, "with another thousand Negro and Latin American workers marching on the sidelines."[45]

In addition, the Party helped organize a Scottsboro benefit at the Rockland Palace on May 15 which demonstrated both the appeal of the Scottsboro issue to black and white intellectuals, and the willingness of Harlem Communists to temporarily depart from Party policies mandating hostility to the "black bourgeousie." Sponsored by the National Committee for the Defense of Political Prisoners, an organization of left-wing intellectuals, the meeting drew upon the resources of leading black and white writers, artists, and entertainers, and claimed several socially prominent black women as its "patronesses."[46] At a time when glorification of things "proletarian" dominated Communist cultural activity, and when work songs represented the most approved forms of black music, the program displayed surprising artistic diversity. Beginning with speeches by James Ford, Eugene Gordon, Louise Thompson, and Waldo Frank, a well-known white novelist and critic who had recently moved to the left, the evening concluded with presentations by Rose McLendon and the cast of "Porgy," Martha Graham and her dancers, the Hall Johnson choir, and Cab Calloway's orchestra. Over 2,000 people, most of them white, attended the meeting, the *Interstate Tatler* reported, and "got worked up into a sort of religious frenzy over the imprisonment and conviction of these Negro boys." The predominately white audience contributed more than 2,500 dollars in cash to the Scottsboro Defense Fund to help finance future appeals.[47]

Shortly thereafter, the ILD won a legal victory that greatly increased the legitimacy of Party tactics in the Scottsboro case. On May 27, the Supreme Court announced that it would hear the Scottsboro case in October, 1932, and ordered the death sentences for the boys indefinitely suspended. This inspired unprecedented statements of support for the ILD from several Harlem newspapers. "The attention of twelve million Negro citizens," the *Interstate Tatler* wrote, "is focused on the cases of seven doomed boys. . . . Regardless of the outcome of this case, they will remember that the Communist organization helped them to fight. . . . In this, the infamy of mankind is partially atoned for by the fair intentions of a few friends of humanity. And it will be remembered with gratitude." The *Amsterdam News* divided its praise between the ILD and the NAACP (which had won an earlier case which provided the basis for the Supreme Court's decision to hear Scottsboro), but ended by appealing to blacks to support the defense through the Communist dominated National Committee for the Defense of Political Prisoners.[48]

In the summer of 1932, Harlem Communists organized a Scottsboro Unity Defense Committee, which dramatized both their desire and their ability to attract support for their Scottsboro activities from the very mainstream of the Harlem community. The Communists who founded this committee, in an apparent departure from Comintern "Third Period" policies, kept an extremely low profile, projected a nonpartisan image, and targeted socially prominent and politically influential blacks for membership. The group's first open meeting took place at the Harlem offices of the Urban League (the first time a Communist-led group had ever met there!) and attracted forty-five people, most of them black, several of them quite well known. Among those attending were white critics Lionel and Diana Trilling, John Hammond, Richard Carey, a black assistant district attorney, and J. Dalmas Steele, the popular head of the Harlem Elks (described by black newspapers as the "mayor of Harlem").[49] Aided by its nonpartisan approach (and by its avoidance of open attacks on the NAACP), the Committee soon attracted support from other Harlem notables who had never participated in Scottsboro protests or displayed the slightest sympathy for the left; among them songwriter W. C. Handy and dancer Bill "Bojangles" Robinson. Their participation demonstrated the respect the ILD had gained through its legal victories. "The Scottsboro defense has proved itself beyond all cavil," wrote committee chairperson Viola Carter, a prominent Negro clubwoman. "It has provided the best legal talent available in the United States. . . . It has mobilized the sympathies of the finest, most advanced men and women in the world, leaders in their professions and walks of life."[50]

The committee also demonstrated a growing feeling among blacks that Scottsboro was "their" cause and that they had to play a far more active role in the movement for the boys' release. ". . . it is amazing that in a situation of this kind," Mrs. Carter wrote in a press release, "white citizens of this country have gone to the front and demanded . . . justice for these boys, and that Negroes should be reluctant to come to the front. I feel that this is, after all, a Negro fight and that Negroes should put their shoulder to the wheel and carry on with as great, if not greater enthusiasm than their white friends." An *Amsterdam News* editorial made a similar point: "What part is the Negro himself playing in this world drama to save the lives of the nine Scottsboro boys? . . . Does the appeal for funds to defray the expenses of defending his own against oppression, injustice and death, mean anything to him? The full amount should be subscribed by Negroes before another day passes into history."[51]

The Scottsboro Unity Defense Committee's first project, a "mammoth dance and benefit" at the Rockland Palace, attracted "one of the greatest arrays of stage and radio talent ever seen in Harlem." Those performing included W. C. Handy, Fats Waller, Fletcher Henderson, Duke Ellington, the Mills Brothers, Ethel Waters, Paul Whiteman and the Southernaires, along with Bennie Carter's Orchestra, and "the entire review from Small's Paradise," (a popular black-owned Harlem nightclub). The benefit drew more than a thousand people, and while the majority of the crowd was white, it included a far larger number of blacks than had attended any previous Scottsboro fund-raising event in Harlem.[52]

The tone of this event—so divergent from what Communist critics were writing about black music, and from the Party line in general—dramatized the degree of autonomy which Harlem Communists exercised in planning local tactics. At a time when writers in the *New Masses* regularly attacked jazz as decadent, a Scottsboro committee in which Communists were active had invited the best jazz musicians in the United States to perform. In addition, Communists were cooperating with middle-class leaders in Harlem without making the slightest effort to discredit them, a striking contrast from their actions two years before at the conference on unemployment and the meeting on the Wilkins lynching. Such tactical flexibility—later to be criticized as opportunism—indicates that Harlem Communists active in the Scottsboro movement, particularly William Patterson, Richard Moore, and Louise Thompson, were deeply affected by the groundswell of black support for their activities and were willing to stretch the Party line to accommodate that support. Their actions confound the image of the black Communist as puppet or automaton, unwilling to take initiatives without direct orders from the top. Obedient, in the last instance, to Central Committee directives, they were also influenced by popular feeling in the community they worked in.[53]

The inability of Communists to control their new allies became strikingly visible in October, 1932, when difficulties developed in the production of "Black and White," the Soviet film blacks had been commissioned to make. According to Henry Lee Moon and Theodore Poston, work on the film had been halted, shortly after it had begun, because of pressure from American business interests who wanted to establish diplomatic relations between the U.S.S.R. and the United States. Members of the film party who tried to investigate, Moon and Poston reported, were provided the unconvincing explanation that the film had been postponed because of technical difficulties and were offered a tour of the Soviet Union as an alternative. A majority of the film party accepted this offer, but Poston, Moon, and four other members of the party issued a statement accusing the Soviet government of sacrificing its principles to appease American race prejudice. The editorial board of the *Amsterdam News* endorsed their position. "The Russian Film Fiasco," it wrote,

> should carry a great lesson to all Negroes who have in recent years begun to look toward Communism as the governmental system offering them a better opportunity for development. . . . Communism is interested in the Negro only as a propaganda medium for its own advancement in the world. . . . If the . . . film cannot be produced in Soviet Russia for fear of intimidating American Capitalists, where under the heavens can they produce it. Shakespeare was right. All the glitters is not gold.[54]

These statements provoked a vigorous response from some members of the film group still in the Soviet Union and from black Party leaders in the United States. Much of the film group, having had no previous experience with that medium (and having gone on the trip more for the "adventure" than for the opportunity for artistic expression), seemed almost relieved when the project was cancelled and were excited by the prospect of touring the Soviet Union. Impressed by what they saw, they issued a press release endorsing Soviet claims that the film had been postponed for technical reasons and accusing Moon and Poston of spreading "lying slanders" in order to arouse "distrust in the success of socialist construction in the Soviet Union." Individual members of the group praised the treatment they received. "We have seen with our own eyes," Loren Miller declared, "how this is the one country where all races and peoples . . . have achieved real equality." Another cast member described his experience as a "pleasant dream, like waking from a nightmare." Three members of the cast, actor Wayland Rudd, artist Lloyd Patterson, and postal clerk Homer Smith, decided not to return home, and became permanent residents of the Soviet Union. In the United States, Party spokesmen accused Moon and Poston of trying to "divert the Negro masses from their turn toward Communism" and to undermine their "faith" in the Soviet Union. Harlem Communists sent a delegation to the *Amsterdam News* to demand that the paper print the statement of the remainder of the film group, and tried unsuccessfully to set up a debate between a member of the paper's staff and William Patterson.[55]

Significantly, the conflict over the film did not permanently poison relations between the *Amsterdam News* and the Party. Amidst the charges and countercharges surrounding cancellation of the film, the *Amsterdam News* printed editorials and articles praising the ILD's role in the Scottsboro case and supporting the Scottsboro Unity Defense Committee. Even in its handling of the film incident the paper avoided appearing militantly anti-Communist. It printed the statement of the film group in late October and followed it up four weeks later with a long interview with Louise Thompson explaining why she "preferred Russia to living in America."[56]

The *Amsterdam News*'s care in avoiding a total break with the Party—reciprocated by Harlem Communists—reflected a shrewd but principled stance that influential Harlemites adopted as the Party grew in strength. Despite doubts about the Party's motives, methods, and ultimate ends, some Harlem leaders were beginning to regard the Communist movement as a force that could create pressure for reform in American racial practices. They wanted to take advantage of the Communist movement's aggressiveness, but without cutting themselves off from the mainstream of American politics or coming under Communist influence. This position, articulated by the *Amsterdam News,* required a delicate balance between criticism and support of Communist activities, and a willingness to make alliances with the Party around specific political issues.

Cooperation between Communists and Harlem leaders received an additional spur when the Supreme Court voted to overturn the Scottsboro convictions in November, 1932. The Court's decision, made on the grounds that the defendants had been denied adequate counsel, mandated a new trial in the Alabama courts. In Harlem, Communists greeted the verdict with street meetings, a march, and several indoor rallies, featuring speeches by Party leaders, representatives of non-Communist organizations, and Scottsboro parents. These activities culminated in a citywide meeting at the Bronx Coliseum, attended by an overwhelming white crowd of 12,000 people, to mourn the death of J. Louis Engdahl, a white ILD leader who had died while organizing Scottboro protests in Europe. An *Amsterdam News* editorial praised the deceased leader for giving "national and international prominence to the . . . Scottsboro case." "Thanks to men like Engdahl," the paper declared, "the lynchings, or near 'legal lynchings' and exploitation of the Negro in America are no longer isolated problems to be ineffectively dealt with by the United States alone, for through the spread of the Communist doctrine, Russia, with one sixth of the population of the world, is challenging this iniquitous system of exploitation and murder."[57]

The trial of Angelo Herndon, a black Communist who faced the death penalty for his activities as an unemployed council organizer in Atlanta, elicited equally strong praise for Communist defense activities. Herndon had been charged with "inciting Negroes to insurrection" under a provision of the Georgia law adapted from its slave code, and the ILD had infuriated Georgia authorities by hiring an outspoken black attorney from Atlanta, Benjamin Davis, Jr., to handle Herndon's case. The Party's legal defense work, wrote *Amsterdam News* editor William Kelley, had forced him to thoroughly reevaluate his attitudes toward Communism:

> A little less than a year ago . . . I was suspicious of these gift-bearing Reds . . . lest they should rise to power on the backs of American Negroes and then leave them to their fate.
>
> Since that time, a lot of water has run under the bridge, enough to cause us all to reevaluate the accomplishments of this movement in our cause. The victory thus far of the Communists in the Scottsboro case, the Orphan (Euel Lee) Jones case, the fight they are putting up for colored and white farmers in Alabama and the defense of Angelo Herndon . . . strike forcefully at the fundamental wrongs suffered by the Negro today.[58]

The Party's quest for support from "leading Negroes" still faced strong private opposition from the NAACP national officers, whose mistrust of Communist defense tactics remained undiminished. In November, 1932, Walter White took offense at a Scottsboro Unity Defense Committee resolution which offered "full endorsement of the International Labor Defense policy and conduct" in the Scottsboro case and listed ten prominent Harlemites as signatories. Convinced that the statement did not conform to the views of the persons mentioned, many of whom had been NAACP supporters, White wrote letters to them asking them to publicly repudiate the resolution if it was obtained under misleading circumstances.[59] White's suspicions of Party misconduct proved to be on target. Three of the persons contacted — Rev. William Lloyd Imes of St. James Presbyterian Church, Rev. Adam Clayton Powell, Jr., and Mrs. Inez Richardson Wilson, wrote back saying that their names had been used without their permission and one of them — Wilson — resigned from the Scottsboro Unity Defense Committee in protest.[60]

But if White could retard the Party's access to mainstream institutions (he persuaded Imes to cancel an ILD-sponsored symposium at his church in December, 1932), he could not stop it altogether.[61] In February and March, 1933, Scottsboro defense conferences took place in two of the most prestigious churches in Harlem, Abyssinian Baptist and St. Philip's Episcopal (which Communists had denounced for its real estate dealings four years before!) and featured speeches by Countee Cullen, J. Dalmas Steele, William Kelley, and *Amsterdam News* publisher William H. Davis. Increasingly, the passions around by Scottsboro superseded fears of working with Communists. Many a Harlemite had come to feel, in William Kelley's words, "that the Scottsboro fight is his fight, and that no sacrifice is too great to make in saving the lives of these defendants."[62]

Meanwhile, Party activity among the unemployed, less publicized than its Scottsboro defense work, also displayed the Party's growing effectiveness in stimulating community protest. Unemployed Council organizers, largely from working-class backgrounds, conducted relentless agitation on the streets of Harlem to draw black Depression victims into protests aimed at keeping them in their homes and getting them funds to live on.

Throughout 1932, the Council concentrated its attention on the home-relief system, organizing Harlemites to march on local bureaus to demand immediate cash grants. As unemployment worsened, these protests assumed a grim and desperate character. The bureaus simply did not have enough aid to meet the needs of Harlem jobless and periodically closed down because of lack of funds. Even when they were open, the resources they had fell short of the community's needs. The Urban League estimated that 40,000 jobless families remained entirely without relief more than four months after the bureaus opened, and warned that the black population of New York was "approaching a desperate crisis."[63]

To force the relief system to function more effectively, the unemployed movement settled on a strategy of stimulating disorder. Harlem Council activists organized groups of jobless people, took them to the local relief station, and demanded that they receive aid. If the relief bureau officials refused to see them or claimed they were out of funds, the demonstrators camped in the bureau offices and remained there until they received aid. If police tried to remove them from the bureaus or prevent them from entering, council tactics became more violent. At one demonstration in June, 1932, the *Amsterdam News* reported, a group of council organizers broke down the bureau doors and overturned desks and chairs before police could arrest them. Other demonstrations ended in pitched battles with police that resulted in bloodied heads and numerous arrests.[64]

In carrying out this strategy, the Harlem Council could count on a small but impressive group of rank-and-file leaders to set an example for the Harlem jobless. Council leader Louis Campbell helped develop a group of black organizers who displayed a remarkable ability to risk arrest and physical violence in the course of their activities. Sam Brown, Arthur Williams, William Partin, William Fitzgerald, Norman Smith, and Hammie Snipes were arrested numerous times in demonstrations at relief bureaus or in conflicts with local Garveyites, but continued to lead street meetings and march at the head of demonstrations. They were aided by a small group of white council activists who displayed equal courage — Eugene Nigob, Freida Jackson, Sadie Van Veen, and Eleanor Henderson. Working in the midst of terrible suffering, these organizers rarely had time for Party recruiting. But the victories they won in preventing evictions and forcing bureaus to give out funds, helped the councils acquire a reputation as a place for Harlemites to go when they were penniless and desperate.[65]

Council organizers benefited from strong support from the rest of the Party in carrying out their work. During the summer of 1932, when the struggle at the relief bureaus became particularly intense, the new section organizer in Harlem, Henry Shepard, led several local marches, and black Communists Harold Williams and Solomon Harper temporarily shifted their focus from Scottsboro to work with the unemployed. In addition, Party leaders boosted council morale by moving swiftly to the defense of organizers arrested in demonstrations. In the fall of 1932, Communists organized a major defense movement in behalf of Sam Brown, a council organizer who had been sentenced to six months in prison for a protest at a Harlem relief station, even though Eleanor Henderson, a white council leader arrested with him, received a ten-day sentence. Party members in the courtroom led a spontaneous demonstration that resulted in several arrests, and in succeeding weeks, Communists organized protest meetings in Harlem that led up to a rally at the home of the judge who handed down the sentence. Over 500 Communists, most of them white, came to this meeting and engaged in a free-for-all with police that resulted in twenty-two arrests. When the prisoners appeared in court, Communists greeted them with another demonstration that forced the judge to clear the court and make additional arrests. Similar demonstrations took place at subsequent court appearances, accompanied by street meetings in Harlem that denounced Brown's jailing and the attack on protesters as "local Scottsboros."[66]

The movement in Brown's defense had a profound effect on black council organizers. The willingness of so many white Communists to endure arrests and beatings to protect a black comrade gave Communist arguments in behalf of interracial solidarity a new logic and concreteness. Several of the black council leaders who participated in this struggle, notably Louis Campbell, Hammie Snipes, William Fitzgerald, and Sam Brown, developed into some of the most solid and reliable Harlem Communists, rank-and-file leaders who remained with the Party for several years and carried out difficult and dangerous work with little reward or publicity.[67]

During the winter of 1932–33, council organizers found Harlemites increasingly receptive to their message that only organized protest action could cut through relief bureau red tape. "I stood in the rain for three days and the Home Relief Bureau paid no attention to me," one woman declared at a Council neighborhood meeting. "Then I found out about the Unemployed Council. . . . We went in there as a body and then they came across right quick." "The woman at the desk said I was rejected." another woman added. "I was crying when Comrade Minns told me to come to the meeting of the Unemployed Council. One week later I got my rent check. I got my rent check for two months and I guess I'll get the third." Experiences such as this began to convince many Harlemites that joining the council represented an effective way to pry relief funds from the city bureaucracy. In March, 1933, a council demonstration in Harlem attracted 500 people, by far the largest group ever to join a relief protest in that community, and won food and rent checks for twenty-five people.[68]

Communist successes in organizing the unemployed and in Scottsboro work encouraged Harlem Party leaders to seize the initiative on an entirely new issue: health conditions in Harlem. In January, 1933, inspired by resignations of black doctors from the Harlem Hospital staff in protest against alleged poor patient care, political favoritism in appointments, and lack of opportunities for promotion, the Party announced that it would "support a movement to do away with discrimination against Negro doctors, nurses, and patients in Harlem Hospital and all hospitals in New York City." Criticizing an NAACP committee appointed to look into hospital conditions as a "whitewash" (some Harlemites perceived a conflict of interest in the association's investigation of an institution whose medical board secretary, Dr. Louis Wright, served on the NAACP National Board), the Party called for a popularly elected investigating committee supported by mass pressure tactics. On January 26, it called a protest meeting in Harlem to press its demands, which included improved patient care in Harlem Hospital, the admission of Negro patients to all hospitals in the city, the right of black doctors and nurses to be advanced according to their ability, and the reinstatement of doctors who resigned in protest from Harlem Hospital.[69]

In organizing around this issue, Harlem Communists once again displayed their desire to enlist middle-class Harlemites, and members of church and fraternal organizations, in a campaign of protest—especially since one of the targets of that campaign was the NAACP. The January 26 meeting resulted in the formation of a "People's Committee Against Discrimination in Harlem Hospital" that voted to welcome unemployed and employed workers, "small home owners, small shop keepers, church members, beauty parlor and barber shop workers," and "doctors, lawyers, and teachers," who were "affected by widespread unemployment and discrimination." Although no theoretical pronouncement accompanied this statement—and it could not, given the prevailing Comintern line—Harlem Communists, as they did in the Scottsboro campaign, were seeking a constituency that cut across class lines. Given the extraordinary discrimination black doctors and nurses faced—they were barred from most public and private hospitals in the city of New York—such a policy had considerable logic. People's Committee leaders attended several meetings organized by the North Harlem Medical Society and offered to cooperate with any organization in Harlem willing to "wage a mass fight" to improve hospital conditions.[70]

In the hospital campaign, the Party developed its first working relationship with Rev. Adam Clayton Powell, Jr., then assistant pastor at his father's Abyssinian Baptist Church. Powell's involvement in this campaign symbolized a growing conflict within Harlem's professional strata, partly generational in origin, over the appropriateness of mass protest tactics, and the effectiveness of the NAACP's leadership. One of the first Harlem ministers to support the allegations of the resigning doctors, Powell had not been satisfied by the NAACP's investigation of the dispute, despite his father's presence on the NAACP National Board and the investigating committee itself. In March, 1933, he called a meeting at Abyssinian Baptist Church to prepare for a confrontation with city officials over conditions at Harlem Hospital. Powell invited William Patterson, a member of the "People's Committee," to be a featured speaker at the gathering, which drew 1,500 people. The group voted to mount a series of protest meetings in Harlem and at City Hall, and to send a delegation to see the mayor. Patterson was selected as a member of the delegation, along with Powell, J. Dalmas Steele, William H. Davis, and several doctors. Such a step—unimaginable two years before—demonstrated both the respect Patterson commanded for his individual talents and the Party's newfound credibility as an exponent of practical reform.[71]

The Harlem Party's growing visibility and effectiveness drew cautious words of praise from the Party's Central Committee. "The . . . upsurge among the Negro masses," Earl Browder commented in March, 1933, had reached the point that "even in Harlem . . . we are making tremendous inroads . . . so that the bourgeois press is forced to devote front page and editorial columns to . . . what the Communists are doing and the Communist position on the Negro question." Party leaders seemed particularly gratified by these gains because of the importance they attached to Harlem as a "center of activities for the Negro people all over the world."

"The time has come for action," James Ford told a Party gathering in Harlem. "It is in Harlem that we must lead the struggle against conditions such as 80 percent of Negroes unemployed, high tuberculosis, death and child mortality rates."[72]

The elan of Harlem Communists received a further boost from a manifesto issued by the Comintern in mid-March, 1933, shortly after Hitler's rise to power. Recognizing, rather belatedly, that its sectarian warfare with Socialists had helped bring a government to power that seriously threatened the Soviet Union, the Comintern called for a "United Front of Struggle" between Communists and Social Democrats. In the United States, the Comintern called for limited alliances between the CPUSA and groups that it had previously denounced as "social fascist": the Socialist Party, the Conference for Progressive Labor Action (Musteites) and the American Federation of Labor. Communists were still supposed to accompany such alliances with criticism of socialist leaders and efforts to recruit socialist workers, but the new line initially did give the CPUSA greater latitude in working with non-Communist groups.[73]

In Harlem, the Comintern Manifesto appeared to give legitimacy to policies which Communists were *already pursuing* on an ad hoc basis. Well before Hitler came to power, Communists in the Scottsboro movement had cooperated with black organizations which were not even "socialist"—churches, lodges, professional associations—and the new line gave them added incentive to do so. As a new set of Scottsboro trials approached in late March, 1933, Harlem Communists stood poised to dramatically expand their political influence. The leading force in a cause which aroused powerful emotions—they now had access to important Harlem churches, critical support from the black press, and a theoretical outlook which enabled them to respond with flexibility to potential allies.

The opening of the new Scottsboro trials on March 27, 1933, aroused tremendous excitement and anxiety in Harlem. The Scottsboro boys seemed to be in a far better position than they had been at the time of their first trial. The ILD had retained one of the nation's best criminal lawyers, Samuel Leibowitz, to represent the defendants and had uncovered new evidence which raised doubts as to whether a "rape" had ever occurred. On February 13, 1933, the *Daily Worker* released a letter from Ruby Bates, one of the two Scottsboro "victims," declaring that the Scottsboro defendants had never touched her and that local authorities had forced her to lie.[74]

At the trial of Haywood Patterson, first of the defendants to come before the court, Leibowitz confidently set out to destroy the prosecution's entire case. He tore into Victoria Price, the main prosecution witness, questioning her honesty, her memory, and her moral reputation. Leibowitz insisted that the only sexual relations Price had had took place in a hobo jungle the night before the train ride. When she declined to admit this, Leibowitz called Lester Carter, a secondary witness in the case, to testify that he and a friend had spent the night with the two young women before the incident and Ruby Bates to testify that no rape had occurred. In addition, Leibowitz called on the examining physician to testify that he found no live semen on the two young women and that they showed no sign of injury.

Leibowitz felt confident this evidence could sway the most prejudiced jury. But as the trial continued, observers noted a hardening in the faces of the jurors when Leibowitz spoke and a growing restiveness in the local community. Leibowitz's rough handling of Victoria Price had violated southern canons about the "sanctity of white womanhood," and local citizens began speculating aloud whether the defense attorney would ever leave town alive. National Guard investigators attended a protest meeting of 200 people in which several speakers advocated "riding the New York lawyers out of town on a rail and then lynching the Scottsboro boys."[75]

As the trial proceeded, the Communist Party revived its campaign of mass demonstrations, organizing marches, and street meetings that involved large numbers of non-Communist blacks. After two years of Scottsboro protests, Harlemites of all social classes had developed a strong emotional identification with the Scottsboro boys, and they viewed the hardening atmosphere in the trials as a signal for a show of support. In the first Harlem protest parade during the trial, the *Daily Worker* reported that for the first time, a majority of the marchers were black and that "most of them were Garveyites...and members of Harlem churches." A succeeding Communist protest parade on April 8, one day before the case went to the jury, drew 1,500 people into the streets, according to *Daily Worker* estimates, with thousands more lining the sidewalks and contributing "pennies, nickels and dimes for the Scottsboro defense."[76]

The outcome of the Patterson trial confirmed the worst fears of Harlem demonstrators. After an undisguised appeal by the prosecutor to sectional and racial prejudice ("show them that Alabama justice cannot be bought and sold with Jew money from New York"), the jury, in less than one day of deliberation, found Patterson guilty and fixed his punishment as death in the electric chair.

When news of Patterson's conviction reached Harlem, it turned a subdued Sunday crowd of churchgoers and strollers into a mass of enraged protesters. While Communist organizers fanned out through Harlem to tell people of the jury's decision, *Amsterdam News* publisher William Davis issued a call for a march on Washington to demand that President Roosevelt insure the safety of the Scottsboro boys, and began circulating petitions to that effect throughout the community. Davis's action precipitated an extraordinary response. Thousands of people milled outside the

Amsterdam News offices waiting to sign the petitions, while diverse political groups offered to collect signatures and participate in the march.
"I have never seen such anger and indignation before or since," Party organizer Theodore Bassett recalled: "Everywhere you went, you saw anger
on people's faces, men and women. Some people were ready to march to
Alabama that night. If there were ever a revolutionary situation, I imagine that's what it would be like."[77] Throughout the day, tens of thousands
of Harlemites remained in the streets. "Speakers from the Communist
Party, the Garvey movement, preachers, and the ILD," the *Daily Worker*
reported, "mounted each other's stands," united in their determination to
"save the Scottsboro boys." For the first time, Harlem had witnessed "the
coordination of all her forces," Theodore Poston wrote. The *Amsterdam
News* petition drive, supported by "Republican and Democrat, Communist and Socialist, Garveyite and Lovestoneite," collected 40,000 signatures in less than one day.[78]

On Monday, April 10, Harlem's "continual mass meeting" shifted
downtown. After a rally at Union Square, 3,000 people gathered at Pennsylvania Station to greet Samuel Leibowitz upon his arrival from Alabama. Outside the station, ILD leaders organized a rally and called for a
march to Harlem. Five hundred people in the crowd followed their advice
and began a singing, cheering parade up Broadway that periodically
broke up and regrouped as police attacked it.[79]

The outburst of popular indignation even penetrated conservative
Harlem institutions. On April 10, the Interdenominational Ministers
Alliance, a coordinating body of Harlem churches, voted to endorse the
ILD's role in the Scottsboro case and similar endorsements came from
Harlem fraternal organizations, women's clubs, political organizations
and social and benefit societies.[80] "Harlem has almost gone insane," a
surprised Walter White wrote to I. F. Coles, "but alas, as in other cases
its enthusiasm will soon pass."[81]

The NAACP, alone among black organizations, attacked the ILD, but
discovered that it had seriously misread black public opinion. Two days
after issuing a press release blaming Patterson's conviction on the "injec-
tion of Communism into the case," the NAACP Board, stunned by the
hostility this position evoked among its own branches and the black press,
reversed itself and offered to aid the ILD in raising money for future appeals. In Harlem, the association's actions aroused considerable resentment. "On every corner up here now," I. F. Coles wrote, "the NAACP is
catching hell, and anyone who lifts his voice in the interest of the organization also catches hell."[82] Harlem newspapers proved equally critical.
"The NAACP should deem it a privilege to cooperate . . . with the defense,
whether sponsored by Communists, Socialists, Democrats, or Republicans," the *Amsterdam News* wrote. "If it cannot do this, wisdom dictates

that it should hold its tongue." "Snap out of it Walter White! This is your last chance," wrote a columnist for the *New York Age*. " . . . the ILD is conducting a fight for the lives of these innocent lads in a most praiseworthy manner and it is up to every Negro and pro-Negro organization in the country to rally to their support."[83]

During the weeks following Patterson's conviction, Harlem Communists tried to consolidate Harlem's spontaneous outpouring of militancy into disciplined protest action under its leadership. Seizing on William H. Davis's proposal for a Scottsboro March on Washington—which the *Amsterdam News* publisher had made in the heat of battle and subsequently repudiated in favor of a "delegation of representative citizens"—Communists convened a conference at the Harlem Masonic Temple on April 16 to formulate plans for a march. Taking advantage of the new Comintern line, Communists invited representatives of black churches and fraternal organizations, the NAACP, and white leaders of the Socialist Party. Neither NAACP officials or representatives of Harlem's largest churches showed up, but the Conference attracted representatives of ten fraternal organizations, (including the Odd Fellows, Masons, and Elks), three women's clubs, and eighteen educational and cultural associations. The gathering approved the ILD's plan for a militant interracial march to demand freedom for the Scottsboro boys and enforcement of the Thirteenth, Fourteenth, and Fifteenth Amendments, and set up a National Scottsboro Action Committee to organize the demonstrations.[84]

In addition, the ILD, in vast departure from its previous policies, agreed to accept the NAACP's offer to raise funds for the Scottsboro defense, and set up a series of meetings with association officials to work out a division of labor in the case. Not only did these meetings (attended by William Patterson of the ILD, and Walter White and Roy Wilkins of the NAACP) produce an agreement to cooperate in assuring financial support for the defense, but they also resulted in what Roy Wilkins called a "verbal understanding, a sort of gentlemen's agreement" that "attacks and counterattacks shall be discontinued so that both organizations can concentrate on the winning of the Scottsboro cases."[85] Nevertheless, considerable tension pervaded the relationship between the two organizations. Patterson continually pressed association officials to participate in ILD-sponsored protest meetings and to endorse its overall defense strategy, and association officials just as persistently turned these requests down. "The NAACP is not participating in marches to Washington or anywhere else; it is not presenting any 'demands' . . . ," Roy Wilkins wrote to NAACP branch officers. "The national office strongly recommends that its branches do not join any so-called unity defense committees."[86]

The NAACP was not alone in wishing to disassociate itself from aspects of Communist defense strategy while assuring financial support for the defendants. On April 11, a group of Harlemites led by Rev. Richard Manuel Bolden, pastor of First Emmanuel Church, and Bill "Bojangles" Robinson asked Samuel Leibowitz if he would cooperate in forming a defense fund independent of the ILD. Leibowitz, an organization Democrat, endorsed their proposal and agreed to present it at a meeting of the Interdenominational Ministers Alliance at Salem M. E. Church on April 13. Over 4,000 Harlemites came to the meeting and voted to set up a fund-raising committee which would deal directly with the popular attorney. Communists, who had hired Leibowitz as a legal technician, were infuriated by the prospect of the fund raising in the case escaping their control. They denounced the meeting and demanded that the ministers turn over funds they raised directly to the ILD.[87]

These divisions over fund raising, and over "control" of the Scottsboro movement, surfaced even more dramatically at a protest meeting called by Adam Clayton Powell, Sr., at Abyssinian Baptist Church on April 17. Billed as a "united front" demonstration, the meeting brought together such divergent speakers as Walter White of the NAACP, Benjamin Davis, Jr., of the ILD, Joshua Bushnell of the Harlem Democratic organization, Adam Clayton Powell, Sr., William Davis of the *Amsterdam News,* and ILD Secretary William Patterson. Between the NAACP and the ILD, relative peace prevailed. But Patterson bitterly criticized William Davis, who was still circulating petitions to present to the President, for changing his plan for a 50,000-person march on Washington into one that called for a "delegation of representative citizens" and for collecting funds for the Scottsboro defense without ILD authorization. "If you get out of line we'll whip you back into line!" Patterson reportedly bellowed. "Get into line for by God it will be a hell of a time if you get out of line this time."[88]

Following this meeting at Abyssinian Baptist, the Scottsboro protest movement in Harlem split into two distinct and increasingly antagonistic groups (the NAACP, which confined its Scottsboro activities strictly to the *legal* domain, watched this conflict from the sidelines). On one side stood the members of the Interdenominational Ministers Alliance, some important political and fraternal leaders, and the publishers of the *Amsterdam News* and the *New York Age.* This group wished to register its protest against the Scottsboro verdict, but in a manner that "avoided the stigma of Communism." It supported the petition drive launched by William Davis, but believed the petitions should be presented to the President by a delegation of "representative" Harlem citizens rather than by the leaders of a militant demonstration. The other groups consisted of the Communist Party and ILD activists, a number of younger Harlem ministers and fraternal leaders, and some black and some white intellectuals. They viewed "mass action" as an essential component of the Scottsboro defense and supported a militant march on Washington. They regarded the spontaneous Scottsboro protest in Harlem as an important step in the political awakening of the black population, something to be sustained, consolidated, and extended to other issues.[89]

As the Scottsboro united front crumbled at the top, Harlem Communists intensified their efforts to win popular support for their strategy. Throughout the last two weeks of April, Party activists maintained a continuous schedule of street meetings and rallies in Harlem and tried to turn the Harlem chapter of the ILD into a mass community organization. Under the leadership of William Fitzgerald, a former Garveyite who had joined the Party through the unemployment movement, the ILD recruited hundreds of Harlemites who knew little about Communism but were ready to fight to free the Scottsboro boys. During April, 1933, the ILD formed nine new chapters in Harlem, each named after a different Scottsboro boy. Overwhelmingly black in membership, these groups provided outlets for a "grass-roots" militancy that Party organizations had rarely touched before. With the CP leadership keeping a low profile, the ILD recruits brought a new spirit into the Harlem Scottsboro movement, organizing card parties, teas, and dances, as well as street meetings and rallies.[90] Their enthusiasm especially affected preparations for the march on Washington, scheduled for May 6, 1933.

On April 22, a protest parade sponsored by the National Scottsboro Action Committee had a pageantry and color reminiscent of the Garvey movement in its prime. While black aviator Herbert Julian flew overhead in a plane covered with Scottsboro slogans, the UNIA, the Elks, the Masons, and Harlem church groups joined the ILD and the Party in a march through the community that featured "uniforms, banners and bands." "Your reporter has been to many a demonstration in Harlem," a *Daily Worker* writer claimed, "but none were like this. . . . In other parades, most of those on the sidewalks were spectators, still doubtful, but today, there was no doubt. Today, as one Negro said, 'We are all on the march.' . . . Eighty percent of those in line are residents of Harlem." A bystander expressed the spirit of the occasion: "Yes brother, a new thing is born. It's a new people and we're marching for our rights."[91]

As the march on Washington approached, tension between different factions in the Harlem Scottsboro movement grew dramatically. Rev. J. W. Brown of Mother Zion A. M. E. Church, and J. Dalmas Steele, both members of the National Scottsboro Action Committee, announced their support for Davis's delegation of representative citizens, and were joined in this venture by Rev. Adam Clayton Powell, Sr., librarian and book collector Arthur Schomburg, and A. Philip Randolph. The conflict between the two spilled out into the streets, where Party soapboxers got into verbal and physical confrontations with New York City police and opponents of the march.[92]

Despite the last-minute rush of support for Davis's plan among influential Harlemites, the Scottsboro march retained some important backers. Reverends Shelton Hale Bishop of St. Phillip's Church and Adam Clayton Powell, Jr., of Abyssinian Baptist Church, continued to support the march, while a delegate from the Caribbean Union (a coordinating body of West Indian Organizations), Samuel Patterson, served as chairman of the Scottsboro Action Committee. The participation of Bishop and Powell symbolized the growing generational split within Harlem's leadership. The sons of influential ministers who served on the NAACP's National Board, their open sympathy for the left surprised and scandalized some NAACP supporters. "Why Young Powell," I. F. Coles wrote Walter White, "who is supposed to be a personal friend of yours, has been speaking for the Communists on street corners."[93]

But Powell's action represented more than youthful rebellion—shrewd political instinct also guided his behavior. The mobilization for the Washington march, though led by Communists, revealed a substantial constituency in Harlem for mass pressure tactics. The night before the march took place, over 5,000 people came out to a meeting at St. Nicholas Arena that featured speeches by Powell, Samuel Leibowitz, William Patterson, and Scottsboro witnesses Lester Carter and Ruby Bates. Identifying himself wholeheartedly with the left's protest strategy, Powell proclaimed that "our own NAACP has sold us out" and hailed the Washington March as an important step toward a needed political awakening among blacks. "It's about time," he told the cheering audience, "that Negroes got off their backsides and got into action."[94]

On the morning of May 6, 500 people gathered outside the headquarters of the Scottsboro Action Committee to form the Harlem contingent of the Scottsboro march. Joining up with 1,500 predominately white marchers from other parts of the city, they headed for Philadelphia, and then Baltimore, where they participated in several demonstrations against hotels and restaurants that refused to serve black marchers. Upon their arrival in Washington, the marchers, now 3,000 strong, lined up four abreast, with arms linked, and marched to the White House, where a delegation composed of James Ford, William Patterson, and Ruby Bates demanded to see the President. They were received by Presidential Secretary Louis Howe, who announced that the President was "too busy" to discuss the case with them. The marchers thereupon proceeded to the Capitol, where the delegation presented a twenty-four-part civil rights bill, mandating an end to discrimination, peonage, and lynching, to the Vice-President and the Speaker of the House, and demanded "congressional action for the unconditional release of the Scottsboro boys."[95]

One day earlier, William H. Davis, accompanied by eighteen prominent Harlemites, had followed a similar route, presenting 145,000 Scottsboro petitions to the President's secretary, and conferring with sympathetic congressional leaders over the possibility of legislative action to protect black civil rights. Denouncing Patterson's conviction as a "travesty of justice," the delegation also took pains to emphasize that Harlem's outrage over the Scottsboro verdicts was not confined to Communists and Communist sympathizers.[96]

Harlem Communists, though furious over Davis's actions, regarded their own march as a powerful affirmation of a new spirit of militancy in the black population. On the journey to and from Washington, the marchers had taken over restaurants that refused to serve blacks and defied police who tried to eject them, and the Harlem contingent returned full of "enthusiasm and fighting spirit." "We've never before attempted to fight our way through," an ILD member declared at a gathering of Harlem marchers. "We've always attempted to pray our way through. We must go back to our churches and lodges and put the spirit of fight in them." "The march marks a new stage in the struggle of the Negro people," Cyril Briggs wrote, "with the Negro workers emerging as the leaders of these struggles and . . . supplanting the businessmen, preachers, and professional self-elected leaders who have consistently betrayed our struggle in the past."[97]

In the weeks following the march, Scottsboro protest activity in Harlem continued to attract broad popular support. Throughout May and June, 1933, the ILD, the Communist Party, and the Scottsboro Action Committee sponsored street meetings, rallies, and parades to register Harlem's indignation against the death sentences the defendants had received. The Harlem ILD registered impressive gains in membership. By the middle of June, the group claimed 1,700 members in nineteen different chapters and had opened a series of lectures and leadership classes to supplement its political and social activities.[98]

The support extended for this activity by some prominent blacks inspired an impassioned debate in Harlem newspapers over the Communist Party's role in black life. In May, 1933, Adam Clayton Powell, Jr., reportedly told an ILD mass meeting that he would leave his church if it barred Communist meetings. "I don't mind being called a Communist," the young minister allegedly said. "The day will come when being called a Communist will be the highest honor that can be paid an individual and that day is coming soon." Dr. Mordecai Johnson, president of Howard University, expressed somewhat similar sentiments in a speech to Howard alumni, at Harlem's Mt. Olivet Baptist Church. Johnson called the Russian experiment "the beginning of the emancipation of the human race" and declared that America should move toward the same political ends "without bloodshed." A *New York Age* editorial attacked the two men, telling them to "exercise judgment and discretion when speaking in public" lest they jeopardize the welfare of black institutions.[99]

Divisions on this issue also surfaced in the *Negro World* and the *Amsterdam News.* During May, 1933, the once anti-Communist *Negro World* began featuring two new columnists, H. Donaldson Riley and Thomas Cathcart, who strongly supported Communist Scottsboro activities and advised blacks to join the "working-class movement." Their views attracted considerable opposition from the paper's correspondents, but the *Negro World* continued to print their columns and give the Harlem Scottsboro movement editorial endorsement. In the *Amsterdam News,* political differences emerged between editor William Kelley, who supported the mass Scottsboro march, and publisher William Davis, who had organized the delegation of Harlem notables. By June of 1933, the differences had become irreconcilable and Kelley was forced to resign.[100]

These conflicts reflected the emergence of a distinct "left-wing" in the Harlem community, independent of the Party but sympathetic to its views. After two years of Party Scottsboro organizing, a significant segment of Harlem's intelligentsia had come to regard the Party as a valuable political ally and to work with it closely in the Scottsboro movement. The bulk of Harlem Scottsboro activists remained political independents, joining "united front" committees and the ILD rather than the Party itself, but they shared the Party's belief that only organized protest could halt the discrimination blacks faced throughout the United States.

In late June, 1933, the Party's credibility received an additional boost when Judge James Horton, the presiding magistrate at the Patterson trial, overturned the jury's verdict and ordered a new trial for the defendant. After reviewing the case for several months, Horton decided that there was simply not "sufficient credible evidence on which to base a verdict." The judge's courageous decision did not end prosecution of the Scottsboro cases; the Alabama attorney general announced his intention of retrying the cases "as soon as possible." But the decision removed the Scottsboro boys from immediate danger and gave those who protested the verdicts the feeling that their militancy had achieved results.[101]

With this new legal victory in the Scottsboro case, the Communist Party in Harlem turned its attention to other issues that troubled the community—unemployment, job discrimination, conditions in Harlem Hospital. It did so from a position of considerably greater influence. In a little more than two years, the Scottsboro movement had helped transform the Party from a political "outsider" in Harlem into an important force in the community's life. Despite strong NAACP opposition, the Party had established its right to hold meetings at important churches and lodges and had helped transmit an enthusiasm for mass pressure tactics to large portions of Harlem's populatin. By courting support from black editors, ministers, and fraternal leaders (in seeming defiance of Third Period strategy) as well as maintaining a steady presence on Harlem's streets, the Communioto gradually instilled a powerful emotional identification with the Scottsboro defense in Harlemites of diverse backgrounds. In the period following Haywood Patterson's conviction, Harlemites who had once passively observed Party Scottsboro parades took to the streets by the thousands and turned the Harlem Scottsboro campaign from a "proving ground" for white radicals into a mass community movement. For the first time, Cyril Briggs proudly declared: "the Negro people [have] come forward clearly as an active force . . . in the mass fight to free the Scottsboro boys and put a stop to the flagrant violations of Negro rights. . . . Harlem during the past few weeks has given the Negro people of the whole world a wonderful demonstration in the effectiveness of militant and united struggle."[102]

NOTES

1. Dan T. Carter, *Scottsboro, A Tragedy of the American South* (paperback ed.; New York: Oxford University Press, 1971), p. 50.

2. *Ibid.,* pp. 20–28; William L. Patterson, *The Man Who Cried Genocide* (New York: International Publishers, 1971), pp. 127–28; Haywood Patterson and Earl Conrad, *Scottsboro Boy* (New York: Doubleday, 1950), pp. 11–12; *Daily Worker,* Apr. 7, 1931.

3. *Daily Worker,* Apr. 2, 1931, Apr. 10, 1931, Apr. 13, 1931; International Labor Defense to Governor R. Miller, Apr. 7, 1931, International Labor Defense Papers, Schomburg Collection, Reel 3, hereafter cited as ILD Papers.

4. Carter, *Scottsboro,* pp. 52–52, 56, 61–62.

5. U.S. Congress, House, Special Committee on Communist Activities in the United States, *Investigation of Communist Propaganda* (Washington: Government Printing Office, 1930), pp. 200–201.

6. For evidence of the respect the NAACP had attained in Harlem for its past work, see *New York Amsterdam News,* May 20, 1931; *New York Age,* July 11, 1931.

7. Du Bois lived in the Dunbar Apartments, a Rockefeller-funded development that housed many black businessmen and professionals, and White lived at 409 Edgecombe Avenue, a luxury apartment building in Harlem's "Sugar Hill." For evidence of how association national officials operated through personal networks, see Walter White to Ferdinand Q. Morton, June 18, 1931, NAACP Papers, D 69, and "Ministers to Whom Tickets for Lecture are to be Sent," Jan. 1, 1932, NAACP Papers, C 332.

8. The NAACP Papers, and the Harlem press, provide little evidence of substantive activity by the association's New York branch in the early '30s. Its presi-

dent, James Egert Allen, a black schoolteacher, is not mentioned in any of the correspondence documenting the NAACP's conflict with the ILD, nor are any of the branch's vice-presidents. Moreover, none of these officials are mentioned in articles on Scottsboro in the black or Party press. In addition, from 1933 on, documents regularly appear in the NAACP Papers complaining of the weakness of the New York branch. For an example of one of these, see Bennie Butler to Roy Wilkins, Oct. 4, 1933, NAACP Papers, G 143.

9. *Daily Worker,* Apr. 15, 1931, Apr. 21, 1931, May 5 and 13, 1931; *New York Amsterdam News,* Apr. 29, 1931; *New York Times,* Apr. 25, 1931.

10. *Daily Worker,* May 4, 1931, May 15, 1931; *Liberator,* Apr. 25, 1931. For evidence of the dismay Pickens's comments caused among NAACP officials and board members, see Walter White to Robert Bagnall and Herbert Seligmann, May 3, 1931, NAACP Papers, D 68; Mary White Ovington to William Pickens, Apr. 30, 1931, *ibid.*

11. Interview with Henry Lee Moon, May 1, 1937; interview with John Hammond, Sept. 26, 1978; Patterson, *The Man Who Cried Genocide,* pp. 117–18, 130–35.

12. *New York Times,* May 17, 1931; *Daily Worker,* May 18, 1931; *Liberator,* Apr. 25, 1931.

13. *New York Amsterdam News,* May 20, 1931; *Negro World,* May 23, 1931; *New York News and Harlem Home Journal,* May 23, 1931.

14. On Pickens's disenchantment with the ILD, see William Pickens to Walter White, May 31, 1931, NAACP Papers, D 69. For an example of the NAACP's efforts to win over black editors to their side of the Scottsboro dispute, see Walter White to Carl Murphy, May 16, 1931, *ibid.,* D 68.

15. Memorandum from Mr. Bagnall (Re: Scottsboro Cases), May 6, 1931, NAACP Papers, D 68; Walter White, To Members of the NAACP, June 18, 1931, *ibid.,* D 69.

16. *New York Amsterdam News,* June 2, 1931.

17. *Liberator,* May 30, 1931, June 20, 1931.

18. *Daily Worker,* June 23, 1931.

19. *Young Worker,* May 11, 1931; *Liberator,* June 6, 1931, June 13, 1931.

20. *New York Amsterdam News,* July 1, 1931; *Interstate Tatler,* July 2, 1931.

21. Walter White to Members of the NAACP, June 18, 1931, NAACP Papers, D 69; Walter White to Ferdinand Q. Morton, June 18, 1931, *ibid.;* Walter White to Dr. F. A. Cullen, June 25, 1931, *ibid.*

22. *New York Times,* June 29, 1931; *New York Amsterdam News,* July 1, 1931.

23. *Daily Worker,* June 29, 1931; *Liberator,* July 4, 1931.

24. Carter, *Scottsboro,* pp. 77–79.

25. Eugene Gordon, "The Negro's New Leadership," *New Masses,* 7 (July, 1931), 14–15.

26. *New York Age,* July 11, 1931; *Negro World,* Aug. 8, 1931.

27. *New York Amsterdam News,* Aug. 12, 1931; *New York Age,* July 25, 1931, Aug. 15, 1931; *Negro World,* Aug. 15, 1931, Sept. 26, 1931.

28. *Daily Worker,* Sept. 17, 1931; *New York Amsterdam News,* Oct. 21, 1931; *Liberator,* Oct. 17, 1931.

29. Walter White to Rev. L. H. King, Oct. 13, 1931, NAACP Papers, D 70;

telephone message to White from Rev. L. H. King, Pastor of St. Mark's M. E. Church, Oct. 14, 1931, *ibid.*

30. Carter, *Scottsboro,* pp. 92–99; Patterson and Conrad, *Scottsboro Boy,* pp. 18–19.

31. Carter, *Scottsboro,* pp. 98, 101.

32. Floyd J. Calvin to Walter White, Jan. 16, 1931, NAACP Papers, D 71.

33. *New York Amsterdam News,* Jan. 6, 1932.

34. *Daily Worker,* June 19, 1931, Aug. 14, 1931, Aug. 19, 1931; *Liberator,* Sept. 19, 1931.

35. *Daily Worker,* Oct. 12, 1931; *Liberator,* Nov. 14, 1931, Nov. 21, 1931, Dec. 5, 1931.

36. Josephine Chapin Brown, *Public Relief, 1929–1939* (1940; rpt. New York: Octagon Books, 1971), pp. 89–94.

37. *New York Amsterdam News,* Dec. 23, 1931, Feb. 17, 1932, Feb. 24, 1931.

38. Interview with Louise Thompson, Sept. 14, 1977; interview with Theodore Bassett, Nov. 2, 1973.

39. *New York Amsterdam News,* Feb. 17, 1932, Mar. 9, 1932.

40. Interview with John Hammond, Sept. 26, 1978; interview with Henry Lee Moon, May 1, 1979; *New York Amsterdam News,* June 15, 1932; *Interstate Tatler,* June 16, 1932. On Bearden's role in cancelling an ILD meeting at a Harlem church, see memorandum from Mr. Bagnall (Re: Scottsboro Case), May 6, 31, NAACP Papers, D 68.

41. C. Smith, "The Problem of Cadres in the Party," *Communist,* 11 (Feb., 1932), 114; Robert Jay Alperin, "Organization in the Communist Party, U.S.A., 1931–1938" (Ph.D. dissertation, Northwestern University, 1959), p. 61.

42. *Daily Worker,* Jan. 29, 1932; interview with Abner Berry, Feb. 4, 1978. Although Party "stipends" for functionaries were very small, other fringe benefits came with it: free medical care from Party doctors, visits to Party resorts, places to stay at little or no rent, etc. In a time of Depression, even this minimal security made one better off than the average unemployed worker.

43. Interview with Richard B. Moore, Nov. 14, 1973; Harry Haywood, "The Scottboro Decision; Victory of Revolutionary Struggle Over Reformist Betrayal," *Communist,* 11 (Dec., 1932), 1073–74. Haywood complained of the Party's failure to capitalize on the popular support its Scottsboro activities aroused.

44. Almost no information exists in the Party press about these individuals, other than their place of origins, their occupations, and the fact that they served as section organizers. The limited information I have about them comes from interview data: interview with Richard B. Moore, Nov. 14, 1973; interview with Theodore Bassett, Nov. 2, 1973. But it does seem clear that none of these individuals were of the stature and capability of the top people working under them, and that the Party refused to recognize this as a source of the problem in the Harlem Section.

45. *Daily Worker,* Mar. 25, 1932, Mar. 26, 1932, Apr. 16, 1932, May 9, 1932; *New York Amsterdam News,* Apr. 20, 1932; Carter, *Scottsboro,* p. 160.

46. *Daily Worker,* May 10, 1932. The "well known Harlem figures" listed as sponsors were Mrs. Edna Thomas, Mrs. Bertha Cotton, and Mrs. Belle Edwards.

47. *Daily Worker,* May 17, 1932; *Interstate Tatler,* May 19, 1932; Philip Schatz,

"Songs of the Negro Worker," *New Masses,* 5 (May, 1930), 6. During the 1920s, Frank had been a close friend of Jean Toomer, one of the most important novelists of the Harlem Renaissance, and had spent a great deal of time in Harlem. On Frank's relationship with Toomer, see David Levering Lewis, *When Harlem Was in Vogue* (New York: Knopf, 1981), pp. 66–71, 99.

48. Carter, *Scottsboro,* p. 160; *Interstate Tatler,* June 2, 1932; *New York Amsterdam News,* June 8, 1932.

49. "Minutes on conference held to consider Ways and Means of developing work in Harlem," Aug. 1932, ILD Papers, Reel 2; Minutes, Scottsboro Unity Defense Committee, Monday, Sept. 19, 1932, *ibid.*

50. Scottsboro Unity Defense Committee, press release, *ibid.; New York Amsterdam News,* Sept. 21, 1932.

51. Scottsboro Unity Defense Committee, press release, Sept., 1932, ILD Papers, Reel 2; *New York Amsterdam News,* Sept. 21, 1932.

52. *Ibid.,* Oct. 12, 1932.

53. On Communist attitudes toward black music in the early '30s, see Schatz, "Songs of the Negro Worker," 6; Lawrence Gellert, "Negro Songs of Protest," *New Masses,* 6 (Jan., 1931), 16. "The Harlem cabaret," Mike Gold wrote, "no more represents the Negro mass than a pawnshop represents a Jew, or an opium den the struggling Chinese nation" [*New Masses,* 5 (Feb., 1930), 8].

55. *Ibid.,* Interview with Louise Thompson, Sept. 14, 1977; Langston Hughes, *I Wonder as I Wander, An Autobiographical Journey* (New York: Hill and Wang, 1964), pp. 73–99; *Liberator,* Oct. 15, 1932, Oct. 20, 1932, Nov. 4, 1932; *Daily Worker,* Oct. 6, 1932, Oct. 24, 1932; Lewis, *When Harlem Was in Vogue,* pp. 289–93.

56. *New York Amsterdam News,* Oct. 26, 1932, Nov. 23, 1932.

57. Carter, *Scottsboro,* pp. 161–63; *Daily Worker,* Nov. 10, 1932, Nov.11, 1932, Dec. 20, 1932; *New York Amsterdam News,* Nov. 30, 1932.

58. Charles H. Martin, *The Angelo Herndon Case and Southern Justice* (Baton Rouge: Louisiana State University Press, 1976), pp. 36–61; *New York Amsterdam News,* Jan. 25, 1933. Euel Lee was a black Maryland farmworker sentenced to death for allegedly murdering his employer. In appealing his case, the ILD argued that jury selection procedures in his trial excluded blacks. The Maryland Court of Appeals accepted this argument and threw out Lee's conviction.

59. Walter White to Rose McLendon, Nov. 21, 1932, NAACP Papers, D 72. Copies of this letter were also sent to John H. Hammond, Jr., Mrs. Harry W. Austin, Mr. and Mrs. J. Dalmas Steele, Mrs. Inez Richardson Wilson, Rev. William Lloyd Imes, Rev. A. C. Garner, Rev. Adam Clayton Powell, Jr., and Mrs. Viola Carter.

60. William Lloyd Imes to Walter White, Nov. 23, 1932, NAACP Papers, D 72; Adam Clayton Powell, Jr., to Walter White, Nov. 28, 1932, *ibid.;* Inez Richardson Wilson to Elliott Coen, Nov. 28, 1932, *ibid.*

61. Walter White to William Lloyd Imes, Nov. 30, 1932, NAACP Papers, D 72; William Lloyd Imes to Walter White, Dec. 1, 1932, *ibid.*

62. *New York Amsterdam News,* Feb. 22, 1933, Mar. 15, 1933; Scottsboro Unity Defense Committee, leaflet, Feb. 1933, ILD Papers, Reel 2; *Daily Worker,* Feb. 14, 1933.

63. Brown, *Public Relief, 1929–1939,* p. 90; Ellen Malino James to Mark Naison, Sept. 27, 1974 (Ms. James was then writing a dissertation on the administration of relief in New York City from 1929 to 1934); *New York Times,* Mar. 9, 1932.

64. *New York Amsterdam News,* June 29, 1932; *Hunger Fighter,* Sept., 1932, in ILD Papers, Reel 1.

65. *Liberator,* July 1, 1933.

66. *Hunger Fighter,* Sept., 1932; *Daily Worker,* Sept. 3, 1932, Oct. 17, 1932, Oct. 20, 1932; *New York Times,* Oct. 16, 1932, Oct. 18, 1932, Oct. 20, 1932.

67. Campbell, Snipes, Fitzgerald, and Brown all remained active in the Party till at least 1938. Snipes and Campbell broke with the organization that year, under circumstances which I will describe in a later chapter.

68. *Hunger Fighter,* Mar. 1933; *Daily Worker,* Mar. 3, 1933, Mar. 24, 1933.

69. *Daily Worker,* Jan. 12, 1933, Jan. 21, 1933, Jan. 28, 1933; *New York Amsterdam News,* Dec. 21, 1932, Feb. 1, 1933.

70. *Daily Worker,* Feb. 6, 1933; *New York Amsterdam News,* Feb. 1, 1933.

71. *New York Age,* Jan. 14, 1933, Mar. 11, 1933; *Daily Worker,* Mar. 6, 1933.

72. Earl Browder, "The End of Relative Capitalist Stabilization and the Tasks of Our Party," *Communist,* 12 (Mar. 1933), 225; *Daily Worker,* Jan. 28, 1933.

73. *Daily Worker,* Mar. 18, 1933; Wilson Record, *The Negro and the Communist Party* (Chapel Hill: University of North Carolina Press, 1951), pp. 120–24; Irving Howe and Lewis Coser, *The American Communist Party, A Critical History, 1919*–1957 (Boston: Beacon Press, 1957), pp. 230–31.

74. *Daily Worker,* Feb. 13, 1933; Carter, *Scottsboro,* pp. 181–82.

75. *Ibid.,* pp. 191–234.

76. *Daily Worker,* Apr. 4, 1933, Apr. 9, 1933. *Daily Worker* estimates for numbers of participants in demonstrations are not always accurate. But in this instance, the substance of what the *Worker* reports—i.e., large black participation in its Harlem demonstrations—seems to conform to what other sources suggest is occurring at this time.

77. Carter, *Scottsboro,* p. 239.

78. *New York Amsterdam News,* Apr. 12, 1933; *New York Times,* Apr. 10, 1933; *Daily Worker,* Apr. 11, 1933; interview with Theodore Bassett, Sept. 12, 1974. Non-Communist sources confirm the breadth and nonpartisan character of the spontaneous protests that followed Patterson's conviction. Poston's article appeared in the *New York Amsterdam News,* Apr. 12, 1933.

79. *New York Times,* Apr. 11, 1939.

80. *Daily Worker,* Apr. 11, Apr. 18.

81. Walter White to L. F. Coles, Apr. 14, 1933, NAACP Papers, D 73.

82. *New York Times,* Apr. 13, 1933; *New York Amsterdam News,* Apr. 19, 1933; Walter White to the Branches, Apr. 12, 1933, NAACP Papers, D 73; L. F. Coles to Walter White, Apr. 14, 1933, *ibid.*

83. *New York Amsterdam News,* Apr. 19, 1933; *New York Age,* Apr. 15, 1933.

84. Minutes of the Scottsboro Conference at Harlem Masonic Temple, Apr. 16, 1933, NAACP Papers, D 73; Louise Thompson to Walter White, Apr. 17, 1933, *ibid.*; *Daily Worker,* Apr. 14, 1933, Apr. 18, 1933.

85. *Ibid.,* Apr. 15, 1933; Walter White to William Patterson, Apr. 19, 1933, William L. Patterson to Walter White, Apr. 20, 1933, NAACP Papers, D 73. The

negotiations between the ILD and the NAACP took place at the office of Roger Baldwin, who served as an intermediary. Wilkins's comments about a "gentlemen's agreement" appear in Roy Wilkins to L. Pearl Mitchell, May 24, 1933, *ibid.*

86. William L. Patterson to Walter White, Apr. 28, 1933, NAACP Papers, D 73; Roy Wilkins to Branch Officers, May 4, 1933, *ibid.*

87. *New York Age,* Apr. 15, 1933, Apr. 22, 1933; *New York Times,* Apr. 12, 1933, Apr. 14, 1933.

88. *New York Age,* Apr. 22, 1933; *Daily Worker,* Apr. 19, 1933.

89. *New York Age,* May 13, 1933; *Harlem Liberator,* Apr. 20, 1933.

90. Crusader News Agency, press release, Apr. 22, 1933, NAACP Papers, D 73; *Harlem Liberator,* May 6, 1933, May 27, 1933; interview with Richard B. Moore, Nov. 14, 1973.

91. *Daily Worker,* Apr. 20, 1933, Apr. 24, 1933.

92. Reformist Sabotages of the Scottsboro March, May, 1933, ILD Papers, Reel 2; *Harlem Liberator,* Apr. 29, 1933.

93. L. F. Coles to Walter White, Apr. 22, 1933, *ibid.*

94. *Harlem Liberator,* May 13, 1933; Roy Wilkins to Rev. Adam Clayton Powell, Jr., May 6, 1933, NAACP Papers, D 73. Wilkins was quite upset about Powell's disparaging comments about the NAACP's role in the Scottsboro Case.

95. *Harlem Liberator,* May 13, 1933; *New York Age,* May 20, 1933; Carter, *Scottsboro,* pp. 250–51.

96. *New York Amsterdam News,* May 10, 1933; *New York Age,* May 13, 1933. Significantly, Davis's delegation contained no representatives of the NAACP. Its participants, among whom were A. Philip Randolph, J. Dalmas Steele, and Arthur Schomburg, believed that mass protest action was appropriate in the case, but wanted to distinguish their efforts from those sponsored by Communists.

97. *Harlem Liberator,* May 13, 1933; *New York Amsterdam News,* May 17, 1933.

98. *Ibid.; Daily Worker,* May 13, 1933; *New York Age,* May 20, 1933; *Harlem Liberator,* June 10, 1933.

99. *New York Age,* May 27, 1933, June 3, 1933, June 17, 1933.

100. *Negro World,* June 3, 1933; *Harlem Liberator,* June 17, 1933.

101. Carter, *Scottsboro,* p. 269.

102. *Harlem Liberator,* Apr. 29, 1933.

4

James Ford Comes to Harlem — The Central Committee Reasserts Control

DURING THE LATE SPRING and summer of 1933, the Central Committee of the CPUSA initiated a thoroughgoing review of the policies of the Harlem Communist Party. This action, coming when the Harlem Party displayed unprecedented dynamism, reflected confusion among the CPUSA's top leadership about how to interpret the new Comintern policy calling for a limited "united front" with socialist organizations. Initially, American Party leaders had viewed the policy as a mandate to seek alliances with groups they had previously fought. But when the Comintern criticized them because of the Party's low membership and their failure to discredit socialist leaders with whom they sought alliances, CPUSA leaders responded with an almost hysterical vigilance against unorthodox practices in the Party's local organizations. The Harlem Party, whose manner of functioning was unusually decentralized, and whose pattern of alliances was unusually broad (even before Hitler's rise to power), served for them as a convenient symbol of deviation from Comintern standards. In July, 1933, at an Extraordinary Party Conference which subjected the CPUSA's entire organizing strategy to critical review, the Central Committee designated Harlem as a "national concentration point" of the Party, and appointed its most prominent black leader, James Ford, as special Harlem organizer.[1] Within nine months of his arrival, Ford had pushed Harlem's pioneering black Communists, Richard Moore and Cyril Briggs, out of positions of influence in the Harlem Party and had transformed it from a freewheeling agitational center into a model of political orthodoxy.

Significantly, the Harlem Party's actions in the Scottsboro movement, its most successful single project, provided the initial target for Central Committee dissatisfaction. In the May and June issues of *Communist,* three articles appeared attacking the Party's role in Harlem Scottsboro protests as an "opportunist distortion" of the united-front policy the Party initiated after Hitler's rise to power. The Harlem Communists had been so caught up in the enthusiasm of these protests, *Daily Worker* editor Clarence Hathaway wrote, that they had forgotten that the purpose of the united front was "to destroy the influence of the reformist leaders," and not "to make peace with them." Hathaway criticized Communists for accepting a united front with the NAACP "without serious conditions," for "taking a too tolerant attitude toward Davis and the Amsterdam News," and for allowing J. W. Brown and J. Dalmas Steele to play important roles on the Scottsboro Action Committee. Party theoretician James Allen criticized the Harlem leadership for failing to counteract "illusions about capitalist justice and democracy" among the "Negro masses activized by the Scottsboro case." Allen reminded Harlem Communists that their goal was "to establish the unchallenged leadership of the Communist Party in the Scottsboro struggle," and not merely to organize the broadest mass movement.[2]

This criticism, as intended, shattered the modus vivendi William Patterson had established with NAACP officials. In early June, 1933, Patterson, whose cordial comportment had pleasantly surprised association leaders, suddenly assumed a persona of unyielding stridency.[3] Seizing upon the refusal of the NAACP to pay bills for nonlegal expenses in the case (in their initial agreement with the ILD, NAACP officials had explicitly targeted their fund raising for court costs and lawyers' fees) Patterson issued a propaganda barrage accusing association leaders of "criminally squandering" money, discouraging working-class unity, and forming a "close alliance with the white ruling class." "Friends in the NAACP," one of his epistles declared, "step over the heads of your leadership which has linked itself inseparably with the ruling class of America." Patterson's sudden reversion to sloganeering squandered his personal credibility and seriously weakened the fund-raising campaign for the Scottsboro defense but it satisfied Central Committee leaders that the Scottsboro movement was now being conducted in line with Comintern requirements for alliances with "reformist" organizations.[4]

Shortly thereafter, the Central Committee turned its attention to the Harlem Party's internal weaknesses, particularly its failure to attract, and retain, a large black membership. A Party census taken during the fall of 1933 showed only eighty-seven black members of the Harlem Section, even though Communists had drawn thousands of blacks into Scottsboro marches and rallies. During the frenetic mobilization for the Washington March, Harlem Communists had chosen the ILD, rather than the Party, as a rallying point for Scottsboro militants, since it seemed to offer a more direct expression of popular indignation.[5]

The chaotic atmosphere in the Harlem Party apparatus seemed to present a major obstacle to effective Party building. Unit life in the Harlem Section diverged sharply from the image of unity and discipline the Party sought to project. Observers of Section activities complained of "all kinds of dissatisfied elements pulling in different directions," and "petty personal questions on the order of business at Section meetings." Racial tensions, particularly differences over the meaning of white chauvinism, contributed mightily to this turbulent atmosphere. Although the Party's emphasis on fighting chauvinism had helped sensitize white Communists to the special problems of black workers and to mobilize them to take an aggressive civil-rights stance, it had created an atmosphere which made it difficult for whites to function in positions of authority in the Harlem Section.[6]

The leadership of neighborhood units in Harlem, which had between ten and twenty members apiece, served as a particular bone of contention. Each of these units had three officers—an organizer, an agitprop director, and a financial secretary. They were responsible for making sure that the decisions of higher Party bodies were carried out, for familiarizing the membership with Party ideology and tactics, and keeping track of dues payments and finances. A number of leading black Communists, who had come to the Party out of nationalist movements, felt very strongly that whites should not serve in such positions in predominately black Party units. This placed them at odds with the top Party leadership, which wished to have the administrative and educational apparatus of the Party in the hands of experienced, reliable cadre. Since few blacks had been in the Party long enough to acquire such experience, debates on the proper white "presence" in Harlem erupted regularly at Party meetings, sometimes taking the form of a generalized suspicion of whites.[7] "When I joined the Party," one black member complained during a review of section activities, "the situation within the Party in Harlem was rotten.... Nearly every white comrade was charged with the crime of chauvinism, the vast majority of these charges had no foundation whatsoever. At this time, as a new member, it appeared to me that the duty of a Negro worker in the Party was to accuse a white worker of white chauvinism."[8]

To Central Committee leaders, these derelictions from Party policy suggested that black Harlem Communists had become *too* responsive to the moods and feelings of Harlem's population. At a time when blacks were displaying increasing militancy, Party leaders feared that the Harlem organization was too weak and undisciplined to prevent black activism from taking an antiwhite or anti-Communist direction. The behavior of Harlem Party leaders during the Scottsboro upheaval—their subordination of Party building to mass agitation, their willingness to make alliances with blacks of all backgrounds, and their encouragement of skeptical attitudes towards whites among the Party's black rank and file—all cast doubt on the Harlem Party's political reliability. "It is the first duty of the Negro comrades to create confidence among the Negro masses in the Party and the Central Committee," James Ford declared at the Extraordinary Party Conference. "I do not think there is sufficient of this work done by leading Negro comrades now."[9]

In August, 1933, James Ford arrived in Harlem with a mandate to remold the political life of the Harlem Section. His goals were to strengthen Party discipline, restore the authority of the Central Committee, increase party recruitment, develop a strategy of trade union organization in the Harlem area, and wage a struggle *within* the Harlem Party against nationalist tendencies. In undertaking these tasks, Ford had the full backing of the Central Committee and the benefit of his own personal friendship with Party secretary Earl Browder. In addition, Ford brought with him a group of white college-educated Communists to serve as administrators of the new regime, "behind the scenes" functionaries whose goals were to bring order to chaotic Party finances and membership records and to set up a system of reporting and control which would allow the Section leadership to keep continuous tabs on all units. To head this team of Party "efficiency experts," Ford selected Louis Sass, a Hungarian-Jewish chemist who was known as one of the Party's best administrators. With Sass as organization secretary taking charge of the details of the Party apparatus, Ford was free to devote full attention to changing the atmosphere of the Harlem Party and establishing new political goals.[10]

The changes Ford and Sass initiated immediately brought them into conflict with Richard Moore and Cyril Briggs. Both Briggs and Moore had lived in Harlem for over fifteen years, and had a following in the community based upon their uncompromising commitment to black liberation throughout the world and their considerable personal abilities. Although they were loyal Party members, they had joined the Party as revolutionary intellectuals with an *independent political base,* and they had been allowed to function in a more individualistic manner than less talented or strategically situated comrades. By temperament, Briggs and Moore were agitators rather than administrators and they were accustomed to dominating the political and intellectual life of the Harlem Party without taking responsibility for organizational details. Both had played an important role in prodding the Party to implement its campaign against white chauvinism, and they still viewed that campaign as a precondition for effective work in the black community. The Ford regime's new emphasis on administrative efficiency, Party discipline, and the struggle against black nationalism seemed to mark a movement away from the uncompromising militancy on racial issues that had first attracted them to the Party.[11]

In addition, Briggs and Moore found it difficult to respect Ford's personality and style of wielding authority. Unlike Briggs and Moore, Ford had entered the Party without previous experience in radical movements and had risen through the ranks on the basis of administrative ability and shrewd political instincts rather than theoretical brilliance or verbal and literary talent. A large, powerfully built man who carried himself with conspicuous dignity, Ford was a Communist version of the man in the gray flannel suit. At Fisk University, he had been a star athlete, a good student, and a leader in campus organizations—everyone's image of a talented "young man on the make." An *Amsterdam News* writer reflected:

> Nobody at Fisk University in the years before the World War ever dreamed that 'Rabbit Ford,' the fleet-footed athlete, would become other than what Fisk expected of her sons—a loyal respectable citizen, a school teacher, a doctor, or a lawyer, or perhaps a 'race leader.' A model student, ambitious, hardworking, steady, a baseball and football star, a leader in the YMCA and other student activities, James W. Ford was the kind of Fisk man that the faculty was proud of, the kind for lower classmen to emulate. He had that Fisk spirit.[12]

After graduating from college, Ford served in the Signal Corps in France during World War I, where he participated in protests against the jim-crowing of black troops. But his most disillusioning experience came when he returned to the United States to find that the only white-collar job he could get was a position in the Chicago Post Office. Ford joined the Chicago Postal Workers Union and through it the Communist Party. He rose rapidly through the Party's ranks. In 1929, he became head of the International Trade Union Committee of Negro Workers, in 1930, the head of the Negro Department of the Trade Union Unity League, and, in 1932, the Party's candidate for Vice-President of the United States. Although not a deep thinker or a compelling speaker, Ford had an acute political sense and had developed a special relationship with the most powerful American Communist, Earl Browder. When Ford came to Harlem, he had a reputation as a "Party man" rather than a black revolutionary leader. He had none of the cynicism or irreverence that black Party members sometimes expressed about white comrades on the Central Committee. Ford was distant, efficient, and resentful of any resistance to his authority. For the first time, Briggs and Moore found themselves face to face with a Harlem section organizer whose commitment to Party discipline was total and unyielding and who expected the same from other black Communists.[13]

When he first arrived in Harlem, Ford shrewdly avoided an open break with the people he superseded. The Party was a leading force in a politically aroused community and few of its leaders wished to break with it while its influence was growing. To maintain continuity, Ford sustained Party agitation on unemployment, relief, and health conditions with little modification. He also tried to keep opponents in positions of leadership even when he undercut their political base. One of Ford's first acts in Harlem was to deemphasize the ILD—the mass organization built during the Scottsboro protests—in favor of the League of Struggle for Negro Rights. But in carrying out this policy, designed to place mass movements stimulated by the Party under tighter political control, Ford appointed Richard Moore as national secretary of the LSNR and Herman Mackawain, a talented black street speaker who was closely allied with Moore, as head of the LSNR Harlem Council. So long as they were willing to obey Party discipline, Ford was willing to give his internal opposition a large share in the Party's public agitation.[14]

Ford also preserved continuity in the Party's cultural activities. During the height of the Scottsboro protests, Louise Thompson and Augusta Savage, a well-known black sculptress, had formed an organization called the Vanguard, which aimed to expose Harlemites to "new and progressive" currents in politics and the arts. Left-wing in tone, but not openly Communist, the Vanguard sponsored dance and theatre groups, a summer musical program, a forum on political subjects, and a Marxist study circle. Among its participants were Aaron Douglass, an artist whose home served as a meeting place for Harlem intellectuals, Romeo Beardon, a popular theatre critic, and Langston Hughes. Mixing parties with serious discussion, the Vanguard did much to expose Harlem's elite to intellectual currents on the left and to white left-wingers who worked in related fields. Since it reached only a limited audience and posed no threat to his authority, Ford gave the Vanguard his strong endorsement.[15]

Only on one key issue—that of job discrimination—did Ford precipitate an open clash with the section's previous leadership. During the summer of 1933, Harlem Communists, breaking with established Party policy, decided to initiate a campaign to force chain stores in Harlem to hire black clerks. Alarmed by the success experienced in such "Don't Buy Where You Can't Work" campaigns, sponsored by nationalist-led boycott groups, in winning popular support, Harlem Communists felt they would have to organize a boycott of their own to maintain credibility with Harlem militants. During the summer of 1933, a former Garveyite named Sufi Abdul Hamid had begun picketing stores in the 135th Street area with considerable success, and the popular nationalist street speakers Arthur Reid and Ira Kemp, heads of the African Patriotic League, were exhorting blacks to use the boycott as a first step toward taking control of all Harlem business establishments. Unlike their predecessors, these organizers were employing direct-action techniques and attracting considerable support from Harlem's unemployed. Harlem Party leaders feared that they might spearhead a mass movement to "drive the white workers out of Harlem" unless an alternative campaign could be launched which fought discrimination without arousing antiwhite sentiment.[16]

In July, 1933, Harlem Communists invited church and fraternal groups to join them in a movement to force Harlem chain stores to hire black clerks until blacks composed 50 percent of their workforce. Unlike nationalist boycott leaders, Communists insisted that no white workers be displaced: they wanted jobs to be opened by transferring white employees to other stores of the chain or reducing their hours without lowering their pay. They elected a committee to begin approaching store owners and selected W. T. Grant stores as their first target. Several unsuccessful meetings took place with the Grant management and in mid-August, the committee announced plans to picket the store if it refused to make concessions.[17]

The Communists who engineered this campaign felt it had great popular appeal, but Ford ordered its termination shortly after his arrival in Harlem. To Ford, the campaign signified that Harlem Communists had become so vulnerable to popular pressures that they forgot longstanding Party guidelines for fighting discrimination in employment. At a meeting of the Harlem Section Committee attended by Central Committee observers, Ford argued that the jobs campaign, by focusing on stores exclusively in Harlem, encouraged Harlemites to see their political emancipation as a struggle for control of a segregated district. "These comrades," Ford argued, "forget about the fight against Jim Crowism in other parts of the city and tend to regard Harlem as 'our territory,' playing directly into the segregation policies of the black nationalists and the white ruling class." In addition, Ford argued that the strategy would "antagonize white workers already employed in Harlem stores" and exacerbate divisions between black and white workers. The only way a jobs campaign would cement black-white working class unity, Ford claimed, was if the Party had launched trade union organization among the employees in the unit selected and if those employees could be organized to support the demand that blacks be hired. Organized white workers had to be brought into the jobs movement at every stage, he concluded, or else the movement would degenerate into a struggle of black against white rather than a united working-class struggle against the employers. What Ford was calling for was a decisively new boycott strategy—one which made "Don't Buy Where You Can't Work" campaigns *dependent* on trade union support.[18]

Richard Moore, supported by a small group of black Communists, vociferously opposed Ford's argument. In Moore's view, the position Ford outlined placed the burden for maintaining working-class unity on the *black* workers rather than on the whites. "Why all this talk about antagonizing the white workers," Moore argued. "Are not these white workers in Negro neighborhoods living on the backs of the Negro masses? Are they not occupying jobs that rightfully belong to Negroes?" If the black workers had to wait until white workers endorsed their demands for fair employment opportunities in Harlem, Moore claimed, they might have to wait forever. It was the Party's responsibility to raise the demand for employment of black clerks and *then* to rally the white employees behind it rather than vice versa.[19]

Although Moore's arguments reflected popular sentiment in Harlem far more than Ford's did, the Section Committee, with Central Committee approval, sharply rebuffed him. Having observed the consequences of boycott movements in several black communities, Party leaders wanted to do nothing to encourage blacks to vent their hostility on ghetto storekeepers. Many of these storekeepers were recent immigrants (Jews, Italians, Greeks, etc.) and movements aimed against them invariably generated antiforeign sentiment. Since most white Communists were immigrants themselves, Party leaders desperately wanted to avoid any strategy which might inflame ethnic tensions and make it more difficult to unite blacks with left-wing workers in trade unions and the unemployment movement.[20]

The Section Committee therefore reaffirmed Ford's suggestion that any jobs movement launched by the Party be based on "the development of a united front of Negro workers with the white workers in those institutions against which a struggle was being conducted," and that it be city-wide in scope. In particular, the Section Committee wanted the targets of job protests to be large institutions which were not "immigrant owned" — corporations, public utilities, and government agencies. Communists, it insisted, should not "confine this movement to Harlem, but . . . make it a starting point for . . . a real drive throughout the city for the right of Negroes to work on all jobs, in all trades and professions, against all forms of discrimination, as in connection with relief work and in the issuance of unemployment relief."[21]

After the Section Committee decision, the jobs issue temporarily receded into the background. The Party halted the campaign against the Grant stores and Party activists turned their attention to other issues. But the divisions produced by the jobs debate remained a source of tension within the Harlem Party. Moore and his supporters accepted the Section Committee's line and obeyed Party discipline, but made no secret of their displeasure with Ford's leadership. As Ford consolidated his political base in Harlem by appointing black and white Communists sympathetic to his views to key positions in the Section organization, Briggs and Moore constituted themselves as spokesmen of a "left-opposition" within the Harlem Party, determined to resist any deemphasis of the struggle against white chauvinism and any tendency to replace blacks with whites in key Party posts. They viewed Ford as a political opportunist who refused to fight for special black interests within the Party and who used his influence with top Party leaders to acquire dictatorial control over the Harlem organization. Ford knew of these sentiments and acted forcefully to defend his political position. In October, 1933, he removed Cyril Briggs as editor of the *Harlem Liberator* and assigned him to a full-time position "downtown" as a reporter for the *Daily Worker.*[22]

This marked the end of an era for the Harlem Party. For nearly fifteen years, Briggs had been a key figure in the Harlem Communist movement, its most prolific writer and able theorist. He had been the editor-in-chief of every Party publication in the field of Negro work and was well known among Harlem radicals and in Harlem's West Indian community. But to James Ford, Briggs was the leader of a "second center" in the Harlem Party, a spokesman for a nationalist tendency that had to be defeated if the Party were to forge closer links between the black struggle and the working-class movement. To replace Briggs on the *Harlem Liberator,* Ford brought in Maude White, a black Howard University graduate who had been an organizer for the Needle Trades Workers Industrial Union. With Briggs's removal, the Harlem Party lost one of its major links to the generation of Afro-West-Indian militants that had helped shape Harlem radicalism in the postwar years.[23]

Despite the bitterness Ford's action evoked, both sides, anxious to maintain a facade of Party unity, refused to make their dispute a public issue. During the fall of 1933, black Communists closed ranks in organizing protests against a series of lynchings—one in Alabama (which claimed four lives), two in Maryland, one in Missouri—which dramatized the continuing vulnerability of blacks to mob violence. Richard Moore served as the Party's major spokesman during these protests, acting as the keynote speaker at an antilynching conference in Baltimore and appearing at numerous rallies on the streets of Harlem. Ideologically "suspect" on the jobs issue, Moore was the Party's most effective black orator, and Ford felt compelled to make use of his talents to dramatize the Party's militant opposition to lynching and jim crow. Briggs too played a role in this campaign, printing polemical columns on lynching in the pages of the *Daily Worker.*[24]

Events in the Scottsboro case also temporarily united Ford and his antagonists. The Scottsboro boys came up for new trials in November, 1933, and from the first day they appeared in court, their prospects looked hopelessly grim. The community chosen for the new trials, Decatur, Alabama, seethed with hostility toward the defendants, and the judge chosen to preside, William Callahan, seemed so biased that even the *Birmingham Post* observed that he "combined some of the qualities of the prosecutor with those of the jurist." Hampering the boys' attorneys at every turn, preventing them from introducing key evidence, Callahan openly instructed the jurors how to find the defendants guilty. By the beginning of December, two of the defendants, Haywood Patterson and Clarence Norris, had been sentenced to death.[25]

The Harlem Party, its divisions carefully hidden, sponsored an impressive array of protests during and after the trials. On the day after Patterson's conviction, some 2,000 white Communists paraded through the streets of Harlem with several thousand blacks joining them in line before the day had ended. A protest rally the following day, at the Rockland Palace Ballroom, drew nearly 4,000 people.[26] Though Harlemites seemed more subdued in their protests than they had been the previous spring, partly because guilty verdicts this time seemed a foregone conclusion, Scottsboro still remained a rallying point for community militancy. "The Scottsboro mess and the wave of mob spirit," the *Amsterdam News* wrote:

> ... shows clearly that Negroes must be prepared for a long fight if they want mob murder and legal lynching wiped out. The Scottsboro case may go on for years. The defense may cost hundreds of thousands. Yet the price will be cheap. There must be no let down. Call upon white friends for help, chastise white legislators who refuse to aid in the battle for social justice, and continue to protest.[27]

In organizing Scottsboro protests, Harlem Communists, cognizant of Central Committee criticism, tried to maintain much more rigid control over the political tone of the movement than they had the previous spring. Although they invited many community groups to participate in Scottsboro demonstrations (including the NAACP, which they continued to ritually denounce!), they carefully screened the list of speakers to exclude leaders with popular followings who had displayed independence of Communists in the past—particularly J. Dalmas Steele, William H. Davis, Bill Robinson, and Samuel Leibowitz. Instead, they assigned key roles at rallies to the most effective Communist orators—Richard Moore, William Patterson, and William Fitzgerald—and to political "unknowns" like Patience Williams of the Garvey Club.[28]

In fund raising, the Party proved less sectarian. As the Scottsboro defense prepared for another round of appeals, the ILD encouraged Harlemites of all political persuasions to help it raise money. The Activities Department of the Harlem branch of the YMCA called a meeting of leading Harlem citizens to explain legal developments in the case, featuring speeches by William Patterson and Samuel Leibowitz, and elicited 300 dollars in cash and pledges to raise more.[29] Two Scottsboro benefit dances, held early in 1934, proved even more successful. Held under the auspices of the black and white civil servants of Harlem and the National Committee for the Defense of Political Prisoners, the affairs enlisted the talents of Harpo Marx, Helen Morgan, Buck and Bubbles, Bennie Carter, and Fletcher Henderson. William Davis and Samuel Leibowitz, conspicuously absent from Scottsboro demonstrations under strictly Party auspices, both spoke at these affairs, and the ecumenical spirit extended to the dance floor. "Communists were mingling gaily with Socialists, liberals, and artists of varying political and racial shades," the *Amsterdam News* reported. The two benefits raised over 2,600 dollars. When sectarian considerations were set aside, Scottsboro still had an extraordinary capacity to unite the people of Harlem. Even the NAACP continued to raise funds for the defense, although its officers, embittered by Party attacks, boycotted all Scottsboro gatherings in which Communists participated.[30]

As the Scottsboro case moved into the appeal stage, the Harlem Party turned its attention again to the issue that had so divided it four months earlier—the question of job discrimination. After a lengthy internal debate, the Party decided to focus its attention on discrimination against blacks by government work-relief programs and public utilities, and to coordinate the campaigns with unionization drives among workers in these sectors. In January, 1934, the Harlem chapter of the League of Struggle for Negro Rights initiated protests against discrimination in the registration and assignment of black workers by the Civil Works Administration, the massive public works program set up under Title II of the National Industrial Recovery Act.[31]

The Party had chosen the CWA as a target because of that agency's decision to force blacks from all over the city to register for jobs in Harlem rather than their local communities. This decision greatly limited the access of black workers to the jobs the agency created. Many black applicants were never assigned work and those who were found themselves confined to menial categories. Although the CWA's Harlem office listed a small number of openings in teaching, nursing, and research, most black professionals and skilled workers found themselves assigned to positions as unskilled laborers under white administrators with less education and training.[32]

In challenging discrimination by the CWA, Communists emphasized that *government,* rather than private business, had represented the most logical target of antidiscrimination struggles in Harlem. "All oppression is firmly rooted in the policy of the government," the *Liberator* declared. " . . . If the government owned public institutions discriminate against the Negro, most certainly private institutions will do likewise." Late in January, 1934, the LSNR sent a delegation to Colonel De Lameter, head of the New York CWA, to demand that the agency allow blacks to register for jobs in their own neighborhoods, provide jobs for all those who register, and end discrimination against blacks in job assignments. Their protest achieved some results. Several days after the delegation presented its demands, De Lameter informed the LSNR that blacks would subsequently be allowed to register for federal jobs in their local communities. Although the immediate impact of this decision was minor, since the CWA was phased out by April, 1934, it did establish an important precedent for the nondiscriminatory administration of public-works programs.[33]

Shortly after the CWA changed its policy, the LSNR turned its attention to the Fifth Avenue Coach Company and the New York City Omnibus Corporation, which operated the bus lines traveling through Harlem. The Coach Company, which despite its large black clientele refused to hire black drivers or mechanics, planned to hire several hundred new employees in February, 1934, and the LSNR hoped to create enough community pressure to force them to hire black drivers, mechanics, and conductors. In early February, LSNR activists collected 2,000 signatures in Harlem on a petition demanding that the new jobs be given to blacks. They set up a meeting with company officials, and after being told by the company's president that its policy "not to hire Negroes on buses," would "not be changed," the LSNR began picketing the Coach Company's transfer station at 125th Street and 7th Avenue and urging Harlemites not to ride the buses.[34]

The campaign against the Coach Company marked the first time Harlem Communists tried to link antidiscrimination protests with trade union activity. At the Extraordinary Party Conference, the Central Committee had designated city transport as an important "concentration point" of Party trade union work in Harlem, and a Party-led Transport Workers Union had been formed which developed a small but loyal following among bus and subway employees. When the LSNR began pressing the Coach Company to hire black workers, it hoped to get white workers in the company to support the campaign. To facilitate such support, the LSNR demanded the reinstatement of twenty-eight workers who had been fired for union activity and insisted that no whites be fired when the Coach Company hired blacks. But though Transport Union activists came to several LSNR meetings and expressed their strong support for the campaign, they chose not to participate in the delegations to company officials or to march on the picket line the LSNR established in front of the Coach Company's Harlem terminal. Why this is so is not clear, but it may be that the union leaders, who were still operating "underground" (the TWU was not yet a recognized bargaining agent), were reluctant to reveal their identities in mass demonstrations, especially for a cause which might not be popular with the bulk of company's workers, who were predominately Irish and none too friendly to blacks. The bulk of participants on the LSNR picket line came from neighborhood organizations in Harlem, the Unemployed Councils, the ILD and the Young Communist League, and from Communist-led trade unions not directly involved in the dispute—the Needle Trades Industrial Union, the Furniture Workers Union, and the Boot and Leather Workers Union.[35]

From a programmatic standpoint, the Coach Company boycott was a failure. Lacking strong support from the company's workers, or important Harlem churches and political clubs (the LSNR, fearful of losing "control" of the campaign, did not encourage their participation), the protests ended in early July, 1934, without seriously damaging company patronage or extracting any concessions.[36] But the campaign did provide some examples of the interracial solidarity Communists hoped to encourage. White Communists featured prominently in all the LSNR picket lines in front of the Coach Company's Harlem terminal, and several whites were arrested in the campaign.[37] One of those arrested, a YCL activist named Isadore Dorfman, had been severely beaten several months before when he protected a black woman from police attack during an anti-lynching meeting outside Abyssinian Baptist Church (he was in critical condition for several days), and his willingness to put himself on the line *again* made him something of a hero in the community. "His name was all over Harlem at the time," recalled Abner Berry, a black Party organizer who came to Harlem during the summer of 1934.[38]

Shortly after the bus boycott began, the LSNR launched another and more successful campaign against job discrimination that featured trade union support. Here, the issue under consideration was discrimination by city relief agencies affecting black clients and employees, and the trade union involved was the predominately white, and Communist-led, Home Relief Employees Association. Since the Extraordinary Party Conference, the Party had launched an organizing drive in Harlem relief bureaus and had developed shop units composed of investigators, clerical workers, and lower-level administrators. Operating amidst a work force which was predominately college educated and heavily Jewish, Party union organizers were able to challenge discrimination with less fear of jeopardizing their political base than their counterparts in the Fifth Avenue Coach Company. Several left-wing relief workers had participated in protests against jim crow in the CWA, and on the LSNR's initiative, they now turned their attention to discrimination in the relief system. In April, 1934, the LSNR and the Home Relief Employees Association sponsored a series of meetings charging relief officials with tolerating racial slurs against black clients, refusing to place qualified blacks in administrative positions, and harassing white employees who fraternized with their black coworkers. As a result of their protests—which included delegations to city officials and demonstrations within the bureaus—several blacks were added to bureau grievance committees and two black relief investigators who had protested discriminatory practices were restored to their jobs.[39]

The campaigns against the Coach Company and the relief bureaus, though they mobilized some whites to fight discriminatory practices in their workplace, did not quell dissatisfaction with Ford's strategy of making all jobs campaigns dependent on trade union support. Although he participated in the two campaigns, Richard Moore complained that the Party's line prevented it from taking action against the one form of discrimination Harlemites most resented—that practiced by Harlem stores. The Party had done very little trade-union organizing in Harlem retail establishments, and Ford's strategy dictated postponing campaigns against such stores until their workers had been organized. Moore believed that such a policy would isolate the Party from the mainstream of Harlem sentiment and give the initiative on the jobs question to Garvey movement leaders, and made his views repeatedly known at Harlem section meetings.[40]

However, Moore and his supporters soon found themselves to be a major target of a nationwide offensive against "petty bourgeois nationalism" orchestrated by the Party's top leadership. At the Party's Eighth National Convention in April, 1934, the Central Committee defined the struggle against black nationalism as a major priority, almost coequal with the struggle against white chauvinism. In a period when nationalist movements among blacks were proliferating rapidly—especially the National Movement for the Establishment of the 49th State, the Pacific Movement of the Eastern World (which spoke of Japan as the "defender of the darker races"), and local "Jobs for Negroes" campaigns—Party leaders had become concerned that their black membership might be so swayed by nationalist feeling that they would be unwilling to implement Party policies based on black-white unity.[41] Harry Haywood, the head of the Central Committee's Negro Department, took to the hustings at the convention to articulate the Party's concern. Possessing immense prestige within the Party because of his role in formulating the "self-determination" doctrine, Haywood regarded it as his personal mission to attack any and all deviations from the Comintern theory on the Negro question and to fight for the unchallenged leadership of the Communist Party in Afro-American life. Of working-class background, Haywood had spent his entire adult life in the Communist Party—including four pivotal years in the Soviet Union—and had risen to the top ranks of the international movement by displaying an aptitude for applying Marxist-Leninst categories to Afro-American life and exhibiting an unwavering faith in Stalin's theoretical omniscience. A shrewd analyst of black organizational behavior, Haywood, more than any other black Communist, believed in the applicability of the bolshevik model to American conditions, and would uphold the banner of revolutionary purity irrespective of practical consequences or personal feelings. Despite his deep resentment of James Ford, who had been chosen over Haywood as the Party's national spokesman on black issues (largely on grounds of appearance and platform manner rather than theoretical depth), Haywood's speech at the convention singled out Ford's opponents in Harlem for taking a position on the jobs question which threatened to further divide blacks from the white working class.[42] "The most glaring example of petty bourgeois nationalism," Haywood declared:

> was . . . the attitude of certain Negro comrades in Harlem in connection with the campaign for jobs for Negroes. . . . Against the line of the Section Committee, certain comrades brought forth the . . . line of replacement of white workers by Negroes. . . . The only logical conclusion flowing from this false conception is that the struggle of the Negro toilers for the betterment of their conditions must be directed not against the capitalist, but against the white workers.

Haywood then excoriated Ford's opponents for "fostering distrust and suspicion among less developed comrades as to the integrity of the Party and its leaders regarding the Negro question," and for inferring "that the leading Negro comrades, those who are seriously carrying out the work of the Party, are Uncle Toms."[43] Party leaders followed Haywood's address with a speech by Herman Mackawain, formerly a partisan of Moore's position, denouncing nationalist tendencies within the Harlem Party and praising Ford for bringing them under control. The convention left little doubt in the minds of black Communists that the Party expected them to moderate their race consciousness in moments when it conflicted with the pursuit of working-class unity.[44]

Shortly after the convention, the Central Committee took further steps to eliminate the "nationalist" opposition from the Harlem Party leadership. In late April, 1934, Harry Haywood replaced Richard Moore as national secretary of the League of Struggle for Negro Rights. Although Moore retained his post as field organizer for the ILD, and remained the leading Party spokesman for the Scottsboro movement, his removal from the LSNR effectively excluded him from participating in the economic struggles of the Harlem Party. During the spring and summer of 1934, the Party sent Moore on several speaking tours for the ILD to remove him from the Harlem scene and to reduce his contact with former supporters who had identified themselves with the new Party policies.[45]

In addition, the Party brought in a new group of black Communists to run the *Harlem Liberator,* appointing Benjamin Davis, Jr., as editor-in-chief and Merrill Work as its business manager. The selection of these two men further confirmed the Central Committee's desire to develop a Harlem Section leadership which could not easily be swayed by community pressure. Like James Ford, Davis and Work were southern born, college educated, and had excellent credentials for membership in the black elite. Davis's father was a fraternal leader, a banker, and a Georgia state committeeman for the Republican Party, who was wealthy enough to send his son to Amherst and Harvard Law School. Davis, an all-American football player in college, had risen to national prominence as an attorney for Angelo Herndon, and his experiences in that case had helped move him to Communism. At the time of his appointment to the *Harlem Liberator,* Davis was a marked man in Atlanta, and Party leaders feared for his life if he remained in that city. Equally fluid as a speaker and a writer, Davis combined the boyish charm of a southern politico (Henry Lee Moon, who knew him well, described him as a "good old boy") with the hard-bitten toughness of a Party bureaucrat. In time, he would become the Party's most popular and effective black leader.[46]

Merrill Work's background was equally unusual. His father, John Work, was a professor at Fisk University who had achieved international acclaim as the conductor of the Fisk Jubilee Singers. Work had been educated as a social worker and had directed a settlement house for the Brooklyn Urban League after his graduation from college. His first contact with Communism came in the course of a struggle against segregation in Brooklyn recreational programs and his movement in that direction was accelerated by the hostility he experienced following his marriage to a white social worker. After being removed from his Urban League position, allegedly because of his marriage (this charge appeared in an *Amsterdam News* article, but I have been unable to prove, or disprove, its veracity), he became an open Communist and rose in the Party's ranks to a position of leadership in the Brooklyn Unemployed Councils.[47]

The selection of these two "scions of the Negro aristocracy" as spokesmen gave the Party added legitimacy with Harlem's leadership stratum.[48] Like James Ford, with whom they would be cooperating closely, Davis and Work had the background and past associations—educational, athletic, and familial—to interact easily with leading Harlem churchmen, politicians, and service workers.

But at the same time, Davis and Word could be counted on to uphold the Party line in the face of popular pressure. Unlike Briggs and Moore, they were organizers and politicians rather than revolutionary intellectuals, people who viewed the Party as a route to political power as well as an instrument of rebellion against injustice. Embittered by American racial practices that severely limited their opportunities, they applied their considerable organizational skills to building a career in the Communist Party and were willing to follow Party rules to assure their success. Along with Ford, Patterson, and Thompson, they constituted a core of black Communist leadership in Harlem whose pragmatic political abilities were as great as their loyalty to the Party line.

The leadership changes following the Eighth National Convention completed the shift in the Harlem Party's political direction launched at the Extraordinary Party Conference. With Briggs and Moore both removed from positions of leadership, the Harlem Party had broken its last remaining links with the group of West Indian militants who had provided the first black recruits to the Communist movement. The American-born blacks lacked their background in nationalist movements and their revolutionary enthusiasm, but had a far greater understanding of how to build political organizations and function within coalitions. Under the leadership of James Ford, this new corps of organizers was determined to make the Harlem Party into a powerful and disciplined organization capable of building alliances between blacks and the working-class movement and of persuading black organizations and leaders to work closely with the left.

NOTES

1. On the turmoil in the U.S. Party that preceded the calling of the Extraordinary Party Conference, see Anders Stephenson, "The CPUSA Conception of the Rooseveltian State," (unpublished thesis, New College, Oxford University, 1977), p. 7; Bert Cochran, *Labor and Communism: The Conflict That Shaped American Unions* (Princeton: Princeton University Press, 1977), pp. 72–74. On the selection of Harlem as a "national concentration point," at the Conference, see Louis Sass, "Some Problems of the Harlem Section," *Party Organizer,* 8 (Mar., 1934), 19.

2. James Allen, "The Scottsboro Struggle," *Communist,* 12 (May, 1933), 442; "The Scottsboro Struggle and the Next Steps, Resolution of the Political Bureau," *ibid.,* 12 (June, 1933), 570–82; Clarence Hathaway, "A Warning Against Opportunist Distortions of the United Front Tactic," *ibid.,* 533.

3. Comments on Patterson's comportment during the brief ILD-NAACP "honeymoon" may be found in Roy Wilkins to L. F. Coles, May 16, 1933, NAACP Papers, D 73; and Wilkins to L. Pearl Mitchell, May 24, 1933, *ibid.*

4. Dan C. Carter, *Scottsboro, A Tragedy of the American South* (paperback ed.; New York: Oxford University Press, 1972), p. 252; William L. Patterson to Walter White, June 1, 1933, NAACP Papers, C 402; White to William L. Patterson, June 14, 1933, *ibid.* The long quote from Patterson is from William L. Patterson to the National Association for the Advancement of Colored People, no date, June 1933, *ibid.*

5. James W. Ford and Louis Sass, "Development of Work in the Harlem Section," *Communist,* 14 (Apr., 1935), 323.

6. Sass, "Some Problems of the Harlem Section," 19; Charles Krumbein, "Small Progress in New York District," *Party Organizer,* 7 (Nov., 1933), 18.

7. Interview with Richard B. Moore, Nov. 17, 1973. For information on how "units" functioned in the CPUSA, see Robert Jay Alperin, "Organization in the Communist Party, U.S.A., 1931–1938," (Ph.D. dissertation, Northwestern University, 1959), p. 61.

8. [Herman] Mackawain, "The League of Struggle for Negro Rights in Harlem," *Party Organizer,* 8 (Apr., 1934), 60.

9. James W. Ford, "Against Imperialist War," *Party Organizer,* 7 (Aug.–Sept., 1933), 48.

10. George Charney, *A Long Journey* (New York: Quadrangle, 1968), pp. 93–94; interview with Harry Haywood, May 15, 1973; "Some Problems of the Harlem Section," 19–20; interview with Abner Berry, July 29, 1974.

11. Interview with George Charney, Nov. 7, 1973; interview with Harry Haywood, May 15, 1973; William L. Patterson, *The Man Who Cried Genocide* (New York: International Publishers, 1971), pp. 75–76, 92–93.

12. *New York Amsterdam News,* Feb. 28, 1934.

13. *Ibid.*; interview with Abner Berry, July 29, 1974.

14. Mackawain, "The League of Struggle for Negro Rights in Harlem," 60.

15. *Harlem Liberator,* May 13, 1933, July 22, 1933; *New York Amsterdam News,* Nov. 24, 1934; interview with Louise Thompson, Sept. 14, 1977.

16. *Harlem Liberator,* July 29, 1933, Aug. 5, 1933; Melville Weiss, "Don't Buy Where You Can't Work," (M.A. Thesis, Columbia University, 1941), pp. 56–57; *Negro World,* July 29, 1933, Aug. 12, 1933.

17. *Harlem Liberator,* Aug. 19, 1933, Aug. 26, 1933, Sept. 9, 1933.

18. *New York Amsterdam News,* Aug. 17, 1935; *Daily Worker,* Aug. 23, 1935; Harry Haywood, *The Road to Negro Liberation* (New York: Workers Library Publishers, 1934), pp. 53–54.

19. *Daily Worker,* Aug. 23, 1935; Haywood, *The Road to Negro Liberation,* p. 54; interview with Richard B. Moore, Nov. 14, 1973.

20. *Daily Worker,* Aug. 23, 1935.

21. *Ibid.*; Haywood, *The Road to Negro Liberation,* pp. 53–54.

22. Interview with Harry Haywood, May 15, 1973; interview with Richard B. Moore, Nov. 14, 1973; interview with George Charney, Nov. 7, 1973; interview with William Weinstone, July 2, 1974; *New York Amsterdam News,* Aug. 17, 1935; *Harlem Liberator,* Nov. 11, 1933.

23. Interview with Harry Haywood, May 15, 1973; Patterson, *The Man Who Cried Genocide,* p. 103; *Harlem Liberator,* Mar. 24, 1934.

24. Carter, *Scottsboro,* pp. 276–77; *New York Age,* Dec. 9, 1933; *New York Amsterdam News,* Nov. 29, 1933, Dec. 6, 1933; *Daily Worker,* Nov. 11, 1933, Nov. 15, 1933, Dec. 9, 1933; *Harlem Liberator,* Dec. 9, 1933.

25. *New York Amsterdam News,* Nov. 29, 1933; Carter, *Scottsboro,* pp. 276, 286, 299.

26. *Daily Worker,* Dec. 2, 1933, Dec. 6, 1933; *New York Amsterdam News,* Dec. 6, 1933; *New York Age,* Dec. 9, 1933.

27. *New York Amsterdam News,* Dec. 6, 1933.

28. *Daily Worker,* Dec. 5, 1933, Dec. 6, 1933. Continued Party efforts to solicit NAACP participation in "united front" defense conferences are documented in

Daily Worker, Dec. 4, 1933, and N. Bruce to National Association for the Advancement of Negroe People [sic], Feb. 6, 1974, NAACP Papers C 402.

29. William H. Wortham and Henry C. Parker, Jr., to William Pickens, Dec. 11, 1933, NAACP Papers, D 73; *New York Age,* Dec. 23, 1933, Dec. 20, 1933.

30. *New York Amsterdam News,* Jan. 31, 1934, Feb. 7, 1934, Feb. 21, 1934. Tensions surrounding the NAACP's continued fund raising for the case, and attacks by Communist speakers on association policies, are described in Walter White to Joseph Brodsky, Feb. 28, 1934, NAACP Papers, C 402.

31. *Harlem Liberator,* Dec. 16, 1933, Jan. 20, 1934; Josephine Chapin Brown, *Public Relief, 1929–1939* (1940; rpt. New York: Octagon Books, 1971), pp. 159–63.

32. *Daily Worker,* Dec. 5, 1933, Feb. 17, 1934; *New York Amsterdam News,* Dec. 6, 1933; *Report of the Mayor's Commission on Conditions in Harlem,* xerox copy in Schomburg Collection, pp. 12–13.

33. *Harlem Liberator,* Dec. 30, 1933, Jan. 20, 1934, Jan. 27, 1934; *Daily Worker,* Jan. 22, 1934; Brown, *Public Relief,* p. 160.

34. *Harlem Liberator,* Jan. 27, 1934, Mar. 10, 1934; *Daily Worker,* Feb. 5, 1934, Feb. 7, 1934, Mar. 9, 1934; *New York Amsterdam News,* Jan. 17, 1934, Feb. 7, 1934.

35. On the role of the Communist Party in building the Transportation Workers Union, see Louis Sass, "Harlem Concentration on Transport," *Party Organizer,* 9 (Mar., 1935), 23, and James J. McGinley, S.J., *Labor Relations in the New York Rapid Transit System, 1904–1944* (New York: Kings Crown Press, 1949), p. 317. On the role of transport workers in the protest movement, see *Harlem Liberator,* Feb. 10, 1934, and *Daily Worker,* Feb. 7, 1934. On the role of other unions in the protest, see *Daily Worker,* Apr. 21, 1934.

36. The last article on the bus protests appears in *Harlem Liberator,* July 7, 1934. No analysis appears in print of the LSNR's organizing strategy in Harlem, but the list of supporting organizations does not include one major church, political club, fraternal organization, or the national or local organizations of the Urban League and NAACP. Since Harlem Communists had sought out such organizations as allies during the April and May, 1933, Scottsboro protests, and were then condemned for doing so, one must conclude that their absence from these protests was intentional.

37. On the role of whites in the Coach Company protests, see *Harlem Liberator,* Mar. 10, 1934, and Mar. 17, 1934, and *Daily Worker,* Mar. 9, 1934, and Apr. 19, 1934.

38. Interview with Abner Berry, July 29, 1974. Articles on Dorfman can be found in *Daily Worker,* Feb. 9, 1934, and in *Harlem Liberator,* Feb. 10, 1934, Mar. 10, 1934.

39. Ford and Sass, "Development of Work in the Harlem Section," 322; interview with Abner Berry, Nov. 20, 1973; *New York Amsterdam News,* Mar. 31, 1934, Apr. 7, 1934; *New York Age,* Apr. 7, 1934; *Harlem Liberator,* Apr. 7, 1934, May 12, 1934.

40. Interview with Richard B. Moore, Nov. 14, 1973.

41. On the Party's concern about rising nationalist sentiment among blacks, see

Harlem Liberator, Mar. 17, 1934; Haywood, *The Road to Negro Liberation,* Mar. 17, 1934; Haywood, *The Road to Negro Liberation,* pp. 20–49; and Haywood, *Black Bolshevik: Autobiography of An Afro-American Communist* (Chicago: Liberator Press, 1978), pp. 426–29.

42. Haywood's autobiography, *Black Bolshevik,* provides a quite detailed, and often quite revealing, portrait of his political evolution, including his unabashed adulation of Stalin. Haywood's attitudes toward James Ford were expressed in an interview with me in Detroit on May 15, 1973.

43. Haywood, *The Road to Negro Liberation,* pp. 53–54, 57–58.

44. Mackawain, "The League of Struggle for Negro Rights in Harlem," 60–62.

45. *Daily Worker,* Apr. 26, 1934; *New York Amsterdam News,* Aug. 17, 1935; interview with Harry Haywood, May 15, 1973.

46. *Harlem Liberator,* May 19, 1934; *New York Amsterdam News,* June 20, 1934; interview with Harry Haywood, May 15, 1973; Benjamin J. Davis, *Communist Councilman from Harlem* (New York: International Publishers, 1969), pp. 82–100; interview with Henry Lee Moon, May 1, 1979.

47. *New York Amsterdam News,* Oct. 25, 1933; *Daily Worker,* June 16, 1934.

48. The term "scions of the Negro aristocracy" comes from an article in the *New York Amsterdam News,* June 30, 1934.

5

Harlem on the March—The Party Competes for Leadership

DURING THE SPRING and summer of 1934, Harlem Communists faced their severest challenge to date to their efforts to provide leadership to Harlem protest. A campaign to win jobs in Harlem stores, initiated by nationalist street speakers, spread rapidly to include leading ministers, politicians, and newspapermen, and unleashed a wave of picketing and marching that rivaled the Scottsboro movement at its height. Communists, initiators of much previous Harlem protest, found themselves on the outside looking in. The rhetoric of the movement emphasized race pride and black unity, and a small number of its partisans used antisemitic appeals. In desperation, Communists launched an offensive to change the movement's direction. They sent interracial groups onto movement picket lines, challenged its slogans and rhetoric, and organized jobs campaigns of their own based on black-white solidarity and trade union support. By the end of 1934, their strategy had won the support of key churchmen and service leaders, although nationalists still retained a strong popular following.

The size of this movement reflected an extraordinary change in the political behavior of Harlemites that had occurred since the Depression began. In a community where even the most militant spokesmen—whether nationalists or socialists—had failed to disturb the peace of the postwar era (1919–28) with a major strike or boycott, the "butcher, the baker and the candlestick maker," as one journalist put it, were all taking to the picket line.[1]

Communists had helped to arouse this militant spirit, but it had spread far beyond the Party's ranks. "Rising resentment against the existing social system is the outstanding motif of Harlem at the present time," the *Herald Tribune* reported in October, 1933. "Educated and uneducated Negroes alike are becoming more vocal in their demands for professional . . . and social equality." Since 1929, protest meetings, marches, and demonstrations, often organized by Communists, had been a daily occurrence on the streets of Harlem, and (since Scottsboro) common events in churches and meeting halls. Harlemites had come to see these techniques as natural and legitimate expressions of political discontent and had acquired the confidence to employ them in their own behalf.[2]

This receptivity to direct action transcended the black intelligentsia—it had become a genuine popular phenomenon. Four years of enforced idleness had helped generate a "radical street culture" among sections of Harlem's working class. Since 1932, more then 60 percent of Harlem's population had been out of work, and had been exposed to extraordinary persistent and diverse agitation on the streets of Harlem.[3] Communist Party neighborhood units (of which there were more than ten in 1934) sponsored at least one street meeting per day, not including meetings of the Unemployed Council, the ILD, the LSNR, or Communist trade unions.[4] Many of these meetings led directly into demonstrations, and some of them ended in confrontations with police. Nationalist organizers —Sufi Abdul Hamid, Arthur Kemp, and Ira Reid—were equally visible, and their speeches increasingly called for protest action at Harlem stores. Both groups—the Communists and the nationalists—attracted regular followers, but their activity also affected the great mass of the Harlem poor, who heard their grievances against police, landlords, and storekeepers articulated with furious intensity.

In March, 1934, a police attack on an ILD demonstration in honor of Ada Wright provoked an hour-long riot that offered a dramatic sign of the volatility of ordinary Harlem residents. After marching through the streets of Harlem, the demonstrators were holding a rally at 126th Street and Lenox Avenue when police officers arrived and asked to see their permit. While ILD leaders argued with detectives about how to keep the rally from blocking pedestrians and traffic, a group of squad cars suddenly drove into the crowd on the sidewalk, knocking several people down, and an officer in one of the cars hurled a tear-gas bomb. Pandemonium ensued. As fighting broke out between demonstrators and police, hundreds of Harlemites leaned out of their windows and joined in the fray, "The crowd was in an angry mood," the *New York Times* reported. "Stones, fruit, eggs and sticks were hurled at the detectives." As the police brought in reinforcements, the crowd resorted to hit-and-run tactics, dispersing into the side streets as the police pursued them, only to "swarm back into the avenue" when police turned their attention elsewhere. It took motorcycle policemen from adjacent precincts to finally quell the disturbance, which involved 5,000 people at its height—most of whom were spontaneous participants.[5]

Communists approved the militancy displayed by the Harlem crowd, but were a bit uncomfortable with the specific form it took. One week after the disturbance, Communists sponsored a demonstration against police brutality on the same street corner, but carefully kept crowds assembled from interfering with traffic or engaging in altercations with police (who had been ordered by the Mayor to keep a low profile). In addition, Party leaders brought in hundreds of white Communists from other parts of the city to assure that the demonstration had an interracial character. The *Liberator* praised the "splendid order, discipline and organization" of the protest, and hailed it as a sign of the "unbreakable unity of black and white workers."[6]

In campaigns where Communists had the initiative—such as Scottsboro or relief practices—they had little difficulty incorporating whites into Harlem protests. They controlled the podium and made the strategic decisions. But when protest arose *outside* the Party's ranks, their efforts to impose interracial unity met with considerable opposition. This proved to be the case in the movement to win jobs for blacks as salespeople in white-owned stores on 125th Street, a form of black activism which Communists had long avoided.

Sufi Abdul Hamid provided the spark for this movement. Active in the Chicago boycott of 1929, Sufi had come to Harlem in 1932 to persuade Harlemites to "follow Chicago's example" but had initially attracted little support. Local Garvey movement leaders seemed more interested in the liberation of Africa than day-to-day economic issues, and Sufi was forced to recruit his supporters through "soapboxing" rather than official UNIA channels. However, by the summer of 1933, Sufi had attracted enough of a following to begin picketing stores on 135th Street, and was able to win jobs for several members of his group (called the Negro Industrial and Clerical Alliance) in small "mom-and-pop" stores along that thoroughfare. With this victory under his belt, Sufi was ready for the chain stores and department stores of 125th Street, Harlem's main shopping district. In early May, 1934, he threw a picket line around Woolworth's 125th Street store after the manager had refused to hire members of his group as sales clerks, and appealed to Harlemites to boycott the store.[7]

Sufi's activities, though supported by few prominent Harlemites, impelled other community leaders to employ the boycott tactic. In the last week of May, Rev. John Johnson, the young Columbia-educated pastor of St. Martin's Episcopal Church, approached the management of Blumstein's department store to ask that blacks be hired as sales persons, bringing in 7,000 dollars in cancelled sales slips to give his appeal added weight, When Blumstein's refused to commit itself to a change in hiring policies, Johnson decided to form an alliance of Harlem churches, newspapers, and social and political clubs to "show the owners of the store that they cannot continue to get money from the people of Harlem and at the same time deny them work." Two influential Harlem ministers, Adam Clayton

Powell, Jr., and William Lloyd Imes joined him in the campaign, along
with several fraternal leaders and the editors of the *New York Age*. In
June, 1934, they formed an organization called the Citizens League for
Fair Play, and began picketing and boycotting Blumstein's to reinforce
their demand for jobs.[8]

The Blumstein boycott rapidly assumed the character of a crusade for
racial justice. Virtually all of the largest churches and fraternal organizations in Harlem supported the movement, as did political clubs, women's
groups, and representatives of the Garvey movement. The picketing of
Blumstein's was organized by Ira Kemp and Arthur Reid of the African
Patriotic League, a spinoff of the UNIA which argued that the development of black business and the creation of economically self-sufficient
black communities were essential first steps toward the creation of a successful black nation in Africa. Rough-hewn and effective street speakers,
Kemp and Reid recruited most of the pickets from amongst unemployed
and uneducated Harlemites who attended their rallies, although prominent Harlem citizens and representatives of churches supporting the
boycott also marched on the line. Many Harlemites believed that a victory over Blumstein's, the largest store in Harlem, would force other
stores in the community to hire black clerks, and that hope endowed their
efforts with tremendous enthusiasm. At one boycott meeting, the *Age* reported, "citizens of every trade and profession, creed and class . . . all
rose to their feet . . . and thundered 'Blumstein's Must Go.'"[9]

The Blumstein's boycott put Harlem Communists in a difficult position. Committed—since James Ford's arrival—to initiating campaigns
against job discrimination only when white employees in the discriminating institutions would support them, Party leaders now observed Harlemites uniting around a strategy that emphasized race loyalty, race pride,
and independent black action. Despite its nationalistic overtones, the
movement had far too much community support for the Party to openly
oppose it, so Communists tried to work within the movement to change
its objectives. While the LSNR and Party trade unionists continued their
campaign against the Fifth Avenue Coach Company, Communists joined
the Blumstein's picket line with signs demanding that no white workers
be fired when blacks were hired. The Party "especially urged" whites to
join the Blumstein's picketing, providing a counterweight to nationalist
arguments that the boycott was a struggle of "Negro against white."[10]

Initially, the Party's efforts to influence the movement failed completely. At the very time that the Communists found themselves compelled to
abandon the Fifth Avenue Coach Company boycott because of lack of
community support or concrete results, the 125th Street movement won
some gains. In June 1934, Koch's Department Store, opening under new
management, announced that one third of its sales staff would be black,

and a number of smaller stores made similar concessions. By the first week of August, Blumstein's capitulated; its management agreed to hire fifteen black sales clerks immediately and twenty after September 1. "In union there is strength," the *New York Age* exulted. "It is the Negro's salvation, economic, political or social . . ."[11]

The big Harlem "victory parade" following the Blumstein's agreement further dramatized the Party's isolation. LSNR organizer Bonita Williams had a sign taken away from her by members of the African Patriotic League, and marchers ejected a white female Communist from the parade and told her "this is a Negro fight." To Party leaders, these incidents demonstrated "dangerous trends" within the boycott movement, and they redoubled their efforts to persuade Harlemites to "unite with all sincere whites who are willing to fight with us side by side for Negro rights."[12]

Moreover, in the weeks following the Blumstein's victory, divisions surfaced within the boycott movement which gave greater weight to the Party's arguments. As the Citizens League shifted from planning boycott strategy to selecting people to fill the new positions, the remarkable political unity between Garveyites and middle-class community leaders crumbled, evoking grave doubts about the viability of "race loyalty" as a political strategy. Shortly after the Blumstein's agreement, Sufi's group placed pickets in front of the store to demand that its members be given the jobs that the boycott movement opened up. In the resulting controversy, Harlemites discovered that Sufi collected dues from his followers in return for a promise of placing them in jobs and that he approached the movement as a business proposition as well as a contribution to community betterment. The ministers and journalists who headed the Citizens League, seeing a threat to their credibility as negotiators, denounced Sufi as a "racketeer." Sentiment in Harlem ran strongly against Sufi's actions, and he withdrew his pickets after a week without realizing any of his demands.[13]

Shortly thereafter, an even more bitter conflict erupted between nationalists and moderates in the Citizens League ranks. Ira Kemp and Arthur Reid, the Garveyites who headed the league's "picket committee," became incensed when Blumstein's selected its new clerks from an Urban League training program in which light-skinned women predominated rather than from among the "dark-skinned girls" who had marched on the picket line. Accusing the Citizens League top leaders—Rev. John Johnson, *New York Age* editor Fred Moore, and Richard Carey—of color bias, Kemp and Reid decided to take complete control of any job assignments done by the organization. In early September, they reconstituted the "picket committee" as a dues-paying organization and demanded that merchants select black sales personnel only from among their membership. As Johnson, Moore, and Carey watched in horror, Kemp and Reid's group resumed the picketing of stores which had already hired blacks as well as those which hadn't, demanding that members of their group replace blacks already employed. After several stores acceded to their demands, Rev. Johnson filed suit against the "picket committee" to prevent them from using the Citizens League name, and *Age* writers appealed to the "sane people of Harlem" to help destroy the organization. Leaders of the picket committee, an *Age* columnist wrote, were "human vultures," "chiselers of the lowest type," who were "trying to climb to affluence on the backs of the oppressed and downtrodden."[14]

As the Blumstein's coalition dissolved into a maze of competing organizations and personalities, the Communist Party moved to take back the initiative in the struggle against job discrimination. During the last week of August, the Young Liberators, the youth wing of the LSNR, began picketing the Empire Cafeteria on 125th Street and Lenox Avenue to demand the hiring of blacks as countermen. The Empire had been a target of the labor-organizing drive launched by Communists in Harlem following the Emergency Party Conference, and Party organizers had created an alliance between white workers in the "shop" and the groups picketing outside around a program of common demands. Moreover, the Empire depended heavily for patronage on employees of a home-relief bureau on 124th Street among whom the Party led a very effective unionization campaign. Because of this anticipated support from white workers and patrons, Party leaders defined the campaign as a definitive test of their strategy for winning jobs, and invited Communists from throughout the city to join street rallies and marches in support of the picketers.[15]

The Empire boycott generated great esprit de corps within the Harlem CP. Led by James Ashford, a battle-tested black Party youth leader recently brought in from Detroit, hundreds of black and white Communists and sympathizers marched on cafeteria picket lines and hundreds more joined protest meetings held in the evenings. Police broke up several demonstrations and arrested the participants, but their actions only served to swell the ranks of the protesters. White Communists featured prominently in all of the demonstrations, and among those arrested, and black Communists hailed their presence as a "smashing refutation of the lies of the Negro reformist leaders that white workers cannot be won to the struggle for Negro rights." In addition, the predominately white Home Relief Bureau Employees Association of the 124th Street bureau supported the boycott, depriving the cafeteria of a large part of its noonday business. After a week and a half of protests, the Empire management capitulated and hired four blacks as countermen without firing any whites, and dropped all charges against the protesters.[16]

The Empire victory represented a landmark in the history of the Harlem CP. Coming at a time of rising nationalist sentiment, it helped to legitimize the role of whites in campaigns against job discrimination and to enhance the credibility of the Party.[17] The Empire boycott, a Party leader recalled:

> made the white workers in Harlem who followed the Party altogether different from any other white workers. From that point on, all you had to do was explain, if you got stopped by a black on the street, that you were a Communist, and someone would say, "That's all right boys, he's a Communist," and you could go on your way. This was a case where white workers had taken the lead in organizing to get jobs for Negroes. . . . And because of that, you were better able to go about your organizing duties than before.[18]

In the weeks following the Empire victory, Communists focused their fire on nationalist boycott leaders, who were stirring up racial and ethnic antagonisms in an increasingly explicit manner. Sufi's activities particularly disturbed the Party. After his expulsion from the Blumstein coalition, he had taken to calling himself the "Black Hitler," and appealing to blacks to "drive Jewish businessmen out of Harlem." In early October, the Party organized a series of street meetings in Harlem aimed at Sufi's "race baiting." Communists accused Sufi of "shaking down Negro workers out of jobs they had held for years," and warned that his antisemitic speeches would jeopardize jobs blacks held in other parts of the city.[19] "Such fakers as Abdul Sufi Hamid," the *Liberator* declared,

> cannot win the struggle for the Negro workers, for his doctrine is to make this into a "race struggle" alone—a theory which plays directly into the hands of the white bosses and promotes race antagonisms leading to "race riots." . . . Any movement which claims to win the rights of the oppressed Negro people in Harlem or anywhere else is doomed to failure unless it is based on the solid block of Negro and white unity of the workers, professionals and sympathizers.[20]

The Party's campaign against Sufi coincided with a massive repudiation of nationalist boycott activities by leading Harlem ministers, fraternal leaders, and editors. As the disciplined political activism of the Blumstein's movement gave way to racketeering, antisemitism, and intragroup color conflicts, moderate community leaders moved decisively to condemn street speakers who stirred up racial passions. The *Amsterdam News* and the *Age* printed editorials denouncing Sufi and the picket committee, and the Interdenominational Ministers Alliance and the Harlem chapter of the American Legion passed resolutions against antisemitism in Harlem. At the same time, white Harlem merchants initiated legal action to halt the boycott movement. In October, following a meeting between Jewish businessmen and the mayor, police arrested Sufi on charges of "spreading anti-Semitism in Harlem." After four days of conflicting testimony, Sufi was acquitted, but the court action made him far more circumspect in his public remarks. Three weeks later, State Supreme Court Justice Samuel Rosenman granted the A. S. Beck Shoe Company an injunction against the picketing of Ira Kemp and Arthur Reid on the grounds that their activity might stimulate "racial riots and racial reprisals." The judge recognized the right of organizations to picket in labor disputes but claimed that Kemp and Reid's conflict with the Beck management was solely a "racial dispute." When members of Kemp and Reid's organization continued to picket, they were arrested on charges of disorderly conduct and given ten days in jail, the maximum sentence.[21]

Many Harlem moderates supported these court restraints on nationalist boycott activities. The sudden wave of "race consciousness" that swept through Harlem sufficiently alarmed some of the original boycott supporters to persuade them to work with the merchants in restoring order. "The decision of Supreme Court Justice Rosenman," *Age* columnist Vere Johns suggested, would help end "the period of hysteria and general folly which has prevailed in Harlem since the Blumstein boycott victory." "Intelligent Negroes who want to keep the jobs they have," the *Amsterdam News* declared, "will walk past the pickets and trade, whenever possible, in stores which employ Negroes."[22]

As disillusionment with nationalist boycott movements grew, moderate Harlemites became increasingly receptive to Communist antidiscrimination strategy. In December, 1934, Communists launched a campaign against discrimination in the administration of relief that attracted far greater support from important Harlem churches and civic organizations than any economic protest Communists had initiated in the past. Among the organizations participating in the campaign in its early stages were Abyssinian Baptist Church and St. Martin's P. E. Church (both of which had been active in the Blumstein's boycott), the North Harlem Community Council, the *Amsterdam News,* and the New York branch of the NAACP.[23]

The initiative in this movement came from the Home Relief Bureau Employees Association. In October, 1934, the association issued a bulletin charging administrators of Harlem relief bureaus with discourteous treatment of black clients, hostility to black clerks and investigators, and refusal to promote blacks to supervisory positions. The association followed these charges with a mass meeting of Harlem relief workers, but local administrators failed to make any concessions. Shortly thereafter, central relief officials fired white association chairman Frederick Benedict. This impelled the association to take its grievances to the Harlem community. After acquiring the support of the Unemployed Councils, the ILD, and the LSNR, association leaders invited influential ministers, editors, politicians, and fraternal leaders to an open meeting on relief practices at the Harlem YMCA. The groups assembled formed a Joint Conference on Discriminatory Practices and scheduled a series of community meetings to publicize discrimination in the relief bureaus and call for the dismissal of prejudiced officials.[24]

The activities of the Joint Conference added to the credibility of the Party's strategy for fighting discrimination in employment. The Home Relief Bureau Employees Association had units in every relief bureau in Harlem, composed largely of young, college-educated Jews with radical backgrounds. Respected by the few blacks in the bureaus because of their egalitarian behavior, they had the numbers, and the solidarity, to disrupt bureau operations.[25] Leaders of black organizations, conscious of the power they possessed, welcomed their cooperation. At the Joint Conference's first protest meeting—held at Abyssinian Baptist Church—association leaders together with Harlem Communists Richard Moore and James Ford shared the platform with Rev. Adam Clayton Powell, Jr., Democratic assemblyman-elect William T. Andrews, and James Egert Allen, a schoolteacher and president of the New York branch of the NAACP.[26] Allen's involvement ended there (though the NAACP name, to Walter White's consternation, remained on Joint Conference stationery), but Andrews and Powell continued to work closely with left-wing relief workers in putting pressure on city officials. Throughout the winter of 1934–35, the Joint Conference sponsored numerous demonstrations, petition drives, and delegations downtown. Several black relief workers sympathetic to the left emerged as leaders in this campaign—among them Arnold P. Johnson, who would later achieve prominence as Adam Clayton Powell's right-hand man in the Harlem jobs movement of the late '30s. Moreover, the campaign helped bring about significant changes in relief-bureau policies. In December, 1934, relief officials promoted several blacks to supervisory positions in the 124th Street bureau, and in subsequent months, they appointed so many black investigators that by the summer of 1935, relief workers constituted the largest group of black professionals on the city payroll.[27]

The Party's experience in the Harlem jobs movement boosted the self-confidence of the Harlem Section leadership. Using the strategy Ford had fought for in the Section Committee—an alliance between black community groups and white workers in institutions which practiced discrimination—Communists had shown that they could obtain concrete benefits for blacks without exacerbating ethnic antagonisms. Their accomplishment impressed both the unemployed and underemployed Harlemites who congregated on neighborhood streets, and the leaders of powerful community organizations. Among the former, their activity helped prevent the antiwhite rhetoric of Sufi, Kemp, and Reid from winning general acceptance; among the latter, it helped affirm the value of alliances with the labor movement and the left. Nationalist feeling remained strong among all sections of Harlem's population, but Communists had demonstrated their capacity to channel popular militancy in directions that permitted cooperation with left-wing whites.

NOTES

1. *New York Age,* July 14, 1934.

2. *New York Herald Tribune,* Oct. 8, 1933, Section 2.

3. The estimates on Harlem unemployment come from *New York Amsterdam News,* Nov. 1, 1933, and *New York Post,* Mar. 21, 1935.

4. The figures on Party neighborhood units in Harlem come from Ford and Sass, "The Development of Work in the Harlem Section," *Communist,* 14 (Apr., 1935), 323.

5. Report, A. W. Wirin to Hon. F. H. La Guardia, Mar. 26, 1934, Fiorello H. La Guardia Papers, Municipal Archives, New York City, Box 2550, H #9; Report, From the Chief Inspector to the Police Commissioner, Mar. 26, 1934, La Guardia Papers, Box 2550, H #9; *New York Amsterdam News,* Mar. 24, 1934; *New York Times,* Mar. 18, 1934.

6. Report, A. L. Wirin to Hon. F. H. La Guardia, La Guardia Papers, Box 2550, H #9; *Harlem Liberator,* Mar. 31, 1934.

7. Wilbur Young, "Activities of Bishop Amiru, Al-Mumin Sufi A. Hamid," Federal Writers Project Papers, Reel 1; *New York Age,* Oct. 1, 1932; Melville Weiss, "Don't Buy Where You Can't Work," (M.A. thesis, Columbia University, 1941), pp. 56–57; *New York Amsterdam News,* May 26, 1934.

8. *New York Age,* May 26, 1934, June 23, 1934; Weiss, "Don't But Where You Can't Work," p. 57.

9. *New York Age,* June 16, 1934, June 23, 1934, July 14, 1934; on the activities of the African Patriotic League, see *Negro World,* May 14, 1932; "Discriminatory Practices," Federal Writers Papers, Reel 2.

10. *New York Age,* July 14, 1934, July 28, 1934; *Daily Worker,* June 9, 1934.

11. *New York Age,* June 9, 1934, Aug. 4, 1934.

12. *New York Amsterdam News,* Aug. 4, 1934; *Negro Liberator,* Aug. 4, 1934.

13. *New York Age,* Aug. 11, 1934; *New York Amsterdam News,* Sept. 1, 1934.

14. *New York Age,* Sept. 15, 1934, Sept. 22, 1934, Oct. 6, 1934, Oct. 27, 1934.

15. *New York Times,* Sept. 1, 1934; *Daily Worker,* Sept. 1, 1934, Sept. 11, 1934. On policy of industrial concentration launched in Harlem after the Emergency Party Conference, see Louis Sass, "Harlem Concentration on Transport," *Party Organizer,* 9 (Mar., 1935), 23, and Ford and Sass, "The Development of Work in the Harlem Section," 315–16.

16. *New York Times,* Sept. 1, 1934; *Daily Worker,* Sept. 7, 1934, Sept. 11, 1934; *Negro Liberator,* Sept. 15, 1934.

17. *Ibid.*; Ford and Sass, "The Development of Work in the Harlem Section," 313.

18. Interview with Abner Berry, July 29, 1974.

19. *Ethiopian World,* Oct. 20, 1934; *New York Age,* Sept. 29, 1934; *New York Amsterdam News,* Oct. 6, 1934; *Negro Liberator,* Oct. 6, 1934.

20. *Ibid.*, Sept. 15, 1934.

21. *New York Age,* Oct. 20, 1934, Nov. 17, 1934, Dec. 8, 1934; *New York Amsterdam News,* Oct. 13, 1934, Nov. 3, 1934, Dec. 29, 1934.

22. *New York Age,* Nov. 17, 1934; *New York Amsterdam News,* Oct. 20, 1934.

23. *New York Amsterdam News,* Dec. 15, 1934; *New York Age,* Dec. 22, 1934.

24. *26th and 27th PCTS Bulletin,* Oct. 29, 1934, La Guardia Papers, Box 2550, H #5; *Daily Worker,* Nov. 5, 1934; *New York Amsterdam News,* Dec. 8, 1934; Harry Dolimer and Allan MacKenzie, *The Negro Worker in the ERB* (New York: Association of Workers in Public Relief Agencies, 1937), p. 1, in the National Negro Congress Papers, Reel 1, Schomburg Collection.

25. Interview with Alice Citron, Aug. 20, 1979; interview with Abner Berry, Nov. 20 , 1973.

26. *New York Amsterdam News,* Dec. 15, 1934.

27. Dolimer and MacKenzie, *The Negro Worker in the ERB,* pp. 1, 10–12; leaflet, "Boro Mass Meeting to Protest Discriminatory Practices of Home Relief Bureau Administration," La Guardia Papers, Box 2550, H #5; *Reports of the Mayor's Commission on Conditions in Harlem,* pp. 10–11. For evidence of White's discontent with the NAACP's name appearing on the Joint Conference letterhead, see Walter White, Memorandum to Mr. James E. Allen, President, New York Branch, Feb. 5, 1936, NAACP Papers, G 144.

6

Building the United Front—
The Party Wins Its Spurs

D**URING THE LAST SIX MONTHS** of 1934, the leadership of the Harlem Communist Party, acting in consultation with the Party's Central Committee, undertook a major reformulation of the basis upon which Communists throughout the nation conducted work in black communities. Emboldened by signals from the Communist International encouraging greater "unity against fascism" (and implicitly repudiating the sectarian atmosphere that accompanied the Emergency Party Conference), Harlem Party leaders expanded their network of alliances with Harlem groups and developed a sophisticated rationale for their actions that ultimately became official Party policy. Inklings of this change first appeared in the summer of 1934, but its emergence as a new "line" for the Party nationally came in February, 1935, when an article by James Ford appeared in the theoretical journal *Communist*. Based on the approach Ford outlined, which emphasized working within black organizations rather than trying to undermine them, Harlem Communists achieved a major expansion of their black membership and transformed two potentially difficult crises—the Harlem Riot, and Mussolini's invasion of Ethiopia—into events which solidified the Party's power base.[1]

The evolution of this new policy reflected a fortuitous congruence between the strategic perspectives of Harlem Party leaders and the ever-changing political requirements imposed by Comintern officials. By background and experience, black Communists like James Ford and Benjamin Davis were equipped to work comfortably and easily with leaders of the Urban League, the NAACP, and black fraternal organizations and churches—they attended similar schools, belonged to the same organizations in their youth, and had similar cultural affinities. But they could not fully transform those common experiences into political relationships until the Comintern line—as filtered through the CPUSA top leadership—allowed them to do so. It therefore took a major change in the Comintern view of the fascist danger (first visible in the late spring of 1934) to allow Harlem Party leadership to take advantage of a growing receptivity by black organizations toward mass-protest tactics and an alliance with labor and the left. Just as the Comintern passed signals to the French Communist Party allowing it to negotiate a "unity pact" with French Socialists covering elections, demonstrations, and trade-union activity, so it passed signals to the CPUSA allowing its cadre to make alliances with antifascist socialists and liberals. The Party's Negro work, along with its youth work and trade union organizing, were transformed in the process, removing many sectarian practices that had limited the Party's influence.[2]

The major theoretical innovation in the new policy for work with blacks — which was formulated largely on the basis of experiences in the Harlem Section — was a revised analysis of the nature of black organizations. While retaining the emphasis upon blacks as an oppressed nation, Communists dramatically deemphasized the "war on Negro reformism" which had been a linchpin of Party policy since the two Comintern resolutions on the Negro Question (1928 and 1930).[3] Rejecting the crude characterization of black religious and civic organizations as "agents of the bourgeoisie" in the lives of the black population, James Ford argued, in his article, that most black organizations represented multiclass formations that could be "radicalized in struggle" and that Communists should work with them at the same time as they expanded their own network of organizations. "There are thousands of . . . fraternal organizations, lodges, social clubs, West Indian organizations, independent trade unions, locals of the AFL, youth and Greek letter societies, churches and affiliated social groups," Ford wrote. "We must not come to these organizations with the idea of destroying them, but with the idea of bringing them nearer to the program of the League of Struggle for Negro Rights." To advance the radicalization of black organizations, Ford instructed Party units in black areas to "concentrate on a church, fraternal, or other organization" as though it were a shop, building Party fractions within them to win support for Communist programs.[4]

Even more striking than this shift in strategy was the accompanying imperative to Communists to adapt their behavior to the mores and traditions of the black population. Prior Communist statements on "Negro work," when they discussed culture at all (either in the anthropological or narrowly aesthetic sense), tended to regard both the institutional expressions of black life — churches, insurance societies, etc. — and black artistic production — theatre, music, literature — as "corrupted by bourgeois influence." By implication, if not direct instruction, they pressed Communists to wipe the slate clean and generate an alternative culture based on proletarian values and interracial unity. Black Communists often rejected these prescriptions in practice—especially when organizing Scottsboro protests or working with black intellectuals, but did so largely on an ad hoc basis.[5]

Ford's article represented the first major statement of Party policy which recognized that the organizational forms and cultural traditions of Black America could not be uprooted and that Communists had to adjust to them to expand their influence. "When we are members of . . . [black] organizations," Ford asserted, "we must be sensible and human . . . careful never to assume an attitude of superiority. We must learn the rules of how meetings are conducted and be able to conduct ourselves in such a manner as to gain the respect and confidence of members." Ford called on Communists to be "particularly cautious" in dealing with religious blacks, remembering that "they have pride in their church and in many ways, it meets their social and cultural needs." Ford acknowledged the role of black religion as an expression of black protest and warned Communists not to make an issue of their atheism if it offended potential allies. "Recently," he wrote,

> at an open forum on religion, a Negro woman, a member of church said during the discussion. "You know, you Communists have been sent by God to do the work you are doing, but you don't know it." Should we try to argue with such a woman about this statement when we are trying to make a united front on Scottsboro? Of course not. . . . If this woman believes that her religion can play a revolutionary role to the extent of supporting us on Scottsboro, this gives us a starting point for building the United Front.[6]

This recasting of Communist Negro work, the first since 1930, took place entirely *within* the American Party. Unlike the Comintern Resolutions on the Negro Question of 1928 and 1930, which were drafted in the Soviet Union, with Comintern nationality experts dominating the proceedings, the strategic formulations in Ford's article were developed, and discussed, in three important committees within the American Party of which James Ford was a member—the Harlem Section Committee, the Negro Commission, and the Politburo.[7] Although the analysis in Ford's article was probably approved in some form by the Comintern (it is possible Earl Browder brought it to Moscow in December, 1934, during his annual conference with Soviet officials), its commonsense tactical prescriptions flowed from the large fund of practical experience Communist had accumulated from their work in black communities rather than a theoretical abstraction based on a Soviet model. The new line represented a particular triumph for James Ford, who emerged as the Party's major spokesman on theoretical and strategic issues related to Black America. His major rival for theoretical dominance, Harry Haywood, was transferred from Harlem to Chicago in the fall of 1934, and removed as president of the League of Struggle for Negro Rights. Closely identified with the Party's "war on Negro reformism" — which he had helped to design — Haywood had become expendable to Ford following the successful vanquishing of Ford's "nationalist opposition." Out of touch with the antifascist dynamic gathering momentum in the international movement, Haywood lost the confidence of the CPUSA's top leadership, and was increasingly bypassed as a national spokesman in favor of black Communists who projected a more pragmatic air and were more capable of working cooperatively with influential black organizations and leaders.[8]

The gradual evolution toward a "united front" policy could be observed, within the activities of the Harlem Section, as early as the spring of 1934. At this time, antifascism emerged as a major motif in Party rhetoric, accompanied by a wide-ranging effort to cultivate alliances with the black church. Arguing with considerable force and eloquence, Party organizers linked the persecution of blacks in America with the persecution of Jews in Germany and proclaimed that the defeat of international fascism was essential to black progress. Some influential black ministers found their arguments persuasive. In May, 1934, three of Harlem's largest churches, St. Martin's, Abyssinian Baptist, and St. Phillip's, participated in the first regional conference of the American League Against War and Fascism, a Party-sponsored "united front" concerned with international issues, and endorsed that organization's call for a peace march on August 5.[9]

An even more dramatic example of the Party's new policy was its overtures to the Father Divine Peace Mission, a huge and controversial religious cult with headquarters in Harlem. In May, 1934, Harlem Communists persuaded the leadership of this movement, whose rhetoric emphasized peace and interracial brotherhood, to participate in Party sponsored antiwar demonstrations. Three thousand of Father's "angels" marched in a National Youth Day parade on May 22 and 6,000 more joined the August 5 march against war and fascism. In both demonstrations, they sang their own chants and carried their own banners, mingling antifascist slogans and demands to free the Scottsboro boys with exhortations that "Father Divine is God."[10]

The Party's relationship with Father Divine "startled and confused" many rank-and-file Communists and created an uproar in the Harlem press. The *Amsterdam News,* reviewing the August 5 demonstration, wondered "whether the appearance of a group in the parade proclaiming Divine was God was not incongruous with the Doctrine of Karl Marx, founder of Communism." But Party leaders defended their actions on the grounds that Divine's followers were seeking a "religious way out" of poverty and oppression and might be converted to socialism if they saw that their needs could be met by political struggle. "Father Divine attracts his followers," the *Daily Worker* declared:

> precisely by embodying the desires of the masses in his "new religion." The Negro people, oppressed, persecuted, even lynched, above everything else want "true democracy, justice, freedom, equality, love." This is what he promises, and they now believe that he can fulfill these promises. They believe "Father Divine is God."
> But still, while carrying such strange and foolish placards, they join with Communists and other militants in protest against war and fascism. They can likewise be drawn into strike struggles, the struggles of the unemployed, the Scottsboro-Herndon fight etc. In these class fights under our leadership, they will learn to fight here and now for a heaven on earth, for socialism.[11]

Communists continued their efforts to "politicize" the Father Divine movement. They held regular meetings with leaders of the movement, and persuaded them to issue statements denouncing lynching, segregation, and fascism. But most of Divine's followers remained immune to Communist influence. When people joined the Peace Mission, they gave up their money, their family life, and their sexual activity for a life free from economic necessity; the movement provided them with housing, meals, and employment. The all-encompassing security of this existence limited the need for economic protest, and Communists were unable to draw Divine's followers into the labor movement, or the struggles of the unemployed. But on the questions of peace and resistance to fascism, the alliance survived for more than a year and the Divine movement provided regular participants in Communist demonstrations downtown and in Harlem.[12]

Communists paralleled their overtures to the black church with an equally explicit appeal to the black middle class. Harlem Party leaders like James Ford and Ben Davis began speaking proudly of their college backgrounds and club and fraternity memberships, and telling black professionals they were welcome in Party circles. Party leaders unveiled their new image at an August, 1934, dinner for the black press at the Harlem YMCA, designed to launch the Party's municipal election campaign. Ford introduced the Party's Harlem campaign manager, Samuel Patterson, as a "former executive secretary of the Caribbean Union, an active member of the Odd Fellows and a member of St. James Presbyterian Church," and invited "churches, clubs, business and professional people, and even the Father Divine movement" to endorse the Party's candidates. A *New York Age* columnist, skeptical of the Party's sincerity, described the affair as "Be Kind to the Negro Press Day": "The Harlem Section of the Communist Party leaned far, to the right in its announcement of the broadest united front, and the usual bitter, searing, relentless and uncompromising attack on the Negro press was eloquent by its absence."[13]

The Party's conciliatory approach to the middle class, like its overtures to the black church, brought about no dramatic change in the Party's position. No Harlem leaders of importance endorsed the Communist candidates, and the Party's vote total in Harlem (the 19th and 21st Assembly Districts) remained less than a thousand. Responsive to Communist leadership in mass protest, where Party tactics won tangible results, most Harlemites refused to take Communists seriously as an electoral force. Lacking patronage or influence "downtown" and in Albany (no Communists sat on the Board of Aldermen or in the state legislature), Communists seemed ill equipped to advance black interests in the electoral sphere. In contrast, black Republican and Democratic politicians, with contacts to powerful party structures, had secured nominations to the assembly and the Board of Aldermen, controlled access to scores of minor offices, and had won control (Republicans) or were about to win control (Democrats) of key district leadership positions. Servicing their constituents in the old-fashioned manner — packages at Christmas, jobs shovelling snow, "understandings" between police and businessmen (legal and otherwise) — Harlem politicians attracted support from job hunters, ambitious businessmen and professionals, and ordinary citizens in need of occasional favors. Communists, without comparable services at their disposal — or the realistic hope of acquiring them — drew their votes only from those ideologically committed to socialism, who still represented a tiny minority of Harlem's population.[14]

In addition, the Party's new strategy failed to defuse a deep skepticism of Communist motives among moderate Harlem leaders. Although many influential Harlemites agreed with the Party's strategy of building interracial alliances against discrimination and linking black protest to an international struggle against fascism, they feared that the imperatives for Communists' actions stemmed from sources beyond the black community's control and that the Party's new openness hid an underlying cynicism. The *Amsterdam News* provided the major forum for this criticism. During the summer of 1934, it published a steady stream of articles designed to remind Harlem readers that the Party was controlled "from Moscow" and that it would betray black interests when they conflicted with Soviet policy.

The expulsion from the Comintern of George Padmore, the head of the International Trade Union Committee of Negro Workers, provided the focus of the paper's campaign. Padmore charged that his committee had been liquidated by the Comintern in response to pressure from Great Britain and that the Comintern had deemphasized its anticolonial agitation after Hitler's rise to power in order to win acceptance from western governments. The *Amsterdam News* gave front-page coverage to Padmore's charges and when black Communists tried to discredit Padmore by accusing him of "associating with police spies," it published a number of indignant letters questioning the integrity of Party spokesmen. "I have known Padmore for many years," one correspondent wrote, "and have always known him to be intellectually honest, and that is more than I can say for any of the prominent 'Negro Communist leaders' in this country." An *Amsterdam News* editorial repeated these charges: "No Democratic office holder is more effusively apologetic for the double dealing of Tammany than is any leader of the Communist Party for the opportunistic policies of Moscow. Both are on the payroll of organizations which muzzle dissenters."[15]

In the fall of 1934, the *Amsterdam News* took its criticism of the Party beyond the verbal stage. When two ILD attorneys were arrested for trying to bribe Victoria Price, the publisher of the paper, William H. Davis, joined Samuel Leibowitz in a concerted drive to remove Communists from the Scottsboro case. Supported by two conservative Harlem ministers, Rev. Richard Bolden and Rev. Lorenzo King, Davis and Leibowitz sent a delegation to Alabama and persuaded Haywood Patterson and Clarence Norris to sever ties with the ILD. Shortly thereafter, a group of Harlem businessmen, editors, and ministers joined with Leibowitz in forming an American Scottsboro Committee to coordinate defense activity. Its members read like a "who's who" of Harlem moderates, including the publishers of the *New York Age* and the *Amsterdam News,* members of the Interdenominational Ministers Alliance, and prominent private citizens like Bill Robinson and J. Dalmas Steele. The group selected as its leader George E. Haynes, race relations secretary of the Federal Council of Churches, and initiated an aggressive public relations drive designed to gain financial support for Leibowitz and prevent the Communists from reentering the case.[16]

Communists, surprised by the rapidity of this initiative, tried desperately to regain their foothold in the defense. With the help of Scottsboro parents, they persuaded the defendants to give power to conduct the appeal back to the ILD and instructed ILD constitutional attorneys to continue their work on briefs to win a stay of execution and a new hearing before the U.S. Supreme Court. At the same time, the ILD publicly appealed to the American Scottsboro Committee to restore the "united front" for the boys' defense and cooperate in legal and fund-raising activities.[17]

The American Scottsboro Committee rejected this overture. Leibowitz continued to vie for the loyalty of the defendants, who changed sides five times during October and November, while the committee took its arguments to the people of Harlem. In October, the Interdenominational

Ministers Alliance held meetings in more than twenty churches in Harlem to raise funds for Leibowitz and passed a resolution criticizing the ILD for using "illegal means in the cause of justice" and "propagandizing at the expense of nine Negro boys in trouble."[18]

Communists countered this activity with a mass mobilization of their own. Forming a Scottsboro-Herndon Action Committee headed by three non-Communists sympathetic to the Party—William N. Jones of the *Baltimore Afro-American,* Samuel Patterson of the Caribbean Union, and attorney John Newton Griggs—it sponsored parades, street rallies, and meetings in Harlem churches to win support for a "united front defense committee" including the ILD. As before, the Party buttressed its position by bringing Scottsboro parents to Harlem.[19] One of Harlem's most respected ministers, Rev. Shelton Bishop of St. Philip's Church, was persuaded by the parents to support the ILD, and he criticized American Scottsboro Committee spokesmen for trying to discredit the parents' activities. "I have had contact personally with four of the Scottsboro mothers," he wrote George Haynes, "and they have only confirmed me in my long standing conviction that with all its faults and with all its defections and deflections of finances . . . the International Labor Defense is the sole organization in the country that had kept the Scottsboro disgrace before the world."[20]

Bishop's view, while not representative of the Harlem ministry, dramatized the problems the American Scottsboro Committee faced in trying to *isolate* the ILD. So long as some parents and defendants stuck by the ILD, many important black organizations, including the NAACP, stopped short of the frontal attack on Communist participation in the case that the American Scottsboro Committee wanted. "Our position," Walter White wrote a prominent NAACP supporter, "is hands off until the Communists are completely eliminated and we can go in on our own terms."[21] In late November, 1934, ILD attorneys, who continued working throughout the controversy, won a stay of execution for Norris and Patterson, giving the Party a renewed foothold in the defense.[22] "Despite the strenuous efforts of Attorney Samuel Leibowitz and the American Scottsboro Committee . . . ," the *New York Age* concluded, "recent developments would indicate that the International Labor Defense . . . will have charge of the appeal." Many people had joined with Leibowitz "in an effort to take the case from the radicals," the *Age* commented, but it seemed that "those most concerned with the matter, the nine boys and their parents . . . have given authority to the ILD to continue with their defense."[23]

Despite eroding popular support, the American Scottsboro Committee rejected ILD requests for a "united front" defense organization. But in mid-January, 1935, when the Supreme Court agreed to hear the case, Leibowitz agreed to meet with ILD attorneys to work out a division of

responsibility. The ILD attorneys would argue Patterson's case, and Leibowitz would argue Norris's. This arrangement did not achieve the Party's
major goal — cooperation between the ILD and the Scottsboro Committee in planning legal strategy, fund raising, and protest demonstrations —
but it represented an explicit recognition of the Party's role in the Scottsboro defense.[24] As in the jobs campaign, Communists had demonstrated
that they could survive a concerted effort to exclude them from an important Harlem protest movement.

In January, 1935, Harlem Party leaders conducted a systematic review
of section activities and expressed considerable satisfaction with what
they saw. In the year and a half since James Ford had come to Harlem,
black Party membership in the section had grown from eighty-seven to
over 300, and the general section membership had grown from 560 to
1,000. Communist-led organizations had expanded commensurately.
The Upper Harlem Unemployed Council, with 3,000 registered members,
was the largest in the city, and the Harlem ILD had stabilized its membership at 1,090 in eleven branches. In addition, the program of industrial
concentration launched at the Extraordinary Party Congress had begun
to achieve results. Between April, 1934, and January, 1935, the Harlem
Section had expanded its "shop units" from five to eighteen: two in the
transit system, one in the CWA, five in hospitals, four in the home relief
bureaus, two in the school system, and two in the food industry (cafeterias). These shop units had played an important role in arousing support
among white workers for the Party's antidiscrimination campaigns at the
Fifth Avenue Coach Company, the Empire Cafeteria, and the Harlem
Home Relief Bureaus.[25]

Party leaders took particular pride in their organization's ability to survive political attacks and influence the direction of black protest. "There
is not a single political group among the Negro masses today," James
Ford and Louis Sass claimed, "that has not at one time or another made
gestures of cooperation toward the Party." Although the Party had been
temporarily "outmaneuvered" on several occasions, it had managed to
hold its own in every major crisis, whether it was the Scottsboro Riot, the
jobs movement, or the conflict with the American Scottsboro Committee.
On specific issues, Harlem leaders boasted, Party activists had formed
alliances with the Sufi movement, Father Divine, and Harlem newspapers, churches, and fraternal organizations, "not failing to expose the
leaders of these groups in order to win the masses to our program."[26]

The Party's effectiveness had been significantly increased by an infusion
of new leadership into the Harlem Section. Hurt by the departure of William Patterson, who suffered a physical collapse during October, 1934,
and went to the Soviet Union to recuperate, the Party, during the fall of
1935, imported three of its top black organizers to work in Harlem.[27]

James Ashford, a leader of the Briggs Auto Strike in Detroit, came in to head the Harlem Young Communist League; Manning Johnson, a district organizer from Buffalo, came in to supervise trade union work in Harlem; and Abner Berry, a leader in unemployed work in Kansas City, arrived to replace Harry Haywood as head of the League of Struggle for Negro Rights. Ashford and Johnson, both college educated and articulate men, represented polar opposites in their personal styles. A fluent speaker and an astute tactician, Johnson was an ambitious man with a taste for expensive clothes, fine liquor, and the company of women. Disliked in the Party because of his sharp tongue and questionable personal habits (he was reputed to be a wife-beater), Johnson functioned well in mainstream labor circles, where his hard drinking style and cynical air did not seem out of place.[28] Ashford, by contrast, was a radical "boy scout," a cheerful, selfless worker who disdained material luxury and dealt with comrades in a gentle manner. An inspirational figure in the Party, who put in long hours and suffered numerous arrests, Ashford almost singlehandedly turned the Young Liberators, the youth wing of the LSNR, into an effective protest organization. Had he not been cut down by illness in the fall of 1936, he might have emerged as one of the Party's most effective black leaders—nationally as well as locally.[29]

Abner Berry's appointment proved to be the most important of the three. A warm, soft-spoken man with an incisive mind and a "poetic feeling for people," Berry rapidly won a place as the Harlem Party's main troubleshooter and liaison with Harlem organizations. The scion of a theatrical family—his brothers were well-known tap dancers—Berry's Party work in Texas and Missouri had exposed him to serious danger, but he displayed his political convictions without self-righteousness or bravado. Although he lacked college training, Berry possessed a fine theoretical mind and considerable journalistic skill. Black leaders found him easy to deal with because of his unassuming manner and sense of humor; he had an uncanny ability simultaneously to win people's respect and put them at ease. Operating in the shadow of James Ford, the section's "mass leader," Berry assumed responsibility for much of the day-to-day negotiating that built the united front.[30]

The promotion of Theodore Bassett to education director of the Harlem Party—done in the same period—also provided Ford with an invaluable assistant, one who like Berry would exercise his skills in the background and not compete for top leadership. Bassett had been a member of the Harlem Party since 1931, but had lacked the charisma or street savvy to achieve prominence as a mass leader. A graduate of Howard who had taught school in North Carolina before coming to New York, Bassett had been attracted to the Party by its theoretical concerns, and involvement in international events, as much as its practical activities. A scholarly, responsible person with a rather bland personality, Bassett had the journalistic skills to serve as an effective speechwriter and sufficient knowledge of Party history and doctrine to supervise its training of new members.[31]

The Harlem Party also benefited from the promotion of two talented black women to leadership positions: Bonita Williams as an organizer in the LSNR and the Unemployed Councils, and Audley Moore as an organizer in the ILD and the International Workers Order, the Party's insurance and fraternal society. Unlike Louise Thompson and Maude White, other black women who had been prominent in the Harlem Party, Moore and Williams came from working-class backgrounds and had a "down home" eloquence that enabled them to articulate the feelings of the uneducated black women who constituted the rank and file of the Harlem Unemployed Council. Both were effective street speakers who could argue for Communist policies in the cadence of the Garvey movement and the church. Details about Williams's background are unfortunately quite sketchy—we know she was West Indian and from a family of modest means, but Moore's history epitomizes the fusion of socialist and nationalist traditions within the Party's ranks. Born in Louisiana, Moore had been an enthusiastic participant in the Garvey movement in New Orleans in the early '20s. When she moved to Harlem, she kept her UNIA ties, but also became involved in Republican Party politics. Attracted to the Communist Party by the Scottsboro movement, Moore plunged into its activities with immense energy and enthusiasm, becoming one of its best known women leaders in Harlem, and in New York City as a whole. A big, light-skinned woman with a powerful voice and a taste for flamboyant rhetoric, Moore was a skilled politician, as comfortable with ministers and district leaders as she was with laundry workers or domestics. Her emergence as a Party leader, like that of Williams, symbolized the Party's willingness to adapt to the cultural and organizational proclivities of Harlem's population, a theme Ford emphasized strongly in his writings on the "united front."[32]

The Party's increased "representativeness" brought tensions in its wake. As leaders arose who reflected the perspectives of black working-class women, the Party was forced to conduct internal debates on the explosive subject of relationships between black men and white women. Critics had long accused the Party of using white women as "bait" to attract black men into the movement. Harlem newspapers regularly carried humorous articles on the subject, but the humor veiled resentments that few blacks wished to express as political criticism for fear of condoning segregation. Among black women in the Party, however, the resentments had become too great to suppress. Many black male leaders of the Harlem Section, among them James Ford, Theodore Bassett, Abner Berry, and William

Fitzgerald, had married white women, while the reverse relationship rarely occurred. Moreover, at Party dances and social affairs, black men would often ask white women to dance, leaving black women without partners because few white men were willing to dance with them (in part because of ingrained prejudice, in part because they felt too inadequate as dancers to play the approved male role of initiating contact).³³ By the time Abner Berry arrived in Harlem, a group of black women had taken the extraordinary step of asking the section's leaders to ban interracial marriages in the Party's ranks. Berry, as Party troubleshooter, was assigned to deal with their complaints and he managed with difficulty to convince them that the Party could not take such a step. As he recalled:

> I handled it through theory, quoting from Lenin on the National Question, discussing the experiences of the Jewish Bund in Russia and Eastern Europe, using everything to convince them that it would be counterrevolutionary for the Party to adopt such a position. I agreed that a black man could function better as a revolutionary with a black wife, but said that the Party couldn't take a formal position against such relationships. The whole discussion, for me, was complicated by the fact that I had a white wife myself. Well, I was able to convince them that the Party couldn't outlaw such marriages, that it was something that had to be left to the decision of each individual. We had to change the social conditions within and outside the Party so that the black woman would come into her rightful place.³⁴

The black women's initiative did force changes—albeit subtle ones—in the Party's social atmosphere. A few young black male Communists started what they jokingly called a "movement back to the race," breaking off relationships with white wives and girlfriends in order to find black women as partners. In addition, Party organizers made a concerted effort to teach white male Communists in Harlem to dance, so that they would not be ashamed to ask black women to dance at Party social affairs. These internal "reforms," and the accompanying discussions, did not solve the problem of interracial relationships in the Party; they remained a source of tension as long as the Party was active in Harlem. But the Party's ability to discuss the subject politically and grapple with ways of handling it, reflected its growing sensitivity to the nuances of black life and to the passions and prejudices of the people it hoped to organize.³⁵

During the first three months of 1935, the Harlem Party, buttressed by new leaders and a theoretical orientation emphasizing work within black organizations, served as the hub of an enormous range of activity. In a district-wide recruiting drive, the Harlem Section recruited 314 new members, 92 of them black, bringing the black section membership to nearly 400. Party trade union work in Harlem and its campaign against job discrimination continued to expand, providing a counterweight to nationalist initiatives in the 125th Street area. While Party trade union organizers in Harlem bus and subway terminals, relief bureaus, and stores raised the issue of discrimination against blacks in the course of their organizing, the Young Liberators kept up pressure on the 125th Street chain stores and cafeterias to hire black workers without firing any whites. The Scottsboro-Herndon Action Committee, still at odds with the American Scottsboro Committee, also broadened its base of support. A February, 1935, conference called by the group attracted representatives of the Odd Fellows, the Elks, the Household of Ruth, the Order of Moose, and several black college fraternities.[36]

In addition, Communists formed their first "united front" with the Garvey movement around the question of protecting Ethiopian independence. In December, 1934, the Italian government of Benito Mussolini used the pretext of a border clash between Italian and Ethiopian troops (the Italians were in Somalia) to initiate a campaign to turn Ethiopia into an Italian colony. When Mussolini broadcast a humiliating set of demands upon the Ethiopian government and began mobilizing troops for duty in East Africa, his actions aroused enormous indignation in Harlem, particularly among the fragmented but still vital remnants of the Garvey movement. The UNIA, the Pan-African Reconstruction Association, the African Patriotic League, and the Garvey Club all mobilized to aid Ethiopia, calling variously for a boycott of Italian products, a movement to recruit black American volunteers for the Ethiopian army, and a campaign to drive Italian merchants out of Harlem. To Harlem nationalists, Mussolini's threats seemed an affront to the entire black race and they appealed to Harlem's "race pride" in organizing resistance.[37]

As pro-Ethiopian sentiment in the community grew, Harlem Communists moved swiftly to try to direct the emerging movement into "antifascist" rather than antiwhite channels. In late December, 1934, Abner Berry approached Capt. A. L. King of the New York Division of the UNIA to propose a defense committee which would collect money and supplies for the Ethiopian government and organize mass demonstrations against Italian war plans. The UNIA leaders endorsed the proposal, but declared they would "have nothing to do with whites." Berry expressed this disagreement with King's viewpoint, but decided initially to respect his prejudices. With the help of black Communists Sol Harper and William Fitzgerald, Berry joined Capt. King and I. Alleyne of the UNIA and Arthur Reid of the African Patriotic League in a "Provisional Committee for the Defense of Ethiopia" that brought together a number of Harlem organizations "representing varying degrees of antagonism to all whites."[38]

However, as soon as the group began meeting, the black Communists tried to persuade members of the committee that antifascist whites, particularly antifascist Italians, be involved in the campaign, and that Italian merchants in Harlem not be a target of the committee's attacks. Pointing to picket lines before the Italian consulate by the Italian workers club and demonstrations in East Harlem against the fascist propaganda film "The Man of Courage," black Communists argued that many Italian-Americans were refugees from fascism and would participate in a struggle against Mussolini's government. Most nationalist representatives were suspicious, but Party organizers finally persuaded one leader of the UNIA to appear before the Italian Workers Club to appeal for funds for Ethiopia. "We went to their meeting," Abner Berry recalled, "The chairman called on him to make a speech. Well, he gave the regular speech that a nationalist would be expected to make, the whole business about Ethiopia, what it stood for, and when he got through, he looked at me indignantly and said 'Well, I told them.' And then there was this burst of applause, they gave him money, and he never got through talking about it." Such experiences helped break down some of the hostility to Italian-Americans that Mussolini's action had evoked. Black Communists persuaded the Provisional Committee to accept a program calling for "monster mass meetings . . . a delegation to the Italian consulate, and a city wide parade."[39]

The Committee's first open meeting, held on March 7 at Abyssinian Baptist Church, reflected a complex balance between Communist and nationalist influence. Literature for the meeting emphasized the theme of black unity, and the six featured speakers—Adam Clayton Powell, Jr., J. A. Rogers, A. L. King, Arthur Reid, James Ford, and Willis Huggins, were all black. The "wildly enthusiastic" crowd of 3,000 contained a sizable group of Garveyites, and "Africa for the Africans" appeared on many banners. Nevertheless, most speakers declined to interpret the conflict as a "race war" and tried to deflect hostility away from Italian-Americans. Historian and journalist J. A. Rogers pointed out that "this is not a fight against Italian people" and Rev. Adam Clayton Powell, Jr., defined the culprit as "fascism." Although Ford rejected nationalist suggestions to recruit Afro-Americans for service in the Ethiopian Army, his proposal of a fund-raising campaign and mass interracial demonstrations won praise from some nationalist leaders. "There was some fear that the Communists would not come through with flying colors," Arthur Reid commented, "but the speech of Mr. Ford has stilled that fear. The Communists have proven that all of us can work together." The meeting rejected a proposal for a boycott of Italian merchants in Harlem and approved plans for a protest parade through Harlem and a series of demonstrations at the Italian consulate. For the moment at least, Communists had helped prevent the Ethiopian conflict from stirring up ethnic antagonism between blacks and Italian-Americans, 150,000 of whom lived in East Harlem in close proximity to black neighborhoods.[40]

The Party's actions in this movement offered striking confirmation of James Ford's admonitions to Communists to be "sensible and human" in contact with black organizations and to avoid "an attitude of superiority." By initially respecting the hostility of Garveyites to working with whites, black Communists had won their confidence sufficiently to expose them to experiences that undermined their prejudices.

But in mid-March, 1935, Harlem Communists faced an even more severe test of their effort to forge alliances with important black organizations. After an afternoon and night of rioting provoked by an incident at a Harlem store, Communists found themselves the target of a concerted attempt by the district attorney—supported by several conservative newspapers—to blame them for the disorder, and to restrict their political activities. In response, Communists appealed to black leaders to exonerate them of these charges and join them in a campaign to focus attention on discrimination by the city government. Both campaigns came to a head at a hearing on the Riot sponsored by a mayoral commission, with results that would have a lasting impact on the Party's position in the Harlem Community.

The incident that gave rise to the Harlem Riot took place at the W. H. Kress store on 125th Street, a major target of the Harlem job crusade, and a store which had steadfastly refused to hire black clerks. At 2:30 P.M. on March 19, 1935, the manager of the store observed a teenager named Lino Rivera stealing a knife and dragged him kicking and screaming through the store to place him in the hands of a policeman. When the policeman took the boy to the basement and released him through the back entrance, it set off a rumor among black shoppers that police were beating the boy up. Some began shouting, overturning counters and throwing merchandise on the floor demanding that the boy be taken upstairs. Police sent to quell the disturbance proved unable to quiet the crowd's fears for the boy's safety. At 5:30 P.M., they ordered the store closed and began shoving people through the store's front entrance. By this time the shoppers had been joined on 125th Street by a huge crowd of Harlemites attracted by the tale of the boy's beating, which had become inflated, through retelling, to claims that he was "near death."[41]

These rumors reached the headquarters of the Harlem Communist Party. As dozens of blacks stormed into the Party's offices "in a white heat of rage," Party activists decided to channel their anger into an "orderly, militant protest" against the Kress management. An interracial group of organizers from the Young Liberators, the group which led the Empire Cafeteria boycott, drew up placards with the inscription "Kress

Brutally Beats Negro Child" and established a picket line and a street meeting in front of the store. After the first Young Liberator speakers completed their speeches, which combined denunciations of the Kress management with appeals for black-white unity, someone threw a rock through the window of the Kress store. Police thereupon dragged the speakers from the platform and tried to disperse the crowd.[42]

At this point, a full-scale battle broke out between Harlem residents and police which resembled the Scottsboro riot of the year before. As squads of mounted and foot patrolmen charged into the crowd, enraged Harlem residents threw rocks and bottles at store windows and police. Each time police charged into the crowd, by now numbering 3,000, it dispersed into the side streets, returning to 125th Street when the police retreated. After half an hour of fighting, the police cleared 125th Street, but not before every store window between 7th and 8th avenues had been smashed by the crowd.[43]

Police now expected the disorder to subside, but when a hearse pulled up to its normal parking spot near the back entrance of the Kress store, it gave rise to a rumor that the boy had been killed. Within minutes, the story of the boy's death had spread throughout Harlem, rekindling a new and more ferocious outbreak of rioting. In an area between 120th and 138th streets and Fifth and St. Nicholas avenues, Harlem residents smashed and looted hundreds of stores and showered police with missiles from roofs, hallways, and windows. By the time the disorder ended, one person had been killed, several seriously wounded, and more than 200 Harlemites had been injured or arrested.[44]

Throughout the evening's rioting, black and white Communists circulated throughout the crowds, trying to prevent the outbreak from assuming an antiwhite character and to stop suicidal confrontations between Harlemites and police. Although Young Liberator leaflets repeated the story of the boy's death, other black and white Party organizers began handing out a leaflet which called for "UNITY of Negro and white workers," and warned "Don't let the Bosses Start Race Riots in Harlem." These appeals, reinforced by the long history of white participation in protests against discrimination, may have had some impact on popular attitudes. Almost no whites were physically assaulted in the course of the evening's rioting, and even property attacks lacked a strictly racial character, as some larger black-owned stores were looted by the crowd, and some white-owned stores which hired blacks were left untouched.[45]

Although Communists used their influence to discourage racial conflict, they soon found themselves under attack for fomenting the disorder. Police officials accused Communists of "deliberately spreading the false rumor of the boy's death," and Manhattan District Attorney William

Dodge ordered police raids on Party offices to gather evidence for criminal anarchy indictments. Dodge openly accused Communists of being responsible for the riot, and questioned whether they could safely be extended the right of "free speech."⁴⁶ "We have some pretty good clues," he told reporters. "There's some hot stuff in these pamphlets. Some of them advocate the violent overthrow of the American government. . . . These people take every opportunity, as they did in Harlem this time. That colored boy and the woman who screamed were relatively innocent."⁴⁷

The Hearst newspapers, the *New York Journal* and the *New York American,* endorsed Dodge's accusations. "Investigation . . . by the police and the District Attorney," a *Journal* reporter wrote, "proved beyond doubt that Communist agitators inflamed thousands and led them in an outbreak of violence." An editorial in the *American* described the riot as the "fruit of a long . . . campaign of disloyalty," and wondered whether "Communists have the right to hold public meetings . . . under the false pretext of exercising their right of free speech." Some black Harlem conservatives echoed these charges, claiming foreign-born white Communists were responsible for the trouble. "The peace of Harlem," *Age* editor Fred Moore declared, "was disrupted . . . by people dissatisfied with the place they came from . . . and dissatisfied with American ways," and Urban League official James Hubert claimed that "Communists started the rioting and did most of the damage." Several Harlem ministers called for suppression of Communist speakers, and a white Catholic priest asked his Harlem parishioners to form a movement to "keep white Communists out of Harlem."⁴⁸

The mayor of New York, Fiorello La Guardia, responded more cautiously. While claiming that the disorder was "instigated . . . by a few irresponsible individuals," he declined to name Communists as the "instigators" in question and emphasized that "an outburst like the one which happened . . . doesn't go off unless there was smoldering some underlying feeling." La Guardia appointed a Mayor's Commission on Conditions in Harlem of "eleven representative citizens," with the power to study the disorders in depth and develop proposals to prevent their recurrence. Composed of six blacks and five whites with "distinct liberal leanings," the Commission quickly developed plans to hold public hearings on the riot and on economic and social conditions that jeopardized the "health and safety" of the residents of "colored Harlem."⁴⁹

Harlem Communists responded quickly to attacks on their role in the riot and the prospect of an investigation. On the evening following the riot, Communist streethawkers flooded Harlem with a special issue of the *Daily Worker* that proclaimed "Negro Harlem Terrorized" and called on black and white workers to maintain their unity and avoid "race riot provocations." "The whole world knows that the Communist Party does not believe in . . . provocations, race riots, and looting as a means of solving the terrible conditions of the Negro people," James Ford declared in a press release printed on the *Worker*'s front page. "We have been organizing and teaching the masses that this is not the method to better . . . conditions." Party statements blamed the riot on the "utter misery and suffering" of the people of Harlem and expressed willingness to cooperate with authorities in exposing those conditions. "I believe that if an open investigation is made," James Ford declared, "it would unearth startling facts about the terrible conditions of the Negro people in Harlem. . . . We, the Communist Party, stand ready to give . . . information to such an investigation."[50]

Ford's analysis of the riot coincided closely with that of other black activist leaders. The day after the riot, Rev. Adam Clayton Powell, Jr., invited a select group of Harlemites and white liberals to his apartment to form an Emergency Citizens Committee designed to focus public attention on underlying causes of Harlem unrest. The committee, which included Obie McCullum of the *Amsterdam News,* H. K. Craft of the Uptown YMCA, labor leader Frank Crosswaith, and James Ford, issued a statement attributing the outbreak to "basic economic maladjustments . . . primarily segregation and discrimination against the Negro both private and public as well as in the administration of relief." The group took a strong stand against the "Red Baiting Crusade" launched by the district attorney and the Hearst press, calling it a "miscarriage of justice," and a "tragic diversion of energy."[51]

Comments of liberal Harlem ministers, journalists, and social workers echoed these views. "To make the Communists the scape goat for the riot is only to raise a smokescreen," Rev. John H. Johnson declared. "What happened was actually an economic revolt . . . against the prejudice, exploitation, the unfair practice of many of the stores on 125th Street."[52] Roy Wilkins warned reporters that "the authorities would make a great mistake to dismiss the riot as a demonstration of a few Communists," and *Amsterdam News* editors reinforced this analysis with a series of "Man on the Street" interviews with Harlem residents. The "average Harlemite," the paper concluded, thought "conditions" precipitated the riot: "very few" blamed Communists for initiating the unrest.[53]

Party leaders felt vindicated by such statements and grew increasingly confident that they could survive the political and legal attack leveled against them. They quickly focused their attention on the Mayor's Commission on Conditions in Harlem, which set March 31 as the date of its first hearings and invited "information and suggestions" from the residents of Harlem. Observing the liberal tone of Commission statements,

Party activists concluded they could use the hearings as a platform and began bombarding the Commission with letters asking permission to testify.[54]

At the first hearing, devoted to the immediate causes of the riot, the Party mobilized three of its most articulate black leaders, James Ford, Abner Berry, and Louise Thompson, to present a detailed defense of Communist actions during the disturbance. To add weight to their testimony and to cross-examine police witnesses, it brought in two white ILD lawyers, Edward Kuntz and Joseph Tauber, and Central Committee leader Robert Minor. Minor, a tall, impressive-looking Texan, was one of the Party's best orators, a self-taught student of the law who had defended himself successfully in several political trials and had a reputation for turning courtrooms into forums for Party views. With his help, the Party hoped to demonstrate that the disorders arose spontaneously and to place blame for their occurrence on the Kress management and the police.[55]

The Party's preparation worked to its advantage. The chairman of the hearing, attorney Arthur Garfield Hayes, allowed people from the audience to question witnesses, and Communist attorneys made ample use of this privilege. Backed by a crowd of 600 Harlemites, "most of them volubly Communist," Minor, Tauber, and Kuntz cross-examined over a dozen eyewitnesses to the riot, including representatives of the police, the Kress management, and the Party. The picture that emerged refuted allegations that Communists had purposefully incited violence. Witnesses unanimously agreed that the leaflets issued by the Young Liberators and the Communist Party did not appear on the streets until 8:30 P.M., "fully two hours after the worst of the disorders took place." Although Party spokesmen admitted that they had organized a demonstration without concrete evidence that the boy had been beaten, they received far gentler treatment from the Commission and the crowd than did police. Under cross-examination by Hayes and ILD attorneys, both the police officer who arrested Rivera and the chief police official in Harlem admitted that "the whole outbreak might have been prevented had the police acted differently when the boy was first caught" and had "given proper explanation" to shoppers who feared for the boy's safety. Community residents supplemented this testimony with accounts of police violence in the store and in the streets, evoking cries of indignation from the predominately left-wing audience.[56] "One important fact was established by the Mayor's Committee in its first public hearing," an *Amsterdam News* editorial observed:

> . . . that the shortsightedness of a police officer and not the activities of the Young Liberators and the Communists was the immediate cause of the fatal outbreak. . . . Disappointing as this testimony must be to District Attorney William C. Dodge and Mr. Randolph Hearst . . . it is

well that the issue was settled at the outset by the committee. Now, with the red herring out of the way, the investigating body can set out to probe the basic factors which really precipitated the riots — the discrimination, exploitation and oppression of 204,000 American citizens in the most liberal city in America.[57]

During the next two months, the Harlem Party concentrated the efforts of its best organizers on the Mayor's Commission hearings. The commission divided its work among six subcommittees dealing with major problems in Harlem: crime and police, health and hospitals, housing and recreation, education, discrimination in employment, and discrimination in relief. A total of twenty-five hearings took place under the auspices of these bodies, and the Party used them to present a detailed analysis of discrimination against Harlem residents, backed up by rigorous cross-examination of employers and city officials. This carefully orchestrated performance took place before a very sympathetic audience. The Party called on Harlemites to "pack the courtroom every Saturday at 10 o'clock" to "demand relief, jobs and an end to . . . oppression," and crowds of 700 appeared at some of the hearings. Although many of those who attended came from Communist organizations, the predominately black crowds represented a broad cross-section of Harlem occupations and political perspectives.[58] The most "secure and respectable" joined the poor and unemployed in questioning witnesses, and "popular outbursts" nearly caused the cancellation of several of the sessions.[59]

The Party's activities at the hearings helped strengthen its ties with other Harlem organizations. The representatives of Harlem "labor unions, trade associations, religious, social and political organizations" that came to the hearings shared many of the same concerns about racial problems in New York as Party organizers and cooperated with them closely in exposing Harlem conditions. In style and educational background, the leading black Communists at the hearings, James Ford, Merrill Work, Abner Berry, Ben Davis, Williana Burroughs, and Louise Thompson, had much in common with the middle-class Harlem civic leaders who also testified. Although Communists openly used the hearings as a platform for their political views, they tried to maintain a level of professionalism in the presentation of evidence that would command the respect of their black allies and the Commission. When Party leaders accused a city agency of discrimination, they tried to provide detailed documentation of their charges and supporting testimony from workers in the accused agency.[60] In addition, Party leaders at the hearings conducted their cross-examination of city officials with "consummate skill," translating the "groping, often incoherent queries of the common man into clear searching questions which prevented equivocation and subterfuge." By the end of April, witnesses at the hearings faced a coalition of community activists determined to make discrimination by city agencies a major topic of investigation and to elicit promises from city officials to introduce immediate reforms.[61]

The Party's aggressive posture at the hearings stood in sharp contrast to that of the NAACP, whose New York branch officers lacked a strategy to deal with the issues the riot exposed. "I regretted that the Branch was not represented at the hearings...," Walter White wrote branch president James Egert Allen shortly after the investigation began, "especially as practically every other Harlem group of importance was represented. This was particularly noticeable in that such situations as this is the NAACP's specific job. . . ." Two weeks later, branch officers had still not presented the material on Harlem conditions that the association's national office had made available to them, leaving a vacuum in leadership that Communists were all too glad to fill. "The New York Branch has been completely out of the picture on this riot situation," a disgruntled Roy Wilkins wrote Allen, "and silence and inactivity of the NAACP... is not doing anything to make the organization more popular with the people."[62]

The hearings on relief discrimination, chaired by A. Philip Randolph, offered a particularly effective display of the Party's leadership at the hearings and of the solidarity that emerged between Communists and other Harlem leaders. The Joint Conference on Discriminatory Practices, a coalition between left-wing relief workers and Harlem organizations, had organized protests on this issue since December, 1934, and it used the hearings quite effectively to document its complaints.[63] Relief director Edward Corsi, testifying at the relief committee's first hearing, stirred the audience to fury when he denied that blacks experienced discrimination in work relief programs and lacked access to supervisory jobs in the home relief system. "Among those who harried Corsi continually," the *Age* reported, "were Charles Romney, secretary of the Civil Rights Protective Association..., James W. Ford..., Bernard Riback, representing the Home Relief Employees Association, Robert T. Bess, representing the Consolidated Tenants Leagues...Arnold Johnson, organizer of the Relief Workers organizations...and Rev. William Lloyd Imes, pastor of St. James Presbyterian Church."[64] The questioning of Victor Suarez, supervisor of a Harlem relief precinct, proved even more turbulent. When Suarez engaged in a shouting match with one of his former staff members who accused him of making racist statements, the audience in the hearing grew so disorderly that Randolph ordered the meeting adjourned.[65]

At the next hearing of the subcommittee, Unemployed Council organizers Merrill Work and Fred Benedict, aided by James Ford, presented a lengthy indictment of relief officials—complete with statistics and case histories—accusing them of breaking up families, discouraging needy clients, discriminating against blacks in home and work relief, and failing to appoint black supervisors. Although their presentation drew cheers from the audience, no relief officials appeared to answer their charges. City relief administrator Oswald Knauth, enraged by the atmosphere at the first relief hearing, had instructed his staff not to appear or testify unless the commission took stronger steps to control people in the audience. Knauth's actions proved the beginning of a trend, as other city officials withdrew their staffs from hearings relating to their departments in protest against the freewheeling character of the proceedings.[66]

The withdrawal of city officials from the hearings provoked widespread indignation in Harlem, even among some members of the mayor's commission. "I am unalterably opposed," A. Philip Randolph wrote the commission secretary:

> to any limitation being set upon the freedom . . . to ask questions and give testimony in these hearings. If the people pouring out their pent up wrath and resentment against conditions of oppression, exploitation and discrimination in Harlem . . . takes the form of a "Roman Holiday," then let them have it. The picture and significance of the spiritual and moral awakening on the part of the downtrodden black workers . . . in these hearings are incomparably of much more value than any prim, polite, and pious but timid policy which may elicit the admiration of our critics.[67]

On May 24, the Joint Conference on Discriminatory Practices held a rally at Abyssinian Baptist Church to demand that the mayor give his commission the power to subpoena witnesses and to recommend changes in city policies at the conclusion of each hearing. Shortly thereafter, a group called the "United Societies League for Negro Rights" announced plans for a "Mass trial of employers and city officials" at St. James Presbyterian Church during the last week of June. Although Communists played a role in planning this event and defining its perspective, a number of prominent Harlemites offered cooperation and support. Revs. Adam Clayton Powell, Jr., William Lloyd Imes, and J. W. Brown, Channing Tobias of the YMCA, Elmer Carter of the Urban League, and several physicians and fraternal leaders agreed to serve as "jurors" for the people of Harlem, while Communists Edward Kuntz and Ben Davis and Party sympathizer Loren Miller assumed the role of lawyers for the prosecution.[68]

The breadth of these protests appeared to influence some segments of city government. On June 18, the president of the Board of Aldermen,

Bernard Deutsch, delivered a "vitriolic attack" on discrimination in relief and warned that unless conditions were corrected, Harlem might see a repetition of the March 19 disorders.[69] In a reply to Deutsch's address, relief director Oswald Knauth disclaimed responsibility for Harlem conditions, but announced the appointment of a Negro advisory commission headed by Rev. John H. Johnson to "survey the Harlem situation and make recommendations."[70] During the summer and fall of 1935, home relief officials took several concrete steps to improve relations with the Harlem community. They opened up two new Harlem relief bureaus headed by black supervisors, increased the number of black investigators, and acceded to community demands for the transfer of some "openly chauvinist officials."[71]

The relationships Communists developed at the hearings spilled over into numerous campaigns to improve economic conditions in Harlem. After working with Harlem Communists on a day-to-day basis, and learning to respect their abilities, several influential Harlemites who attended the hearings, and some members of the mayor's commission, became consistent, vocal advocates of a "united front" with Communists. Among these were two popular ministers, Adam Clayton Powell, Jr., and William Imes; a union president, A. Philip Randolph (who had previously been a bitter opponent of the Party); and leaders of the Consolidated Tenants League, the North Harlem Community Council, and the Harlem YMCA. In June and July of 1935, Abner Berry and Ben Davis joined Revs. Powell and Imes in organizing a boycott for jobs at Weisbeckers Market, a large food store on 125th Street, while the Consolidated Tenants League and the Unemployed Council cosponsored several demonstrations demanding increased allocations for relief, full rent payments by the relief bureaus, and the construction of low-rent, public housing.[72]

Later in the summer, these organizations and leaders focused attention on the impact of the newly organized Works Progress Administration on Harlem. Critics of relief practices, recalling the prevalence of discrimination of past public works projects (the CWA and the PWA) feared that the Roosevelt Administration's plan to shift employables on relief to WPA would be disastrous to blacks. With the help of the relief workers' union, a Communist-led coalition of Harlemites organized rallies, marches, and delegations to WPA offices to insist that blacks received their fair share of jobs on WPA projects and had access to skilled positions. These protests, aided by a large concentration of liberals in the WPA hierarchy, achieved some results. The New York WPA office publicly committed itself to the nondiscriminatory administration of local projects and displayed a far greater willingness to hire blacks in skilled positions than previous works administrators.[73]

The protests on relief and housing, in large part, represented the fruit of alliances with middle-class organizations and leaders. The Consolidated Tenants League, organized during a 1934 rent strike in "Sugar Hill," drew its members from the upper and middle strata of the community, and the ministers closest to the Party, Revs. Imes, Powell, and Bishop, represented some of Harlem's largest and wealthiest churches. But Communists still possessed the capacity to organize protests among Harlem's poor, using street meetings and marches as mobilizing vehicles. In June, 1935, Communists led a Harlem-wide campaign against the high price of meat which produced an unprecedented display of coordinated protest activity by black working-class women.[74]

The campaign, launched by Party activists in Jewish sections of the city (where Communists had their strongest neighborhood organizations) spread quickly to Harlem. Harlem Communists, led by Bonita Williams, and aided by nationalist and religious groups, organized a flying squad of black housewives to march through the streets of Harlem demanding that butchers lower their prices by 25 percent. Hundreds of "aroused Negro women" joined the demonstrations, warning butchers of a "repetition of March 19" if they failed to reduce their prices. This appeal, along with the volatile behavior of protesters, helped break the resistance of many Harlem stores.[75] "The strike swept through Harlem with great speed during the weekend," the *Daily Worker* boasted:

> More than a thousand consumers formed a flying squad and moved down Lenox Avenue holding meetings in front of all open stores. All stores between 129th Street and 145th Street, with the exception of L. Oppenheimer's . . . have reduced prices 25%. So great was the sense of power of the workers that when butchers agreed to cut prices, housewives jumped up on tables in front of stores and tore down old price signs and put up new ones. . . . No store held out for more than five minutes after the pickets arrived.[76]

In the second week of the campaign, Communists tried to increase pressure on the meat packers by forcing butcher shops to close completely for four days. More than 300 Harlem butcher shops committed themselves to such a closing after being "visited" by delegations of angry women. But the meat packers, supported by the City Markets Commission, exerted strong pressure on Harlem butchers not to participate in the strike and many reopened their stores before the four-day period ended. With only black and Jewish neighborhoods participating in the strike (reflecting the Party's weakness among other ethnic groups), the movement lacked sufficient power to force concessions from the packers, and butchers had to bring their prices back up in order to make a profit. But meat prices remained lower than they had before the protest, and Party leaders viewed the campaign as an important step in giving Communists greater credibility among black working-class women, a group which had only recently been represented in the leadership of the Party.[77]

The effectiveness Communists displayed in organizing protests at the hearings and in mobilizing broad-based community movements against high rents and prices gave the Party's strategic perspectives far greater weight in Harlem. The Riot, and the hearings that followed, placed Communists on center stage, allowing them to explain the "united front" policy to a large and attentive audience. Never before had black Communists had such an opportunity to rub shoulders with other community leaders, and they used each encounter to emphasize that Communists were "regular folk" and responsible political allies. Party leaders told Harlemites they worked with that Communists could be members of churches and lodges and that Communists would not try to impose their whole political program on their partners in coalitions. Some longtime critics remained skeptical of this approach. "The Communists," Frank Crosswaith wrote Norman Thomas, "having at last discovered that they cannot make headway in Harlem by their usual chauvinistic racial and irresponsible appeal and conduct have been busy forming innocent organizations through which they hope to contact unguarded and misguided people. . . . I have steered clear of their net, for I am convinced . . . that they are not to be trusted with the socio-economic problems of the Negro or the workers as a whole."[78] But other Harlemites seemed willing to take Communists at their word. A. Philip Randolph, a bitter opponent of the Party since the early '20s, became a strong exponent of the united front in the spring of 1935, eliminating anti-Communist themes almost entirely from his speeches and writings. Urban League official Lester Granger, never previously sympathetic to the Party, startled an audience of black social workers in June of 1935 by suggesting that blacks abandon the "dignified approach" and "join the reds in fighting with vulgarity and profanity."[79] And the Father Divine movement newspaper printed a long editorial refuting the "myth" that Communists stood in opposition to "American ideals and government":

> Intelligent members of the Communist Party . . . are rapidly coming to the realization that violence or force cannot contain the answer to their problems. They are . . . becoming convinced that a united front and a peaceful orderly process of the electorate is the best means of obtaining their ends.
> The Communists are the only outstanding organization or party with

enough courage to stand flatly for social equality or equal opportunity, regardless of race, creed, or color. . . . With the unrest gripping the world at the present time . . . every true American and Christian should unite himself with these principles of peace and equality, even if it brings upon him the label of "Communist."[80]

What gave the Party's appeals such force, and made the united front an ethos as much as a strategy, is that its vision extended into culture as well as politics and linked developments in black communities with national and international events. By the spring of 1935, Communists had convinced a good many black intellectuals that the broad forces the Party identified with — the labor movement, the leftist intellectual community, and "sincere opponents of war and fascism" — should be actively courted as allies of black protest. That Communists would play a leading role in such alliances all took for granted, but much of the united front's appeal stemmed from the vagueness of its political categories. In the rhetoric employed by Party spokesmen, you did not have to be a Communist to hitch your wagon to the future — you could contribute almost as much as an ally as a fellow traveller. This gave blacks sympathetic to the left a wide variety of options — they could remain outside the Party, or even join it and leave it, and still be considered part of the "family" so long as they did not attack the Party openly.

The united-front policy opened the way for a significant expansion of Party activity among Harlem's creative intelligentsia — writers, artists, musicians, and theatre people. For the first time, enough of these individuals began to join the Party and its affiliated groups to generate a black cultural movement explicitly identified with the left — aesthetically as well as politically. Shortly after the Harlem Riot, black and white intellectuals close to the Party formed a united-front cultural organization called the "Friends of Harlem" which planned to create "theatre, dance, movie and musical groups based on material dealing with social realism and protest." As its first major project, the group organized a Negro People's Theatre composed of more than twenty black and white actors and actresses drawn from the casts of *Stevedore* and *Green Pastures,* and directed by two black performers with extensive Broadway experience, Rose McLendon and Chick McKinney.[81]

The decision to found a theatre was significant because it was in theatre that the genre of social protest had perhaps the greatest impact on black artists. Prior to the mid-'30s, Broadway dealt with black life largely through the medium of the musical revue, or the romantic folk drama, highlighting the most "exotic" and colorful features of black life. Of the major white playwrights (black dramatists rarely got to Broadway), only O'Neill depicted black characters capable of assertion and rebellion, and the most dramatically challenging roles presented blacks as victims rather than confident agents of change. But in 1934, experimental theatre groups "downtown" produced two dramas that had an enormous impact on the black theatrical community: *They Shall Not Die,* a reconstruction of the Scottsboro case, done by the Theatre Guild, and *Stevedore,* a story of black and white longshoremen on the New Orleans docks, done by the Theatre Union.[82]

Stevedore made a particularly strong impression. Featuring the brilliant dramatic actor Rex Ingram, and the Hall Johnson Choir, the play exposed the feelings of black workers engaging in their first protest action—toward their employers, toward white workers, and toward a group of white radicals offering them support. Harlem performers and critics, with the sound of marches and demonstrations reverberating through their own neighborhoods, thrilled to the opportunity of expressing this dramatically. "For the first time." J. A. Rogers wrote, "Negroes are given the opportunity on stage to talk back to white people and say what's on their minds." But blacks also responded to the play's utopianism. The final scene, where white radical workers joined the black longshoremen in facing a white mob, aroused enormous enthusiasm among blacks in the audience (seated throughout the theatre in defiance of standard Broadway practice); at one performance, dancer Bill Robinson reputedly became so excited that he leaped onto the stage and joined in the fight. Among Harlem's intellectuals, the image of black and white workers uniting in protest had acquired considerable force as a dramatic symbol, reflecting the spread of left-wing political views far beyond the Party's ranks. The final scene may have been "unreal," J. A. Rogers wrote, but it was nevertheless "the best, for it enacts before our eyes, and fixes in our consciousness, what is probably the only real solution to the 'race problem.' . . . The Negro and white workers put the white mob, the henchmen of the capitalist, to flight, as they surely will some day."[83]

Given such enthusiasm for protest themes, it is not surprising that the Negro Peoples Theatre chose for its first presentation the most popular protest drama of the era, Clifford Odets's *Waiting for Lefty.* This play about a New York City taxi strike drew its characters from a Jewish ethnic milieu, but the company "adapted it to Harlem conditions," by substituting the word "Negro" for "Jewish" wherever it appeared in the text and making minor changes in the dialogue to remove inconsistencies. Since black cabdrivers had participated in the strike Odets portrayed, the cast viewed such changes as artistically and politically legitimate. After several weeks of rehearsal, the company unveiled its product to Harlem in a gala "Theatre Night" at the Rockland Palace Ballroom.[84]

The community's response to the event, if not the play itself, thrilled the group's supporters. Some 5,000 people came to the Rockland Palace, "by far the largest group of people ever . . . to see a play in Harlem" and seemed thoroughly to enjoy the performance and the dancing that followed. The company's interpretation of *Lefty* satisfied few critics: even the *Daily Worker* and the *New Masses* felt that it should have rewritten the play extensively in order to better convey "the experiences of the Negro people." But the enthusiasm of the cast and the audience, which included many Harlem notables from the theatre, politics, and the arts, excited even those who found the performance artistically flawed. "Did you think that Father Divine could pack the Rockland Palace," Marvel Cooke wrote in the *Amsterdam News,*

> or the Elks or the International Labor Defense or the Most Righteous Order of Grand So and So? With my hand reaching to heaven, I declare that the Friends of Harlem and the Negro People's Theatre made all of them look puny when these groups interpreted (or should I say, rather, misinterpreted?) Waiting for Lefty at the good old Palace Saturday night.
>
> Although Waiting for Lefty proved to be a tiresome business, partly because Lefty's pals did not quite convince us that they belonged "deep down in the working class," . . . the evening of fun, theatre and festival left me with a good taste in my mouth.

Shortly after the performance, the company announced plans to stage additional full-length dramas based on a "program of social realism."[85]

The movement toward a black theatre of protest posed difficulties for black artists. "Social realist" drama had numerous cliches and conventions: e.g. the conversion, the crisis, and the obligatory concluding strike —that made it difficult to portray human relationships that were not explicitly political. Such difficulties increased in a black setting, where writers and their left-wing critics often felt compelled to emphasize the theme of black-white unity and to counteract popular stereotypes of black behavior. When an artist portrayed blacks as criminals, religious enthusiasts, or hedonists, no matter how accurate that might be in a particular setting, s/he risked the displeasure of Communist critics. Such a fate befell Rex Ingram. At a theatrical benefit for the ILD, Ingram's company put on a play called *Drums Along the Bayou,* which portrayed the radicalization of black workers in Louisiana and their rejection of voodoo for Communism. The final scene, in which the "previously superstitious" workers began "shouting Communist slogans" and the voodoo drums beat a new "supposedly Communist rhythm," horrified *Daily Worker* writer Alice Evans:

> This treatment, presenting Communism for the Negro as a sort of sublimated voodooism, full of hysteria and drum beats, is very danger-

ous, in that it confirms the vicious capitalist myth about the Negro as a jungle creature instead of a human being.

Thinking of the fine self-control, remarkable discipline, and quiet reasoning power of Negro workers, proved in hundreds of struggles ... it becomes extremely regrettable that Rex Ingram should have given us so frenzied a picture of Negro conversion to Communism.[86]

The puritanical and paternalistic perspective taken by this piece—rejecting much that was vital and inventive in black working-class culture—characterized much Communist writing on the black arts in 1935 and before. But despite the crude formulations of some critics, who fortunately did not select which pieces were performed, many black writers and performers found the left-wing community far more supportive of their work than Broadway producers or commercial publishers: it offered them a place to perform, an enthusiastic and generous audience, and contact with well-known white artists in their respective fields.[87] Moreover, many black artists believed that literature or theatre should present an attack on segregation and racism and regarded the protest mode as an outlet for emotions that their predecessors often suppressed. After performing two plays at a Communist summer resort, Negro People Theatre's director Rose McLendon told the audience: "If I die tomorrow, I will die happy. At last, we have a theatre of our own, something I have been wanting for the last fifteen years. Tonight's performance proved it and it proved another thing: that we belong in the left-wing theatre and only in the left-wing movement can we build and maintain such a theatre."[88]

The left's growing political and moral influence among black intellectuals—inspired, but not narrowly defined, by the activities of the Communist Party—emerged with equal clarity in a 1935 petition drive in behalf of Angelo Herndon. In May of that year, the U.S. Supreme Court voted to refuse to hear Herndon's appeal or review the "slave insurrection law" on which his conviction was based, and Communists began a campaign to obtain two million signatures demanding that the Governor of Georgia drop all charges against him (Herndon was currently out on bail). Communists approached the campaign as a prototype of the united front, welcoming support "from every individual and organization ... who believes in free speech ... and the cause of Negro rights." It attracted support from an impressive array of organizations and leaders, many of whom had never previously supported a Communist-initiated movement, among them Father Divine, Norman Thomas, the Harlem Baptists Ministers Alliance, the NAACP, the ILGWU, and several members of the Mayor's Commission on Conditions in Harlem.[89]

Of the supporters of the petition drive, none proved more eloquent than A. Philip Randolph. In a letter to the *New York Age,* Randolph declared that although he did not share the "Communist views of Herndon," he regarded the denial of his appeal as a "serious challenge and a dangerous threat to Negro Americans." "The only way to free Herndon," he declared, "is for Negroes to develop a united front in church, fraternal society, social, political, professional and labor organizations and join with the white radical and liberal movements that are fighting for the downtrodden and the oppressed."[90]

The growing convergence on strategic questions between Communists and influential black ministers, social workers, and trade unionists emerged with equal clarity in the Ethiopian defense movement, whose carefully orchestrated interracialism faced a challenge from Ira Kemp and Arthur Reid. In May, 1935, Kemp and Reid tried to organize a boycott of Italian icemen in Harlem, arguing that money given to Italian merchants went directly to Mussolini and that blacks could advance black interests at home and abroad by "supporting Negro business." Fearful of Reid and Kemp's popularity with Harlem crowds, Communists set up street meetings adjoining theirs to challenge their arguments and tried to isolate them from their base in the Garvey movement. The latter effort proved partially successful. Several leaders of the New York Division of the UNIA, impressed by Italian-American militants that they met at demonstrations and meetings, spoke out against a boycott of the icemen and supported alternative plans for a boycott of Italian imports. In June and July, 1935, the Provisional Committee for the Defense of Ethiopia approached Harlem store owners to demand that they refuse to carry Italian merchandise, and a number of stores, including some owned by Italians, agreed to cooperate. This activity, combined with the participation of Italian radicals in Committee protests at the Italian consulate, helped justify the Party's claim that many of the "most active fighters against Mussolini . . . are the Italian workers." In July, the Provisional Committee voted to condemn the boycott of the icemen and expel Kemp and Reid from its ranks.[91]

With Kemp and Reid temporarily checked, the Party moved to expand the base of the Ethiopian protest movement. On July 11, the Provisional Committee signed an agreement with the American League Against War and Fascism calling for a huge antiwar march through Harlem on August 3 that would unite "all opponents of Italian Fascism." This proposal attracted wide support from Harlem liberals and moderates. Many community leaders welcomed an opportunity to provide Harlem with a display of black-white solidarity at a time when racial feeling was aroused and shared the Party's desire to avoid a conflict with Harlem Italians. Rev. William Lloyd Imes agreed to serve as chief marshal of the parade and leaders of the Urban League, the Brotherhood of Sleeping Car

Porters, and many churches and lodges persuaded their members to endorse it.[92]

This endorsement of left-wing strategy, significantly, came at a time when Soviet policy toward Mussolini's government had come under sharp attack from the NAACP. At the April, 1935, meeting of the League of Nations, Soviet delegate Maxim Litvinov had failed to condemn Italian aggression, and the NAACP sent him a telegram, which it released to black newspapers, asking whether Russia had "abandoned its alleged opposition to imperialism and its much publicized defense of weaker peoples." To add weight to its criticism, the NAACP magazine published an article by George Padmore which argued that the Soviets' evasive stand on Ethiopia stemmed from its decision to cultivate relationships with Western governments as protection against a rearmed Germany. To avoid offending France and England, Padmore argued, the Soviets had changed their image from advocates of revolution and colonial revolt to cautious proponents of European security and had become a reluctant partner in the "united front of white Europe against black Africa." Harlem newspapers gave these charges front-page coverage and endorsed them editorially. "Let the Soviets hope for some gain that seems important to the rulers of that country," the *Amsterdam News* concluded, "and the axe falls, it matters not upon whose neck."[93]

Communists responded to these charges with bitter personal attacks on Padmore and NAACP officials, treating their arguments as "slander" rather than serious criticism. Refusing to debate the content of Soviet diplomacy, Party spokesmen issued sweeping pronouncements about Soviet achievements in building socialism and providing self-determination for oppressed minorities. Straining the credulity of their critics (and some Party supporters) they argued that the interests of the Soviet government and those of oppressed colonial people were *identical,* and that all Soviet policies, however conservative they seemed, served to weaken imperialism and advance world revolution. Such efforts to place Soviet actions entirely above criticism had little effect. Throughout the summer of 1935, Harlem newspapers continued to take every available opportunity to expose inconsistencies in Soviet policies, to poke fun at Soviet pretensions, and to remind black Americans that they could not trust Soviet leaders to make a principled defense of their interests at all times and all places.[94]

Nevertheless, many Harlem organizations worked closely with Communists in planning for the August 3 march. While critical of Party dogmatism regarding Soviet actions, they regarded Communists as an important counterweight to the activities of black nationalists and respected their ability to attract white support for black causes. As endorsements for the march arrived from white "trade unions, church groups, foreign language groups, youth and children's groups, fraternal organizations, organized and unorganized workers," even some of the sharpest critics of Soviet actions rallied to the movement. By the end of July, support for the march in Harlem extended from conservatives like James Hubert and J. Dalmas Steele, to liberals like Roy Wilkins and William Pickens, to militants like Adam Clayton Powell, Jr., and A. Philip Randolph. The presence of two national officers of the NAACP among the sponsors (Wilkins and Pickens) dramatized the march's appeal, although association secretary Walter White, reluctant to form any alliance with Communists, withheld his support.[95]

In preparing for the march, Communists and their allies emphasized the theme of black-Italian unity. "We have no bitterness toward the Italian people," parade marshal William Lloyd Imes told the *Amsterdam News*. ". . . peace-loving and anti-fascist Italians will be marching with us." The physical arrangement of the parade dramatized the effort to unify the two national groups. The parade was to begin as two separate contingents, one led by Italians, the other by blacks, merging into a unified line of march at 129th Street and Seventh Avenue and concluding with a massive outdoor rally.[96]

Sparked by a citywide mobilization of Communists and party sympathizers, the march attracted more than 25,000 participants, making it one of the largest interracial protests in Harlem's history. "Organizations of every description participated in the gathering," the *Age* reported. Pullman porters in uniforms and white gloves, Garveyites in military regalia, followers of Father Divine, Socialists, trade unionists, war veterans, and members of Communist nationalities clubs with banners in fifteen languages, all joined to proclaim their support for Ethiopia and their opposition to war and fascism. But the group that received the warmest reception was the antifascist Italians. The sight of hundreds of Italian-Americans shouting "Down with Mussolini," "Death to Fascism," and "Hands Off Ethiopia," raised "wave after wave of spontaneous cheering" from spectators along the line of march. At the end of the parade, marchers and spectators joined in an open-air meeting, where they listened to speeches, chanted antifascist slogans, and passed resolutions against Mussolini and Hitler.[97]

The August 3 demonstration added greatly to the Party's reputation as a catalyst of mass protest and a force for racial harmony. The *Amsterdam News* praised Italian radicals who "lifted their voice against premier Mussolini as eloquently as any Negro pent up with race consciousness," and editorially denounced nationalist efforts to start a boycott against Italian-American merchants. *Amsterdam News* columnist J. A. Rogers argued that the demonstration called for major changes in black strategic thinking. "When white workers march in such numbers in such cordiality through a Negro neighborhood," he declared, "it is something for Negroes to think very deeply about." Rogers praised Communists for bringing this about, and urged blacks to ally themselves with the Party without relinquishing their independence. "There is a dogmatism and a despotism in Communism," he wrote, "that will always be repellent to liberal minds. It is promised that when Communism gets stronger, these will disappear. But we can take no chances. In any case, it is best not to cultivate these weeds now. We can, however, travel with the Communists as far as they go on our road, and that is a darn sight further than any of the other groups go."[98]

Rogers's comments, ambivalent though they were, offered a striking testimony to the growth of the Party's influence. In the five months since the Harlem Riot, black journalist Loren Miller observed, the Communist Party had "implanted itself in Harlem's life," and had acquired a reputation as an organization that could get things done.[99] After discrediting those who sought to blame them for the riot, Communists had organized numerous protest movements on issues raised in the hearings, organized large interracial coalitions in defense of Ethiopia and Angelo Herndon, and expanded their following among black intellectuals and artists. The Party's black membership had grown commensurately. Between January and August, 1935, the number of black Party members in Harlem rose from 300 to 700 and included recruits from Harlem churches, lodges, professional associations, and nationalist groups.[100]

These successes in Party organizing, significantly, came at a time when Communists publicly deemphasized revolutionary objectives in favor of broad coalitions around practical political issues. Throughout the spring and summer of 1935, Harlem Communists conducted almost all their political work in alliances with non-Communist groups and regularly proclaimed their respect for the organizational and political diversity of the Harlem community. Although this pluralistic position may have been tactical rather than philosophical—a fact dramatized by the Party's crude attacks on critics of Soviet diplomacy and its suppression of internal dissent—it made the Party more acceptable as an ally to Harlemites who retained their faith in the American political system.

So long as Communists did not ask them to relinquish their organizational affiliations or political and religious beliefs, Harlemites could form coalitions with the Party on an issue-by-issue basis without feeling they compromised their integrity. If some voluntarily suppressed criticism of Party policies in order to keep alliances smooth, others made a point of periodically dramatizing their independence.

But the united front, despite cynicism on both sides, had an elan and emotional force which should not be underestimated. The victories achieved by Harlem protests organized by the left, employing direct-action tactics and interracial alliances, had a profound impact on many black intellectuals and political leaders. Deeply shaken by the Depression, which had disrupted their careers as well as their hopes of peaceful change, they now agreed with Communists that relentless protest, in alliance with the labor movement and the left, held the key to black progress. Like Communists as well, they identified the rising power of international fascism with the lynch mobs, employers and politicians who kept black Americans in submission. In this difficult and dangerous period, the united front emerged as a strategy that would end black isolation, that could unite their just claims with the struggles of other insurgent groups. Though first proposed by Communists, it became the property of a new generation of protest leaders, expressed with equal if not greater eloquence by Adam Clayton Powell, Jr., and A. Philip Randolph than any Communist leader.

NOTES

1. For evidence of the new orientation in Party Negro work, see *Daily Worker,* Aug. 6, 1934; *New York Age,* Aug. 25, 1934; and James W. Ford, "The United Front in the Field of Negro Work," *Communist,* 14 (Feb., 1935).

2. On changes in the Comintern view of the fascist danger, and on the origins of the PCF's unity pact with French Socialists, see Fernando Claudin, *The Communist Movement: From Comintern to Cominform* (Hammondsworth, England: Penguin Books, 1975), pp. 171–82, and Daniel Brower, *The New Jacobins: The French Communist Party and the Popular Front* (Ithaca, N.Y.: Cornell University Press, 1968), pp. 11–65. On changes in the CPUSA's strategic outlook during the same period, see Anders Stephanson, "The CPUSA Conception of the Rooseveltian State," (Unpublished thesis, New College, Oxford University, 1977), pp. 23–24; Al Richmond, *A Long View from the Left* (Boston: Houghton Mifflin, 1973), pp. 225–27; and Bert Cochran, *Labor and Communism: The Conflict that Shaped American Unions* (Princeton: Princeton University Press, 1977), pp. 71–77.

3. Perhaps the best examples of the Party's attack on "Negro reformism" were two theoretical articles by Harry Haywood, "The Crisis of the Jim-Crow Nationalism of the Negro Bourgeoisie," *Communist,* 10 (Apr., 1931); and "The Scottsboro Decision: Victory of Revolutionary Struggle Over Reformist Betrayal," *Communist,* 11 (Dec., 1932).

4. Ford, "The United Front in the Field of Negro Work," 169–73.

5. From the Sixth Comintern Congress until the latter part of 1934, none of the major Party theoretical writings of "Negro work" mentioned culture, yet they all described black organizations and their leaders as adversaries. The last theoretical exposition of this position was Harry Haywood's pamphlet, *The Road to Negro*

Liberation, produced for the Eighth Convention of the CPUSA in the spring of 1934. Explicit Party writings on the black arts had an equally sectarian quality, taking an antagonistic stance toward black music or literature that did not flow out of a leftist milieu, or a context of open political struggle. See Eugene Gordon, "Negro Novelists and the Negro Masses," *New Masses,* (May 15, 1934), 29–30.

6. Ford, "The United Front in the Field of Negro Work," 170–73.

7. Interview with Abner Berry, Dec. 2, 1973.

8. Interview with Harry Haywood, May 15, 1973.

9. *Daily Worker,* July 11, 1934; *New York Amsterdam News,* May 26, 1934.

10. Claude McKay, *Harlem, Negro Metropolis* (1940; rpt. New York: Harcourt, Brace, Jovanovich, 1968), pp. 47–49; interview with Abner Berry, Dec. 2, 1973; *Daily Worker,* May 31, 1934, Aug. 6, 1934.

11. *New York Amsterdam News,* Aug. 11, 1934; *Daily Worker,* Aug. 6, 1934.

12. Roi Ottley, *New World A-Coming* (1943; rpt., New York: Arno, 1969), p. 95; McKay, *Harlem, Negro Metropolis,* pp. 35–49; Sara Harris, *Father Divine* (1953; rpt., New York: Macmillan, 1971), pp. 45–48; interview with Abner Berry Dec. 2, 1973.

13. *New York Age,* Aug. 25, 1934.

14. John A. Morsell, "The Political Behavior of Negroes in New York City," (Ph.D. dissertation, Columbia University, 1950), pp. 25–47; George Martin Furniss, "The Assimilation of the Negro into New York City Politics, 1900–1960," (Ph.D. dissertation, Columbia University, 1969), pp. 285–327; Henry Lee Moon, *Balance of Power: The Negro Vote* (New York: Doubleday, 1949), pp. 166–68.

15. James Hooker, *Black Revolutionary: George Padmore's Path from Communism to Pan-Africanism* (New York: Praeger, 1970), pp. 6–10; *New York Amsterdam News,* June 16, 1934, July 14, 1934, July 28, 1934, Aug. 4, 1934, Sept. 1, 1934, Sept. 22, 1934; *Daily Worker,* Aug. 2, 1934.

16. Dan T. Carter, *Scottsboro: A Tragedy of the American South* (New York: Oxford University Press, 1971), pp. 310–13; *New York Amsterdam News,* Oct. 13, 1934; *New York Age,* Oct. 20, 1934; *New York Times,* Oct. 11, 1934, Oct. 13, 1934.

17. *Daily Worker,* Oct. 12, 1934, Oct. 14, 1934, Oct. 31, 1934; *New York Times,* Oct. 12, 1934, Oct. 13, 1934; Carter, *Scottsboro,* p. 313.

18. *Ibid.,* p. 314; telegram, American Scottsboro Committee Inc., to the Hon. Franklin D. Roosevelt, Nov. 15, 1934, ILD Papers, Reel 2, C 39; *New York Amsterdam News,* Oct. 13, 1934, Nov. 24, 1934.

19. *New York Age,* Oct. 27, 1934; press release, Provisional Scottsboro Defense Committee, Oct. 18, 1934, ILD Papers, Reel 2, C 175; *Daily Worker,* Oct. 20, 1934, Oct. 32, 1934, Nov. 10, 1934; *New York Amsterdam News,* Nov. 3, 1934.

20. Rev. Shelton Hale Bishop to Mr. George E. Haynes, Nov. 1, 1934, ILD Papers, Reel 3, C 48.

21. Walter White to Will Alexander, Oct. 23, 1934, NAACP Papers, D 73. Also Walter White to Arthur Spingarn, Nov. 19, 1934, *ibid.,* D 74.

22. *Daily Worker,* Nov. 28, 1934, Dec. 7, 1934; Open Letter, National Scottsboro-Herndon Action Committee to American Scottsboro Committee, Nov. 28,

1934, ILD Papers, Reel 3, C 47; Slater Brown, "We'll Let Them Take Their Medicine," *New Masses*, 13 (Dec. 4, 1934), 14.

23. *New York Age*, Dec. 15, 1934.

24. Carter, *Scottsboro*, p. 319.

25. Ford and Sass, "The Development of Work in the Harlem Section," 316–23.

26. *Ibid.*, 312.

27. In mid-October, 1934, Patterson's name abruptly disappeared from the Party press. Over half a year later, an article appeared in the *Negro Liberator*, May 15, 1935, saying that "Patterson's health was broken through almost superhuman effort in behalf of the Scottsboro boys" and that he had gone to the Soviet Union for medical treatment. Whether this is an accurate explanation of Patterson's departure is difficult to corroborate. Patterson's autobiography, *The Man Who Cried Genocide*, does not mention the collapse and merely indicates that he went to the Soviet Union and returned in the late '30s to become a top Party leader in the Chicago district (and to marry Louise Thompson). It also mentions nothing about his four years in the Soviet Union. One possible explanation for Patterson's departure is dissatisfaction with his handling of the Scottsboro defense, which broke up into competing factions shortly before his "colllapse," but no available evidence confirms this speculation. Certainly, Patterson's standing in the Communist movement remained high; three articles appeared under his imprimatur during the summer of 1935 — "The Abyssinian Situation and the Negro World," *International Press Correspondence*, 15 (May 11, 1935); "Negro Harlem Awakens," *Negro Worker*, 5 (July–Aug., 1935); "World Politics and Ethiopia," *Communist*, 14 (Aug. 1935). Was he on "special assignment" in the Soviet Union? The whole episode deserves further investigation.

28. Interview with Abner Berry, Dec. 2, 1973; interview with Theodore Bassett, Dec. 15, 1973; interview with George Charney, Nov. 7, 1973. On Johnson, see also McKay, *Harlem Negro Metropolis*, p. 216.

29. On Ashford, see *Daily Worker*, Sept. 21, 1936; and *Young Communist Review*, 1 (Oct., 1936), 2.

30. *Negro Liberator*, Dec. 1, 1934; Charney, *A Long Journey*, p. 97; interview with Samuel Coleman, Apr. 20, 1970.

31. Interview with Abner Berry, July 29, 1974; interview with Theodore Bassett, Nov. 2, 1973.

31. *Daily Worker*, July 22, 1934; *Negro Liberator*, July 1, 1935; Max Steinberg, "Achievements and Tasks of the New York District," *Communist*, 14 (May, 1935), 453; Charney, *A Long Journey*, p. 102; interview with Abner Berry, Nov. 20, 1973; interview with Audley Moore, May 3, 1974.

33. *New York Amsterdam News*, Sept. 15, 1934, Feb. 9, 1935; *New York Age*, Jan. 19, 1935; McKay, *Harlem Negro Metropolis*, pp. 204, 232–37; interview with Theodore Bassett, Dec. 15, 1973.

34. Interview with Abner Berry, Nov. 20, 1973.

35. Interview with Abner Berry, Dec. 2, 1973; interview with Theodore Bassett, Dec. 15, 1973; Charney, *A Long Journey*, pp. 102–3.

36. Steinberg, "Achievements and Tasks of the New York District," 449; *Daily Worker*, Feb. 1, 1935, Feb. 26, 1935, Mar. 9, 1935; *Negro Liberator*, Feb. 15,

1935; leaflet, "To All Store and Office Workers on 125 Street, Negro and White," La Guardia Papers, Box 668; "The Red Signal," no date, *ibid.*

37. Thomas M. Coffey, *Lion By the Tail* (New York: Viking Press, 1975), pp. 6–42; George W. Baer, *The Coming of the Italian-Ethiopian War* (Cambridge: Harvard University Press, 1967), p. 101; *Daily Worker,* Mar. 25, 1935; William Patterson, "The Abyssinian Situation and the Negro World," *International Press Correspondence,* 15 (May 11, 1935), 542.

38. James W. Ford, "For Defense of Ethiopia," *Negro Worker,* 5 (May, 1935), 5–6; interview with Abner Berry, Dec. 2, 1973; *Daily Worker,* Mar. 25, 1935.

39. *Daily Worker,* Feb. 13, 1935, Feb. 15, 1935, Mar. 25, 1935; *Negro Liberator,* Jan. 15, 1935; interview with Abner Berry, Dec. 2, 1973.

40. Leaflet, "Mass Protest Meeting!! Defend Ethiopia!!," Universal Negro Improvement Association Papers, Schomburg Collection, Box 15, Reel 6 (hereafter referred to as UNIA Papers); *New York Amsterdam News,* Mar. 9, 1935; *Negro Liberator,* Mar. 15, 1935; Ford, "For Defense of Ethiopia," 6.

41. *Report of the Mayor's Commission on Conditions in Harlem,* pp. 2–4; *New York Times,* Mar. 20, 1935, Mar. 31, 1935; *Daily Worker,* Mar. 29, 1935; *New York Age,* Mar. 20, 1935, Mar. 23, 1935.

42. *Daily Worker,* Mar. 29, 1935; *New York Age,* Apr. 6, 1935; *Report of the Mayor's Commission on Conditions in Harlem,* p. 3.

43. *Ibid.,* p. 3; *New York Herald Tribune,* Mar. 20, 1935.

44. *New York Times,* Mar. 20, 1935; *Report of the Mayor's Commission on Conditions in Harlem,* p. 3.

45. *Ibid.,* p. 3; *New York Times,* Aug. 10, 1935; leaflet, "Child Brutally Beaten," La Guardia Papers, Box 668; leaflet, "For UNITY of Negro & White Workers!," *ibid.*; interview with Abner Berry, Dec. 2, 1973; *Daily Worker,* Mar. 21, 1935; *New York Evening Journal,* Mar. 23, 1935; William Patterson, "Negro Harlem Awakens," *Negro Worker,* 5 (July–Aug., 1935), 26–27.

46. *New York Herald Tribune,* Mar. 20, 1935, Mar. 22, 1935; *New York Times,* Mar. 21, 1935, Mar. 22, 1935; *Daily Worker,* Mar. 25, 1935.

47. *New York Herald Tribune,* Mar. 26, 1935.

48. *New York American,* Mar. 20, 1935, Mar. 21, 1935, Mar. 22, 1935; *New York Evening Journal,* Mar. 20, 1935, Mar. 23, 1935; *New York Age,* Mar. 23, 1935; *New York Herald Tribune,* Mar. 21, 1935; *New York Amsterdam News,* Mar. 30, 1935.

49. *New York Herald Tribune,* Mar. 21, 1935; *New York Times,* Mar. 21, 1935, Mar. 26, 1935.

50. *Daily Worker,* Mar. 21, 1935.

51. *New York Times,* Mar. 21, 1935; *New York Herald Tribune,* Mar. 21, 1935; *New York Amsterdam News,* Mar. 30, 1935,

52. *New York Age,* Mar. 30, 1935.

53. *New York Amsterdam News,* Mar. 30, 1935. Wilkins's comments appeared in *New York Times,* Mar. 22, 1935.

54. *Daily Worker,* Mar. 23, 1935, Mar. 25, 1935; *New York Times,* Mar. 26, 1935; Harlem Section, International Labor Defense, to Chairman, Mayor's Committee to Investigate Harlem Conditions, Mar. 25, 1935, La Guardia Papers, Box 667; James W. Ford to Chairman, Mayor's Committee of the Investigation on

Conditions in Harlem, Mar. 25, 1935, *ibid.,* Box. 2550 H #11.

55. *Daily Worker,* Mar. 23, 1935; interview with Abner Berry, July 29, 1974.

56. *New York Herald Tribune,* Mar. 31, 1935; *New York Age,* Apr. 6, 1935.

57. *New York Amsterdam News,* Apr. 6, 1935.

58. *Negro Liberator,* May 1, 1935; *Hillside Leader,* May 29, 1935, in La Guardia Papers, Box 2550, H #10; "Murder in Harlem," *New Masses,* 15 (Apr 6, 1935), p. 6.

59. *Report of the Mayor's Commission on Conditions in Harlem,* pp. 5-6.

60. *New York Times,* Apr. 14, 1935; May 12, 1935, Section 4; *Daily Worker,* Apr. 20, 1935.

61. *Report of the Mayor's Commission on Conditions in Harlem,* p. 6.

62. Walter White to James Egert Allen, Apr. 1, 1935, NAACP Papers, G 144; Roy Wilkins to James E. Allen, Apr. 15, 1935, *ibid.*

63. Arnold P. Johnson to Mayor's Commission Investigating Conditions in Harlem, May 3, 1935, La Guardia Papers, Box 2550, H #5; *Negro Liberator,* Apr. 15, 1935.

64. *New York Age,* May 4, 1935.

65. *Ibid.; New York Times,* Apr. 25, 1935.

66. *New York Times,* May 12, 1935, Section 4; *New York Age,* May 18, 1935.

67. A. Philip Randolph to Mrs. Eunice H. Carter, May 29, 1935, La Guardia Papers, Box 2550, H #7.

68. Leaflet, "Big Mass Trial," La Guardia Papers, Box 2550, H #7; *Negro Liberator,* June 1, 1935, June 15, 1935, July 1, 1935; *New York Amsterdam News,* June 22, 1935.

69. *Ibid.; New York Times,* June 19, 1935.

70. *Ibid.,* June 20, 1935.

71. *Report of the Mayor's Commission on Conditions in Harlem,* p. 10; *New York Age,* Sept. 28, 1935; *Daily Worker,* July, 1935.

72. Interview with Abner Berry, Dec. 2, 1973; *Daily Worker,* July 22, 1935, Jan. 13, 1936; leaflet, "Protest Terror at Mayor's Committee Hearings," La Guardia Papers, Box 667; *Negro Liberator,* May 1, 1935, June 15, 1935; Draft Program Joint Conference on Discriminatory Practices, Aug. 22, 1935, La Guardia Papers, Box 667; leaflet, "An Open Letter to Harlem Tenants," *ibid.*; leaflet, "Harlem Tenants Wake Up!," *ibid.*

73. Josephine Chain Brown, *Public Relief, 1929–1939* (1940; rpt. New York: Octagon Books, 1971), pp. 324-25; Harry Dolimer and Allan MacKenzie, *The Negro Worker in the ERB* (New York: Association of Workers in Public Relief Agencies, 1937), pp. 5-9; *Negro Liberator,* July 15, 1935; *New York Age,* Sept. 28, 1935, Oct. 26, 1935; *New York Amsterdam News,* Oct. 5, 1935, Mar. 14, 1936; *Daily Worker,* Oct. 19, 1935; *New York Times,* Nov. 14, 1935.

74. *New York Amsterdam News,* Aug. 19, 1935; *Daily Worker,* June 3, 1935.

75. *Ibid.,* June 3, 1935, June 4, 1935; *New York Age,* June 15, 1935.

76. *Daily Worker,* June 3, 1935.

77. *New York Age,* June 22, 1935; leaflet, "Housewives, Consumers of Harlem!" La Guardia Papers, Box 667; Ann Barton, "Revolt of the Housewives," *New Masses,* 15 (June 18, 1935), 18-19.

78. Frank R. Crosswaith to Norman Thomas, June 17, 1935, Norman Thomas

Papers, New York Public Library.

79. *New York Age,* June 15, 1935. The comments by Granger appear in an article in the *Daily Worker,* June 15, 1935.

80. *The Spoken Word,* May 25, 1935.

81. Interview with Abner Berry, Nov. 20, 1973; *Daily Worker,* May 28, 1935, May 29, 1935; Lofton Mitchell, *Black Drama* (New York: Hawthorn Books, 1967), p. 100. The "Friends of Harlem" included prominent Harlemites from the arts, the church, and local politics. Among its sponsors were Reverends Adam Clayton Powell, Jr., and Shelton Hale Bishop, writers Jean Toomer and Countee Cullen, artists Augusta Savage and Aaron Douglass, and sports promoter Robert Douglass. John E. Velasco to UNIA, no date, UNIA Papers, Real 4, Box 11, E 62.

82. Jay Williams, *Stage Left* (New York: Charles Scribner's Sons, 1974), pp. 16–18; Mitchell, *Black Drama,* pp. 94–96; *New York Amsterdam News,* Feb. 28, 1934, May 5, 1934.

83. Williams, *Stage Left,* pp. 114–17; Mitchell, *Black Drama,* pp. 97–98. The quotes from Rogers are taken from an article he wrote in *New York Amsterdam News,* May 26, 1934.

84. "The Negro People's Theatre," *New Masses,* 15 (June 4, 1935), 28; *New York Amsterdam News,* June 1, 1935.

85. *New York Times,* June 30, 1935, Section 10; *Daily Worker,* June 5, 1935; "The Negro People's Theatre," *New Masses,* 15 (June 11, 1935), 27; *New York Amsterdam News,* June 8, 1935.

86. *Daily Worker,* May 16, 1935.

87. Interview with Ernest Rice McKinney, Nov. 1, 1973; *Daily Worker,* July 18, 1936.

88. *Ibid.,* Aug. 16, 1935.

89. *Negro Liberator,* June 1, 1935; *Daily Worker,* May 23, 1935, July 20,1935; *New York Amsterdam News,* June 22, 1935, July 27, 1935; "Comrade Browder (U.S.A.)," *International Press Correspondence,* 15 (Aug. 28, 1935), 1062.

90. *New York Age,* June 15, 1935.

91. *New York Amsterdam News,* Apr.27, 1934; *Negro Librator,* July 1, 1934, July 15, 1935; leaflet, "Defend Ethiopia, Don't Buy Italian Merchandise, Buy from NEGROES!" UNIA Papers, Reel 4, Box 11; *New York Times,* July 7, 1935; *Daily Worker,* July 25, 1935, July 27, 1935.

92. *Daily Worker,* July 12, 1935; *New York Amsterdam News,* Aug. 3, 1935; *New York Age,* Aug. 3, 1935.

93. *New York Age,* June 1, 1935; George Padmore, "Ethiopia and World Politics," *Crisis,* 42 (May, 1935), 138–39; *New York Amsterdam News,* June 15, 1935, July 27, 1935.

94. *Daily Worker,* June 29, 1935; William L. Patterson, "World Politics and Ethiopia," *Communist,* 14 (Aug., 1935), 723–24.

95. *New York Amsterdam News,* Aug. 3, 1935; *Daily Worker,* July 21, 1935, July 23, 1935; William Pickens to Allen Taub, July 22, 1935, NAACP Papers, C 297. White received an invitation to sponsor the demonstration, which included mention of Wilkins's and Pickens's support, but he filed the letter "No Reply." See Allen Taub to Walter White, July 24, 1935, *ibid.*

96. *New York Amsterdam News,* Aug. 3, 1935; *New York Age,* Aug. 3, 1935; *Daily Worker,* July 31, 1934.

97. *Ibid.*; Aug. 4, 1935; *New York Times,* Aug. 4, 1935; *New York Amsterdam News,* Aug. 10, 1935; *New York Age,* Aug. 10, 1935; *Baltimore Afro-American,* Aug. 10, 1935.

98. *New York Amsterdam News,* Aug. 10, 1935

99. Loren Miller, "Harlem Without Make-Up," *New Masses,* 16 (Aug. 13, 1935), 14.

100. Interview with Abner Berry, July 29, 1974; *Daily Worker,* Aug. 3, 1935.

PART TWO

7

The Popular Front and the Origins of the National Negro Congress

DURING THE SUMMER OF 1935, Communist Parties throughout the world gathered in Moscow to confirm a new political strategy that made resistance to fascism the International's preeminent objective. Frightened by the growing belligerence and power of Hitler's Germany and the rise of fascist movements throughout much of Europe, the Soviet leadership decided to seek collective security agreements with Western democracies and to focus the energies of Communist Parties on preventing right-wing governments from coming to power. Using the World Congress—the highest Comintern body—as their stage, the Soviets called on Communists everywhere to abandon temporarily their goal of a revolutionary conquest of power and join with Socialists, trade unionists, and liberals in a "Broad People's Front" to stop the rise of fascism and prevent a new world war. To give Communist policies greater appeal, they instructed parties in Western democracies to assume the role of defenders of the democratic tradition, fighting to "extend the hard won democratic rights of the masses," and prevent the abolition of bourgeois democratic liberties. They hoped that such a program would attract the middle class as well as workers and broaden the base of antifascist activity.[1]

The new Comintern program aroused considerable excitement within the CPUSA. Even before the World Congress, many sections of the American party, recognizing the absence of revolutionary (or even socialist) sentiment among the people with whom they were working, had in practice abandoned revolutionary agitation in favor of coalitions for practical reforms. As seen in Chapter 6, this had been occurring with considerable force in Harlem. But the Comintern now invested this change in policy with a romantic aura and a sense of revolutionary duty. The new Comintern program simultaneously instructed Communists to put themselves at the service of the Soviet state ("We do not only defend the Soviet Union in general," Italian Party leader Palmiro Togliatti told the Congress, "we defend concretely its whole policy and each of its acts,") and identify with the national traditions and culture of the countries they lived in. Contradictory though this was, it spoke perfectly to the split personality of many American Communists, who, while loyal to the Soviet Union, were anxious to transcend their position as outsiders (ethnic as well as political) in the American nation. Seeing an opportunity to expand their influence, American Party leaders began to dramatically recast the Party's image, "to come forward as the bearers and pioneers of that revolutionary tradition out of which the United States was born." They returned from the Congress with a program that emphasized work within established trade unions (AFL or independent), the organization of a Farmer-Labor Party, and the development of alliances with liberals and Socialists to protect civil liberties, extend Negro rights, and prevent the domestic and international growth of fascism.[2]

The Seventh World Congress inaugurated a period of Party history— the Popular Front—which represented the high point of Communist influence in the United States. During the next four years—until the Nazi-Soviet Pact undermined its credibility and forced the abandonment of its antifascist stance—the American Communist Party launched a dramatic attempt to adapt its ideology, tactics, and structure to American political conditions. Beginning in 1936, the CPUSA leadership, anxious to increase its electoral influence and to develop smooth working relations with antifascist liberals, deemphasized conspiratorial features of the Party's local organizations and sought to cultivate an image as a "responsible American organization." Party leaders enlarged their neighborhood units, renamed them "branches," and encouraged them to open public headquarters, reorganized their sections to conform with election district lines, and reduced the workload of Party members to allow more time for leisure and family life. In addition, Party leaders, beginning in 1938, dissolved their "shop units" or fractions in industry to remove the suspicion that Communists aimed to dominate the trade unions they worked in and thus gave Communist trade union leaders considerable freedom to work out policies that protected their position in the CIO hierarchy.[3]

The Party's program and rhetoric also changed substantially. During the 1936 Presidential election campaign, Party candidate Earl Browder, discarding bolshevik terminology, declared that "Communism is 20th Century Americanism" and that Communists "were the most consistent fighters for democracy for the enforcement of the democratic features of our Constitution, for the defense of the flag and the revival of its glorious revolutionary traditions." In succeeding years, Browder spoke of the possibility of an American path to socialism that deviated from the Soviet model, claiming that the Party abjured force and violence except in self-defense, and had no wish to impose socialism on the American people if the majority of the population opposed it. To show that the Party's commitment to democracy was sincere, Browder proclaimed that the Party respected differences of opinion among "progressives" and would deal with them in a principled manner. "To our allies in the fight against fascism," he wrote, "we pledge the use of democratic methods as the sole means of resolving disputes between us."[4]

Significantly, this public endorsement of American democracy involved no change in the hierarchical process of decision making *within the Party*. At the very same time that the Party proclaimed its respect for the Bill of Rights, it warned members that it would continue to ban factions, limit political discussion to issues defined by the leadership, and "burn out any tendency to irresponsible political gossip with a red hot iron." An outline for new members classes, printed during December, 1936, reaffirmed the authority of the Comintern over the U.S. Party and the basic principles of democratic centralism—"subordination of the minority to the majority," "subordination of the lower bodies to the higher bodies," and "iron party discipline."[5]

Nevertheless, the changes in the Party's organization and program proved to be far more than cosmetic. Once initiated, the policy of alliance with American liberalism set in motion forces which were difficult to reverse. As institutional power within American society became the Party's major objective, and "socialism" receded to the status of a distant dream, it attracted a large number of American-born cadre who viewed it as the most efficient vehicle available for combatting fascism and accelerating social reform. Educated in American schools, brought up on radio and movies and sports, they felt the pull of the "American Dream," tarnished though it was by depression and poverty, and they longed for respectability and success in their native land. Unwilling to challenge the principles that stood at the core of the Party's identity—and which Comintern authority enforced—they pushed the Party as far as they dared to accommodate it to practical politics and American popular culture, and with Browder's blessing, tried to infuse Party life at the grass roots with greater dynamism and flexibility. Rising quickly to positions of influence in the Party apparatus, these young Communists, many of them of Jewish ancestry, invested Americanization with a romantic aura and displayed considerable aptitude for the coalition building and political maneuvering that the new policies implied.[6]

In Harlem, Americanization, which made the Party's program and rhetoric indistinguishable from that of many black liberals, brought Communists an easy acceptance in community affairs that had been denied them in the past. "The launching of the Popular Front," Claude McKay wrote, "simultaneously with the New Deal WPA, gave the Communists . . . vast influence among colored professional groups." Although

Party membership in Harlem grew only marginally beyond 1936 levels, Communists became a recognized force in Harlem politics, exerting a power far beyond their numbers. "Communist Party headquarters," a *Saturday Evening Post* writer observed:

> is a place where every Negro with a grievance can be sure of prompt action. If he has been fired, the Communists can be counted on to picket his employer. If he has been evicted, the Communists will guard his furniture and take his case to court. If his gas has been cut off, the Communists will take his complaint, but not his unpaid bill, to the nearest office. . . . There is never a labor parade, nor a mass meeting of any significance in the colored community, in which Communists do not get their banner in the front row and their speakers on the platform.[7]

Unlike the early '30s, the Party's influence in Harlem came to rest on a significant degree of institutional power. Communists obtained an influential, and sometimes dominant role, in numerous city unions, in the relief system and the WPA, and in a newly formed third party that promised to become a force in city politics—the American Labor Party. Wheeling and dealing like Tammany stalwarts, they developed close working relationships with many leading Harlem ministers, social workers, and politicians. During the Popular Front years, Adam Clayton Powell, Jr., referred to Communists in his weekly column as "my brothers in red," and Lester Granger described James Ford, in an *Opportunity* book review, as "my good friend." Liberal Harlem politicians worked closely with Communists in drafting legislation and coordinating lobbying at the state legislature and occasionally sought and won Communist endorsement for their election campaigns. A writer for *Interracial Review,* a Catholic journal devoted to countering Communist influence, observed sadly that "Communism has come off the street corners of Harlem and is appealing to the educated Negroes, winning among them leaders who shall bring the black race to Marx."[8]

The Party's movement into the mainstream of black life, as we have seen, began well before the Seventh Comintern Congress—as early as the summer of 1934, the Party had begun pursuing "united-front relationships" with important black organizations. But the changes in Party policy that followed the Seventh World Congress, some immediate, some gradual, brought about a qualitative change in its relations with nonradical blacks, making the Party seem far more accessible, and less threatening.

During the fall of 1935, the Party leadership took several steps to make

the guiding principles of Party "Negro work" more in tune with the pragmatic policies and outlook of major black organizations. At the November, 1935, meeting of the Central Committee, Party leaders formally
abandoned "self-determination in the Black Belt" as an agitational point
in the Party's organizing and decided to concentrate on immediate issues
such as disfranchisement, discrimination in employment and denials of
civil rights. Dissolving the League of Struggle for Negro Rights, the organization most identified with the self-determination program, it redirected its energies into building support for the National Negro Congress,
a nationwide federation of black organizations which it had helped to
launch. The congress idea, which had arisen almost simultaneously in
Party circles and among some influential black liberals critical of New
Deal racial policies, became the primary focus of Party "Negro work."
To facilitate its growth, vestiges of earlier, more "sectarian" policies were
removed. In December, 1935, the Party disbanded the *Negro Liberator,*
the newspaper of the League of Struggle for Negro Rights, and moved its
editorial staff to the *Daily Worker.* From this time, the Party concentrated
its coverage of black political, cultural, and economic life in the pages of
the *Daily Worker* and the *New Masses* and tried to increase circulation of
these organs in black communities.[9]

In Harlem, the strategic orientation mandated by the Seventh World
Congress gave Communists additional flexibility in pursuing alliances
with black organizations and leaders, particularly those representing
middle-class constituencies. Without relinquishing an emphasis on mass
protest action, Party leaders began to speak of extending the "united
front" into electoral politics, of forming a labor party embracing "liberals, radicals and all workers, manual, white collar and professional."[10]
This recognition of the importance of elections helped narrow the gap between the Party and influential Harlemites who took questions of political power and patronage seriously. Combined with other new features of
Party policy—notably its willingness to let other leaders serves as spokespersons for Party-organized coalitions—it reinforced the Party's image
as a "respectable American organization" able to wheel and deal effectively in the world of practical politics.[11]

But the introduction of the People's Front in Harlem took place against
a background of controversy. In mid-August, 1935, during the height of
the Seventh World Congress, Herman Mackawain, the once-prominent
leader in the Harlem section, resigned in protest from the Party, issuing a
long statement of explanation to the black press. Mackawain complained
of the suppression of internal dissent by the Harlem Party leadership,
both during the Harlem jobs movement (1933–34) and in current protests
in behalf of Ethiopian independence. Attacking the Soviet Union's refusal to halt trade with Italy or publicly condemn its aggression, he accused

Russia of abandoning revolutionary activities in Africa and Asia to appease its European allies and spoke of a "campaign of harassment" against Communists who brought the issue up.[12]

A *New York Times* story in early September, reporting Soviet sales of coal tar, wheat, and oil to Italy at below market price, added fuel to Mackawain's charges. Although the Soviets finally spoke out against Italian aggression at a meeting of the League of Nations, Harlem newspapers seized upon their trade policies as yet another sign that "the Soviet Union cannot be counted to stand steadfast as far as Negroes are concerned." The October, 1935, *Crisis,* speaking for the NAACP, contained an editorial complaining of the "shameless" opportunism of the Soviet Union and the "holier-than-thou" attitude of Communists, accompanying it with a year-and-a-half-old "Open Letter," from George Padmore to Earl Browder explaining his disillusionment with Comintern policies.[13]

Such charges—repeated and embellished by nationalist street speakers —appeared to have an impact on the Party's rank and file. Although Party leaders denied the *Times* story and pointed to demonstrations by Communists worldwide protesting Italian aggression, they did not quell the doubts of all their supporters, especially those who came from nationalist backgrounds. Pressed to explain to friends and family members why "Russia sold Ethiopia out," many found Party membership too great a burden and quietly left the organization. Although the black membership in Harlem did not go down, it ceased its rapid growth, as losses sustained on Ethiopia almost equalled gains made during other campaigns.[14]

Nevertheless, the turmoil about Soviet diplomacy did not hinder cooperation between Communists and most Harlem organizations. Communists took an extraordinarily conciliatory approach to non-Party critics, gently chiding them for "slander mongering" when unity was the order of the day. "Would it not be better," Earl Browder asked NAACP leaders in a *Crisis* article, "if instead of attacking us, you would combine forces with us in fighting for Negro rights, for Angelo Herndon, for the Scottsboro boys, and for the defense of Ethiopia. We would welcome cooperation with you for these things, in place of having to answer your attacks, which is indeed an unpleasant duty."[15]

NAACP leaders, in turn, showed little inclination to quarantine the left on the Ethiopian question. Walter White and W. E. B. Du Bois were among the featured speakers at a September "Hands Off Ethiopia" rally at Madison Square Garden sponsored by the American League Against War and Fascism, and following Mussolini's full-scale invasion of Ethiopia in October, the New York branch of the NAACP endorsed a League-sponsored "People's March for Peace." Whatever doubts association leaders possessed about Communist sincerity, groups like the league represented the only force mobilizing large numbers of people in behalf of

Ethiopia's independence (9,000 at the Garden rally, 15,000 at the March). Association leaders did not want to isolate themselves from that constituency, especially since no restraints on "free speech" governed their participation in League protests.[16]

In addition, many black leaders stood shoulder-to-shoulder with Communists on questions of protest strategy. At the Madison Square Garden rally, Benjamin McLaurin of the Brotherhood of Sleeping Car Porters, Capt. A. L. King of the UNIA, and Rev. William Lloyd Imes all made speeches describing the fight for Ethiopian independence as a worldwide struggle of the oppressed of all races. "This is a fight of the masses against the classes," King declared. "We black people will join you liberal whites all over the world not only to protect the rights of Negroes, but in the interest of all mankind." Rev. Imes called on the audience to "stop sneering at radicals for they serve as a gadfly to goad us from our complacency," and Benjamin McLaurin "brought down the house" with an impassioned plea for working-class unity. "When the next war is fought," McLaurin declared, "it must be a workers war — a war of the workers, Negro and white, against their oppressors."[17]

Communists accompanied such demonstrations with a campaign to provide material aid for the Ethiopian government. In cooperation with several black physicians, they set up a "Medical Committee for the Defense of Ethiopia" in August, 1935, that worked to collect funds and medical equipment for the Ethiopian army. Harlem's medical community rallied enthusiastically to the committee's work. Setting up booths on Harlem street corners and holding meetings in churches and lodges, it collected two tons of medical equipment and nearly a thousand dollars in cash.[18]

In December, 1935, Communists followed up this campaign by organizing a federation of some of the largest Ethiopian aid organizations in Harlem — the Medical Committee for the Defense of Ethiopia, the Provisional Committee for the Defense of Ethiopia and the Friends of Ethiopia. Called "United Aid for Ethiopia," the group won endorsement of the Ethiopian government as its "official representative" in Harlem and sought to coordinate fund raising in that community to insure that it reached its proper destination (a few enterprising street speakers had discovered that "fund raising for Ethiopia" was a quick way to fill their pockets). Although Communists brought the groups together, made the contacts with the Ethiopian government, and did much of the fund raising and paperwork, they encouraged non-Communists to serve as United Aid's major spokesmen, confident that an "antifascist" perspective would be projected nevertheless. The Party's representative, Cyril Philip (a former youth leader of Salem M. E. Church) served as secretary of the group, while its meetings featured speeches by Rev. Adam Clayton Powell, Jr.,

Dr. Willis Huggins, Capt. A. L. King, Dr. P. M. H. Savory, and Rev. William Lloyd Imes.[19]

The antifascist orientation of these groups attracted bitter opposition from some Harlem nationalists. In October, 1935, Ira Kemp and Arthur Reid, now militantly anti-Communist, began holding street meetings and picket lines in front of Italian-owned stores in Harlem. Rejecting cooperation with white workers, who they claimed "couldn't be trusted," they appealed to Harlemites to act politically on a strictly racial basis and to drive outsiders from positions of power in Harlem's economy. Though their message of black solidarity struck a responsive chord "on the street" — some of their rallies attracted thousands and ended in near riots — they proved unable to attract support from the black intelligentsia, black professionals, or the black clergy. With few exceptions, Harlem's established leaders supported Ethiopian defense groups which solicited white support, allowing Communists to remain influential in this important protest movement.[20]

A very similar coalition emerged during a boycott of the *Amsterdam News* provoked by the dismissal of seventeen editorial employees. When the dismissed workers, who had joined the American Newspaper Guild, began picketing the paper's offices and demanding their reinstatement, their activities became a rallying point for Harlemites who viewed labor organizations as essential to black progress. Frank Crosswaith and Elmer Carter, working closely with Guild officials, organized a Harlem Citizens Committee in support of the boycott that included representatives of the Urban League and the NAACP (Walter White and New York branch president James Egert Allen both participated), several large churches, and the Socialist and Communist Parties. Joining black and white guildsmen on the picket line, along with representatives of other unions, Harlem activists welcomed the boycott as the harbinger of a new labor militancy that would cut across racial lines.[21] "I believe fundamentally in the cause of the workers when they come into conflict with the employers," Rev. Shelton Hale Bishop told a *New York Age* reporter who interviewed him on the picket line. "Unionism is the only hope of all," Rev. Adam Clayton Powell, Jr., added, "especially Negroes."[22]

The *Amsterdam News* publisher, Mrs. Sadie Warren Davis, tried to rally Harlemites against the boycott on nationalist grounds. She denounced the Newspaper Guild as a "white man's union" and attributed the unrest on her staff to the influence of Communist employees intent on "destroying all capitalist enterprise." Letters to the editor buttressed her position, denouncing the boycott as "an attempt to make a Negro business submit to the dictates of white influence," and decrying the importation of "white radicals to harangue the Harlem public."[23]

But though she received aid with her campaign from Ira Kemp and Arthur Reid, she proved unable to match the Citizens Committee in breadth of support. As the dispute dragged on, more and more ministers and civic leaders took to the picket line and urged their followers to boycott the paper. By mid-December, the protests had so reduced *Amsterdam News* revenues that Mrs. Davis filed a petition for bankruptcy and put the paper up for sale. It was quickly purchased by two wealthy Harlem physicians with prolabor sympathies, Dr. P. M. H. Savory and Dr. C. B. Powell, who opened negotiations with the Guild and returned all discharged employees to their previous posts. In early January, they signed a two-year contract with the Guild establishing a union shop and providing editorial workers with a 10 percent wage increase, a grievance committee, severance notices, vacation time, and a forty-hour week. It was the first such agreement reached between the Guild and a black-owned newspaper.[24]

The new publishers, though more conservative than they first appeared, expressed strong editorial support for alliances between black organizations and the left. "It is the task of every intelligent Negro in America," one of their first editorials stated, "to begin to combat the rising forces of fascism in this country. . . . Support the . . . Scottsboro defense. Fight for the freedom of Angelo Herndon and the Mississippi sharecroppers. Demand federal anti-lynching legislation. Join hands with the many organizations now combatting the rise of fascism in America and elsewhere."[25] The publishers reaffirmed this activist stance by hiring Rev. Adam Clayton Powell, Jr., as a weekly columnist. Powell quickly established himself as a forceful advocate of political and economic cooperation between black and white workers, and of broad protest coalitions to force improvement in Harlem conditions.[26]

The alliances which the Party forged in the Ethiopian protests and the *Amsterdam News* boycott carried over, at least in part, into the campaign to create a National Negro Congress. The story of this movement's origins, or at least that portion of it that we can reliably reconstruct, dramatizes the growing convergence of outlook between Communists and activist black intellectuals that took shape in the protests of the mid-Depression years (1933–35) but reached full fruition in the Popular Front. Building on a consensus on three important issues — support for organized labor, resistance to the rise of fascism, and the use of mass-protest tactics to challenge racial discrimination — Communists were able to help create a black organization of national significance whose constituency and leadership extended considerably beyond the Party's ranks.

The congress movement was "officially" launched at a May, 1935, conference at Howard University in Washington under the auspices of the

Joint Committee on National Recovery, an "ad hoc lobby" to protect black interests in the federal government, that was partially funded by the NAACP.[27] The 150 participants, drawn together by Joint Committee leader John P. Davis, represented a cross-section of black intellectuals critical of New Deal racial policies, who proved receptive to Davis's suggestions, echoed by other conference speakers, that blacks form a national coalition of church, labor, and civil rights organizations to coordinate protest action in the face of deteriorating economic conditions for blacks. At the conclusion of the conference, Davis and Howard political science professor Ralph J. Bunche invited a "select group of negro leaders" to Bunche's apartment to put the idea into operation.[28]

Neither the Howard Conference nor the congress itself was openly promoted as a Communist initiative, but the Party played a significant, and possibly determinative role in setting the stage for the congress's creation. According to Abner Berry, the idea for a congress arose within the Harlem Section of the Party, in late 1934, in response to the Party's success in creating alliances with a wide variety of black organizations. Impressed by the growing militancy of black religious, fraternal, and civil rights organizations, Harlem Party leaders felt that the Party could take the lead in launching a nationwide coalition of black organizations concerned with eliminating racial discrimination, fighting lynching and disfranchisement, and encouraging black participation in unions. After bringing the idea to the Party Politburo for approval, black Party leaders tried to promote the congress within their own publications and meetings.[29] In January, 1935, James Ford spoke in favor of a congress in a Harlem debate with Frank Crosswaith and black Chicago Congressman Oscar DePriest, and Communists won endorsement of the congress idea at a Harlem conference of the Scottsboro-Herndon Action Committee in February of the same year.[30] But the limited response to these initiatives persuaded Party leaders to hand responsibility for launching the project to John P. Davis, a Washington-based economist who was not publicly identified with the Communist Party (though he was possibly a secret member) and who had good contact in black government, academic, and civil rights circles. Davis argued forcefully for a Negro congress in an article in the May, 1935, issue of *Crisis,* and used the Conference at Howard as a means of setting the plan in motion.[31]

Black Communists were active in the Howard conference and in subsequent efforts to launch the congress, but they did not stand out politically from other participants. Eschewing references to violent revolution, Communists instead cultivated an image as "radical democrats," exponents of militant protest action to win blacks full equality within American society. With this orientation, they fit easily with the group of leaders Davis had invited to Bunche's apartment to plan the congress and write its call. The sponsors of the movement represented a fairly diverse group of liberal and radical black intellectuals: Bunche and Alain Locke of Howard University, A. Philip Randolph of the Brotherhood of Sleeping Car Porters, James Ford from the Communist Party, Lester Granger and Elmer Carter of the Urban League, and Charles Houston, a prominent attorney close to the national leadership of the NAACP.[32] Significantly, the consensus they reached—with little Communist prodding—had an anticapitalist tone. "The keynote of the Howard conference," former Howard University dean Kelly Miller wrote, " . . . was that the Negro must combine with white labor and overthrow the existing order in order to wrest their common rights from capitalism which exploits them both." But Miller's distress was not widely shared by conference participants, who felt that a militant, national protest organization could fill an important need. "With all due respect," Charles Houston wrote Walter White, "we have not worked out a solution, nor has any of the other organizations best known in the field. The YW has not done so. Nothing but the Socialist and Communists left. . . ."[33]

In Harlem, Communists made the congress an important focal point of their organizing and worked closely with others on the National Sponsoring Committee in popularizing congress objectives. On May 29, 1935, James Ford, Lester Granger, and John P. Davis jointly conducted a panel discussion on Negro labor sponsored by Alpha Phi Alpha fraternity at Abyssinian Baptist Church. While Ford spoke of the plight of sharecroppers and farmers under the New Deal, Davis and Granger told the audience that the key to the "betterment of the race" lay in the organization of black workers in mixed unions in their industries.[34] Similar meetings took place in Harlem throughout the summer and fall, during which Communists consciously limited their role to the elaboration of a few principles of unity and allowed Randolph and Davis to serve as the congress's major spokesmen. When the National Sponsoring Committee set February, 1936, as the date of the congress's founding convention, a large and diverse group of Harlemites joined to organize the New York contingent. Important members of the New York sponsoring committee for the congress, organized at a December 10 meeting at the Harlem YMCA, included Lester Granger of the Urban League, Benjamin McLaurin of the Brotherhood of Sleeping Car Porters, Roi Ottley of the *Amsterdam News,* Roy Wilkins and Charles Houston of the NAACP, Revs. William Lloyd Imes and Adam Clayton Powell, Jr., Democratic Assemblyman William T. Andrews, Building Service Employees Union organizer Clifford McLoed, Communists James Ford, Benjamin Davis, and Louise Thompson—a cross-section of Harlemites who expressed support for organized labor.[35]

Once a New York Sponsoring Committee was formed, the Communist

Party concentrated its efforts on winning political and financial support
for the congress. Every Communist organization in Harlem, from the
Young Liberators, to the Unemployed Council to the ILD sent representatives to the Sponsoring Committee, and the Communist-influenced
unions helped pay some of the group's expenses. But Communists in the
movement tried to keep their contribution as unobtrusive as possible.
While people like McLoed, Imes, and Granger served as spokesmen for
the New York Committee, Communists arranged meetings, handled correspondence and organized fund raising.[36]

The low-keyed Party presence helped define the congress, at least initially, as considerably more than a Communist front. A small number of
churches and fraternal organizations (among them Abyssinian Baptist,
St. James Presbyterian, and Phi Beta Sigma Fraternity) agreed to send
delegates to the congress, and the movement received endorsements from
Harlem leaders of the YMCA, the NAACP, the Urban League, and the
UNIA.[37] But the most enthusiastic response to the congress came from
black intellectuals and professionals who viewed trade unionism and
mass protest as keys to black advancement and were attracted by the vision of a united front against fascism. The New York delegation to the
congress convention included relief workers, teachers, doctors, musicians,
writers, and artists, many of them representing unions in their fields.
Some were Communists, but many more functioned as part of an amor-
phous Harlem "left wing," which provided critical support for the Party's
activities. To people in the latter group, which included clergymen like
Adam Clayton Powell, Jr., artists like Augusta Savage, and much of the
staff of the *Amsterdam News,* the congress provided an opportunity to
join with Communists in fighting "lynching, discrimination, and inequal-
ity of social and economic opportunity," without identifying themselves
as Communists or subjecting themselves to Party discipline.[38]

Not all Harlem activists supported the congress movement. Most black
nationalists refused to participate, and the National Board of the NAACP,
acting in December, 1935, voted against endorsing the congress or participating in its founding convention on the grounds that "the NAACP does
not know the objective of the proposed National Negro Congress and
does not see how anything can possibly be gained by such superficial discussion as is indicated by the pamphlet advertising the Congress."[39] This
action, taken despite the presence of two association officers on sponsoring committees for the congress (Assistant Secretary Roy Wilkins and
Special Counsel Charles Houston) bore the imprimatur of association
Secretary Walter White, who feared that the congress might come under
Communist influence and be used to undermine the NAACP.[40] Despite
some support for the congress within the association—among some

branch leaders and a few national officers—White persistently turned down personal invitations from John P. Davis and A. Philip Randolph to speak at the congress convention or lend association sponsorship to the movement.[41] "Do hope Congress is not permitted to be 'sold down the river' to any political group," White replied to one Randolph letter."Have heard many disturbing rumors." The NAACP board assigned Roy Wilkins to attend the convention as an observer, but remained highly skeptical of the congress's purposes. "It is my impression," Walter White wrote *Baltimore Afro-American* publisher Carl Murphy, "that the Board action is final unless there should be some very good reason for reopening the matter."[42]

In addition, the small, but influential group of black Socialists who ran the Harlem Labor Center, an organization financed by the city's needle-trades unions to familiarize blacks with the labor movement, withheld their endorsement of the congress. Harlem Labor Center Chairman Frank Crosswaith, though willing to work with Communists on an issue-by-issue basis, regarded them as too politically and intellectually corrupt to entrust with leadership in black organizations, and judged their role in the congress too large for his taste. Officers of the New York Sponsoring Committee tried to win Crosswaith over by promising to "prevent political domination by any Party," and offering him a place in the congress leadership, but the most he would agree to was to send observers to the convention. In addition, Crosswaith advised key trade unions that he worked with, the Amalgamated Clothing Workers Union and the International Garment Workers Union, not to endorse the congress and to reject the congress's plea for financial support. As a result, two of the city's largest and most influential unions, with sizable black membership, refused to cooperate in a major effort to link black protest with organized labor.[43]

The congress's trade union support in New York came in large part from unions in which Communists played a role—the Teachers Union, the Musicians Union, the Newspaper Guild, the Relief Workers Association, the Fur Workers Union. In addition, the congress nationally won the endorsement of John L. Lewis and John Brophy of the Committee on Industrial Organization, the coalition of AFL unions committed to breaking down craft barriers and "organizing the unorganized." But the most forceful trade union voice for the congress was that of A. Philip Randolph, President of the Brotherhood of Sleeping Car Porters. Randolph applied the full force of his personal prestige to persuading blacks in "church, lodge . . . business and labor" organizations to send delegates to the congress convention.[44] "While the hydra-headed monster of fascism is threatening our rather weak democratic institutions in America," one of his press releases stated, "it is . . . imperative that the mass voice of Negroes and all their common allies be spoken through a National Negro Congress."[45]

The congress's founding convention had some of the breadth that Randolph hoped for: 817 delegates came to the convention, and its plenary sessions drew 3,000 to 5,000 people. "Negroes in every walk of life were there," Lester Granger reported, "ministers, labor leaders, businessmen, mechanics, farmers, musicians, housewives, missionaries, social workers. . . . There were representatives of New Deal departments and agencies; old line Republican wheel horses and ambitious young Democrats exchanged arguments; Communists held heated altercations with proponents of the Forty Ninth State Movement, and Garveyites signed the registration books immediately after the Baha'ists."[46] Despite the diverse background of those attending, Roy Wilkins was struck by the youth of key participants. "The Congress at Chicago . . . enlisted great sections of young colored and white people under thirty five years of age"; he wrote in a report to the NAACP Board, "the delegates were from the so-called working class and mass organizations, who came at great personal sacrifice and who owed their allegiance only to organizations committed to a militant fight for the Negro."[47]

The tone of the gathering, by intention and default, was set by the left. Because several moderate speakers turned down invitations to appear, among them NAACP Secretary Walter White, *Chicago Defender* editor Robert Abbott, and the mayor of Chicago, advocates of labor organization and militant protest tactics dominated the plenary sessions.[48] The keynote speaker, A. Philip Randolph, whose speech was read in his absence, devoted much of his attention to attacks on the "profit system" and called upon blacks to unify their ranks and join with white sympathizers in a "common attack upon the forces of reaction." Such a movement, Randolph claimed, had to use different tactics than blacks traditionally employed, depending on "parades, picketing, boycotting, mass protest (and) the mass distribution of propaganda as well as legal action."[49] In addition, radicals played a dominant role in most of the workshops and small group discussions where the congress's program was forged. "There are key Communists in every discussion, such as Richard B. Moore, Louise Thompson, Ben Davis," Roy Wilkins wrote to Charles Houston, ". . . not actually leading, but always with their hands in."[50]

The atmosphere of the convention troubled black conservatives. Three bishops who had signed the original call — James A. Bray, R. A. Carter, and W. J. Walls — denounced congress organizers for limiting the clergy's role to "making invocations and pronouncing benedictions" and Kelly Miller complained that "religion, philanthropy, and patriotism, the three pillars upon which the life and hope of the race have built, were either ruthlessly flouted or tepidly tolerated. . . ."[51] But most of the delegates seemed to welcome the convention's break with traditional tactics and leadership. "Never have I seen any group of people as serious and stern and willing as the delegates to the National Negro Congress," Adam Clayton Powell, Jr., wrote, Lester Granger attributed the enthusiasm of convention delegates to a "deep rooted and nationwide dissatisfaction of Negroes" that was rapidly mounting "into flaming resentment."[52]

Communists played an important role in handling the administrative work of the convention and in shaping its political outlook, but they were careful not to express views that might offend moderate delegates. The presence of white Communist secretaries in Davis's Chicago office aroused more controversy than the content of remarks by Party representatives in speeches and discussions.[53] In all their presentations, Communists emphasized their desire to work "equally and cooperatively" with other black organizations and projected a program of minimum demands that evoked little controversy—"the fight for unionism, for adequate relief, for civil and political rights, for equality in economic opportunity, for the suppression of lynching, and the abolition of Jim Crowism." In addition, Communists filled their speeches with references to American history and proclaimed their respect for the American political tradition. "It was not Marx, Lenin and Stalin" whom Communists cited in their addresses, the *Amsterdam News* reported. "Rather it was Douglass, Lincoln and the heroes of the American Revolution from whom they drew their inspiration."[54]

When the convention ended, Communists declined to push any of their acknowledged leaders for important congress positions. A. Philip Randolph was elected president of the new organization, John P. Davis as secretary, and Ms. Marion Cuthbert, a YWCA official and a member of the NAACP national board, as treasurer. Three leading Harlem Communists, Abner Berry, Ben Davis, and James Ford, were elected to the congress executive committee, but Communists composed a small number of its seventy-five members. The Party's main influence on the congress's direction came through its relationship with Davis, who represented the new organization's only paid, full-time staff member (Randolph and Cuthbert served as volunteers). Set up to function as a federation of organizations, the congress created two major centers of initiative: Davis's Washington office, which handled the congress's national affairs, and the congress's regional councils, which tried to create coalitions of organizations which shared congress objectives and to develop programs of action on local and national issues. At least initially, this structure seemed too democratic—too cumbersome—to be easily dominated by Communists, or any other political group.[55]

The Party's circumspect behavior at the convention helped consolidate its ties with many black activists and intellectuals who supported the congress movement. "Negroes who elect to be Communists need make no apology for it," A. Philip Randolph wrote in a reply to congress critics, "that is their right. It is guaranteed by the Federal Constitution. Communists are not criminals. The Communist Party is a legitimate political party and has city, state and national tickets like Republicans and Democrats."[56] Historian Carter G. Woodson, long skeptical of Communist philosophy, argued that the black Communists he met at the congress seemed more interested in fighting for equal rights than in overthrowing the government. "I have talked with any number of Negroes who call themselves Communists," Woodson wrote in the *New York Age,* "and I have never heard one express a desire to destroy anyone or anything but oppression. . . . Negroes who are charged with being Communists advocate the stoppage of lynching, the abrogation of the laws of disfranchisement, the abolition of peonage, equality in the employment of labor. . . . If this makes a man a 'Red,' the world's greatest reformers belong to this class, and we shall have to condemn our greatest statesmen, some of whom have attained the presidency of the United States."[57]

Significantly, the national leadership of the NAACP did not echo these sentiments; despite repeated overtures from Davis, it refrained from any formal endorsement of the congress, or of the "united front" strategy. But enough members of the association board and staff—among them Roy Wilkins, Marion Cuthbert, Charles Houston, and William H. Hastie (a Washington-based lawyer on the NAACP board)—supported an association presence in the congress to prevent the NAACP from condemning the congress, or discouraging local branch officers from participating in congress activities. Wilkins and Houston both argued forcefully that the NAACP, to avoid being outflanked by the Negro congress, had to either formally participate in its governing structure, or generate initiatives of its own in fields where the congress displayed special strength—especially youth work and labor education. ". . . the very fact that there was such a wide representation at the Congress," Houston wrote Walter White, "shows that the NAACP must re-analyze its program."[58]

Harlem Communists, who played an important role in the congress convention as speakers and workshop leaders, viewed the event as a decisive sign of their Party's movement into the black political mainstream. The convention marked a "definite break with the narrow 'stew in your own juice' attitude of Communists," Ben Davis wrote. "Communists found themselves at home among Negroes in all walks of life." James Ford boasted of a "significant development toward the Left" among black organizations in the congress movement, as well as a "better understanding on the part of Negro Communists of how to work among the Negro masses."[59] When the New York Regional office of the congress opened in late February, the Party made it a focal point of activity, working closely with regional chairmen Lester Granger and Clifford McLoed to coordinate community support for trade unions conducting strikes in the Harlem area.[60]

Shortly after the congress ended, the Central Committee ordered a reorganization of the Harlem section to help accommodate the rapid growth of its membership and the expansion of its political activities. The Harlem section now became a Harlem division composed of three separate sections coinciding with the major ethnic divisions in the area: a Lower Harlem section covering Italian and Puerto Rican neighborhoods, an Upper Harlem section, covering black neighborhoods, and a Washington Heights section, covering Irish and Jewish neighborhoods. The Central Committee appointed James Ford organizer of the entire division, and Abner Berry organizer of the Upper Harlem section.[61]

This reorganization marked the beginning of a new stage in which electoral politics and trade union work became major foci of Party activity. Between the spring of 1936 and the signing of the Nazi-Soviet Pact, Communists concentrated their attention on building broad coalitions for "independent political action" and helping to win black support for the organizing drive of the CIO. Active in numerous movements to improve Harlem conditions—in housing, employment, education, health care, and relief—the Party approached these issues with a new sophistication, using lobbying and electoral bargaining as well as direct action tactics.

To facilitate their implementation of these new policies, Party neighborhood organizations in Harlem gradually assumed a totally different persona than they had in the early '30s, when Communists made contact with Harlemites largely through soapbox rallies or protests the Party organized. Protest activity remained a central feature of the Party's work, but the Party also assumed community-service functions that it had once disdained as reformist. Neighborhood branches in Harlem, replacing the much smaller "street units," stopped meeting in apartments and opened up storefronts and meeting halls to which Harlemites were encouraged to come when they had a grievance, much in the manner of a local Democratic club. Named after martyred black Communists and black revolutionary heroes, the branches sponsored forums and classes, organized tenants groups and PTA's, and in one instance, ran a day care center using WPA teachers. Seeking recruits from all classes, Party organizers took great pains to emphasize that the Party did not confine itself to the angry and disillusioned.[62] A *Daily Worker* article on Harlem's Milton Herndon branch (entitled "Swell People, the Kind You Meet Any Day in Harlem") suggested the kind of ambience the Party tried to project:

The people composing this unit are ordinary people . . . domestic workers, drill workers, truck drivers, carpenters, social workers, unemployed persons.

The branch is composed of 100 people, 95 of whom are Negro. . . . they are fast making their center a place where people in the neighborhood visit. Their headquarters are simple and attractive. Three posters adorn their walls. A large picture of Milton Herndon, with an American flag draped over it, a poster of Abraham Lincoln which says, "Give Aid to Spain," and a *Daily Worker* poster which says, "It Gives Us a New Outlook."[63]

Communists also sought to increase popular acceptance by trying to "incorporate into branch meetings the cultural forms of struggle of the Negro people." Defining the struggle for cultural recognition as a central feature of the Party's program, Communists organized choral societies, dance groups, and sports clubs, sponsored community theatres, and played an active role in PTA's and the Association for the Study of Negro Life and History. In addition, Communists enthusiastically promoted black arts within their publications and organizations and tried to draw black artists, musicians, writers, and theatrical people into the Party and its affiliated organizations. In their writings and public pronouncements, Communists extolled the contribution of black artists, particularly musicians, as a democratizing force, the source of much within the nation's culture which was distinctively "American."[64]

In addition to an emphasis on cultural questions, Americanization in Harlem brought about a relaxation of Party discipline, especially among intellectuals. In its quest for prestigious members, the Party allowed prominent blacks who joined almost complete freedom from routine Party duties such as distributing leaflets and canvassing for votes, or even from attending meetings regularly. If they were writers, the Party interfered little with what they wrote so long as they defended the Party line in public appearances and did not raise troubling questions about issues like the purge trials and the campaign against Trotskyism. Such a "double standard" had always existed in the Party—for trade-union leaders as well as intellectuals—but it became more explicit in the Popular Front, when the Party sought to win a large portion of the American intelligentsia and the labor movement over to an antifascist and pro-Soviet stance.[65]

Despite its appeal to black intellectuals, the loosening of discipline for "influentials" had some troubling implications for Party work in Black America. The imperative to expand the Party's practical influence, and adapt its activity to local customs, exposed individual Communists to strong pressures to dilute their racial militancy. For Communists in positions of influence—union leaders, politicians, Hollywood writers—whose position rested on the support of people not always distinguished by ra-

cial liberalism, the temptation to avoid an aggressive fight for black interests proved particularly strong, yet it was precisely such individuals
who experienced the greatest freedom from Party discipline. From the
standpoint of the black community, therefore, liberalization was a two-
edged sword: While it made the Party more sensitive to black culture and
the demands of its black constituency, it removed a key mechanism that
had prevented white Communists from falling prey, however subtly, to
the racial conservatism of the surrounding society.

Moreover, liberalization raised difficult questions about the nature—
and ultimate appeal—of Party membership. If the public face of "Communism" differed little from that of black liberalism, what did the Party
have to offer black recruits? True, the Party did have a distinctive set of
concerns that it pressed upon its members (as opposed to the general public): its commitment to socialism as a long-term goal, its militant defense
of the Soviet Union, its quest for a "scientific" view of human events, and
its architectonic vision of strategy that linked events in Spain and China
with trade union and electoral tactics in the United States. But those features of Party life appealed largely to people with an intellectual bent,
whether formally educated or not.

Communists also distributed a certain amount of patronage through
the unions they controlled, through their power in the WPA and the relief
system, and through the Party apparatus and Party-controlled businesses.
But since the Popular Front placed such a premium on alliances—the
Party tried to conduct most of its Harlem organizing within coalitions—
fellow travellers as well as members benefited from the Party's good
graces.

In the Popular Front Party, the boundaries separating Communists
from Party sympathizers became increasingly vague. Party functionaries
remained a tightly knit and disciplined group, functioning in a highly
charged and insular political milieu, but the rank-and-file membership,
who went in and out of the Party at a rapid rate, found that the organization no longer sought to organize their every waking hour into purposeful activity. Party branches, especially among privileged strata—
such as those on the WPA Negro Theatre and the staff of the *Amsterdam
News*—came to resemble discussion groups more than units of a disciplined revolutionary army, and it became difficult to distinguish card-
carrying members from sympathizers on the basis of either their life-styles
or their intellectual work.[66]

When analyzing Popular Front Communism, it is important to discard
the "totalitarian" model that dominates Party historiography: the image
of an obedient and docile membership that jumps up and down in unison
when the leadership snaps its fingers. The Party remained "bolshevik" at
the core, making most of its key decisions without consulting the mem-

bers; but it lost the power, and even the will, to reshape the total lives of its more prominent adherents, and much of its rank and file. The Party was run by a professional staff, but in other respects, it came to resemble a movement, with a free-floating group of members and sympathizers who publicly endorsed its basic objectives and agreed to follow the Party line — but displayed considerable diversity, and even division in areas where the line did not apply. This fluidity must be kept in mind in assessing the Party in the Popular Front, for its power derived not so much from its actual membership as from the much larger group of people who regarded it as a center of initiative and voluntarily identified with its policies. To the Party's enemies in Harlem, this sometimes made it seem that the Party was everywhere, controlling and manipulating everything from the jobs movement to the WPA, but it was a power that rested largely on consent, and was extremely vulnerable to shifts in the international Communist movement, and the political climate in the United States.

NOTES

1. Wilson Record, *The Negro and the Communist Party* (Chapel Hill: University of North Carolina Press, 1951), pp. 128–32; "Concluding Speech of Comrade Dmitrov," *International Press Correspondence,* 15 (Aug. 31, 1935), 1098; *Daily Worker,* Aug. 5, 1935; Fernando Claudin, *The Communist Movement: From Comintern to Cominform* (Hammondsworth, England: Penguin Books, 1975), pp. 184–95.

2. *Ibid.,* p. 187; George Charney, *A Long Journey* (New York: Quadrangle, 1968), p. 60; Al Richmond, *A Long View From the Left* (Boston: Houghton Mifflin, 1973), p. 254; Joseph Starobin, *American Communism in Crisis, 1943–1957* (Cambridge: Harvard University Press, 1972), p. 29; Irving Howe and Lewis Coser, *The American Communist Party: A Critical History* (New York: Praeger, 1962), p. 339; "Comrade Browder (U. S. A.)." *International Press Correspondence,* 15 (Aug. 23, 1935), 1062; Earl Browder, "The United Front — The Key to Our New Tactical Orientation," *Communist,* 14 (Dec., 1935), 1075–1129. The Togliatti quote is taken from Claudin; the Browder quote about American revolutionary traditions from *International Press Correspondence.*

3. Starobin, *American Communism in Crisis,* p. 39; Charney, *A Long Journey,* pp. 94–97; Robert Jay Alperin, "Organization in the Communist Party, U.S.A., 1931–1938," (Ph.D. dissertation, Northwestern University, 1959), pp. 45, 74–75; Howe and Coser, *The American Communist Party,* pp. 332–35; Bert Cochran, *Labor and Communism: The Conflict that Shaped American Unions* (Princeton: Princeton University Press, 1977), pp. 135–36; F. Brown, "New Forms of Party Organization Help Us Win the Masses," *Party Organizer,* 10 (July-Aug., 1936), 11.

4. Earl Browder, *The People's Front* (New York: International Publishers, 193, pp. 105, 145–49, 167–72, 266–69.

5. *Ibid.*, p. 147; "Outline for New Members Class," *Party Organizer,* 10 (Dec., 1936), 24–30.

6. Starobin, *American Communism in Crisis,* preface, pp. 28–47; Howe and Coser, *The American Communist Party,* pp. 336–39; Charney, *A Long Journey,* pp. 30–31; Arthur Leibman, *Jews and the Left* (New York: John Wiley and Sons, 1978), pp. 30–31; Maurice Isserman, "The 1956 Generation. An Alternative Approach to the History of American Communism," *Radical America,* 14 (Mar.–Apr., 1980), 47–48.

7. Claude McKay, *Harlem, Negro Metropolis* (1940; rpt. New York: Harcourt, Brace, Jovanovich, 1968), p. 239; Stanley High, "Black Omens," *Saturday Evening Post* (June 4, 1938), 38.

8. *New York Amsterdam News,* May 8, 1937; Lester B. Granger, "Along the Party Line," *Opportunity,* 17 (Mar., 1939), 90–91; "As Youth Sees It," *Interracial Review,* 10 (Aug., 1937), 126.

9. Browder, "The United Front," 1119–20; Record, *The Negro and the Communist Party,* p. 113; James W. Ford, *The Negro and the Democratic Front* (New York: International Publishers, 1938), pp. 83–84; James W. Ford, "The Negro People and the Farmer-Labor Party," *Communist,* 14 (Dec., 1935), 1136–37; interview with Abner Berry, Nov. 20, 1973.

10. *New York Amsterdam News,* Sept. 28, 1935.

11. The term "respectable American organization" comes from Howe and Coser, *The American Communist Party,* p. 337.

12. *New York Amsterdam News,* Aug. 17, 1935.

13. *New York Times,* Sept. 8, 1935; George W. Baer, *The Coming of the Italian-Ethiopian War* (Cambridge: Harvard University Press, 1967), pp. 316–17; *New York Age,* Oct. 5, 1935; "Soviet Russia Aids Italy," *Crisis,* 42 (Oct., 1935), 305.

14. *Daily Worker,* Sept. 6, 1935, Sept. 7, 1935, Sept. 9, 1935; Record, *The Negro and the Communist Party,* pp. 139–40; interview with Abner Berry, Dec. 2, 1973; Max Steinberg, "Problems of Party Growth in the New York District," *Communist,* 15 (July, 1936), 647. Mackawain was the only Harlem Communist in a leadership position to leave as a result of Soviet Ethiopian policy. However, Party leaders felt that the Ethiopian controversy did slow the growth of the Party's black membership.

15. *Daily Worker,* Oct. 6, 1935); "Earl Browder Replies," *Crisis,* 42 (Dec., 1935), 372.

16. *New York Age,* Oct. 5, 1935; *Negro Liberator,* Oct. 1, 1935; *New York Amsterdam News,* Nov. 2, 1935; *Daily Worker,* Oct. 24, 1935; *New York Times,* Sept. 26, 1935.

17. *New York Age,* Oct. 5, 1935.

18. *Ibid.,* Aug. 10 , 1935; Ford, "The Negro People and the Farmer-Labor Party," 1137; *Daily Worker,* Sept. 25, 1935; *New York Amsterdam News,* Sept. 28, 1935; leaflet, "Ethiopia Calls to Us. 'We Need Your Help,'" UNIA Papers, Reel 5, Box 12; leaflet, "Answer the Fascist Murderers, Send a Hospital to Ethiopia," *ibid.*

19. *Daily Worker,* Dec. 26, 1935; *New York Amsterdam News,* Feb. 1, 1936;

conference minutes, United Aid for Ethiopia, no date, UNIA Papers, Reel 5, Box 13; interview with Theodore Bassett, Nov. 2, 1973.

20. *Daily Worker,* Oct. 6, 1935, Oct. 10, 1935; *New York Amsterdam News,* Oct. 5, 1935; *New York Times,* Oct. 4, 1935; *New York Age,* Oct. 12, 1935; James W. Ford, *The Communists and the Struggle for Negro Liberation* (New York: Workers Library, 1936), pp. 60–62.

21. Daniel J. Leab, *A Union of Individuals: The Formation of the American Newspaper Guild, 1933–1936* (New York: Columbia University Press, 1970), pp. 233–37; *New York Age,* Oct. 12, 1935, Oct. 19, 1935, Oct. 26, 1935; *Daily Worker,* Oct. 14, 1934, Oct. 17, 1935; Ford, "The Negro People and the Farmer-Labor Party," 1136–37; Loren Miller, "Labor Trouble in Harlem," *New Masses,* 17 (Oct. 22, 1935), 20; *Reporter,* Nov. 7, 1935, in UNIA Papers, Reel 4, Box 11.

22. *New York Age,* Nov. 23, 1935.

23. *New York Amsterdam News,* Oct. 19, 1935, Oct. 26, 1935.

24. *New York Age,* Nov. 2, 1935, Nov. 23, 1935; *New York Amsterdam News,* Jan. 11, 1936; "Victory for the Guild," *New Masses,* 18 (Jan. 6, 1936), 6.

25. *New York Amsterdam News,* Jan. 25, 1936.

26. *Ibid.,* Feb. 15, 1936, Mar. 7, 1936.

27. On the origins of the Joint Committee on National Recovery, see Raymond Wolters, *Negroes and the Great Depression: The Problem of Economic Recovery* (Westport: Greenwood Press, 1970), pp. 110–11.

28. Ralph Johnson Bunche, "The Programs, Ideologies, Tactics and Achievements of Negro Betterment and Interracial Organizations," unpublished manuscript, Myrdal Memoranda Collection, Schomburg Collection, pp. 319–23; Record, *The Negro and the Communist Party,* pp. 153, 354; Raymond Wolters, *Negroes and the Great Depression,* pp. 353–58.

29. Interview with Abner Berry, Dec. 2, 1973.

30. *Negro Liberator,* Feb. 15, 1935, Mar. 15, 1935. That Harlem Communists had begun publicly calling for a Negro congress early in 1935 offers good circumstantial evidence of the accuracy of Berry's view.

31. Interview with Abner Berry, Dec. 2, 1973; John P. Davis, "A Black Inventory of the New Deal," *Crisis,* 42 (May, 1935), 55. Whether Davis was a Communist remains a matter of some dispute, but two of Richard Wright's biographers suggest that Davis was acting for the Party in his dealings with Wright. See Michel Fabre, *The Unfinished Quest of Richard Wright* (New York: William Morrow, 1973), p. 126, and Addison Gayle, *Richard Wright: Ordeal of a Native Son* (Garden City: Doubleday, 1980), pp. 89–90.

32. *Daily Worker,* May 23, 1935; "A National Negro Conference," *New Masses,* 15 (June 4, 1935), p. 9; *Negro Liberator,* June 15, 1935; Wolters, *Negroes and the Great Depression,* p. 358.

33. *New York Age,* June 1, 1935; Charles Houston to Walter White, May 23, 1935, NAACP Papers, I-A64.

34. *New York Amsterdam News,* June 1, 1935; *Negro Liberator,* June 15, 1935.

35. John P. Davis, *Let Us Build a National Negro Congress* (Washington, D.C..: National Negro Congress, 1935), p. 3; L. B. Granger to Dear friend, Dec. 6, 1936, NAACP Papers, C 383; *Daily Worker,* Dec. 16, 1935; *New York Am-*

sterdam News, Dec. 28, 1935; Ben J. Davis, Jr., to John P. Davis, Dec. 13, 1935, National Negro Congress Papers, Reel 2, Box 4 (hereafter referred to as NNC Papers).

36. *Daily Worker,* Jan. 10, 1936, Feb. 7, 1936; Dolimer and MacKenzie, *The Negro Worker in the ERB,* p. 16; Ford, "The Negro People and the Farmer Labor Party," 1140; James W. Ford to John P. Davis, Nov. 14, 1935, NNC Papers, Reel 2, Box 4; Benjamin J. Davis to John P. Davis, Nov. 26, 1935, *ibid.*; James W. Ford to Clifford McLoed, Jan. 6, 1936, *ibid.,* Reel 3, Box 5; Benjamin J. Davis to John P. Davis, Dec. 28, 1935, *ibid.,* Reel 2, Box 4.

37. *Daily Worker,* Dec. 16, 1935, Jan. 11, 1936; *New York Amsterdam News,* Dec. 28, 1935; Emmet M. May to John P. Davis, Jan. 10, 1936, NNC Papers, Reel 3, Box 5.

38. The quote about "lynching, discrimination . . . " etc., comes from an editorial in the *New York Amsterdam News,* Feb. 8, 1936. The Feb. 15, 1936 issue of the *New York Amsterdam News* contains a listing of much of the New York delegation to the congress convention.

39. Minutes of the Meeting of the Board of Directors, National Association for the Advancement of Colored People, Dec. 9, 1935, NAACP Papers.

40. Wolters, *Negroes and the Great Depression,* p. 358; Walter White to Harry E. Davis, Jan. 27, 1936, NAACP Papers, C 383.

41. For examples of efforts to solicit White's support of the Congress, see John P. Davis to Walter White, Jan. 20, 1936; telegram, John P. Davis to Walter White, Jan. 24, 1936; Maurice Hubbard to Walter White, Jan. 31, 1936; A. Philip Randolph to Walter White, Feb. 4, 1936, all in NAACP Papers, C 383.

42. Walter White to A. Philip Randolph, Feb. 1, 1936, and Walter White to Carl Murphy, Dec. 28, 1935, NAACP Papers, C 383; Minutes of the Meeting of the Board of Directors, National Association for the Advancement of Colored People, Jan. 6, 1936, NAACP Papers.

43. *Daily Worker,* Dec. 19, 1935, Feb. 7, 1936; Benjamin J. Davis to John P. Davis, Dec. 13, 1935, NNC Papers, Reel 2, Box 4; Clarence Senior to John P. Davis, Jan. 1, 1936, NNC Papers, Reel 4, Box 7.

44. *New York Amsterdam News,* Feb. 15, 1936; James W. Ford, "The National Negro Congress," *Communist,* 15 (Apr. 1936), 325–26; James W. Ford and A. W. Berry, "The Coming National Negro Congress," *Communist,* 15 (Feb. 1936), 141; Lawrence S. Wittner, "The National Negro Congress: A Reassessment," *American Quarterly,* 22 (Winter, 1970), 896.

45. *Daily Worker,* Jan. 13, 1936.

46. *Official Proceedings of the National Negro Congress, February 14, 15, 16, 1936* (Washington, D.C.: National Negro Congress, 1936), p. 3; Wolters, *Negroes and the Great Depression,* p. 359; Lester Granger, "The National Negro Congress —An Interpretation," *Opportunity,* 14 (May, 1936), 151–52.

47. Memorandum, from Roy Wilkins to the Board of Directors on the National Negro Congress, Mar. 9, 1936, NAACP Papers, C 383.

48. Roy Wilkins to Charles Houston, Feb. 18, 1936, *ibid.*; Wolters, *Negroes and the Great Depression,* p. 360.

49. *Official Proceedings of the National Negro Congress,* p. 11.

50. John P. Davis to James Ashford, Jan. 26, 1936, NNC Papers, Reel 2, Box

4; John P. Davis to Abner Berry, Jan. 26, 1936, *ibid.*; Roy Wilkins to Charles Houston, Feb. 18, 1936, NAACP Papers, C 393.

51. Wolters, *Negroes and the Great Depression,* p. 363; *New York Age,* Mar. 7, 1936.

52. *New York Amsterdam News,* Feb. 22, 1936; Granger, "The National Negro Congress—An Interpretation," 152.

53. Roy Wilkins to Charles Houston, Feb. 18, 1936, NAACP Papers, C 383.

54. *Official Proceedings of the National Negro Congress,* p. 17; *New York Amsterdam News,* Feb. 22, 1936.

55. Wittner, "The National Negro Congress: A Reassessment," 887; *Official Proceedings of the National Negro Congress,* p. 40; James W. Ford, "Build the National Negro Congress Movement," *Communist,* 15 (June, 1936), 561; memorandum, Roy Wilkins to the Board of Directors on the National Negro Congress, Mar. 9, 1936, NAACP Papers, C 383.

56. *Chicago Defender,* Feb. 29, 1936.

57. *New York Age,* Mar. 14, 1936.

58. Wolters, *Negroes and the Great Depression,* pp. 364–365; memorandum, Roy Wilkins to the Board of Directors on the National Negro Congress, Mar. 9, 1936, NAACP Papers, C 383; Roy Wilkins to John P. Davis, Mar. 11, 1936, *ibid.*; Charles Houston to Walter White, Feb. 29, 1936, *ibid.*

59. *Daily Worker,* Mar. 18, 1936; Ford, "The National Negro Congress," 317.

60. *Daily Worker,* Mar. 30, 1936, July 10, 1936.

61. *Ibid.,* Mar. 13, 1936, Mar. 25, 1936; interview with Abner Berry, Nov. 20, 1973.

62. *Proceedings, 10 Convention, Communist Party, New York State* (New York: New York State Committee, Communist Party, 1938), pp. 159–90; *Daily Worker,* July 10, 1937, Aug. 16, 1937, Sept. 11, 1937, Sept. 17, 1937, Oct. 29, 1937, Nov. 2, 1938, Feb. 16, 1939, Feb. 19, 1939.

63. *Ibid.,* May 20, 1938.

64. George Blake, "The Party in Harlem, New York," *Party Organizer* 12 (June, 1938), 17; *Proceedings, 10 Convention, Communist Party, New York State,* pp. 298–99; Ford, *The Negro and the Democratic Front,* pp. 74, 205–7; Francis Franklin, "The Cultural Heritage of the Negro People," *Communist,* 18 (June, 1930), 562–71.

65. On the role of "influentials" in the CPUSA, see Starobin, *American Communism in Crisis,* pp. 39–41.

66. Interview with Abner Berry, July 5, 1977; James W. Ford, "Uniting the Negro People in the People's Front," *Communist,* 18 (Aug., 1937), 728–29. Berry recalled that the *Amsterdam News* branch of the Party, had, among others, a cartoonist and a gossip columnist. There is no evidence that the gossip columnist took a particularly "Communist" stance on her work, except for mentioning left-wing dances and cultural functions. Ford describes the *Amsterdam News* branch as something of a problem for the Party.

8

Communism and Harlem Intellectuals in the Popular Front—Antifascism and the Politics of Black Culture

BETWEEN 1936 AND 1939, the Communist Party emerged as an important focal point of political and cultural activity by Harlem intellectuals. "My memory and knowledge," Party organizer Howard Johnson recalls, "is that 75% of black cultural figures had Party membership or maintained regular meaningful contact with the Party." Harlem critics of the Party spoke bitterly of Party dominance of the black intelligentsia and feared they would use this to "capture the entire Negro group." "Most of the Negro intellectuals," Claude McKay wrote, "were directly or indirectly hypnotized by the propaganda of the Popular Front," and George Streator complained in the Catholic *Interracial Review* of the smug social cohesiveness of black "anti-fascists": "Most of our intellectuals were led to believe that the cause of Negro freedom was at stake in Spain. . . . The same social set that engineered these cocktail parties for Spain handled the [National] Negro Congress."[1]

Although the Party had successfully cultivated black intellectuals in the early '30s—particularly via the Scottsboro defense—its efforts to win their support became far more explicit during the Popular Front years. The new Party strategy called for the incorporation of the entire black community into antifascist alliances with white liberals and radicals, and it viewed the black intelligentsia as a pivotal group in its quest for "sustained and fraternal cooperation" with the most powerful groups in black life—the NAACP, the Urban League, and the black church.[2]

The Popular Front Party's success among Harlem intellectuals and professionals, however, whether measured in membership or political influence, proportionately far exceeded its impact on Harlem's working class. Abner Berry and Howard Johnson, important Party leaders in the period (Johnson was a leader of the Harlem Young Communist League), both recall that the Party had a very high percentage of middle-class members — perhaps half — in a community where the overwhelming majority of the population was working class and poor. Although articles in the Party press did not discuss the Harlem Communist Party's social composition, the one Party branch in Harlem consistently singled out for praise during the Popular Front era, the Milton Herndon branch, was located in "Sugar Hill," probably Harlem's wealthiest neighborhood. The set of symbols and affinities that marked Popular Front politics in Harlem — linking the cause of Ethiopia with that of China and Loyalist Spain; identifying the persecution of Jews in Germany with that of blacks in the United States; viewing the New Deal and the labor movement as harbingers of black progress — had more weight among black doctors than they did among black domestics, or among parishioners of St. Philip's than worshippers in storefront churches.[3]

This phenomenon reflected the special attraction of intellectuals to an internationalist vision — which Popular Frontism emphatically was — but it also bespoke profound social and economic changes in Harlem in the mid-'30s that gave Communist optimism regarding racial reform particular weight among black intellectuals and white-collar workers. Between 1935 and 1937, white-collar employment opportunities for Harlem blacks expanded enormously, partly as a result of liberal policies of the La Guardia and Roosevelt administrations, and partly as a result of protests against discrimination led by left-wing unions and Harlem community groups. In the Emergency Relief Bureau, a center of leftist agitation, more than 1,100 blacks found employment, most in skilled positions, and thousands more received jobs on WPA projects set up during 1935 and 1936. Although most WPA jobs were in blue-collar fields — e.g., sewing or construction — the WPA represented a special boon for educated Harlemites; more than 350 found employment on the theatre project as actors, directors, and designers; others found jobs as writers and researchers and teachers on adult education programs; musicians and artists found employment in their specialties; and WPA health centers hired black doctors and nurses.[4] Many Negro WPA employees had "the best jobs they've ever had in their lives," the *Amsterdam News* declared. "Thousands of Negro clerks and other white collar relief workers found the kind of employment they are trained for."[5]

This expansion of opportunities in government employment, coming at a time of stagnation and decline in black business enterprise, tended to undermine the prestige of strategies emphasizing black self-sufficiency and give credence to those emphasizing interracial alliances. In all of the key sectors where educated blacks found employment in large numbers — in the relief system, the WPA, the school system, and Harlem Hospital — white-collar unions, led by the left, had fought to expand employment opportunities for blacks and protect their jobs (as those of other workers) from austerity measures urged by conservative legislators.[6] This phenomenon endowed interracial protest strategies with an air of practicality. "Negro workers on the WPA should enlist immediately in . . . the Teachers Union or the City Projects Council," Adam Clayton Powell, Jr., wrote. ". . . Our battles are only going to be won to the same degree that we unite with all other fighting for the same ideals."[7]

These positive experiences with the left, along with a profusion of new opportunities, gave educated blacks something of a buffer against nationalist ideologies which had a hold among less privileged sectors of Harlem's population. As the economic crisis persisted, and Harlem's poor fell into nearly total dependency on the relief system, street speakers preaching variations on Garvey's message expanded their popular following. Embittered by their isolation from positions of power and near-exclusion from the Harlem media, they combined shrewd critiques of interracialism with raw agitation of prejudice against Italians and Jews. Admirers of Japan, the first "colored nation" to become a world power, they bitterly rejected any internationalism which lacked a racial component and urged Harlemites to "think black, talk black, act black, and see black."[8]

The pessimism inherent in this vision had deep roots in Afro-American culture — as Garvey's appeal demonstrated — but it failed to strike a chord among an upwardly mobile black intelligentsia and white-collar group that saw its position in American life *materially improving* and perceived antifascism as a worldview which gave legitimacy to their aspirations.

The evolution of Ethiopian defense efforts in Harlem, especially after Mussolini completed his conquest, demonstrated the deep resistance of Harlem's intellectuals and professionals to movements which tried to sever the community's links to white radicals and liberals. A wave of popular unrest followed news of Mussolini's victory: new attacks occurred on Italian-owned businesses, some of them involving hundreds of people; Italian icemen were driven out of business, and dissidents forced the removal of Capt. A. L. King as head of the New York Division of the UNIA for cooperating with Communists in organizing Ethiopian support actions. But United Aid for Ethiopia — Harlem's major coordinating committee for Ethiopian protests — survived the loss of its nationalist component. In the fall of 1936, it sent a delegation to Europe to meet with Emperor Haile Selassie and won recognition as the official Harlem coordinator of fund raising and publicity for the Ethiopian government in exile. During the first half of 1937, the group held numerous rallies and parades in support of Ethiopian independence, all featuring representatives of the Italian-American left, and participated in picket lines at the

Italian consulate sponsored by the American League Against War and Fascism. Despite its left component, United Aid elicited the endorsement of the national office of the NAACP, which urged its branches to coope-rate with United Aid in organizing fund raising or protest activity in Ethi-opia's behalf.[9]

Support for United Aid seems to have been especially strong in Har-lem's West Indian community. Many of the physicians in the group were of West Indian ancestry as were the *Amsterdam News* owners (Drs. Sa-vory and Powell), several of its ministers (Revs. David Licorish and Wil-liam Imes) and the Communist Party representative, Cyril Philip. Though members of the group differed sharply on many questions — Savory and Powell were loyal Tammany Democrats and periodically warned their readers against Communist manipulation — they came from markedly similar backgrounds. Though a loyal Communist, Cyril Philip was a suc-cessful businessman (he owned a print shop) and a sophisticated and well-traveled person. Like James Ford, the other Communist in the leadership of United Aid, he could interact comfortably with Ethiopian government representatives, European left-wing intellectuals, or members of Har-lem's elite.[10]

But above all, United Aid was held together by opposition to nationalist street orators who spoke of Ethiopia as a race war, encouraged attacks on Italian-Americans, and affected a paramilitary air reminiscent of European fascism (Carlos Cooks, one of the leading nationalist spokes-men, formed a uniformed group called the "Black Shirts"). From his col-umn in the *Amsterdam News,* Adam Clayton Powell, Jr., an exponent of the principle of black unity in the electoral arena, regularly attacked Harlem Garveyites for racketeering at Ethiopia's expense ("Give the Ital-ian haters Antonio's fish cart, Tony's ice business, and Patsy's fruit stand and they'll forget all about Haile Selassie"), and for obfuscating the ma-jor political threat to blacks throughout the world — fascism.[11] "The cause of Ethiopia is not a lost cause," he wrote, "but it is lost if we look at it from a nationalist viewpoint. . . . It is not a union of darker races, but a union of the oppressed that will triumph. . . . The militancy of Garveyism must be retained, the solidification of Garveyism must be carried on, but we must move within a greater program . . . the union of all races against the common enemy of fascism."[12]

Because this perspective was widely shared among educated blacks, Communists had little difficulty in developing an enthusiastic support network in Harlem for the Spanish Loyalist cause. In the spring of 1937, Communists, using the slogan "Ethiopia's fate is at stake on the battle-fields of Spain," worked to make the Spanish Civil War the preeminent cause for internationally-minded blacks. They encouraged blacks to serve in the International Brigades as soldiers and medical workers and to contribute money and medical supplies which they had collected for Ethiopia to the Spanish government. "The material aid which they could not give to the Land of the Ethiopians," William Patterson wrote, "separated as they were by thousands of miles and innumerable difficulties imposed by . . . capitalist governments, can be given through Spain."[13]

Nationalist leaders bitterly attacked this initiative, but many black intellectuals adopted the Spanish cause with great fervor. Several nurses and doctors active in United Aid for Ethiopia (including Dr. Arnold Donawa, the former head of Howard University dental school) volunteered for the Abraham Lincoln Brigade; Harlem churches and professional organizations sponsored rallies for the Loyalist cause; and black relief workers and doctors raised enough funds to send a fully equipped ambulance for Spain. Two blacks who died in Spain—Alonzo Watson and Milton Herndon—were honored with memorial services at leading Harlem churches (St. James Presbyterian and Abyssinian Baptist) and torchlight parades through the community. A Carnegie Hall Concert for Spain, sponsored by a Harlem and Musicians' Committee for Spanish Democracy, featured people like Cab Calloway, Fats Waller, and Count Basie, and a dinner in honor of Salaria Kee, a black nurse who served in Spain, drew virtually the entire black nursing staff from Harlem and Lincoln Hospitals. By 1938, support for Spain had assumed an almost fashionable air, becoming a symbol of sophistication and political awareness among Harlem's intelligentsia.[14] "There was much speech making, singing, and dancing for Spain," George Streator recalled. "Spanish freedom and Negro freedom were made to be synonymous."[15]

The left-wing peace movement attracted a similar Harlem constituency. Marches and conferences organized by the American League Against War and Fascism won endorsements from J. Finley Wilson, head of the International Brotherhood of Elks, Roy Wilkins of the NAACP, Elmer Carter and James Hubert of the Urban League, Democratic Assemblyman William Andrews, and six influential Harlem ministers who were regular participants in Popular Front causes—Rev. Adam Clayton Powell, Jr., of Abyssinian Baptist Church, Rev. William Lloyd Imes of St. James Presbyterian Church, Rev. Shelton Hale Bishop of St. Philip's Episcopal Church, Rev. John H. Johnson of St. Martin's Episcopal Church, Rev. David Licorish of St. Matthew's Baptist Church, and Rev. John Robinson of Christ Community Church. Though they often differed with Communists on specific international issues—the interpretation of the Moscow Trials, support for Jewish immigration—these leaders felt blacks had much to gain by working in antifascist organizations that had large popular followings and displayed special sensitivity to civil rights issues. At the fall, 1937, conference of the League for Peace and Democracy (the new name of the American League Against War and Fascism) attended by fifty black delegates, white conventioneers mounted a huge spontaneous demonstration against hotels in Pittsburgh which refused to accept blacks. This protest, coupled with resolutions on behalf of Ethiopia and the Scottsboro defense passed by the convention, reinforced the feeling that the ideology of antifascism was conducive to support for racial equality.[16] "If the traditional prejudices can be battered down by the radical and liberal elements in their organizations such as the American League," Roy Wilkins wrote in the *Amsterdam News,* "the Negro will become a stalwart part of the movement for peace and democracy."[17]

Events in the Soviet Union strained, but did not destroy, cooperation on international issues between Communists and Harlem liberals. The Moscow Trials elicited sharp rebukes from Adam Clayton Powell, Jr., and the *Amsterdam News* used them as the basis for editorials attacking Stalin's "dictatorship," but such criticism only partially offset the glowing accounts of Soviet life that regularly appeared in the Harlem press, offered by black professionals who visited or lived in the U.S.S.R. With the exception of Claude McKay, who presented a brilliant critique of Soviet nationality policy and treatment of intellectuals, prominent blacks who had been there presented what in retrospect looks like wildly romantic pictures of life in the midst of Stalin's terror.[18] Jean Blackwell, a general assistant at the 135th Street branch library (and later to become head librarian at the Schomburg Collection) claimed that "in no city in America had she seen such well fed people as in Soviet cities."[19] Two Virginia-educated agricultural experts solemnly averred that "you have more right to criticize in Russia than you could hope to have in Mississippi or in my own Virginia."[20] Paul Robeson, black America's most respected actor, declared his approval of the purge trials and announced that he was educating his son in Russia in order to "escape racial prejudice."[21] And black writer Alain Locke spoke of the "cultural minorities art programs being consistently and brilliantly developed . . . for the various racial and cultural folk traditions of that vast land."[22]

Such comments on Soviet life, echoed even in the NAACP journal *Crisis* (which printed an article extravagantly praising the Soviet constitution for declaring racial and ethnic prejudice illegal),[23] subtly influenced the tone of political discourse in Harlem, especially in protest meetings. Whatever their private feelings about the nature of the Soviet regime, ministers like Adam Clayton Powell, Jr., and William Lloyd Imes, and union leaders like A. Philip Randolph, when speaking at rallies in behalf of Spain or Ethiopia, or at meetings of the National Negro Congress, never made reference to Stalin's brutality. Even Frank Crosswaith and leaders of the NAACP, bitter and sophisticated critics of Soviet society, rarely expressed their views publicly between 1936 and the signing of the Nazi-Soviet Pact (the NAACP journal *Crisis,* edited by Roy Wilkins, which had excoriated the Soviet Union over Ethiopia in 1935, contained *not one article* critical of Soviet society during the period in question). The reluctance of black intellectuals and political leaders to systematically criticize Soviet society infuriated Claude McKay. "Despite the blood purges and wholesale uprooting of peasant populations," he wrote, the notion of Soviet Russia as the "one political state which stands for social justice for oppressed peoples . . . remained fixed in gullible minds."[24]

But gullibility offers only a partial explanation of Harlem attitudes on this issue. If some black intellectuals lost their critical faculties in the face of Soviet racial liberalism, others simply decided that an attack on Soviet policies had low priority in a world where fascist movements based on race hatred were making rapid gains. Significantly, most black intellectuals remained clear-headed enough to ignore the crusade against Trotskyism that Communists tried to inspire at the beginning of the Moscow Trials: Harlem Party leaders could not get most of their own *members,* much less their fellow travelers, to attend meetings on the subject and not one prominent Harlem liberal defended the trials in print. In middle-class Harlem circles, pro-Sovietism, though widespread as a political attitude, represented something less than a passion; when circumstances changed, it could be deemphasized, or abandoned with little personal trauma.[25]

The breadth of leftist influence among Harlem's middle class, as well as it limits, emerged clearly in the development of the National Negro Congress. Among Harlemites of an activist bent, the congress aroused great expectations. Adam Clayton Powell, Jr., spoke of it as the "only . . . mass organization dedicated to our problem here in America," and the *Amsterdam News* praised it as a "rank and file organization" that "offers a rallying point for all individuals who are interested in justice for black folk."[26] Communists envisioned it as the institutional form of a "Negro People's Front" that would unite the great organizations of Black America with the left and organized labor and hoped that the NAACP and the Urban League would participate in it and support it.[27]

But in Harlem, the congress found it difficult to translate the enthusiasm it aroused into institutional power. After the first congress convention, members of the New York sponsoring group, composed of representatives of the Urban League, the Communist Party, and local white-collar unions (most trade union representatives came from the Association of Workers in Public Relief Agencies and the Brotherhood of Sleeping Car Porters) found themselves possessed of an organization that had no money, no staff, and no program. Designed as a coalition of organizations, the Congress needed to find issues that could spur other groups to affiliate, and contribute funds and manpower. But strike support and trade union education, bulwarks of congress activity in other cities, could not be made its focus in New York. Harlem already had an organization devoted precisely to that purpose—the Negro Labor Committee—and its leader, Frank Crosswaith, told congress organizers that he would regard their entry into that area as "competition."[28]

Lacking the resources to initiate protest activity, the New York Regional Council of the congress, during the first year of its operation, functioned largely as an educational body, organizing forums and conferences on Harlem's housing and educational problems, on trade union discrimination, on Roosevelt's Court Reform Plan, on the Spanish Civil War, and on the Eastern Seaboard maritime strike. Held in the YMCA and Harlem churches, these meetings, the young Baptist minister Rev. David Licorish, who worked in the Congress, recalled, "brought together a cross section of black people in labor, the church, the professions and the Greek letter fraternities and sororities." Along with luncheons and dances which the congress sponsored, these events institutionalized regular communication between leading black Communists and Harlem ministers, social workers and labor leaders and helped create a milieu in which the causes of the Popular Front—unionism, civil rights, and antifascism— received sympathetic attention from Harlem's "college crowd."[29]

The congress youth work, in particular, demonstrated the degree to which left-wing views had penetrated mainstream black organizations. The sessions on youth had been among the most lively and well attended of those at the congress's founding convention and had led to the creation of a youth division of the NNC which included representatives of the Young Communist League, NAACP junior branches, the YM and YWCA, the Urban League, and alumni clubs of black colleges. Openly left in its political outlook ("it concretized," a *Crisis* writer argued, " . . . a tendency to substitute for a narrow racial outlook an orientation based on class composition"), the NNC youth program helped spur the NAACP to implement a youth movement of its own with an activist orientation.[30] "Already, the youth division of the NNC is comparatively well organized nationally and is making a great inroads," Juanita Jackson, youth coordinator of the NAACP, wrote in a memorandum to the association board. "The NAACP . . . must concentrate and throw its strength and resources immediately into the field."[31]

In Harlem, the youth councils of the NNC and NAACP worked cooperatively on several occasions (even though the national offices of the two organizations—on the NAACP's initiative—never undertook joint projects), and projected a similar political outlook. In February, 1937, NAACP youth coordinator Juanita Jackson solicited NNC and Communist Party support in organizing a "United Youth Committee Against Lynching" that orgnized a well attended series of protests in support of the antilynching bill. The following February, the Committee revived this campaign, also with left-wing support.[32] Similarly, when the NNC Harlem youth council, late in 1937, organized the "Federated Youth Clubs of Harlem," it attracted support from the Harlem Youth Council of the NAACP, as well as from the Urban League, the Y's and many church and student organizations. Later that year, the NNC Youth Council sponsored an All-Harlem Youth Conference, chaired by Dorothy Height (later head of the National Council of Negro Women) to dramatize the need for more recreational space, improved schools, and greater employment opportunities in the Harlem community.[33] Whether launched by the the NNC or the NAACP, such youth programs displayed a common preoccupation with the rise of fascism and a desire to attract support from predominately white trade unions and student groups. "The problems of Negro youth," Juanita Jackson wrote, "seemingly unique and individual, have their roots in basic social and economic adjustments that affect all."[34]

The black Communists who worked in the congress youth council were well equipped to function effectively among the more upwardly mobile sections of Harlem's youth. James Burnham, a City College graduate, had headed the Frederick Douglass Society at the College, and had led the fight for its first black history course; Claudia Jones, of West Indian background, was a skilled journalist and public speaker; Howard "Stretch" Johnson had been a dancer at the Cotton Club and an actor in the Negro People's Theatre, and Angelo Herndon, now a permanent Harlem resident, was a former political prisoner who held national office in the American Youth Congress, a predominately white student organization. Sophisticated, confident, and personally attractive (Jones and Johnson were both strikingly good-looking people) they gave the left an almost glamorous aura that contrasted with the tough "proletarian" image that it once sought to project.[35]

The Second Convention of the National Negro Congress, held in Philadelphia in October, 1937, confirmed the left's image as a center of initiative in Afro-American life. Funded largely by the Communist Party and left-wing unions, the convention attracted thousands of participants —500 from Harlem alone—and speakers such as Walter White of the NAACP and F. A. Patterson of Tuskegee Institute, neither of whom were noted for their pro-Communist views. But despite the pluralistic atmosphere, symbolized by a telegram of greetings from FDR, the official spokespersons for the congress offered a virtually identical version of the Popular Front line of support for organized labor, opposition to Italy, Germany, and Japan, and participation in coalitions with "labor and the progressive and liberal forces of the nation" to win full citizenship rights for blacks and defend "democracy against reaction."[36] "The Congress," an *Interracial Review* writer complained, "convened to achieve a greater degree of social justice for the race, . . . accepted the leadership of Communists and the methods of Communism."[37]

The session on Negro culture represented a special showcase of leftist influence. "The Negro artist who will be worth his salt," poet Sterling Brown told the gathering, "must join with those who are recording a world of injustice and exploitation" and critic Alain Locke argued that the "class proletarian art creed" of the black artists of the '30s had the same commitment to the "expression of Negro folk life" as the "cultural racialism . . . of the 1920's."[38] Indeed, participants in the congress, whether in the cultural or political sessions, continually tried to suggest that they saw no contradiction between seeking greater unity among blacks and expanding black participation in the labor movement and the left. "This is the only nationalism that, in the long run will be effective," Adam Clayton Powell, Jr., wrote of the congress, "a nationalism that aims toward solidifying our race into a militant oneness and to cooperate with other groups in the fight for social justice."[39]

Following this convention, congress Secretary John P. Davis tried to mount a campaign of lobbying and mass protest to secure passage of antilynching legislation being debated in the U.S. Congress. In doing so, he sought the cooperation of the NAACP, which had been carefully orchestrating passage of the bill for many years. But NAACP leaders deeply resented Davis's initiative, which they regarded as a duplication of effort and a cheap device to get funds and publicity for the NNC. Walter White stonewalled all Davis's efforts to arrange sessions between leaders of the two organizations and refused to endorse or participate in congress conferences and demonstrations devoted to the antilynching issue. Even Roy Wilkins, initially more open toward the congress, became disillusioned with Davis, feeling that he was trying to "cut in" on the NAACP program, "to keep the name of his organization before the public."[40]

But if the antilynching drive permanently poisoned Davis's relations with the national leadership of the NAACP, in Harlem it helped put the congress on the map as a protest organization. In April, 1938, the Manhattan Council of the congress (the New York Regional Council had divided into Brooklyn and Manhattan sections) sponsored an antilynching rally in Union Square that attracted 8,000 people and followed it with several demonstrations and indoor rallies in Harlem. In the fall of 1938, the Manhattan Council sent a large delegation to an Eastern Regional Conference of the NNC in Baltimore which made the antilynching bill its major focus.[41]

The educational and cultural programs of the NNC in Harlem, along with its youth work, also displayed considerable dynamism. Early in 1938, the Harlem CP mobilized its affiliated organizations to become sponsors of the Manhattan Council, providing it with the beginnings of a secure financial base. In the spring and summer of 1938, the congress organized a meeting on women's problems, a protest against the threatened closing of the WPA Negro theatre, and a fund-raising cabaret satirizing the Senate filibuster against the antilynching bill. This latter event, called "The Bourbons Got the Blues," offered historical sketches of black life from slavery to the Depression, presented by actors and playwrights in the WPA Negro Theatre.[42]

By the end of 1938, the issue of cultural opportunities for blacks had become a major concern of the NNC's Manhattan Council, equalled only by the antilynching crusade. In the fall of that year, after budget cuts forced the Federal Theatre Project in Harlem to close temporarily, the NNC organized a demonstration demanding a permanent government-funded cultural center in Harlem that would present "legitimate stage plays, marionette shows and plays for children, lectures on painting and sculpture." In May, 1939, in response to an attack by the U.S. Congress on the entire WPA arts program, it organized a two-day conference "to consider present day opportunities for the stimulation of Negro art and culture," and "to arouse community support for maintaining existing opportunities for the employment of Negroes in the cultural field." In doing so, the congress was accurately expressing the priorities of its Harlem constituency, composed largely of intellectuals, professionals, and white-collar workers. But it also expressed the determination of Communists— who now supplied the bulk of the congress's funding—to identify themselves wholeheartedly and enthusiastically with the striving of black artists for security and recognition.[43]

The Communist Party's approach to the black arts, and to black culture generally, remains one of the most controversial features of its activity in Black America. Some critics have claimed that its values were integrationist, while others have claimed they were nationalist. In addition, several critics have argued that the Party milieu "stifled and choked" black creative expression, and that the Party regarded black culture with less respect and understanding than it did other ethnic cultures. One critic has unfavorably compared black writing of the '30s with that of the Harlem Renaissance, claiming that metaphors of left-wing struggle and triumph prevented black writers from achieving a uniquely ethnic voice.[44]

Upon close examination, none of these generalizations prove particularly helpful in understanding the kind of cultural atmosphere that surrounded the Harlem CP during the Popular Front years. The Party's concern with black culture extended far beyond its involvement with the prominent black artists whose work normally frames the debate—Richard

Wright, Langston Hughes, and Paul Robeson. It involved support for black theatre, WPA-sponsored and independent; efforts to encourage the teaching of black history in colleges and schools; the sponsorship of concerts and musical theatre aimed at winning recognition for black musicians; and campaigns to end discrimination in amateur and professional sports. Through Party organizing on the WPA arts projects and in the Harlem schools, and through the cultural activities of its own organizations, it touched the lives of hundreds of black artists and thousands of "ordinary" Harlem citizens. Only by examining these activities in their variety can one make conclusive statements about the values that underlay the Party's approach.

Secondly, analysts of Communist cultural policies often exaggerate their theoretical and political consistency and underestimate how much they varied at different times in the Party's history. In the Popular Front, the Party diverged sharply from the perspectives on black culture which it had espoused in the early '30s — when its critics demanded a black music free from "commercial influences" and a literature totally dominated by a social protest message. As the line of the Party changed from encouraging class struggle in the black community to building a "Negro People's Front" including the middle class, Party leaders began to speak of the black arts (with the exception of vaudeville and musical comedy with sexually explicit themes) as politically "progressive," in and of themselves. Among Party functionaries, the preference for protest themes still carried great weight, but it coexisted with an opportunistic understanding that black artists could not be won to the Party if it continually tried to force their work into a narrow mold. In addition, black and white intellectuals came into the Party who unaffectedly enjoyed black music and dance and tried to develop a political justification for their tastes. The resulting conflict between old and new critics, visible on the pages of the *Daily Worker,* meant that black artists close to the Party did not feel consistent pressure to adapt their work to an abstract political standard and were able to fall back on their own experience and cultural preferences.[45]

But if a more flexible and sophisticated set of aesthetic values made the Party more attractive to black artists, the greatest source of its prestige stemmed from its efforts to secure institutional support for the black arts — an effort which, in Harlem, revolved primarily around the WPA arts projects.

The arts projects had a dramatic impact on Harlem's cultural scene. They included a Federal Negro theatre that employed 350 people, put on sixteen plays, and gave black playwrights, actors, directors, and technicians the best opportunities of their lives; a Federal Writers Project branch that undertook a study of the history of New York blacks and of the cultural, political, and economic life of Harlem's residents; a Harlem

Community Art Center which provided studio space for Harlem's best known artists and offered art classes free of charge; a music project that sponsored orchestras, bands, and music appreciation classes; a puppet show; and an African dance troupe. Fully operative in 1936, these programs gave an extraordinary boost to the morale of Harlem's artistic community, which had lost much of its audience and private patronage since the Depression struck and which still suffered crippling discrimination in "downtown" clubs, theatres, and publishing houses.[46]

Communists, whose ties with black intellectuals were strong even before 1935, rapidly assumed a position of great influence on the Harlem arts projects because of their campaign to unionize project workers. From the time WPA went into operation, it came under attack from Congressional conservatives, and periodic layoffs and budget cuts kept its employees in a state of turmoil. During 1936 and 1937, the City Projects Council, a coordinating committee of WPA unions, aided by the Workers Alliance, responded to each budget cut with a wave of mass protests, strikes, sit-ins and marches. In the summer of 1937, WPA strikes in Harlem, including an all-night sit-in by the entire staff of the Federal Theatre project, shut the program down for days, and the movement was strong enough to force 1,000 stores to shut down in "sympathy" with the strikers. Activist ministers, politicians, and social workers supported these actions, but it was the Party, with large "shop units" on the Theatre project, the Writers project, and the adult education program, that made them happen.[47] "It must be admitted," Claude McKay wrote in the *Amsterdam News,* "that more than any other group, Communists should be credited with the effective organization of the unemployed and relief workers."[48]

The implications of Communist influence on the arts projects served as the focus of considerable debate in Harlem. Several black intellectuals —among them Willis Huggins, a respected black teacher and school administrator—claimed that the Party used its control of hiring and promotions on the Federal Writers Project to insure that all its published work took a "revolutionary slant."[49] The Urban League accused Communists of wielding "wide and in many cases disruptive influence in various projects" and the *Amsterdam News* spoke of the dominance of protest themes as a reason for Congressional attacks on their activities. "The Theatre and the other arts projects are the most articulate of all WPA projects," the paper declared. "Through their work, they have laid bare to the bone the absurdity of an economic system which produces a glut, and yet permits men and women and children to starve."[50]

But the aesthetic consequences of Communist influence on the projects were not as clear-cut as these comments suggest. Other than a strong populism and identification with the downtrodden, the works that came out of those projects with strong Party units had few distinguishing features. The Writers Project document most vigorously attacked by black conservatives—the portrait of Harlem in the WPA *New York City Guide*—never even mentions the Communist Party and gives only passing reference to the National Negro Congress. The author of the portrait, probably Richard Wright, wrote vividly of the social and religious customs of Harlem's population, their patterns of entertainment, and their growing militancy in the face of discriminatory practices, but he gave far more space to Harlem's nightlife than he did to leftist causes.[51]

In the Federal Theatre Project, a strong Party presence proved compatible—not always by intention—with considerable artistic diversity. From the very first, Communists had offered enthusiastic support for the project. Its first director, Rose McLendon, had been co-founder of the Negro People's Theatre, and many of the black actors, writers, and technicians on the project had come from the same group. McLendon died of cancer shortly after the project began, but her white co-director John Houseman continued her procedure of meeting regularly with Harlem Party leaders, who expressed their desire for "plays of social protest and a voice in the assignment of executive jobs."[52]

Nevertheless, none of the Theatre's first three plays, all appearing in 1936, represented the kind of stylized working-class dramas Party leaders liked best. Its opening production, *Walk Together Chillun,* dealt with tensions between southern and northern blacks and called for unity between them; its second production, *The Conjure Man Dies,* used the format of a mystery to present musical numbers and vaudeville routines that Harlemites found hilarious, but few whites could understand; and its third production was the extraordinary voodoo version of *Macbeth,* directed by Orson Welles, that swept critics off their feet and was later taken to Broadway. Only after these plays were produced did the Party faction on the project get the kind of play it wanted, a protest drama called *Turpentine,* that dealt with conditions in southern turpentine camps and the efforts of black and white workers to find a basis for joint action.[53]

Despite private doubts about the theatre's early offerings, Party critics gave it extravagant praise. Mike Gold, writing in the *New Masses,* hailed the Negro Theatre's opening as a sign that a national Negro theatre was emerging which could express the special artistic gifts of the Negro people and "elevate the whole of the American stage." Gold praised the company for offering the work of a black playwright in its first production and made an extraordinarily forceful argument for black cultural autonomy. "Just as no Frenchman or Russian can ever hope to create an Amercan literature . . . ," Gold wrote, "so must a true Negro theatre remain unborn until Negro playwrights have banded themselves for the task. . . .

Negroes have given America all the truly native music it has thus far produced, and I believe that they can give us our first truly poetic theatre."[54]

It is hard to know if Gold — or other Communist critics — fully accepted the implications of this argument — namely that the most distinctive aspects of black artistic expression might emerge in form rather than content, and that open-ended support for the black arts would enhance the entire American culture — but they did begin to act on some of its premises. The Party encouraged its followers to attend Negro theatre plays and supported Harlem's demand for black direction of the project. In August, 1936, the transfer to black leadership took place; John Houseman resigned and was replaced by a "triumvirate" of Harry Edwards, Carlton Moss, and J. Augustus Smith. This change in administration further enhanced Party influence on the project; Smith and Moss were both very close to the Party (if not actual members) though they had differing personalities and artistic tastes. For Harlem Party leaders, the lesson was clear; a muted "cultural nationalism" was consistent with the consolidation of left-wing power.[55]

During the period of black administration, the theatre became a center of protest activity, with almost its entire staff, from stagehands to directors, participating in strikes and demonstrations against reductions in its budget. Changes also took place in the theatre's offerings. The three major plays the project produced following Houseman's departure, *Sweet Land, The Case of Philip Lawrence,* and *Haiti,* all had protest themes — the first dealt with a rebellion of southern sharecroppers, the second with an Olympic athlete whose encounters with discrimination led him to crime, the third with the Haitian Revolution. But within the framework of dramatic realism, they represented a wide variety of approaches to the black experience. Only *Sweet Land,* which ended in an interracial strike, represented a didactic application of the agitprop form; *Philip Lawrence* showed the crippling effects of racial prejudice without offering political solutions; and *Haiti* — the most successful of the productions invoked the color, drama, and distinctive cultural milieu of the slave revolt that led to the founding of the West's first black nation. These productions (occurring between January, 1937, and July, 1938) suggest that during the Popular Front — contrary to the assertions of some critics — the Party did not consistently try to prevent black authors from exploring themes internal to black life.[56]

Nevertheless, it does seem clear that Party cultural policies were far more attuned to the artistic tastes (or more to the point *aspirations*) of Harlem's middle class, than they were to those of its working class and poor. Communists spoke repeatedly of the need to incorporate black "folk themes" into art, but the theatrical forms they endorsed moved educated and sophisticated blacks far more than they did "the folk." Like their counterparts in the Urban League and the NAACP, Communists tried to exclude musical comedy and vaudeville from the WPA Negro theatre, even though these were the forms black working-class audiences traditionally enjoyed. None of the protest dramas the WPA produced attracted a large black audience; the only play which brought out more blacks than whites was *The Conjure Man Dies,* which had music and a good many Harlem in-jokes. Black literary critics agonized over small black attendance at the WPA Negro theatre at a time when "Harlemites of all groups . . . jam pack every can can house in Harlem daily," but with few exceptions, they failed to discuss whether it was possible for a community composed largely of first-generation rural migrants to support its own "legitimate theatre." To bring out those people, a theatre would have to provide the bawdy, funky, and humorous entertainment they were accustomed to, but doing so might have threatened the artistic respectability of the enterprise and reinforced hated racial stereotypes. Faced with that dilemma, Communists threw their weight in favor of a theatre that would display the "serious" artistic talents of black writers, actors, and directors and counted on "education" to ultimately cultivate a large black audience.[57] "The success of the Lafayette thus far," Richard Wright argued in the *Daily Worker,* "merely serves to demonstrate the imperative need of even larger subsidies and more theatre for the Negro people . . . developing a theatre literature for the Negro theatre, organizing and educating an audience, training and developing new talent and making the children of the Negro people theater conscious."[58]

Despite their inability to imagine theatre based on the *existing* folk culture of the black urban masses, and their preference for art which instructed rather than entertained, Communists fought consistently to spread the "instrumentalities of culture" beyond the hands of an elite. Through the National Negro Congress and the WPA unions, Communists pressed for the conversion of the WPA projects in Harlem into permanent institutions. "WHEREAS for the first time in the history of our country," the 1937 Convention of the NNC resolved: " . . . millions of Negro people have received the benefit of cultural enlightenment beyond an elementary education. . . . Thousands of Negro artists, writers, musicians, actors, and dancers have had the opportunity to express the traditional culture of the Negro people to all of the American people. THEREFORE BE IT RESOLVED that the National Negro Congress declares the need for an expanded and permanent Federal Arts program."[59]

At a time when the *right* to be taken seriously within the commercial media was a major concern of black artists, this resolution represented something close to a consensus of the black creative intelligentsia. The WPA had—for one brief moment—changed the world of black artists, transcending the humiliating difficulties of relations with white patrons, booking agents, and producers. For the first time, it made the forms and traditions of Western "high culture" widely accessible to the black population, promising to narrow the yawning cultural gap between the black intelligentsia and the black masses. In defining the fight for WPA as a fight for "cultural democracy" Communists struck a responsive chord among educated blacks who hoped to see black cultural accomplishments recognized—and rewarded—within the American mainstream. "There is still a chance," *Amsterdam News* columnist Marvel Cooke wrote during protests to save the Arts projects, "that the Mabel Harts and Perry Watkins will be able to contribute to democracy and the cultural advancement of the Negro people if you . . . fight for the . . . continuance of the arts projects, the education projects and every other WPA project in which the colored workers and the working masses of people are getting a change to develop and contribute to the advance of civilization."[60] Though the WPA arts projects ultimately lost their funding, the left's role in fighting to save them rebounded to its credit in Harlem's artistic community.

Communist sponsorship of black arts also took place within its own organizations. In 1938, the Harlem section of the International Workers Order opened the "Harlem Suitcase Theatre," a repertory company organized by Langston Hughes and Louise Thompson. Its first production, Hughes's *Don't You Want to Be Free?*, was an agitprop drama which, in the words of one critic "plunges the Negro, fresh from the sweet barbaric freedom of Africa, into the degrading slavery of America, depicts his glorious fight in throwing off the shackles of slavery to the tune of 'Go Down Moses' and gives hope for the bright new day in the unity of black and white workers."[61] Despite the didactic ending, the play created considerable excitement in Harlem, attracting crowds for more than a year and a half and eliciting help from people in the WPA Negro Theatre in designing sets, training actors, and directing the performance. Hughes interspersed the action with his own poetry, and a musical background of blues, spirituals, and jazz, and developed a dialogue accurately attuned to the rhythms of black speech. Black critics perceived a tension between the play's "ethnic" spirit and overt political message, but found the experience powerful nevertheless.[62] At the time of the Nazi-Soviet Pact, the company was preparing to present two additional works by black authors: an adaption of Richard Wright's *Bright and Morning Star,* by Theodore Ward; and a blues opera *The Organizer,* written by Langston Hughes and James Johnson.[63]

Communist involvement in black literary circles did not assume the proportions that it did in theatre, largely because fewer blacks made a living from writing than from the stage and because the best known black left-wing authors, Langston Hughes and Richard Wright, were far more interested in writing than in organizing other writers. A black left-wing literary magazine, *New Challenge,* produced one issue with Party support, but failed to survive because of financial difficulties and the diverse political and professional commitments of its founders.[64]

Nevertheless, the Party derived considerable prestige from the writings of black Communist authors, particularly Richard Wright. Wright came to Harlem in 1937 and served as head of the *Daily Worker*'s "Harlem Bureau" for six months, writing on subjects ranging from black female Communists, to Joe Louis's fights, to blues singer Huddie Ledbetter's (also known as Leadbelly) music. When his first book of stories, *Uncle Tom's Children* (1938), won national acclaim, he quit his job on the *Worker,* but remained visible in Party cultural circles, serving as a sponsor of the Harlem Suitcase Theatre and several benefits for the National Negro Congress.[65]

The books Wright wrote while a member of the Communist Party, *Uncle Tom's Children* and *Native Son,* were perceived at the time as a major breakthrough in Afro-American writing. Presenting the black-white encounter in the United States with unprecedented harshness, Wright created characters who, in the words of Ralph Ellison, possessed an "emotional and psychological complexity never before achieved in American Negro writing," and who struggled with political and personal solutions to their plight with the grandeur and dignity of characters in Dostoevski. Virtually alone among black "proletarian" authors, Wright refused to assign the left greater weight in fiction than it possessed in real life. The Communists in his work were cast in a human mold, sometimes awkward, sometimes paternalistic, sometimes dedicated and unassuming, and the black people who met them were rarely willing to relinquish their suspicions. Wright presented the encounter between blacks and Communism as a question mark, rather than a solution, and depicted the cultural and psychological obstacles that prevented Communists from "reaching" the black masses with an accuracy that made Party leaders flinch.[66]

That Wright could sustain a tone of ambiguity and offer such trenchant criticism of personal styles and cultural biases in the Communist movement, *while still remaining in the Party,* illustrates both his own integrity as an artist, and the Party's willingness to tolerate a certain amount of heterodoxy in order to keep a valued black artist within its fold. Although James Ford hated and mistrusted Wright, several key figures in the New York Party apparatus (particularly Ben Davis and V. J. Jerome, the Party's cultural "commissar") protected him from political attack so long as he defended Party policy on key international issues and publicly credited the Party for his development as a writer. Wright seemed willing to accept the bargain, at least for a period of time (he left the Party in 1942).[67] "I owe my literary development to the Communist Party and its influence, which has shaped my thoughts and creative growth," he declared in

1938. "It gave me my first full bodied vision of Negro life in America."[68]

But if Wright displayed considerable orthodoxy in his political pronouncements, his literary work fell into no fixed mold. In the space granted him as a Party "influential," Wright created a literature that simultaneously reached toward the worldview of black working folk and the main political and philosophical currents in the Western world. In a provocative essay in *New Challenge,* Wright gave the tension in his work theoretical expression, arguing that black writers who wished to contribute to the "interdependence of peoples" had to express the nationalist psychology embedded in black folk culture and institutions. "Negro writers," Wright declared, ". . . must accept the concept of nationalism, because in order to transcend it, they must *possess* it and *understand* it." The young Ralph Ellison, a left-winger but not a Communist, elaborated on Wright's views in an article in *New Masses,* but official Party spokesmen neither endorsed them nor condemned them, contenting themselves with facile comments about Wright's "militancy" that systematically ignored ways in which he challenged, or transcended, conventional leftist literary modes.[69]

The Party's approach to black music represented a similar tension between the imaginative instincts of rank-and-file intellectuals and the sectarian impulses of Party leaders. During the Popular Front years, a group of young American-born Communists, some of them writers for the *Daily Worker,* became convinced that Afro-American music represented the keystone of an American musical culture that was "democratic" in spirit and form and embodied the best elements of the national character. Unlike previous Communist critics, who saw virtue primarily in protest songs or rural black music undiluted by "commercialism," these young turks displayed their greatest interest in black musical idioms which were commercially successful—swing and hot jazz. The Popular Front coincided with an explosion in the popularity of big band dance music, played by black and white bands alike, and some Communists saw a unique opportunity, in identifying with this music, to dramatize the Afro-American contribution to American culture and the cultural benefits of interracial cooperation. The first laudatory article on "swing" appeared in the September 12, 1937, issue of the *Daily Worker.* Written by Max Margulies, it emphasized that "Negro musicians . . . have been the decisive element behind its history, development, and course."[70]

The exponents of this viewpoint, though regarded contemptuously by some Party hardliners, met with little resistance in expressing their opinions in the Party press or using Party-affiliated groups to sponsor concerts and historical surveys of the black musical heritage. Between the fall of 1938 and the spring of 1939, three different "united front" organizations in which Communists participated sponsored ambitious programs of contemporary black music. The first of these, a benefit at Carnegie Hall for the Spanish Children's Milk Fund, featured W. C. Handy (whose birthday was being honored), Fats Waller, Cab Calloway, Jimmy Lunceford, Noble Sissle, Eubie Blake, and several church choirs. The organizers took an historical approach, devoting the first section to "spirituals and art songs" and the second to contemporary big band music and hot jazz. The second concert, held under the auspices of the *New Masses,* represented a self-conscious effort to promote black music as America's "great original art." Put together by John Hammond, the music impresario who did so much to open opportunities for black musicians in the recording industry, the concert tried to show the evolution of black music from its southern rural roots to its contemporary urban manifestations. Among the featured artists were the Mitchell Christian singers, blues artists Bill Broonzy and Joe Turner, boogie-woogie pianists Albert Ammons and Meade Lewis, and Count Basie and his orchestra. The third production, "Negro Music, Past and Present," took place under the auspices of the Labor Club of the American Labor Party. Conceived of and written by Carlton Moss, one of the directors of the WPA Negro Theatre, the program followed the model of the Hammond concert, opening with a presentation of African music and dance, followed by a choir singing work songs and spirituals, succeeded by blues numbers performed by Leadbelly, and the boogie woogie piano of Albert Ammons and Meade Lewis. The program's aim, in the words of its sponsors, was "to draw attention to the fact that one of the main sources of American popular music has been the folk music of the Negro."[71]

This effort to promote black music as a prototypical American art did not sit well with all sections of the Party. Although young "hipsters" in the Party and the YCL appreciated jazz and blues on their own terms, some Party critics regarded the playfulness and sexual banter of performers like Fats Waller and Cab Calloway, and the appreciative shouts of their black audiences, with open contempt, insisting that "true art" could only be appreciated in an atmosphere of solemn concentration. After the benefit for the Spanish Children's Milk Fund, one Party critic so infuriated John Hammond with his patronizing comments ("it was assumed the audience consisted of jitterbugs . . . who were given their money's worth of noise and vaudeville") that he demanded, and received an apology from the *Daily Worker.*[72] In addition, some sections of the Party rank and file, particularly the foreign-born comrades, still regarded music that dealt with nonpolitical themes as bourgeois and decadent. Left-wing composer and songwriter Earl Robinson described an embarrassing occasion when he brought blues singer Huddie Ledbetter to a "progressive" summer camp for adults: "After an evening of him singing 'Ella Speed,' 'Frankie and Albert,' and songs of gun-toting gamblers and bad women, the camp was in an uproar. Arguments raged over whether to censure him, me, or both of us. By the next day, things had calmed down and that evening when he sang 'Bourgeois Blues,' and the ballad he had composed about the Scottsboro Boys, the air cleared."[73]

As these incidents suggest, the Popular Front Party represented something of a battleground between different approaches to popular culture, with an old-fashioned puritanism still holding considerable sway. But the momentum temporarily lay with the Americanizers, who used their access to the Party press to openly identify the Party with the unfettered spirit and energy of black popular music. When Mike Gold criticized John Hammond and James Dugan for claiming, at a concert they promoted, that "hot jazz music is . . . the most important cultural exhibit we have given to the world," he was deluged with hostile letters — many of which he printed. ". . . if American music happens to be predominately Negro," one writer declared, "that is just too bad for us white folks. Why the hell haven't we developed any of our own?"[74] Such enthusiasim for popular music — especially when black-derived — strongly influenced the cultural atmosphere of the Popular Front Party. The Harlem CP founded an interracial "swing club," and encouraged "jitterbugging" at its social affairs ("She could dance like a dream, and she was a Communist," Mike Gold commented about a black social worker he met at a Harlem benefit for the *Daily Worker*); the YCL sponsored a "Swing America" pageant at its 1939 convention, and the *Daily Worker* began printing regular reviews of jazz albums that were remarkably free of didacticism and extraneous political commentary. To some young Communists, the growing popularity of black music represented a key manifestation of a broad democratic tendency in American life. "Swing is as American as baseball and hot dogs," James Dugan wrote in the *YCL Review*. "A good hot band can claim as many raucous rooters as the Dodgers. There is a good deal of audience participation in swing, a kind of give and take and mutual inspiration for the musician and the crowd, a rough democratic air invading the sacred halls of music."[75]

In a very similar spirit, Communists identified themselves with Black America's effort to end discrimination in sports. The Party's Negro Commission, meeting in 1936, made it a priority to "break down discrimination in all fields of sport, especially big league baseball," and the *Daily Worker* sports page, founded the same year, defined this as its central concern. Featuring regular articles on the accomplishments of black athletes and interviews with white ball players advocating integration of their sport, the *Worker* argued that all sports would benefit from the presence of black athletes, and that jim crow represented the one "flaw" in the "democratic set-up" that characterized American sports.[76] "American sportsmanship can no more be denied than American democracy," wrote Lester Rodney, noting growing popular support for the integration of baseball. "They go together and grow together."[77]

In Harlem, the Party devoted increasing attention to sports-related issues. The *Daily Worker* sponsored a basketball team composed of Harlem's top high school players and persuaded black professional football teams to play a benefit game for its expansion drive; left-wing trade unions sponsored sports leagues involving large numbers of black athletes; and Party youth groups lobbied for more recreation space and distributed petitions denouncing baseball jim crow. In addition, the Party enthusiastically joined in Harlem's love affair with Joe Louis, holding "Joe Louis radio parties" to coincide with his fights, and hailing him in the party press as a symbol of black accomplishment and working-class dignity and strength. Communists marched in the spontaneous Harlem parade that followed Louis's victory over German boxer Max Schmeling, shouting antifascist slogans and exulting in the "joyous fraternization of whites and Negroes" that they observed.[78] These interracial demonstrations, Ben Davis wrote, "expressed the sentiment of . . . all who treasure the American traditions of liberty and clean sportsmanship. . . . Nothing is more indicative of the power of Negro and white unity for progress and democracy—once it hits full stride."[79]

The position Communists espoused in their sports journalism—that black participation in American institutions represented the acid test of democratic values—also pervaded their approach to education. During the Popular Front era, the Party won the respect of many Harlem leaders through its effort to improve conditions in Harlem schools, to have black history recognized and taught, and to remove racially biased teachers and textbooks.

The major focus of this effort was the Harlem Committee for Better Schools, a coalition of parents associations, churches, and teacher and community groups that lasted from 1935 until the early 1950s. As in the relief system, the initiative for reform came from radicalized professionals who used their union to fight discriminatory practices. During the early '30s, a large group of radical teachers, overwhelmingly Jewish, were assigned to jobs in Harlem. Themselves the subject of ethnic harassment (college instructors told prospective teachers to remove their "Jewish accents" and if possible to change their names), they were shocked by the physically deteriorated conditions of the Harlem schools and the contempt for the capacities of black children expressed by many teachers and administrators. Seeking support from black teachers in the system, they set to work forming parents associations and chapters of the Teachers Union. By the time of the Harlem riot, they had developed close working relationships with black teachers in almost every school in Harlem and had begun to lobby for physical improvements, free lunches, and better conditions for teachers.[80]

At hearings on education held by the Mayor's Commission on Conditions in Harlem, chaired by Rev. John W. Robinson, teacher activists discovered that their concerns were shared by almost every important organization in Harlem. In the fall of 1935, with Rev. Robinson's support, they issued a call for a two-day conference on educational conditions. More than 350 people showed up, representing groups ranging from the NAACP to the Communist Party, and agreed to form a permanent committee that would press city officials to construct new schools (none had been built in Harlem for over twenty years) and "secure for the children of Harlem educational opportunities equal to the very best available to the most privileged child in New York City."[81]

Almost immediately, the committee began sending teacher community delegations to the mayor and the Board of Education, but the incident that put it on the map was a case of corporal punishment. In the fall of 1936, a 250-pound principal named Gustav Schoenchen allegedly assaulted a 14-year-old black child who had come to pick up his younger brother at a Harlem elementary school. The Committee for Better Schools, with the aid of seasoned Communist street speakers like Audley Moore and Richard Moore, immediately established picket lines at the school and organized demonstrations designed to force Schoenchen's expulsion from the school system. These protests attracted thousands of participants, ranging from Harlem parents to top-ranking black politicians, to leaders of the Harlem branch of the NAACP, and culminated in a mass trial of the School Board at Abyssinian Baptist Church. Three months after the incident, Schoenchen was transferred to a school outside Harlem.[82]

From this point on, the committee emerged as a force to be reckoned with in the city school system. Succeeding in its fight for the construction of new facilities (two new school buildings were built in 1938), it devoted an increasing portion of attention to the content of education offered black children and the way blacks were dealt with in the entire school curriculum. In cooperation with the Teachers Union, the committee sponsored workshops and forums on black accomplishments in American life and fought to remove racist textbooks from the city school system. Condemning the practice of channeling blacks away from academic careers, they agitated for the right of black students to participate in college-bound programs and to attend high schools out of the Harlem district.[83]

The Party's presence pervaded the committee. Theodore Bassett, its secretary, and Emmett May, its vice-chairman, were both Party members, and conducted most of the committee's administrative tasks. Born in the south and trained as schoolteachers, they did their work with a quiet efficiency that won the respect of the black ministers and school-teachers who composed the group's other leaders. In addition, Party neighborhood branches participated actively in the committee's work. Communists served as members of PTA's in most Harlem schools and placed their best street speakers at the Committee's disposal when it organized demonstrations.[84]

But the most significant Party presence came in the schools themselves, where white Communist schoolteachers maintained close working relationships with black teachers, parents, and community leaders. Spearheading this group was a remarkable woman named Alice Citron, who headed Party teacher branches in Harlem. Born in East Harlem of an impoverished Jewish family, Citron grew up in a home where activism was "imbibed with my mother's milk": "My mother was a lifetime member of the ILGWU and our house would have discussions on the strikes of the workers, how they were fighting the bosses. . . . We also had to fight the landlord. My mother would paint the signs, 'this house on strike,' and I would write the leaflets."[85] Assigned to Harlem on her first teaching job, Citron felt an immediate identification with her black students and made it her personal mission to demonstrate their capabilities, both to themselves and to a skeptical school bureaucracy. She wrote plays for her classes dramatizing themes from black history, took them on field trips and invited them to her home, compiled bibliographies on black history for other teachers in the system, and joined black teachers in agitating for the celebration of Negro History Week in the city school system. Under her leadership, activity of this kind became something of a trademark of Communist teachers, who displayed an idealism and enthusiasm in dealing with black children that deeply impressed blacks who worked with them.[86] "Most of the teachers who they said were Communists and kicked out of the school system," Rev. David Licorish recalled: "were much more dedicated to teaching black children the way out of the crucible of American life than the teachers we have now. When they left, Harlem became a worse place. They stayed after school with the children and gave them extra curricular attention to bring them up to level. You didn't have these reading problems like you have today. These people were dedicated to their craft."[87]

The work of these teachers, sustained over twenty years, suggests the degree to which the Party's position on the Negro question had transcended its origins as a Comintern imperative and had linked up with powerful cultural impulses in American society. By defining Black America's struggle for cultural recognition as a source of creative energy for the entire nation, Party spokesmen helped give their white constituency a sense that they had a personal stake in black empowerment and that cultural interchange between the races represented a *defining* feature of the American experience, something to be celebrated and dramatized rather than hidden, or made the butt of jokes. In the Popular Front era, writers close to the Party spoke of the attraction whites historically displayed toward black music, dance, and theatre—or even black language and the black sense of style—as the affirmation of a democratic impulse rather than a journey to the heart of darkness. In doing so, they helped give the strug-gle for racial equality the aura of a movement of cultural regeneration. The uniqueness of this perspective cannot be emphasized enough. His-torically, opponents of civil rights had argued that racial equality meant cultural degeneracy, that black culture embodied a barbarism that would undermine American civilization if blacks were not prohibited from "so-cial intercourse" with whites and excluded from positions of political power. Popular Front critics turned this argument on its head, arguing that the distinctive culture of blacks contributed to much that was vital and original in American life and that their full emancipation would strengthen the entire nation. "The Negro People," wrote Francis Frank-lin, a white southern Communist, ". . . are capable of giving the whites as much as the whites are capable of giving them. The Negro people form an integral part of America. Their cultural heritage is an American her-itage. The American people have a right to this cultural heritage. Jim Crowism denied them the inalienable right to come in intimate contact with Negroes and to know their history and culture."[88]

It was this vision of cultural interdependence, deeply American in its symbolism and psychology, that helped inspire white Communist teachers to approach black education as a mission of special importance, YCL or-ganizers to fight baseball jim crow, and young Communist scholars like Herbert Aptheker and Philip Foner to investigate slave revolts and black abolitionism.

But equally important, the vision had a powerful emotional impact on black intellectuals and helped give the Party roots among that strata that survived into the McCarthy era. No one symbolized this phenomenon more than Paul Robeson. A brilliant actor and singer, Robeson believed that blacks could make their most profound contribution to world civili-zation by emphasizing their African heritage and maintaining their "cul-tural and political autonomy." During his self-imposed exile in Europe, Robeson learned ten African languages, wrote scholarly articles on Afri-can culture, and won worldwide recognition for Afro-American folk mu-sic—always emphasizing the distinctiveness of black art and his own pride in his African ancestry. Yet upon returning to Harlem in the spring of 1939, Robeson openly identified himself with the Communist left. He performed concerts and benefits for left-wing organizations, defended Party policies on international events, and participated in theatre groups, forums, and cultural organizations sponsored by the Harlem Communist

Party. Never a Party member in the conventional sense (he was treated with extreme deference by top Party leaders), he became the left's leading exponent of cultural pluralism, a person who in speeches and performances dramatized the richness of the diverse ethnic cultures that contributed to the American nation.[89]

Robeson's presence dramatized the degree to which cultural issues had become central to the Party's program in Black America during the Popular Front years. Discarding the rigidities of the "proletkult" era, Communists emerged as forceful champions of economic support for black artists (via the WPA), recognition of black cultural accomplishments, and expanded educational opportunities for black youth. In response to these initiatives, an extraordinary number of black intellectuals and creative artists gravitated toward Party circles in Harlem, as members, as fellow travelers, or as participants in discussions or social events. "Richard Wright was in the WPA," Louise Thompson recalls: "We used to have discussions in our home with him, Paul Robeson, Langston [Hughes] and Jacques Romain, a Haitian poet we greatly admired. We had jam sessions, long discussions. . . . Ralph Ellison used to be part of that scene as well. He used to be at my house almost every day." Abner Berry recalled discussing "Proust, Joyce, Doestoyevsky, and the role of symbolism in literature" with Wright, Ellison, and Theodore Ward, and Howard Johnson's Party work brought him in contact with Henry Armstrong, Lena Horne, Billie Holliday, and Lionel Hampton.[90]

For many prominent blacks, particularly the entertainers, the relationship with the left was not marked by towering political passions. The Popular Front Party carefully avoided pushing its black sympathizers beyond their limits and allowed black intellectuals in its ranks considerable freedom to maintain bohemian lifestyles or participate in the spirited social world of Harlem's middle class. "Many people didn't take the political stuff too seriously," Louise Thompson admitted. "It was fashionable at the time and we enjoyed it."[91]

Nevertheless, for a brief historical moment, the Harlem Party served as the hub of an immense range of cultural activities. By defining the Afro-American's contribution to American culture as an important political question, Communist Party leaders unleashed a flood of creative energy among black and white intellectuals attached to their movement. Though top Party spokesmen, trapped in Stalinist categories, usually spoke of black aspirations in platitudes and cliches, rank-and-file Communist cultural figures, released from rigid aesthetic guidelines, began to explore the black-white encounter in America with an accuracy and depth only partially distorted by the values of "socialist realism." In a culture where blacks had typically been regarded as marginal and exotic, the Popular Front left inspired its partisans to see Afro-American and American identity as inextricably linked. Drawing optimism from the programs of the New Deal and the interracial solidarity of Depression era protest, they invoked a vision of the American future in which blacks would be recognized — and appreciated — as both culturally distinctive and quintessentially American.

NOTES

1. Interview with Howard Johnson, July 23, 1977; Claude McKay, *Harlem, Negro Metropolis* (1940; rpt. New York: Harcourt, Brace, Jovanovich, 1968), pp. 248–49; *New York Amsterdam News,* Sept. 17, 1938; George Streator, "Books," *Interracial Review,* 13 (Sept., 1940), 145.

2. "Unite the Negro People for the People's Front," *Communist,* 16 (Nov., 1937), 1038; *Daily Worker,* June 20, 1937, June 29, 1937.

3. Interview with Abner Berry, Nov. 20, 1973; interview with Howard Johnson, July 23, 1977; on Milton Herndon branch, see *Daily Worker,* May 20, 1938, and *Proceedings, 10 Convention, Communist Party, New York State* (New York: New York State Committee, Communist Party, 1938), pp. 159–60.

4. Harry Dolimer and Allan MacKenzie, *The Negro Worker in the ERB* (New York: Association of Workers in Public Relief Agencies, 1937), p. 4; Harvard Sitkoff, *New Deal for Blacks, The Emergence of Civil Rights as a National Issue: The Depression Decade* (New York: Oxford University Press, 1968), pp. 71–76; *New York Amsterdam News,* Dec. 5, 1936, Dec. 19, 1936, July 3, 1937; *New York Age,* Dec. 9, 1939; "The WPA and After," *Opportunity,* 17 (Nov., 1939), p. 322.

5. *New York Amsterdam News,* Feb. 11, 1939.

6. Sitkoff, *New Deal for Blacks,* p. 252; Celia Lewis Zitron, *The New York City Teachers Union, 1916–1964* (New York: Humanities Press, 1968), pp. 64–107; Dolimer and MacKenzie, *The Negro Worker in the ERB,* pp. 5–9.

7. *New York Amsterdam News,* Jan. 16, 1937.

8. Roi Ottley, *New World A-Coming* (1943; rpt. New York, Arno, 1968), pp. 119–21, 328–29; *New York Amsterdam News* Jan. 2, 1937, Feb. 6, 1938; McKay, *Harlem, Negro Metropolis,* pp. 211–13; Claude McKay, "Labor Steps Out in Harlem," *Nation,* 45 (Oct. 16, 1937), 399–402; James W. Ford, *Communists and the Struggle for Negro Liberation* (New York: Communist Party, Harlem Section, 1936), pp. 6–7; Charles Peaker, *Black Nationalism* (New York: African Nationalist Pioneer Movement, 1967), pp. 54–59.

9. Ford, *Communists and the Struggle for Negro Liberation,* pp. 60–65; *New York Age,* May 9, 1936, July 18, 1936, July 25, 1936, Aug. 8, 1936; Tony Martin, *Race First: The Ideological and Organizational Struggles of Marcus Garvey and the Universal Negro Improvement Association* (Westport: Greenwood Press, 1976), p. 256; *New York Amsterdam News,* Feb. 13, 1937, Feb. 20, 1937, Mar. 6, 1937, Mar. 27, 1937; *Daily Worker,* Sept. 28, 1936, Jan. 26, 1937, Feb. 25, 1937, Mar. 3, 1937; Roy Wilkins to James E. Allen, Mar. 5, 1936, NAACP Papers, C 298.

10. *Daily Worker,* May 13, 1937; interview with Howard Johnson, July 23, 1977; interview with Abner Berry, Dec. 2, 1973.

11. *New York Age,* June 13, 1936, July 25, 1936; *Daily Worker,* May 25, 1936.

Powell's quote about "Antonio's fish cart," etc. is from *New York Amsterdam News,* May 20, 1936.

12. *New York Amsterdam News,* Jan. 30, 1937.

13. *Daily Worker,* Mar. 14, 1937. Patterson's quote is from *Daily Worker,* Mar. 10, 1937.

14. McKay, *Harlem, Negro Metropolis,* p. 239; J. R. Johnson (C. L. R. James), "Preliminary Notes on the Negro Question," Apr. 12, 1939, typescript in possession of Martin Glaberman, Detroit, Mich.; leaflet, "For a Fully Equipped Negro Ambulance in Spain," NNC Papers, Reel 7; *New York Amsterdam News,* Feb. 20, 1937, June 26, 1937, July 24, 1937, Jan. 8, 1938, Apr. 23, 1938, May 21, 1938, May 28, 1938; *Daily Worker,* June 2, 1937, Nov. 20, 1937.

15. George Streator, "Books," p. 145.

16. Sitkoff, *New Deal for Blacks,* p. 165; *New York Age,* Aug. 7, 1937; *Daily Worker,* May 8, 1937, July 26, 1937, Aug. 5, 1937; *New York Amsterdam News,* Nov. 13, 1937, Nov. 27, 1937.

17. *Ibid.,* Dec. 4, 1937.

18. Powell's comments appeared in *ibid.,* Apr. 3, 1937; McKay's in *ibid.,* May 27, 1939.

19. *Ibid.,* Aug. 21, 1937.

20. *Ibid.,* Sept. 4, 1937.

21. *Daily Worker,* May 10, 1936.

22. *Official Proceedings of the National Negro Congress, 1937* (Washington, D.C., National Negro Congress, 1937), p. 17.

23. Chatwood Hall, "For Full Equality of Races and Nations," *Crisis,* 43 (Sept., 1936), 269–70; see also Hall, "A Black Woman in Red Russia," *Crisis,* 44 (July, 1937), 203–4.

24. McKay, *Harlem, Negro Metropolis,* p. 252.

25. George Charney, *A Long Journey* (New York: Quadrangle, 1968), p. 105; interview with Abner Berry, July 5, 1977.

26. Powell's quote appeared in *New York Amsterdam News,* Sept. 18, 1937; the editorial on the NNC in *ibid.,* Oct. 30, 1937.

27. James W. Ford, "Uniting the Negro People in the People's Front," *Communist,* 16 (Aug., 1937), 727.

28. James W. Ford, "The National Negro Congress," *ibid.,* 15 (Apr., 1936), 325; "Minutes of Negro Labor Committee," June 7, 1937, NLC Papers, Schomburg Collection, Reel 1; Manning Johnson and George Brown to John P. Davis, June 18, 1936, NNC Papers, Reel 3; John P. Davis to A. Philip Randolph, Sept. 5, 1936, *ibid.,* Reel 7; John P. Davis to Frank Crosswaith, June 8, 1936, *ibid.,* Reel 2.

29. *New York Amsterdam News,* Nov. 21, 1936, Dec. 12, 1936, Mar. 13, 1937; "Tentative Draft of Outline of Organization for NNC," 1937, NNC Papers, Reel 5; *New York Age,* Jan. 23, 1937; *Daily Worker,* Dec. 12, 1936; McKay, *Harlem, Negro Metropolis,* pp. 255–56. Licorish's comments are derived from interview with Rev. David Licorish, May 11, 1978.

30. Lyonel Florant, "Youth Exhibits a New Spirit," *Crisis,* 43 (Aug., 1936), 237; *Young Worker,* Mar. 3, 1936.

31. Memorandum, from Juanita Jackson to Mr. White, Mr. Wilkins, Mrs.

Lumpkin, Miss Ovington, Mr. Pickens, Mr. Houston, undated NAACP Papers, E 1.

32. On the "United Youth Committee Against Lynching," and the NAACP's role in it, see "NAACP Youth Council News," *Crisis,* 44 (Mar., 1937), 89; "NAACP Youth Council News," *ibid.,* 44 (Apr., 1937), 121; Michael Martini to Juanita Jackson, Feb. 1, 1937, NAACP Papers, E 1, leaflet, "For a Lynchless America—Citywide Mass Demonstration Against Lynching," no date, 1937, *ibid.;* Juanita Jackson and Dorothy Height to Dear Pastor, Feb. 3, 1938, *ibid.;* George Blake to Juanita E. Jackson, Feb. 3, 1938, *ibid.;* Juanita Jackson to Louise Thompson, Feb. 9, 1938, *ibid.*

33. On the activities of the NNC Harlem Youth Council, see Claudia Jones, "Recent Trends Among Negro Youth," *YCL Review,* 3 (July, 1938), 15–17; Ethel James to Walter White, May 9, 1938, NAACP Papers, C 383; Marion Forrester, "Young Folks Sit Up and Take Notice," *Opportunity,* 16 (Jan., 1937), 25.

34. Juanita Jackson, "Young Colored America Awakes," *Crisis,* 45 (Sept., 1938), 289.

35. *Young Worker,* Feb. 29, 1936, June 14, 1937; Selma Gordon, "'Stretch' Johnson, People's Candidate," *YCL Review,* 5 (Sept. 16, 1940) 11; interview with Alice Citron, Aug. 28, 1979; interview with Abe Shtob, Apr. 28, 1976; interview with Abner Berry, Feb. 4, 1978.

36. Lawrence S. Wittner, "The National Negro Congress: A Reassessment," *American Quarterly,* 22 (Winter, 1970), 890; Wilson Record, *Race and Radicalism: The NAACP and the Communist Party in Conflict* (Ithaca, N.Y.: Cornell University Press, 1964), pp. 95–96; *Official Proceedings of the Second National Negro Congress,* pp. 3–12; *New York Amsterdam News,* Oct. 16, 1937.

37. "Fighting the Epidemic of Prejudice," *Interracial Review,* 11 (Aug., 1938), 115.

38. *Official Proceedings of the Second National Negro Congress,* pp. 15–17.

39. *New York Amsterdam News,* Sept. 18, 1937.

40. On Davis's efforts to get NAACP cooperation in the NNC's antilynching campaign, see Wolters, *Negroes and the Great Depression,* pp. 365–67; John P. Davis to A. Philip Randolph, Apr. 7, 1938, John P. Davis to A. Philip Randolph, Dec. 20, 1938, A. Philip Randolph to John P. Davis, Dec. 30, 1938, all in NNC Papers, Reel 7. On the NAACP's hostile response to Davis's initiative, see Walter White to Arthur Huff Fauset, Apr. 4, 1938; memorandum, Walter White to Roy Wilkins and Charles Houston, Mar. 8, 1938; Walter White to John P. Davis, Apr. 1, 1938; To Organizations Cooperating on the Anti-Lynching Bill and N.A.A.C.P. Branches, Mar. 14, 1938; Roy Wilkins to William Pickens, Apr. 19, 1938, all in NAACP Papers, C 383. Roy Wilkins, in the period of the NNC's formation, seemed far more willing to envision an alliance between the NAACP and the NNC than did Walter White. Wilkins attended meetings of the NNC's New York Sponsoring Committee, attended the NNC founding convention as an observer, and recommended to the board of the NAACP that the "Association go in and have a voice in the making of policies" (Roy Wilkins, memorandum to the Board of Directors on the National Negro Congress, Mar. 9, 1936, NAACP Papers, C 383). Wilkins's "enthusiasm for a possible alliance of the NAACP with the National Negro Congress" (Roy Wilkins to John P. Davis, Mar. 3, 1936, *ibid.*)

proved of relatively short duration, but it demonstrated an important, though subtle, difference between Wilkins and White in their approaches to the Communist left. Wilkins was sharply critical of Communist ideology and tactics, but he seemed to lack White's visceral hatred of the Party. During the Popular Front, Wilkins seemed quite willing to work with Communists on an issue-by-issue basis, and the *Crisis,* under his editorial direction, did not print one article directly critical of the Communist Party or the Soviet Union between April, 1936 — when he assumed full editorship — and the Nazi-Soviet Pact. This did not make Wilkins a Party sympathizer; rather, during the Popular Front he seemed to regard Communists as a "fact of life" in Black America whose participation in civil rights activities was acceptable, though not necessarily welcome. After the Pact, Wilkins became far more vociferous in his expression of anti-Communist views, and more determined to exclude Communists from the mainstream of black protest.

41. John P. Davis to Gladys Stoner, Apr. 15, 1938, NNC Papers, Reel 8; *New York Amsterdam News,* Apr. 9, 1938; *New York Times,* Apr. 3, 1938; *New York Age,* Apr. 23, 1938, Sept. 24, 1938, Oct. 22, 1938; George Blake, "The Party in Harlem, New York," *Party Organizer,* 12 (June, 1938), 19.

42. On the Party's effort to assure financial and political support for the NNC, see *Proceedings, 10 Convention, Communist Party, New York State,* pp. 36, 253–55, 298; and James W. Ford, "Rally the Negro Masses for the Democratic Front," *Communist,* 17 (Mar., 1938), 267–68. On the activities of the Manhattan Council of the congress, see Gladys Stoner to John P. Davis, June 16, 1938, Aug. 12, 1938, NNC Papers, Reel 8; Dorothy Height to John P. Davis, Apr. 25, 1938, *ibid.,* Reel 7; Max Yergan and Vivienne France to Dear Friend, June 29, 1938, *ibid.*; *Daily Worker,* May 6, 1938; *New York Amsterdam News,* Apr. 30, 1938, May 21, 1938.

43. Max Yergan and Vivienne France to Dear Friend, June 29, 1938, NNC Papers, Reel 7; *Daily Worker,* Apr. 25, 1939, May 3, 1939; *New York Amsterdam News,* June 3, 1939, June 24, 1939, Aug. 5, 1939; *New York Age,* Apr. 29, 1939, May 6, 1939.

44. Harold Cruse claimed that Party's values were integrationist, Robert Bone claimed that they were nationalist. Cruse also used the phrase "stifled and choked" to describe the Party's impact on black artists, a charge which James O. Young has echoed. Harold Cruse, *Crisis of the Negro Intellectual* (New York: Frederick Morrow, 1967), pp. 148–49, 186–87; Robert Bone, *The Negro Novel in America,* (rev. ed., New Haven: Yale University Press, 1968), p. 116; James O. Young, *Black Writers of the Thirties* (Baton Rouge: Louisiana State University Press, 1973), p. 40.

45. A perusal of the *Daily Worker* during the Popular Front years reveals greatly varying critical stances toward black art. Occasionally, open conflict over this issue erupted in the paper. One controversy erupted over a jazz benefit for the Spanish Children's Milk Fund in Nov., 1938; and another over a "Spirituals to Swing" concert sponsored by the *New Masses* in Dec., 1938. See *Daily Worker,* Nov. 24, 1938, Dec. 2, 1938, Jan. 3, 1939, Jan. 12, 1939.

46. James W. Baker, "Art Comes to the People of Harlem," *Crisis,* 46 (Mar., 1939), 78–80; "The WPA," *Opportunity,* 17 (Feb., 1939), 34; *Daily Worker,* July

10, 1937, June 25, 1939; *New York Amsterdam News,* Jan. 16, 1937, Feb. 11, 1939; *New York Age,* Apr. 29, 1939, May 6, 1939.

47. *New York Amsterdam News,* Dec. 19, 1936, June 26, 1937, July 10, 1937, July 24, 1937, Jan. 7, 1939; *New York Times,* June 20, 1937, July 18, 1937; *New York Age,* June 19, 1937, June 15, 1937, July 2, 1937, July 28, 1937.

48. *New York Amsterdam News,* Sept. 17, 1938.

49. McKay, *Harlem, Negro Metropolis,* pp. 240–50; *New York Age,* July 9, 1938, Sept. 24, 1938, Oct. 8, 1938, Oct. 22, 1938.

50. "The WPA," *Opportunity,* 17 (Feb., 1939), 34; *New York Amsterdam News,* July 8, 1939.

51. *New York City Guide: A Comprehensive Guide to the Five Boroughs of New York* (New York: Random House, 1939), pp. 132–51; Constance Webb, *Richard Wright: A Biography* (New York: G. P. Putnam's Sons, 1968), p. 145.

52. John Houseman, *Runthrough, A Memoir* (New York: Simon and Schuster, 1972), pp. 175–81; Lofton Mitchell, *Black Drama* (New York: Hawthorne Books, 1967), p. 100; *New York Age,* Jan. 9, 1937; *New York Amsterdam News,* Dec. 28, 1935.

53. Houseman, *Runthrough,* pp. 184–206; Mitchell, *Black Drama,* pp. 100–102; *New York Amsterdam News,* Oct. 24, 1936; *Daily Worker,* June 29, 1936.

54. *Daily Worker,* May 10, 1936; *Young Worker,* Apr. 7, 1936; Michael Gold, "At Last, A Negro Theatre," *New Masses,* (Mar. 1, 1936), 18–19.

55. Houseman, *Runthrough,* pp. 206–10; *New York Amsterdam News,* Apr. 24, 1937, June 25, 1938; *New York Age,* Jan. 9, 1937; *Daily Worker,* June 15, 1937, July 10, 1937, Oct. 15, 1937; interview with Abner Berry, July 5, 1977. The Harlem CP consistently supported Harlem's demand for black leadership on the Federal Theatre Project. In December, 1935, they expelled two white Communists on the project for "white chauvinism" for refusing to relinquish their administrative positions in favor of blacks. Whether this represented a principled stand or an opportunistic one is difficult to determine. Certainly, the Party had nothing to lose politically by supporting black administration, since so many leading black theatrical people had left-wing sympathies. For accounts of the 1935 incident, see *New York Amsterdam News,* Dec. 28, 1935; *New York Age,* Dec. 30, 1935; and Houseman, *Runthrough,* p. 181.

56. On protest actions involving the WPA Negro Theatre, see *New York Times,* June 17, 1937; *New York Amsterdam News,* June 26, 1937, July 10, 1937; *New York Age,* July 17, 1937; *Daily Worker,* June 17, 1937, June 29, 1937, July 2, 1937. On the plays produced under the triumvirate of black administrators, see Mitchell, *Black Drama,* pp. 102–3; *New York Amsterdam News,* Jan. 30, 1937, May 14, 1938, June 4, 1938, June 25, 1938; *New York Age,* July 24, 1937, Jan. 8, 1938, June 4, 1938; *Daily Worker,* June 15, 1937, Oct. 15, 1937.

57. Houseman, *Runthrough,* pp. 180–81; *Daily Worker,* Aug. 21, 1937; *New York Amsterdam News,* June 4, 1938; Edward Lawson, "Androcles and the Lion, A Review," *Opportunity,* 17 (Jan., 1939), 15. The quote about "can can houses" is from *New York Amsterdam News,* May 14, 1938. For analysis of the social basis of black theatrical preferences, see Arthur Paris, "Cruse and the Crisis in

Black Culture," *Journal of Ethnic Studies,* 5 (Summer, 1977), 63–66; and Anne Powell, "The Negro and the Federal Theatre," *Crisis,* 43 (Nov., 1936), 340.

58. *Daily Worker,* Oct. 15, 1937.

59. *Official Proceedings of the Second National Negro Congress, 1937,* pp. 17–18.

60. *New York Amsterdam News,* July 15, 1939.

61. Norman McLoed, "The Poetry and Argument of Langston Hughes," *Crisis,* 45 (Nov., 1938), 358–59.

62. *New York Amsterdam News,* Apr. 30, 1938; *Daily Worker,* Apr. 20, 1938, May 15, 1938, Nov. 23, 1938.

63. *Ibid.,* Aug. 7, 1939, Aug. 9, 1939.

64. Webb, *Richard Wright,* pp. 143–46; Michel Fabre, *The Unfinished Quest of Richard Wright,* (New York: William Morrow, 1973), pp. 142–47.

65. *Ibid.,* pp. 147–51, 161–62; *Daily Worker,* Feb. 25, 1938, Dec. 29, 1938, Apr. 25, 1939, May 9, 1939, June 9, 1939.

66. Richard Wright, *Uncle Tom's Children: Four Novellas* (New York: Harper, 1938); *Native Son* (New York: Harper, 1940); Ralph Ellison, "Recent Negro Fiction," *New Masses* (Aug. 5, 1941), 22.

67. On Wright's relationship with the Party hierarchy, particularly James Ford and Ben Davis, see Webb, *Richard Wright,* pp. 142–55; Fabre, *The Unfinished Quest of Richard Wright,* pp. 184, 228–29; Addison Gayle, *Richard Wright: Ordeal of a Native Son* (Garden City: Doubleday, 1980), pp. 90–100, 141; interview with Abner Berry, Sept. 5, 1977.

68. *Daily Worker,* Feb. 25, 1938.

69. Richard Wright, "Blue Print for Negro Writing," in Ellen Wright and Michel Fabre, eds., *Richard Wright Reader* (New York: Harper and Row, 1978), p. 42; for the best interpretation of Wright's literary work while he was associated with the Party in New York, see Fabre, *The Unfinished Quest of Richard Wright,* pp. 146–233. See also Ellison, "Recent Negro Fiction," 22–26.

70. *Daily Worker,* Sept. 12, 1937. On the emergence of "Swing" as a musical phenomenon, see Marshall W. Stearns, *The Story of Jazz* (1958; rpt. New York: Oxford University Press, 1972), pp. 197–217; Leroi Jones, *Blues People* (New York: Morrow, 1963).

71. Interview with John Hammond, Sept. 26, 1978; *New York Age,* Dec. 3, 1938, Feb. 25, 1939; *Daily Worker,* Nov. 17, 1938, Nov. 24, 1938, Dec. 11, 1938, Dec. 29, 1938, Mar. 7, 1939; *New York Amsterdam News,* Dec. 24, 1938, Feb. 11, 1939.

72. *Daily Worker,* Nov. 24, 1938, Dec. 2, 1938; interview with John Hammond, Sept. 26, 1978.

73. Jay Williams, *Stage Left* (New York: Charles Scribners' Sons, 1974), p. 155.

74. *Daily Worker,* Jan. 3, 1939, Jan. 12, 1939.

75. E. L. Dmitry to John P. Davis, May 3, 1938, NNC Papers, Reel 6; *Daily Worker,* Nov. 20, 1937, May 3, 1939; James Dugan, "Stop Before You Jitter," *Young Communist Review,* 4 (July, 1939), 2, 22. Critics of Communist cultural policy have completely overlooked the enthusiasm for jazz and swing that characterized much of the Party in the Popular Front. In 1938 and 1939, the *Daily*

Worker and the *New Masses* printed regular reviews of jazz albums, interviews with black musicians like Duke Ellington and Count Basie (*Daily Worker,* June 4, 1939), and even had an article speaking positively of "Amateur Night at the Apollo" (*Daily Worker,* Aug. 3, 1939). This seems to contradict Harold Cruse's assertion that "The Negro radical leftwing leadership of Harlem had *always* [italics mine] shown a snobbish and intolerant attitude towards the type of stage fare featured weekly at the Apollo" (Cruse, *Crisis of the Negro Intellectual,* p. 15).

76. "Minutes of Negro Commission," Aug. 3, 1936, Robert Minor Papers, Columbia University; Mark Naison, "Sports for the Daily Worker: An Interview with Lester Rodney," *In These Times,* Oct. 12–18, 1977; Mark Naison, "Lefties and Righties: The Communist Party and Sports During the Great Depression," *Radical America,* 13 (July–Aug., 1979), 54–58; *Daily Worker,* June 14, 1939.

77. *Daily Worker,* July 19, 1939.

78. *Daily Worker,* Apr. 5, 1937, June 22, 1937, June 24, 1937, Dec. 27, 1937, July 15, 1939, July 21, 1939, July 25, 1939; "Striking Out Jim Crow," *Young Communist Review,* 4 (Sept., 1939), 5; George Charney, *A Long Journey* (New York: Quadrangle, 1968), p. 104.

79. *Daily Worker,* June 23, 1938.

80. Zitron, *The New York City Teachers Union,* pp. 85–107; interview with Alice Citron, Aug. 28, 1979; interview with Morris Schappes, Aug. 24, 1979; Alice Citron, "An Answer to John Hatchett," *Jewish Currents,* (Sept., 1968), 12–13.

81. *New York Times,* Apr. 11, 1935, May 9, 1935; Charles Hendley to Dear . . . , Dec. 10, 1935, UNIA Papers, Reel 5, Box 13; Charles Hendley to Capt. A. L. King, Feb. 1, 1936, *ibid.,* Box 14; *New York Amsterdam News,* Mar. 28, 1936; *New York Age,* Mar. 27, 1937; New York State Temporary Commission on the Urban Colored Population, *Public Hearings,* vol. 6, pp. 1053–54; Zitron, *The New York City Teachers Union,* pp. 88–89.

82. Theodore R. Bassett and Emmett M. May to John P. Davis, Oct. 8, 1937, NNC Papers, Reel 5; *New York Amsterdam News,* Sept. 26, 1936, Nov. 21, 1936, Jan. 23, 1937, Jan. 30, 1937; *New York Age,* Nov. 4, 1936, Jan. 16, 1937, Jan. 30, 1937; *Daily Worker,* Aug. 5, 1936, Oct. 23, 1936, Oct. 27, 1936, Oct. 31, 1936, Nov. 10, 1936, Dec. 3, 1936, Jan. 29, 1937. On the NAACP's participation in the Committee for Better Schools, see memorandum, Walter White to Roy Wilkins, Charles Houston, Juanita Jackson, no date, 1936, NAACP Papers, C 332; minutes, "Delegates Organization Meeting," Mar. 8, 1936, *ibid.*

83. *New York Age,* Mar. 27, 1937; *New York Amsterdam News,* Apr. 17, 1937, July 17, 1937, Jan. 15, 1938; Zitron, *The New York City Teachers Union,* pp. 89–91, 94; New York State Temporary Commission on the Urban Colored Population, *Public Hearings,* vol. 6, pp. 1053–79; *Daily Worker,* Jan. 31, 1939; Edith Stern, "Jim Crow Goes to School in New York," *Crisis,* 44 (July, 1937), 201–2.

84. *Daily Worker,* June 1, 1937; interview with Theodore Bassett, Nov. 2, 1973; interview with Abner Berry, July 29, 1974; interview with George Charney, Nov. 7, 1973; *Proceedings, 10 Convention, Communist Party, New York State,* p. 159; Blake, "The Party in Harlem, New York," p. 15.

85. Interview with Alice Citron, Aug. 23, 1979.

86. Charney, *A Long Journey,* pp. 98–99; Zitron, *The New York City Teachers Union,* pp. 94–105; Citron, "An Answer to John Hatchett," p. 13.

87. Interview with Rev. David Licorish, May 11, 1978.

88. Francis Franklin, "The Cultural Heritage of the Negro People," *Communist,* 18 (June, 1939), 57–71; James Dugan, "Stop Before You Jitter," *Young Communist Review,* 4 (July, 1939), 3, 22.

89. Philip Foner, ed., *Paul Robeson Speaks, Writings, Speeches, Inverviews, 1918–1974* (New York: Brunner/Mazel, 1978), pp. 9–13; Sterling Stuckey, "I Want to be African: Paul Robeson and the Ends of Nationalist Theory and Practice, 1941–1945," *Massachusetts Review,* 17 (Spring, 1976), 84; *Sunday Worker,* May 10, 1936, June 4, 1939; Sitkoff, *New Deal For Blacks,* p. 164; *Daily Worker,* July 2, 1939; *New York Age,* July 8, 1939; *New York Amsterdam News,* May 27, 1939, July 15, 1939.

90. Interview with Louise Thompson, Sept. 14, 1977; interview with Abner Berry, Sept. 5, 1977; interview with Howard Johnson, July 23, 1977.

91. Interview with Louise Thompson, Sept. 14, 1977.

9

Communists in Harlem Politics

FOR HARLEM COMMUNISTS, the Popular Front brought with it a vastly increased emphasis on electoral politics. Throughout the early 1930s, Communists had approached elections primarily as educational vehicles, devoting the bulk of their energy to labor organizing and mass protest, but in 1936, they began to seriously try to affect the outcome of local and national elections. The changes in Party structure, tactics, and rhetoric which its leaders mandated, all aimed at helping Communists compete electorally as a "regular American party," capable of drawing a sizable vote for its own candidates and "labor and progressive" candidates whom it supported.[1]

Harlem Communists, following the cues of the Party's national leadership, engaged in a wide variety of strategies to influence voters in black neighborhoods. In 1936, they tried to form a third-party movement based exclusively in Harlem (the All People's Party) which could attract voters hostile to the Democratic and Republican machines and serve as the Harlem nucleus for a Farmer-Labor Party. In 1937, as the prospects for a national Farmer-Labor Party dimmed, they abruptly dissolved the All People's Party and sent their cadres into the American Labor Party, a statewide political body formed by leaders of New York's needle-trade unions to amass socialist support for Roosevelt and alternately compete with and influence New York's conservative Democratic organization. From 1937 on, the American Labor Party served as the primary, but not the exclusive, focus of Communist work. Communists campaigned for all ALP candidates, but also ran their own candidates for the New York City Council, and congressman-at-large, and made a few tentative efforts to influence primary elections and district leadership fights in Harlem's Democratic party organizations.[2]

Considering the effort Communists extended, these various campaigns did not produce impressive results. Communists not only failed to get a significant vote for their own candidates in the two predominately black Harlem assembly districts (the 19th and 21st), but also they proved unable to build the American Labor Party in Harlem into an effective competitor of the dominant Tammany machine.[3] Between 1936 and 1939, the highest vote total any Communist candidate received in either of the two Harlem assembly districts was 556 (drawn by Israel Amter in the 21st AD in 1938 when he ran for congressman-at-large), which represented 2.19 percent of the total votes recorded in the district. American Labor Party candidates did somewhat better, getting 15 percent and 9 percent of the Harlem vote in the 1937 and 1938 elections, but this still fell far short of the totals amassed by either major Party, and of ALP percentages in the city as a whole.[4]

The Party's greatest success in the community came not as the architect of political campaigns, but as a catalyst for lobbying and legislative action. It took the initiative in forming a Harlem Legislative Conference in 1938, which drew together assemblymen from four Harlem districts to press for action to improve housing, health facilities, and schools in the Harlem community. It also played a key role in the activity of a Manhattan Citizens Committee which lobbied for the passage of a group of anti-discrimination bills drawn up by the New York State Commission on the Conditions of the Urban Colored Population.

But the Party's inability to develop local electoral machinery, either under its own name or that of the ALP, which could compete with the Democratic and Republican organizations in Harlem, troubled it greatly. In no other dimension of Harlem life did the Party's efforts to seize the initiative from indigenous leaders produce such limited results. Communists proved unable to translate their power as leaders of mass protest into support at the polls. Their failure reflected the strength of the community's attachment to the two-party system, the popularity and effectiveness of black machine politicians, and the limited ideological appeal of "Communism" or "labor politics" among the masses of Harlem's population in a context where neither could easily yield tangible results.

Electoral politics represented one sphere of Harlem's life in which the community had made significant advances during the early Depression years without the support, or even the sustained input, of Communists and other radicals. From the time Harlem first became a black community, black editors, politicians, and church and civic leaders had united behind the demand for black representation in the Board of Aldermen and the state legislature, and for black leadership of the 19th and 21st Assembly District organizations in both major parties. The first black assemblyman won office in 1917, but the district leadership struggles, which involved control over party patronage, only began to succeed in the Depression years. In 1930, blacks won control of Republican district leadership in the 21st and 19th AD's, and in 1935, over the Democratic leadership in the 21st AD. These leadership victories represented the culmination of years of planning and political infighting, involving lawsuits, the formation of new political clubs, and tens of thousands of dollars in expenses. Both Harlem newspapers offered their support, along with prominent black leaders from all over the country, and the campaigns had the atmosphere of racial crusades as well as inner Party disputes.[5]

These political battles attracted so much attention because they simultaneously offered ethnic recognition and access to patronage. In the Democratic Party particularly, district leaders controlled access to numerous city jobs, exerted influence with policemen, judges and city inspectors, and had access to a sizable campaign fund which they distributed to loyal workers. Though the Tammany machine was declining in the 1930s, particularly after scandals rocked the Walker administration and La Guardia came to power in 1933, it still wielded considerable power in the city.[6] In 1933, the "job list" of the Democratic district leader in the 21st AD (the city jobs he controlled access to) had salaries totalling $600,000, and the 19th AD leader reputedly had even more patronage than that at his disposal.[7] Winning control of a district leadership not only meant access to more city jobs for ambitious Harlemites, but greater protection for black businessmen, legitimate and otherwise, greater influence with the city bureaucracy for black lawyers and civil servants, and more opportunity for black politicians to be nominated to judgeships and city commissions. Because of discriminatory practices in both parties, blacks did not benefit from the perquisites of district leadership to quite the extent of other ethnic groups, but the rewards were sufficient to attract large numbers of talented Harlemites to the political game and to invest the victors in leadership struggles with considerable prestige.[8]

The black leaders who came out of this milieu proved to be far more skilled at running election campaigns than were Harlem Communists. Most Harlem politicians had served long apprenticeships with white district leaders and knew how to motivate campaign workers and voters with a judicious combination of racial appeals, favors, and direct financial incentives. Committed to advancing their own careers as well as black ethnic interests, they tended to approach politics as a "cold-blooded business proposition" in which distribution of patronage and protection of illegal activities were unavoidable parts of the political landscape.[9] Few of them had charismatic personalities or raised ideological issues beyond the sphere of racial self-interest, but they understood the needs of their impoverished constituents and tried to serve them effectively with the practical powers at their disposal—helping them get extensions on their rent, speaking to the police when they got in trouble, supplying them with Christmas presents if they couldn't afford them. "Any problem you had, Tammany could help you with," recalled Rev. David Licorish, a participant in many anti-Tammany election campaigns in Harlem. "They were the social workers. They gave out baskets of food at Christmas time; if people got in trouble, they would send a lawyer." Abner Berry echoed this view: "They had the only organization in Harlem that was exactly like the one that the Communists wanted to build. They had a hold on the people down below in the election districts. When you met a Tammany election district captain, you met a real man of the people." But Harlem politicos were not just machine hacks. When holding elective office, they sometimes became forceful opponents of racial discrimination and strong supporters of social legislation, taking positions considerably to the left of the parties they represented.[10]

Harlem Communists, in their first major election campaign in the Popular Front years, vastly underestimated the strength, resilience, and flexibility of Harlem politicians and political organizations. When James Ford began to hint at the possibility of a new third-party movement in Harlem in March, 1936, he acted as though ideological affinity, or agreement on a common program of demands, would be sufficient to get masses of Harlemites to abandon the political organizations they had worked in for years. In a speech at the National Negro Congress, Ford called for a movement for "independent political action" in Harlem which could unite "Democrats, Republicans, Socialists, and Communists," around a program that called for full civil rights in the South, higher wages and more adequate relief, defense of labor's right to organize, and resistance to fascism internationally. He proposed that such a movement link up with groups around the country seeking to form a Farmer-Labor Party.[11]

The *program* Ford set forth did not clash with the views of Harlem intellectuals and trade unionists who attended the Negro Congress. But the *idea* of a third party—a Farmer-Labor Party at that—owed far more to the political line Communists brought back from the Seventh Comintern Congress than it did to the experience of political activists in the Harlem milieu. Farmer-labor movements and local labor parties existed in many midwestern states, but few Harlem leaders had even talked about such a movement before Ford made his pronouncement, and the Communist leader seemed to assume that his Party's prestige, and the prolabor views of many Harlem leaders, represented sufficient conditions for its success.[12]

Shortly after the Negro Congress ended its meetings, Communists moved to implement Ford's proposal. The Joint Conference on Discriminatory Practices, the Communist-led coalition that fought discrimination in the relief system, issued a call for a conference at Mt. Olivet Baptist Church to discuss "independent political action," and won the endorsement of several Harlem trade unionists, social workers, and community activists who had worked closely with Communists in Harlem protest organizations, among them Lester Granger and James Hubert, Donellan Phillips of the Consolidated Tenants League, Capt. A. L. King, Ashley

Totten of the Brotherhood of Sleeping Car Porters, Theodore Poston of the *Amsterdam News* unit of the Newspaper Guild, and Dr. P. M. H. Savory. Conspicuously absent from the list of sponsors, either because of suspicions of Communist motives, or because of long-established working relations with Harlem's Democratic and Republican leaders, were ministers of Harlem's largest churches and leaders of the Harlem branch of the NAACP. (The only minister to participate was Rev. David Licorish of St. Matthew's Baptist Church, chairperson of the church committee of the National Negro Congress.) Literature advertising the conference made the enterprise seem a logical extension of the pressure groups that had developed after the Harlem riot; it spoke of the mayor's refusal to release the Riot Commission Report or to act on its recommendations, and described independent political action as a way of forcing concessions from government officials. Nothing in the propaganda mentioned the formation of a third party, although that remained the ultimate objective of Communist leaders.[13]

The meeting at Mt. Olivet attracted a large audience. Some two hundred people attended as delegates and observers, including representatives of the Urban League, the UNIA, and some Democratic and Republican clubs, and they listened to a diverse group of speakers denounce the inaction of city officials in the face of Harlem's needs. But at future meetings of the group, when the focus of discussion shifted from detailing Harlem's grievances to proposing candidates for office, the size and breadth of the audience diminished considerably.[14]

By June, 1936, when the organization sponsored a two-day convention to found the All People's Party, several important sponsors had quietly withdrawn support, among them Dr. Savory of the *Amsterdam News,* and Lester Granger and James Hubert of the Urban League. Among non-Communist Harlemites present, only trade unionists were well represented, joined by a few lawyers and leaders of tenants' organizations. The most dynamic group at the convention came from the Italian sections of Harlem where Vito Marcantonio, the Party's most reliable ally in Congress, faced a tough fight for re-election. Marcantonio, officially a Republican, found himself getting so little support from that party's leaders that he needed another line to run on in the election, and the All People's Party seemed to fill the bill.[15]

The All People's Party convention nominated three candidates for office in the 1936 campaign: Vito Marcantonio for Congress in the 20th CD; Horace Gordon for assembly in the 19th AD; and Angelo Herndon for assembly in the 19th AD. Both black candidates, unlike Marcantonio, were newcomers to electoral politics who had achieved prominence for their protest activities. Gordon, an attorney, had been active in exposing police misconduct at the Riot Commission hearings. Their campaign

platform also had an insurgent tone. Their literature denounced the unwillingness of the mayor to act on his Riot Commission Report, the refusal of Tammany leaders to allow black control of the 19th AD district
leadership, the refusal of both major parties to carve out a black congressional district in Harlem, and the inadequacy of schools, hospitals, and
housing in the Harlem community.[16]

But the validity of the issues they raised could not compensate for their
lack of support from Harlem churches and political clubs, or the weakness of their campaign organization. The All People's Party only set up
its campaign machinery in July, 1936, operating with a staff composed
largely of Harlem Communists. (The only non-Communists participating in it were Donellan Phillips, Dr. August Petioni, and Benjamin Mc-
Laurin of the Brotherhood of Sleeping Car Porters.) As a purely local
party, it received neither funding nor publicity from the presidential
campaign and acquired no endorsements from prominent politicians. In
addition, its opponents in the assembly races had the benefit of campaign
machinery that functioned all year round, composed of district captains
and lieutenants attracted by the promise of material gain as well as more
intangible satisfactions. Compared to them, the People's Party workers
were rank amateurs.[17]

In addition, the All People's Party suffered important defections from
its already meagre ranks as a result of the formation of the American Labor Party in the summer of 1936. Initiated by leaders of the Amalgamated
Clothing Workers Union and International Ladies Garment Workers
Unions, the ALP aimed to provide a line on the ballot which would en-
able New York's socialists and left-wing unionists to cast their votes for
President Roosevelt without registering as Democrats and supporting
New York's Tammany machine. Although some needle-trades union
leaders saw the ALP as the first step toward the development of a third-
party movement in the country, their sole objective in 1936 was to insure
that Roosevelt carried New York State. Because of Roosevelt's great personal popularity with trade unionists in the state, their efforts attracted
considerable support. Virtually every CIO union in New York joined the
new party and helped it set up campaign machinery in New York's assembly districts. In Harlem, where the trade union movement was not as
strong or well rooted as in Jewish and Italian neighborhoods, the response
was somewhat less impressive, but Layle Lane of the Teachers Union,
and Ted Poston of the Newspaper Guild, who had made speeches at the
first conference for All-Harlem Political Action, switched allegiance to
the ALP, and they were joined by two key Harlem ministers who were
sympathetic to organized labor, Rev. Adam Clayton Powell, Jr., and
Rev. John H. Johnson.[18]

The formation of the new party presented Communists with a dilemma.

Though they had no role in the decision to create the ALP, it conveniently reinforced Communists' strategy in the presidential election, which was to present a rationale for supporting Roosevelt behind the facade of a campaign for Browder. In addition, the ALP, though it was led by old-time Socialists, represented precisely the kind of trade union involvement in politics that Communists endorsed. Because they were not ready to "officially" support Roosevelt, Communist leaders withheld comment on the ALP, but they quietly encouraged Party trade unionists to work within the ALP and help it set up local organizations. Three Communist-led unions—the Teachers Union, the Fur Workers Union, and the Transport Workers Union—participated in the first ALP campaigns, and Michael Quill of the TWU was selected to sit on its state executive committee. (Quill would win election to the City Council on the ALP ticket in 1938.)[19]

In Harlem, Party leaders encouraged a small number of Communists and Party sympathizers to get a foothold in the American Labor Party. Emmett May, a black Communist active in the Teachers Union and the Committee for Better Schools, became head of the ALP organization in the 19th AD. Communists continued to campaign for All People's Party candidates, but gave less and less publicity to their activities in the Party press. The *Daily Worker,* which had editorially endorsed the All People's Party five separate times in July and August, virtually ceased to discuss it from September on. Party leaders still hoped for a strong "independent vote" in Harlem, but they no longer saw the All People's Party as the only vehicle to achieve it, and were keeping a close eye on the ALP to see if that party had more potential to serve as the nucleus of a third-party movement, in Harlem and throughout the city.[20]

The results of the 1936 elections demonstrated rather forcefully that third-party activity, under any banner, had great difficulty winning the support of black voters. In the 19th AD, Horace Gordon drew 248 votes on the Communist line and 256 on the All People's Party line, as compared to 19,557 and 4,575 for his Democratic and Republican opponents. In the 21st AD, Angelo Herndon drew 294 votes on the Communist line and 72 votes on the All People's Party line, as compared to 24,158 and 6,172 for his Democratic and Republican opponents. The American Labor Party, active only in the presidential election, did a little better, drawing 811 votes for Roosevelt in the 19th AD and 1,113 in the 21st AD, representing 3 percent and 3.27 percent of the votes cast, but its performance hardly represented a groundswell of anti-Tammany sentiment among Harlem voters.[21]

Had Communists based their assessment of the potential for third-party activity in New York strictly by the results in black neighborhoods, they might have abandoned the effort. But the impressive size of the ALP vote in the city convinced Communists that a third-party movement did have a future there, though its potential remained questionable in other parts of the country. The American Labor Party polled 238,845 votes for Roosevelt in New York City, drawing particularly strong support from Jewish neighborhoods. Communists felt the ALP's potential constituency was much larger if it developed strong local election machinery and had the full benefit of Communist support.[22]

In the Harlem area, Communists felt the strong vote tallied by independent candidates in Italian and Puerto Rican neighborhoods partly compensated for their poor showing among blacks. In the 20th Congressional District, encompassing a predominately Italian and Hispanic electorate, Vito Marcantonio tallied 5,000 votes on the All People's Party ticket. In the racially diverse 17th AD (black, Puerto Rican, and white) in Lower Harlem, Jose Santiago tallied 2,000 votes as the Communist candidate for assemblyman. Communist leaders concluded that if one combined the total of American Labor Party, All People's Party, Communist, and Socialist votes in *all* neighborhoods of Harlem, one could perceive a solid base for third-party politics. Paradoxically, Negro Harlem, where the Communist Party had the largest membership and the greatest involvement in local protest movements, seemed to be the weak link in this electoral chain, but Party leaders hoped they could overcome this problem by more concentrated efforts to build an election apparatus in black neighborhoods.[23]

Shortly after the election, Communists decided that they could best expedite the development of a third-party constituency in New York by entering the American Labor Party. In February, 1937, Communists announced that they endorsed the ALP's program and would work to achieve "unity of labor and progressive forces" behind its candidates. Because of ALP regulations, Communist Party organizations could not affiliate as whole units, but Communist trade unionists and neighborhood activists began joining ALP district organizations as individuals.[24]

In Harlem, Communists withdrew their support from the All People's Party, which immediately disappeared, and began working within ALP local bodies in black, Italian, and Puerto Rican neighborhoods. They also assigned a new organization secretary to oversee this strategic shift, George Charney, who replaced Louis Sass. Charney, a white University of Pennsylvania graduate who had done graduate work at Harvard, possessed more knowledge of American history and politics than his Hungarian-born predecessor, and seemed more equipped, by temperament and background, to helping the Party adapt to electoral activity. An enthusiastic advocate of the "Americanization" of the Communist Party, Charney plunged into the task of coordinating electoral strategy in diverse Harlem neighborhoods with considerable enthusiasm, and rapidly developed a good working relationship with the Party's most important political ally, Vito Marcantonio.[25]

The decision to work within the American Labor Party gave Communists their first opportunity to participate in a prolabor electoral coalition that had significant political influence. With its broad trade union base and its close ties with the Roosevelt and La Guardia administrations, the ALP had the potential to become a strong rallying point for the diverse liberal and left-wing groups that Communists hoped to unify to protect "democracy against reaction." Although Communists had little influence on ALP policies, they felt the ALP's positions on civil liberties, labor, housing, and education represented a sound minimum program for a "People's Front" in New York State, and offered Communists a respectable platform from which they could expound their views on these issues.[26]

In addition, the introduction of a new system for city council elections in 1937, proportional representation, virtually guaranteed a party of the ALP's size a significant role in city government. The system gave minor parties who could poll 75,000 votes in a particular county an excellent chance to elect one or more city councilmen, even if they were weaker than the major parties on a district-by-district basis. Based on its vote total in 1936, the ALP seemed assured of electing councilmen in Manhattan, the Bronx, and Brooklyn.[27]

To take advantage of the ALP relationship, Communists had to make some political sacrifices. Officially barred from membership by ALP statute, Communists found they could work within the ALP easily so long as they did not challenge the policies set by the ALP founders, who, through their control of the state executive committee, had the power to make all nominations and endorsements and write the ALP platform. Moreover, even if Communists *wanted* to constitute themselves as an opposition caucus—a step which might shatter the fragile "unity" with their former enemies—they possessed no formal mechanism to do so. Not until the fall of 1938, the date of the first ALP primary, would ALP state executive committee decisions be subject to political action and debate by members of ALP organizations.[28]

In Harlem, the insulation of Communists from ALP decision making posed some special problems which partially offset the advantages Communists accrued by participating in the organization. Because of its citywide constituency and influence, the ALP represented a force which Harlem politicians and voters had to take seriously; it had the power to elect candidates to the city council and state legislature and affect the outcome of close elections by making endorsements. But though it possessed some of the attributes necessary to compete with Democratic and Republican organizations, it had to demonstrate to a cynical Harlem electorate that it would use the powers at its disposal to fight for antidiscrimination measures and black representation in government. Unfortunately for Harlem Communists, the ALP leadership proved indifferent to such concerns. They appointed only two blacks to the thirty-four person ALP state executive committee (Lillian Gaskins of the ILGWU and Thomas Young of the Building Service Employees Union), had no black as an important party officer, and had no plank in the ALP platform attacking lynching and segregation in the South, or discrimination in employment, housing, and public accommodations in the North. Liberal on economic issues, in dealing with the race question they seemed to follow the tradition of the Socialist Party, which claimed that blacks would be helped more by measures which aided the working class as a whole than by policies which appealed to their special interests. Communists disagreed vehemently with such an approach, but they found that their weak bargaining position in the ALP made it difficult for them to fight openly for the civil rights platform and the recruitment of black leadership they thought was necessary. The one Communist (or Party sympathizer) on the ALP state executive committee, Michael Quill, did not challenge the ALP's "color-blind" policies at committee meetings, even when those policies came under attack in the Party press.[29]

The 1937 election campaign in Harlem illustrated some of the compromises Communists had to make as part of their accommodation with the ALP leadership. Early in 1937, Communists announced that they would "accept ALP discipline," which meant supporting all of that party's nominations and campaigning for its candidates. When the ALP declared its support for La Guardia's re-election, Communists agreed to campaign for him, arguing that the Tammany Hall machine represented the local embodiment of "fascism" and that La Guardia's re-election would prevent Tammany's resurgence. This endorsement caused some embarrassment to Harlem Communists because most of their 1936 election campaign, especially in behalf of All People's party candidates, had been directed against the La Guardia administration. In addition, many protest movements Communists sponsored, from the Workers Alliance, to the Committee for Better Schools, to the movement to improve conditions in Harlem Hospital, engaged in regular confrontations with city officials.[30] Local Communist leaders dutifully shifted gears and endorsed the mayor, but without their usual enthusiasm. "I do not say that La Guardia has done all he could for the people of Harlem," James Ford wrote, "yet he has made a beginning." The "chief shortcoming" of La Guardia, Ben Davis argued, was his failure to wage a battle against the Tammany-controlled board of aldermen, and blacks had to support him as the lesser of two evils. "The issue confronting the . . . Negro people," he declared, "is fascism and reaction, represented by the Tammany, Liberty League, Mahoney ticket, versus progress and democracy represented in the ALP."[31]

Harlem Communists felt more enthusiastic toward the ALP's nominee for assembly in the 19th AD, Benjamin McLaurin. McLaurin, an official of the Brotherhood of Pullman Porters who had strong ties with Harlem trade unionists, intellectuals, and civil rights leaders, ran against incumbent Democrat William Justice and Republican Ira Kemp, the virulently anti-Communist head of the Harlem Labor Union. Communists regarded McLaurin as a strong candidate and campaigned for him actively, but were distressed by the failure of the ALP executive committee to invest funds and energy into his campaign or to devote much attention to building up ALP clubs in the 19th and 21st AD's.[32]

Communists also had problems with the ALP leadership's tactics in the Manhattan City Council race. The ALP nominated no black person as a candidate for city council, even though both the Democrats and the City Fusion Party (an organization set up by La Guardia to attract voters reluctant to use the Republican line) had put up black candidates as part of their slates. Late in the campaign, the ALP executive committee endorsed the black City Fusion candidate Rev. John H. Johnson, but didn't distribute literature for him or urge white ALP supporters to give Johnson second- or third-choice votes on their ballots. Communists tried to compensate for this by holding rallies for Johnson in Harlem, and urging left-wing voters throughout the borough to place him third on their ballots behind the Communist council candidate, Israel Amter, and the ALP nominee, B. Chrney Vladek, but their efforts proved insufficient to affect the outcome of the election.[33]

Despite the ALP leadership's unwillingness to campaign aggressively for black candidates, the party made a fairly respectable showing in Harlem. In the city as a whole, La Guardia got 482,790 votes on the ALP line, or 21.6 percent of the votes cast. In the 21st AD, he got 4,289 votes, 16.24 percent of the votes cast; in the 19th AD, he got 3,147 votes on the ALP ticket, 14.9 percent of the votes cast. These tallies, though short of the ALP's citywide average, represented far more than any left or labor tickets had ever achieved in Harlem during the Depression years.[34]

In the 19th AD race for state assembly, where William Justice won reelection, the ALP's performance proved less impressive. McLaurin, the ALP candidate, only got 9.68 percent of the votes. But in the 17th AD, a multiethnic district, the ALP provided the balance of power. Oscar Garcia-Rivera won election to the assembly there on a combined Republican, ALP, and City Fusion ticket, becoming the first Puerto Rican to sit in the state legislature. In the 21st AD, William T. Andrews, running without ALP or Communist opposition, won re-election over his Republican opponent.[35]

The success of the American Labor Party in its first citywide election—

it elected five city councilmen and five state assemblymen—made a strong impression in Harlem. Both Harlem newspapers commented that the ALP had been the balance of power in the mayoralty election and represented a new political force in the life of the nation that blacks could not afford to ignore. "Its appearance at this time," the *New York Age* commented, "marks the definite end of that era in the United States when the ideal of every laborer was to become a capitalist. . . . In years to come, there is bound to be less emphasis on things that labor and capital have in common, and more on those things in which they have no share. . . . The Negro group is largely workers . . . and their interests will naturally lie with the laborers of other races."[36] Adam Clayton Powell, Jr., an early ALP supporter, projected an equally optimistic view of the ALP's significance, but expressed grave reservations about the Party's failure to include blacks in positions of leadership or endorse black strivings for ethnic representation. "I feel that the Labor Party offers the Negro his last chance to come into his own in the political life of America," Powell wrote. "We must be careful, however, for fear that we shall be led into the same old rut. . . . We demand an able Negro in one of the highest positions in the American Labor Party. When this is done, Negroes in New York . . . will fully support this new third party."[37]

Communists echoed all Powell's criticisms of the ALP, but felt the election results confirmed their judgment that the ALP represented the major electoral form of the "People's Front" in New York City. While admitting that the ALP and its mayoralty candidate "left much to be desired" as far as blacks were concerned, Ben Davis firmly equated the ALP with the "forces of progress" and called on blacks to join the party and fight to change its policies. "The question before Harlem," he averred, "is . . . the necessity for building the ALP as a weapon for Negro rights and for the people."[38]

How blacks could wage such a fight, given the policy-making monopoly exercised by the ALP executive committee, Davis didn't say. Like other Communist spokespersons, he offered no specific strategy to modify the racial policies he condemned. After the ALP's impressive showing in the 1937 election, Communists seemed more reluctant than ever to take any initiatives against ALP leaders which might draw attention to their "illegal" presence in the organization. Instead, they urged black trade unionists and "progressives" to join them in strengthening ALP groups in the Harlem Assembly Districts, postponing the task of racial reform to a later date.

With ALP work as their focal point, Harlem Communists began to look for other ways to expand their political influence in the community. In December, 1937, they helped engineer an ambitious attempt to form a nonpartisan coalition to press for programs favorable to Harlem in the

New York State Legislature. George Charney, Harlem division election strategist, felt that the ALP's gains in the 1937 election made it possible to create a multiethnic pressure group and lobby that combined the forces of Harlem's protest organizations and its elected political leaders. To avoid having the proposal too closely identified with the Communist Party, Charney persuaded ex-Congressman Vito Marcantonio to assume leadership of the new group, called the Harlem Legislative Conference, and to use his prestige and influence to win the cooperation of the four Harlem assemblymen: Democrats Robert Justice and William Andrews of the 19th and 21st AD's, and Republican-ALP designees Oscar Garcia-Rivera and Walter Fitzgerald of the 17th and 20th AD's. Marcantonio, anxious to win left and minority group support for his 1938 Congressional race, proved to be an energetic and effective leader. Aided by Emmett May, one of the most capable black administrators in the Harlem CP, Marcantonio won the endorsement of a large number of trade unions, churches, and political clubs in the black, Puerto Rican, Irish, and Italian neighborhoods of Harlem. The first public meeting of the Conference, held in late December, 1937, drew over 400 people.[39]

Interest in the legislative conference, while a tribute to Marcantonio's popularity and influence, also reflected the impact of public hearings of the New York State Temporary Commission on the Conditions of the Urban Colored Population. These hearings, though less uproarious affairs than those of La Guardia's Riot Commission, dramatized the black population's extreme difficulty in securing adequate housing, education, health care, and employment opportunities. Members of the commission, openly sympathetic to Harlem's problems, subpoenaed city school, hospital, and housing officials, heads of important trade unions, and officials of banks, insurance companies, and utilities corporations to defend their racial policies, while inviting Harlem activists to present the community's grievances against them. Bitter confrontations took place between the head of the city hospital system and Harlem nurses' and physicians' groups; between school board officials and representatives of the Committee for Better Schools; between AFL leaders and black trade unionists; but the most extraordinary revelations took place during the cross-examination of utility company officials. Heads of the phone company, the BMT subway lines, and the Fifth Avenue Coach Company not only admitted discriminating against blacks in certain job categories, but defended such discrimination as essential to the harmony of the work force. Phone officials insisted service would be disrupted if blacks were hired as operators, and bus and subway spokesmen claimed their white customers would object to black drivers and conductors. Such testimony enraged Harlemites present at the hearings and helped impel the commission to develop a series of bills aimed at banning discrimination against blacks by trade unions, utility companies, state and city agencies, and stores, restaurants, and places of amusement.[40]

The momentum of these hearings carried over into the legislative conference, which held bimonthly meetings throughout the 1938 session of the New York State Legislature. Before large and vocal audiences, activist groups presented their grievances to Harlem legislators, while liberal politicians from other parts of the city came to offer their support. Communist-led trade unions—the Teachers Union, the Transport Workers Unions, and the State, County and Municipal Workers Union—along with the Workers Alliance, played a particularly important role in the proceedings, but church and professional organizations, the Urban League, and members of the State Temporary Commission also contributed to the discussion. The conference mobilized support for the commission's package of antidiscrimination bills, for slum clearance and the construction of public housing, for increased relief, and for a sixty-hour work week for domestic workers. Although few measures endorsed by the conference passed in the 1938 legislative session, the politicians involved in the conference seemed pleased with the results, and agreed to work together in 1939.[41]

Exhilarated by the results of the legislative conference, Harlem Communists undertook a very ambitious program of activities for the 1938 elections. They strengthened their foothold in the Harlem ALP, achieving control of the 21st AD ALP organization and waged an aggressive campaign for the ALP ticket. They participated in a nonpartisan coordinating committee to elect a black representative to Congress. They made their first entry into a Democratic primary campaign, seeking to defeat the hand-picked candidates of 19th AD Tammany boss, Harry Perry. And they tried to run a vigorous campaign in Harlem for Israel Amter, the Communist Party candidate for congressman-at-large.[42]

However, Communists were forced to implement this complex strategy with a relatively small number of people. In black neighborhoods of Harlem, where the Party had built its reputation as a leader of mass protest, its cadres were stretched to their limits by unemployed work, tenants' organizing, campaigns against job discrimination, committees to improve schools and hospitals, and support groups for Spain and Ethiopia. In addition, the Harlem division election committee, led by George Charney, decided to concentrate most of its resources on the election of Vito Marcantonio in the 20th Congressional District and the re-election of Oscar Garcia-Rivera in the 17th. Some practical considerations justified such an allocation. Marcantonio and Rivera represented close allies of the Communist Party, almost fellow travelers, who faced sharp challenges from Tammany candidates; no campaign in black Harlem posed the ideological issues so sharply and offered Communists an opportunity to serve as the balance of power. But the concentration on Lower and East Harlem exacerbated the Party's weakness in the 19th and 21st AD's, where no prominent politicians identified with it that closely.[43]

In addition, the ALP compromised some of its credibility, and that of Communists with it, by having no antidiscrimination program in its 1938 platform and by refusing to endorse or designate a black candidate for Congress in the 21st District. During the spring of 1938, Communists had participated in a nonpartisan committee to elect a black representative to Congress, and had offered no public objection when the committee selected Rev. Lorenzo King as its candidate. The Republican Party endorsed King, and he began a vigorous campaign, along straight ethnic lines, against white Democratic incumbent Joseph Gavagan, the congressional sponsor of the antilynching bill and a strong supporter of New Deal legislation. Communists did not like King's campaign strategy, but hesitated to oppose him because of their promise to support a black candidate. ALP leaders, however, who had made no such commitment, announced their support for Gavagan in August, 1938. Their action caused a furor in Harlem.[44] "Probably the biggest surprise to Harlemites," *Amsterdam News* columnist Earl Brown wrote, "is the fact that the ALP took a political run out powder on them and refused to support a Negro for Congress in the 21st Congressional District."[45] Adam Clayton Powell, Jr., angrily proclaimed his support for King and urged blacks to challenge ALP decisions that violated their ethnic interests. "This should be a lesson to us," he wrote, "to make the price of Negro political fellowship as high as possible and . . . to serve notice that the voting strength of the race must be bargained for."[46]

The ALP's action provided Communists with a difficult choice: They could support Gavagan, and offend key Harlem allies, or they could campaign for King and create a conflict in the ALP. After much hesitation, they decided the ALP relationship had greater political importance. Early in the fall, they quietly indicated their support for Gavagan's candidacy and campaigned for him in Harlem on the ALP line, as they did for ALP gubernatorial candidate Herbert Lehman, a Democrat.[47]

The 1938 election results in Negro Harlem represented a setback for the left-wing parties. In the 19th AD, Lehman got 1,894 votes on the ALP line, 9.26 percent of the votes cast; in the 21st AD, he got 2,167 votes, 8.57 percent of the votes cast. In the congressional race, Gavagan got 702 votes in the 19th AD on the ALP line, 7.07 percent of the votes cast; and 1,947 votes in the 21st AD, 7.7 percent of the votes cast. (He was elected by large pluralities on the Democratic line.) Israel Amter, the Communist candidate for congressman-at-large, got 306 votes in the 19th and 556 votes in the 21st AD, more than a Communist ever received on a combined total in the two districts, but still only a miniscule percentage of the votes cast (1.49 percent and 2.19 percent). In East and Lower Harlem, where Communists concentrated more of their resources, the results proved more satisfactory. Oscar Garcia-Rivera won re-election to the assembly on the ALP ticket without Republican endorsement, and Marcantonio won election to Congress with almost 9,000 votes on the ALP line. But the results in black neighborhoods suggested that the ALP had lost ground there in the 1938 campaign, and that Communist acquiescence in ALP policies that alienated black leaders and voters hindered the progress of both organizations.[48]

The left's poor election showing in Negro Harlem, though it upset Communist leaders, did not cause them to modify their role in the ALP. Their deference toward the ALP's leadership represented the logical outcome of a *national* Communist policy, growing steadily more explicit, which defined "unity of progressive forces" as the highest priority, superseding the demands of any particular ethnic group or section of the working-class movement. In Harlem, such a policy led to a series of new controversies with black leaders which further diminished the moral credibility of the left and its ability to make headway in elections.[49]

The most serious conflict between Communists and Harlem politicians and civic leaders came during a 1939 campaign to win enactment of the legislative package offered by the New York State Commission on the Condition of the Urban Colored Population. In January of that year, Gerald Allen, a black Urban League employee and secretary of the commission, called a meeting at the New York Urban League to form a Citizens Committee to put pressure on the state legislature to pass the fourteen antidiscrimination bills which the commission had drawn up. Harlem Communists quickly became the dominant force on this committee and used their formidable contacts with trade unions, peace groups, and cultural and ethnic organizations to flood the Capitol with petitions, telegrams, and postcards supporting the bills. But Communists vehemently opposed three of the bills which the commission proposed, aimed at preventing unions which practiced discrimination from receiving certification as official bargaining agents under the State Labor Relations Act. AFL and CIO officials in the state opposed such legislation on the grounds that it might serve as an opening wedge to weaken the state's "little Wagner Act," and Communists, who had supported the bills when they were first proposed in hearings, now pulled out all the stops to prevent them from passing. Communist trade unionists and neighborhood activists, elected spokespersons for the fifty-person delegation which the Citizens Committee sent to Albany, lobbied energetically for eleven of the commission bills, but asked Governor Lehman to veto the labor bills if they passed the legislature.[50]

The Party's about-face on this issue, which placed it at odds with both

the NAACP and the Urban League (the two organizations had been lobbying vigorously for antidiscrimination provisions in federal and state
labor relations laws since 1934) occurred without explanation, or even
acknowledgment. In December, 1937, Communists testifying before the
State Commission on Conditions of the Urban Colored Population had
endorsed proposals to bar unions that discriminated from the protection
of the State Labor Relations Act, and a *Daily Worker* editorial appeared
the same month which endorsed their position. But by January, 1939,
when antidiscrimination bills had actually been drafted, Communists in
unions and in black communities began lobbying against them, and the
Daily Worker began denouncing them as "divisive." Although the precise
timing of this extraordinary shift, and the political logic that underlay it,
does not appear in the public record, Max Gordon, who represented the
Party in Albany at the time, told me in an interview that the determining
factor in the Party's shift was the support given the bills by the Republican caucus in the state legislature, which aroused suspicions that the bills
would be used by employers to retard labor's drive for recognition. This
may well have been true, but by failing to explain its actions frankly, the
Party gave credence to accusations that it placed its ties with important
union officials above its relations with civil rights organizations.[51]

The opposition to the labor bills waged by union representatives and
black Communists on the Citizens Committee aroused the ire of many
Harlemites involved in the lobbying effort. "Organized labor is seeing a
ghost," Assemblyman William Andrews claimed. "The bills cannot and
will not be used by the enemies of labor."[52] The *Amsterdam News* questioned the claims of black Communists that the bill undermined black-
white unity. "We are all in favor of a united front of black and white
workers," the paper editorialized. "In fact, that's labor's only salvation.
But we also know that it hasn't worked yet, and that it's now just as important for Negroes to get a foothold in labor unions through legislation
as it is to gain jobs through legislation."[53] The three bills, strongly supported by Republican legislators, passed the state senate and assembly,
but despite the pleas of Harlem's two assemblymen, Governor Lehman
vetoed the bills and suggested they be redrawn to minimize labor's objections. He also signed two bills which the Citizens Committee had successfully lobbied for, one providing special hearings for civil-service workers
who charged discrimination, and another enlarging the state's civil rights
law to include retail shops, beauty parlors, and elevators of apartment
houses with two or more tenants.[54]

Communists regarded their role in the 1939 legislative session with
considerable satisfaction. Through superior organizational skill, they had
projected an unpopular viewpoint as the "official" Harlem position, and
had avoided a direct confrontation between black leaders and organized

labor. But their maneuvering cast further doubt upon the Party's claim that blacks could gain more from an alliance with the "progressive movement" than from traditional ethnic politics. More than ever, Harlemites sympathetic to organized labor concluded that unions could not be trusted, on the basis of imputed "class solidarity," to accommodate themselves to the black community's needs; they had to be agitated against, and bargained with, to force them to act justly. "Human nature being what it is," Roy Wilkins concluded, "we had best put laws against Jim Crowism in our present labor statutes."[55]

The Communist Party's role in the 1939 election campaign in Harlem demonstrated to what degree its influence, and that of "labor politics" generally, had been stripped of its aura of grandeur and promise and converted into a matter of hard-nosed political bargaining much akin to the machine politics it purported to replace. Two major events took place in the political life of Harlem that year: a campaign to win black control of the district leadership in the 19th AD and a campaign to elect a black member of the Manhattan City Council. In each, the Communist Party's role reflected, in a rather precise manner, its ability to affect the outcome of the voting.

In the 19th AD leadership fight, Communists watched from the sidelines. The challengers to the local Tammany boss, Harry Perry, felt they could win the district leadership on the basis of a straightforward racial appeal, and did not need Communist or labor support. Led by an assistant district leader named J. Raymond Jones, they formed a new Democratic club in the district, then enrolled 8,500 members and came to the primary with enough votes to defeat Perry. Perry threw the issue into the courts by challenging the validity of Jones's petitions, but the campaign created an atmosphere which made it impossible for him to rule directly, and he stepped down from the leadership in favor of Assemblyman Daniel Burrows. In most respects, the campaign was indistinguishable from earlier leadership struggles in Harlem. The money, manpower, and political skill that went into it demonstrated that Democratic Party politics still represented the focus of political energy in Harlem, and that Communists and the ALP had failed to build an alternative to the Tammany machine in the key black assembly districts.[56]

In the city council race, however, Communists proved to be more influential. Because of proportional representation, a straightforward ethnic strategy could not easily yield results; black voters could not elect a councilman by themselves unless the Democratic and Republican parties agreed on a black candidate, an extremely unlikely occurrence. Many Harlemites were therefore quite receptive to political strategies which elicited white left-wing and labor support for a black council candidate, and when Communists proposed one, they received a respectful hearing.

In April, 1939, Harlem Communists organized a Trade Union Non-Partisan Committee to elect a Negro to the city council, which had the specific purpose of selecting a candidate who could appeal to left-wing whites as well as blacks. A statement issued by the Committee attracted support ranging from Communist trade union leaders like William Gaulden of the State, County, and Municipal Workers Union and Ferdinand Smith of the National Maritime Union, to liberal ministers like Adam Clayton Powell, Jr., and William Lloyd Imes, to more conservative community spokesmen like Rev. Lorenzo King and Commissioner Hubert Delaney.[57] It emphasized the need to attract "thousands of white voters who endorse this democratic step," and to elicit the "fullest cooperation from the mass of citizens who vote independently in city elections."[58]

Communists could not promise black leaders the entire ALP vote, but they did make an effort to mobilize their own constituency, concentrated in Jewish neighborhoods of Manhattan, and in East Harlem and the Lower East Side (where the Party also mobilized Italian, Hispanic, and Eastern European voters) to support a black candidate. This represented a sizable voting block: In 1938, Israel Amter, running for congressman-at-large on the Communist ticket, got 25,000 votes, only 862 of which came from the 19th and 21st AD's.[59] Communists began their city council campaign in the spring with the slogan, "Vote for Amter and a Progressive Negro," and tried to persuade their followers to give their first-choice votes to the Communist candidate and their second-choice votes to a black. Amter proclaimed that his major goal was to "unite white public opinion" for the election of a black candidate, and to persuade the "progressive movement as a whole" to endorse such a step.[60]

Throughout most of the spring and summer, the Communist campaign for a black candidate took place in a vacuum, since no such candidate appeared on the ballots of any party. But in August, 1939, a curious series of events transpired which demonstrated that Communists, despite grave weaknesses, had assumed the role of a power broker in one important dimension of Harlem politics.

Shortly after the Nazi-Soviet Pact, ALP state secretary Alex Rose announced that Frank Crosswaith, head of the Harlem Labor Committee would be the American Labor Party's only nominee for Manhattan city councilman. Had this announcement taken place one month earlier, Communists would have been extremely pleased; Crosswaith had the respect of many Harlemites and advocated close cooperation between black organizations and the labor movement. But in the confused political atmosphere introduced by the Pact, Communists withheld comment on his candidacy, preferring to see how Crosswaith, once a bitter anti-Communist, decided to conduct himself if ALP leaders initiated a campaign to drive Communists out of the party.[61]

Crosswaith's candidacy attracted considerable attention in Harlem. The *New York Age* and the *Amsterdam News* suggested that his nomination was "tantamount to outright election," since the 1938 ALP vote in Manhattan had been large enough to elect someone to the council. A. Philip Randolph formed an independent citizens committee of 1,000 to support Crosswaith's candidacy, which included most of the non-Communist trade unionists in Harlem, and several prominent ministers. When the Republicans and Democrats failed to nominate black council candidates, prospects for his election looked even stronger.[62]

But in October, 1939, Crosswaith became embroiled in a controversy that drastically weakened his candidacy. Early that month, the ALP leadership, infuriated by Soviet actions in the European War, called a meeting of its affiliated organizations and district clubs to vote on a resolution denouncing the Nazi-Soviet Pact and the role of American Communists in defending it. After getting the resolution approved by a sizable vote, they defined support for the resolution as a condition of ALP membership. Communists refused to accept this dictum, and launched a counteroffensive to maintain their position in the ALP. They called a meeting of the Manhattan ALP organization, in which they had a majority, voted disapproval of the resolution, and elected a new slate of officers headed by Vito Marcantonio. With the ALP now split into "right" and "left" wings, the election campaign became an extension of the power struggle in the party, and Communists carefully observed Crosswaith's actions, as they did those of other ALP candidates, to see which faction he would line up with. In mid-October, Crosswaith issued a statement to the black press supporting the ALP leaders' resolution and calling on black leaders to drive Communists out of positions of influence in black life.[63]

From this point on, Communists directed their energies to preventing Crosswaith's election. They mobilized Communist neighborhood branches in Manhattan, and the ALP district clubs they controlled to urge black and white voters not to cast their ballots for Crosswaith, whom they described as a "discredit to his race and an enemy to labor." Worse yet, from Crosswaith's point of view, they surreptitiously joined with Harlem Democrats in challenging the validity of his petitions.[64]

The results of the election proved pretty sobering to Harlemites who hoped to build ALP support for a black candidate without Communist help. Crosswaith, kept off the ballot by the Tammany challenge, received only 775 write-in votes. Not only did this showing reflect the weakness of non-Communist ALP forces in Harlem, it reflected the total inability of the ALP "right wing" in the borough of Manhattan to mobilize white voters for Crosswaith's candidacy. The ALP anti-Communist faction represented a distinct minority in Manhattan district organizations to begin with, but worse yet, from the vantage point of Harlem leaders, it had neither the will, nor the ability to deliver a solid bloc of white voters willing to support black candidates and black community issues.[65]

The fate of the Crosswaith candidacy thus provided Harlemites with an indication of the ALP left wing's power in Manhattan at a time when it was under sharp attack because of its identification with the Nazi-Soviet Pact. All pro-Communist groups in Harlem suffered a loss of moral credibility because of their defense of the Pact; a good many liberals and Socialists in Harlem broke indignantly with their Communist allies after it occurred. But once the indignation wore off, a number of politically ambitious Harlem leaders concluded that certain cold political realities made it advantageous to reopen communications with the Communist Party. In Manhattan County, the Communist-dominated wing of the ALP, alone among major political groups, had worked hard to educate its white constituency as to the importance of electing a black to the City Council. It represented a key group black politicians had to bargain with in order to assure a black candidate's election. Adam Clayton Powell, Jr., who kept up ties with both wings of the ALP, understood this particularly well. After pillorying Communists for their venality in his newspaper column for several months following the Pact, he began quietly to resume cooperation with leftist organizations and won Communist and Manhattan County ALP support for his campaign for city council in 1941, the race which successfully launched his political career.[66] (The background of Powell's race will be treated in detail in a later chapter.)

Communists thus emerged from the Popular Front era with a limited degree of influence in Harlem politics. Unable to compete effectively with the Democratic and Republican Parties in Harlem assembly districts, Communists built enough of a base in white Manhattan neighborhoods to control the American Labor Party in Manhattan County and help shape the terms under which a black city councilman could be elected to office. Because of the indifference of the ALP's founding group (later its "right wing") to black aspirations, Communists also became a major conduit between the Harlem community and the "labor political movement" that crystalized in New York around the American Labor Party and the CIO. They made effective use of these contacts to develop two important political pressure groups—the Harlem Legislative Conference and the Manhattan Citizens Committee—which helped determine the shape of legislative proposals affecting black communities in the state in 1938 and 1939.

Still, the Party's attempt to enter the mainstream of Harlem politics hardly produced results commensurate with the effort it expended, or matched the influence Communists exerted in other dimensions of Harlem life. Getting Harlemites to cast their ballots for third-party candidates, whether on the Communist or American Labor Party line, proved extremely difficult to do. The Communists had the misfortune of launching their first serious electoral offensive at precisely the time when blacks were beginning to win leadership struggles and patronage in the Democratic and Republican parties. In such circumstances, the burden of proof lay squarely on Communists to show they could get more for the community from third-party efforts than black politicians could through the old line political machines.

Communists had difficulty meeting that challenge. By Americanizing the Party's image and toning down its militancy, Communists were able to develop an alliance with Socialists and liberals who had real power in city politics, but the price of that alliance, in the ALP at least, seemed to be collaboration in programs and policies which neglected important political goals of the Harlem community. To succeed in Harlem, a third-party movement needed to have power and patronage downtown *and* an aggressive program for civil rights and black representation in government. Due to their own weakness, and the racial conservatism of their allies, Communists found they could not achieve one without sacrificing the other.

NOTES

1. On the relationship between changes in party structure and electoral strategy, see I. Begun, "Taking Part in State and City Politics," *Party Organizer,* 10 (Mar., 1936), 38; SWG [Simon W. Gerson], "State of Affairs," *Party Organizer,* 10 (Mar., 1936), 45–46; F. Brown, "New Forms of Party Organization Help Us Win the Mass," *Party Organizer,* 10 (July–Aug., 1936), 11; Charney, *A Long Journey,* (New York: Quadrangle, 1968), pp. 94–95.

2. There is no good analysis of Communist election strategy in New York City during the 1930s and '40s. However, there are two unpublished dissertations which treat the role of Communists in the American Labor Party in considerable depth: Robert Frederick Carter, "Pressure from the Left, The American Labor Party, 1936–1944," (Ph.D. dissertation, Syracuse University, 1965); and Kenneth Alan Waltzer, "The American Labor Party: Third Party Politics in New Deal-Cold War New York, 1936–1954," (Ph.D. dissertation, Harvard University, 1977).

3. In 1930, the 19th AD was 69.7 percent black; in 1940, it was 95.3 percent black. In 1930, the 21st AD was 70.2 percent black, in 1940 it was 73.2 percent black. The 17th AD gradually became a predominately black district; in 1930, it was 30.1 percent black, in 1940, it was 61 percent black. Statistics are from John A. Morsell, "The Political Behavior of Negroes in New York City," (Ph.D. dissertation, Columbia University, 1950), p. 26.

4. New York City, Board of Elections, *Annual Reports, 1936–1939;* Waltzer, "The American Labor Party," p. 157. I computed the ALP percentages from the two key assembly districts, the 19th and the 21st, using the mayoral election of 1937 and the gubernatorial election of 1938 as the basis. The citywide ALP

percentages in those years, as computed by Waltzer, were 19.2 percent (1938) and 17.7 percent (1938). It should be noted, however, that these citywide totals were pushed strongly upward by the ALP vote in Jewish working-class and lower-middle-class districts, which sometimes reached 50 percent of the total in those areas.

5. On the struggle for black leadership in Harlem politics, see Morsell, "The Political Behavior of Negroes in New York City," 25–47; George Martin Furniss, "The Assimilation of the Negro into New York City Politics, 1900–1960," (Ph.D. dissertation, Columbia University, 1969), pp. 295, 327; Gilbert Osofsky, *Harlem, The Making of a Ghetto* (New York: Harper and Row, 1968), pp. 159–78; Claude McKay, *Harlem, Negro Metropolis* (1940; rpt. New York: Harcourt, Brace, Jovanovich, 1968), pp. 121–42; Roi Ottley, *New World A-Coming* (1943; rpt. New York: Arno, 1968), pp. 213–16.

6. On the way Tammany functioned in Harlem and on the power wielded by its district leaders and those of the Republican party, see Furniss, "The Assimilation of the Negro into New York City Politics," pp. 285, 303; Osofsky, *Harlem, The Making of a Ghetto,* pp. 174–75; Morsell, "The Political Behavior of Negroes in New York City," p. 40.

7. On the "job list" of the 21st AD regular Democratic organization, see Furniss, "The Assimilation of the Negro into New York Politics," p. 324; on the reasons for the persistence of white control in the 19th AD, see Morsell, "The Political Behavior of Negroes in New York City," pp. 45–46.

8. There is some controversy among scholars regarding the meaning of victories in Harlem leadership struggles. Morsell and Furniss both suggest that black district leaders did not have the same power as most of their white counterparts. On the basis of their data, Katznelson challenges Gilbert Osofsky's assertion that blacks made impressive gains in Harlem politics. But contemporary accounts of the leadership struggles consistently refer to them as events of great importance and their protagonists as heroes in the community. Ira Katznelson, *Black Men, White Cities; Race, Politics and Migration in the United States, 1900–1930, and Britain, 1948–1968* (New York: Oxford University Press, 1974), pp. 62–83; McKay, *Harlem, Negro Metropolis,* pp. 120, 123, 130–31; Ottley, *New World A-Coming,* pp. 213–15; *New York Age,* Nov. 9, 1935, Dec. 7, 1935, Oct. 28, 1939; *New York Amsterdam News,* Mar. 14, 1936.

9. On corruption in Harlem politics, see Morsell, "The Political Behavior of Negroes in New York City," pp. 38–39; Osofsky, *Harlem, The Making of a Ghetto,* pp. 173–74; Furniss, "The Assimilation of the Negro into New York City Politics," pp. 302–3, 398. Furniss quoted a Harlem politician as follows: "Negro politics . . . is based upon crap game politics, whether I can run my game or you let me sell my liquor. See, because I can't get a job, will you let me run my house up here (Harlem). And reform would have his house closed. With reform, he wouldn't be able to go in and talk to a man who could talk to the Police Department."

10. Interview with Rev. David Licorish, May 10, 1978; interview with Abner Berry, Sept. 5, 1977. On the contributions made by Harlem legislators, see Osofsky, *Harlem, The Making of a Ghetto,* pp. 171–72; and Morsell, "The Political Behavior of Negroes in New York City," pp. 39–40. On the role of Harlem's

elected officials in protest movements, see *New York Amsterdam News,* Aug. 28, 1936, and James W. Ford, *Communists and the Struggle for Negro Liberation,* p. 60.

11. *Official Proceedings of the National Negro Congress, February 14, 15, 16, 1936,* pp. 16–19; *New York Amsterdam News,* Apr. 4, 1936; James W. Ford, *The Negro People and the Farmer-Labor Party* (New York: Harlem Division of the Communist Party, 1936), p. 6.

12. On the mandate of the Seventh Comintern Congress calling for the formation of a "Farmer Labor Party," and on labor-party sentiment within the United States, see Kenneth Waltzer, "The Party and the Polling Place: American Communism and an American Labor Party in the 1930's," *Radical History Review,* 23 (Dec., 1980), 108–12. On the Communist rationale for forming a version of the Farmer-Labor Party in Harlem, see Ford, *The Negro People and the Farmer Labor Party,* pp. 6–9. The only non-Communist Harlem leader who referred to such a party was A. Philip Randolph, who mentioned it briefly in his speech at the National Negro Congress.

13. "Call, Conference to Discuss All-Harlem Independent Political Action," UNIA Papers, Reel 4, Box 11; Ignatius Lawlor to Capt. A. L. King, *ibid.,* Reel 5, Box 12; *New York Amsterdam News,* Apr. 19, 1936; *Daily Worker,* Apr. 13, 1936, Apr. 16, 1936, Apr. 23, 1936, Apr. 25, 1936, Apr. 27, 1936.

14. On the meeting at Mt. Olivet, see "Agenda, Conference to Discuss All-Harlem Independent Political Action," UNIA Papers, Reel 4, Box 11; *New York Amsterdam News,* May 2, 1936; *New York Age,* May 9, 1936; *Daily Worker,* Apr. 29, 1936. After the continuations committee of the new organization decided to form a new party, the list of individuals sponsoring it grew steadily smaller. *Daily Worker,* May 9, 1936, May 13, 1936, May 27, 1936, June 5, 1936, June 9, 1936, June 17, 1936; *New York Age,* June 20, 1936; *New York Amsterdam News,* June 20, 1936.

15. Waltzer, "The American Labor Party," pp. 193–94; *New York Amsterdam News,* June 27, 1936; *New York Age,* June 27, 1936; *Daily Worker,* June 30, 1936, July 10, 1936; Frank O'Brien, "Harlem Shows the Way," *New Masses,* 20 (Aug. 18, 1926), 17–18.

16. *New York Amsterdam News,* July 18, 1936; *Daily Worker,* July 2, 1936, July 9, 1936, July 15, 1936, July 20, 1936, Aug. 6, 1936, Aug. 7, 1936, Aug. 26, 1936, Oct. 3, 1936.

17. On the establishment of the All People's Party "campaign machinery," see *Daily Worker,* July 15, 1936, Aug. 10, 1936, Aug. 28, 1936. On the campaign organizations of the Republican and Democratic Parties in Harlem, see Morsell, "The Political Behavior of Negroes in New York City," pp. 106–7; Furniss, "The Assimilation of the Negro into New York City Politics," pp. 145, 275–76.

18. On the formation of the American Labor Party, see Carter, "Pressure from the Left," pp. 1–35; and Waltzer, "The American Labor Party," pp. 73–95. On the formation of the ALP in Harlem, see *New York Age,* Oct. 24, 1936, and *New York Amsterdam News,* Oct. 3, 1936.

19. Carter, "Pressure from the Left," p. 15; Waltzer, "The American Labor Party," pp. 92–93; *New York Amsterdam News,* Oct. 3, 1936.

20. On May's position in the Harlem ALP, see *New York Amsterdam News,* Oct. 3, 1936, and *Daily Worker,* Nov. 2, 1936. The last *Daily Worker* editorial endorsing the All People's Party appeared Sept. 3, 1936.

21. New York City, Board of Elections, *Annual Report, 1936,* pp. 120, 198–99.

22. On the distribution of ALP votes in New York City in the 1936 election, see Waltzer, "The American Labor Party," pp. 95–100. On the CP's view of the ALP after the election, see I. Amter, "The Elections in New York." *Communist,* 15 (Dec., 1936), 1148–49.

23. *Ibid.,* 1149; New York City, Board of Elections, *Annual Report, 1936,* p. 198; *Daily Worker,* Nov. 21, 1936; James W. Ford, "The Negro People and the Election," *Communist,* 16 (Jan., 1936), 72. Santiago may have received such a high vote total on the Communist ticket because he was the only Puerto Rican in the assembly race in the 17th AD.

24. *Daily Worker,* Feb. 25, 1937, Mar. 29, 1937; Carter, "Pressure from the Left," pp. 69–70; Waltzer, "The American Labor Party," pp. 107, 123–25.

25. Interview with Abner Berry, Feb. 4, 1978; Charney, *A Long Journey,* pp. 94–96, 105–11.

26. *Daily Worker,* Feb. 25, 1937, Mar. 29, 1937, May 13, 1937; I. Amter, "Significance of the Coming Municipal Elections in New York," *Communist,* 16 (July, 1937), 648–49, 655–59.

27. Proportional representation, introduced largely to break Tammany's power, replaced the old board of aldermen, elected from relatively small local districts, with a city council elected on a county-wide basis. Candidates in each county got on the ballot by accumulating 2,000 signatures on a petition, and voters indicated their preference by ranking the candidates in order. The number of councilmen chosen in each county equalled the number of times 75,000 divided into the total ballots cast in that county (for example, if 400,000 people voted in Manhattan, five councilmen would represent that borough). Candidates who received 75,000 first-choice ballots were elected immediately, but since the number of those usually fell short of the designated total, the others were selected by a complicated system of vote transfers. After the first count, the second-choice votes on all ballots cast for winners, and on those of candidates dropped from the field (the candidate with the lowest first-choice total was dropped on each count) *became* first-choice votes, and were transferred to the persons designated by each voter. This process was repeated until the right number of candidates ended up with 75,000 first-choice votes, or until the number of candidates left in the field equalled the number of seats to be filled. Carter, "Pressure from the Left," pp. 71–72; Charles Garrett, *The La Guardia Years: Machine and Reform Politics in New York City* (New Brunswick, N.J.: Rutgers University Press, 1961), p. 232.

28. Carter, "Pressure from the Left," pp. 30–35; Waltzer, "The American Labor Party," pp. 84, 91, 103–5.

29. On the racial policies of the ALP, see *New York Amsterdam News,* Nov. 13, 1937; *Daily Worker,* Jan. 10, 1938; James W. Ford and George E. Blake, "Building the People's Front in Harlem," *Communist,* 18 (Feb., 1938), 166–67. On the Socialist Party's perspectives on the Negro Question, see Frank R. Crosswaith and Alfred Baker Lewis, *True Freedom for Negro and White Labor* (New

York: Socialist Party, U.S.A., 1934); *Daily Worker,* June 5, 1937, June 7, 1937, June 8, 1937. On Quill's silence on the race issue within the ALP executive committee, see Waltzer, "The Party and the Polling Place," 120.

30. During the summer of 1936, the *Daily Worker* had acquired, and printed, sections of the Report of the Mayor's Commission on Conditions in Harlem, which La Guardia had refused to release. The All People's Party, and other Communist-influenced protest organizations in Harlem, used these reports as "ammunition" for their activities. *Daily Worker,* July 2, 1936, July 3, 1936, July 4, 1936, July 6, 1936, July 7, 1936.

31. *Ibid.,* Oct. 20, 1937, Oct. 28, 1937.

32. *Ibid.,* Oct. 28, 1937, Oct. 29, 1937; Ford and Blake, "Building the People's Front in Harlem," 165–67.

33. *Ibid.,* 162–66; *Daily Worker,* Oct. 29, 1937, Nov. 2, 1937, Feb. 11, 1938.

34. Waltzer, "The American Labor Party," 17; New York City, Board of Elections, *Annual Report, 1937,* p. 124.

35. *Ibid.,* pp. 166–67.

36. *New York Amsterdam News,* Nov. 6, 1937; *Daily Worker,* Nov. 4, 1937; *New York Age,* Nov. 13, 1937.

37. *New York Amsterdam News,* Nov. 13, 1937.

38. *Daily Worker,* Nov. 14, 1937.

39. Charney, *A Long Journey,* pp. 113–15; interview with George Charney, Nov. 7, 1973; *New York Age,* Dec. 25, 1937; *Daily Worker,* Dec. 11, 1937, Dec. 21, 1937, Feb. 11, 1938, Feb. 14, 1938; James W. Ford, *The Negro and the Democratic Front* (New York: International Publishers, 1938), pp. 193–95.

40. New York State Temporary Commission on the Urban Colored Population, *Public Hearings,* vols. 6–8, copies at the Schomburg Collection; *New York Age,* Dec. 25, 1937; *New York Amsterdam News,* Dec. 19, 1937, Dec. 25, 1937, Feb. 19, 1938; *New York Times,* Dec. 14, 1937, Dec. 15, 1937, Dec. 17, 1937, Dec. 23, 1937; *Daily Worker,* Dec. 14, 1937, Dec. 15, 1937, Dec. 16, 1937, Dec. 17, 1937, Dec. 21, 1937.

41. *New York Times,* Jan. 9, 1938; Vito Marcantonio and Emmett May to Dear Friend, Jan. 14, 1938, Feb. 21, 1938, Jan. 21, 1939, UNIA Papers, Box 11, Reel 4; *New York Amsterdam News,* Jan. 15, 1938, July 1, 1939; *Daily Worker,* Jan. 2, 1938, Jan. 7, 1938, Jan. 22, 1938, Feb. 11, 1938, Feb. 27, 1938, Mar. 13, 1938, Mar. 14, 1938, Feb. 26, 1929, Mar. 23, 1939, Mar. 25, 1939; Waltzer, "The American Labor Party," 207.

42. Ford and Blake, "Building the People's Front in Harlem," 167–68; Ford, "Rally the Negro Masses for the Democratic Front," 271; *Daily Worker,* Feb. 11, 1938, Feb. 14, 1938, Feb. 16, 1938, Apr. 14, 1938, Apr. 28, 1938.

43. In a series of articles entitled "The Battle for Democracy, the 1938 Elections in Harlem," James Ford provided a rationale for the concentration of Harlem division energies in East and Lower Harlem. *Daily Worker,* Sept. 7, 1938, Sept. 8, 1938, Sept. 9, 1938. Charney also hints at such an emphasis in the chapter of his book dealing with Harlem, and suggests it was one of the reasons for his being transferred out of that community in 1939 (Charney, *A Long Journey,* pp. 119–20).

44. *Daily Worker,* Apr. 28, 1938; Ford, "Rally the Negro Masses for the Democratic Front," 271; *New York Amsterdam News,* May 7, 1938, June 4, 1938.

45. *Ibid.,* Aug. 13, 1938.

46. *Ibid.,* Oct. 22, 1938.

47. *Daily Worker,* Sept. 8, 1938; *New York Age,* Sept. 24, 1938. Communists never came out with a formal announcement endorsing Gavagan's candidacy, but Communists in the ALP did campaign for him and James Ford emphasized that "the Communist Party in Harlem loyally supports the American Labor Party. We accept its discipline."

48. New York City, Board of Elections, *Annual Report, 1938,* pp. 46, 52–53, 106, 120–21. Gavagan's vote totals on the Democratic ticket were 5,206 in the 19th AD, and 11,399 in the 21st AD, more than five times the totals he received on the ALP ticket.

49. For a presentation of the Party's position on "unity of progressive forces," see Herbert Benjamin, "Meeting Reaction's Assault on the Unemployed," *Communist,* 18 (Sept., 1939), 828.

50. On the 1939 campaign to pass antidiscrimination bills in the state legislature, see *New York Age,* Feb. 11, 1939, Feb. 25, 1939, Mar. 4, 1939, Apr. 8, 1939, Apr. 15, 1939; *New York Amsterdam News,* Apr. 22, 1939; *Daily Worker,* Mar. 5, 1939, Mar. 7, 1939, Mar. 13, 1939, Mar. 15, 1939, Mar. 17, 1939, Mar. 25, 1939, Mar. 27, 1939, Mar. 30, 1939, Apr. 5, 1939, Apr. 9, 1939, Apr. 14, 1939, Apr. 17, 1939, Apr. 19, 1939, Apr. 23, 1939.

51. On efforts of black organizations to put antidiscrimination clauses in the Wagner Act, see Herbert Hill, *Black Labor and the American Legal System* (Washington, D.C.: Bureau of National Affairs, 1977), pp. 104–6. For evidence of the Party's support of antidiscrimination clauses in the state Labor Relations Act in 1937, see New York State Temporary Commission on the Urban Colored Population, *Public Hearings,* vol. 8, pp. 1612, 1615, 1618–19, 1724; *New York Age,* Dec. 25, 1937; *Daily Worker,* Dec. 17, 1937, Dec. 21, 1937. Gordon's comments about the shift in the Party position were made in an interview with me on Oct. 27, 1981.

52. *New York Amsterdam News,* May 13, 1939.

53. *Ibid.,* May 27, 1939.

54. *Ibid.,* May 27, 1939, July 1, 1939; *Daily Worker,* May 7, 1939, May 11, 1939.

55. *New York Amsterdam News,* May 27, 1939.

56. *Ibid.,* Jan. 21, 1939, July 29, 1939; *New York Times,* Oct. 6, 1939; *New York Age,* Feb. 4, 1939, Oct. 14, 1939; *Daily Worker,* Apr. 19, 1939, June 4, 1939; Furniss, "The Assimilation of the Negro into New York City Politics," pp. 290, 326–27.

57. Open Letter, Trade Union Non-Partisan Committee for the Selection of a Negro to the City Council, Reel 5, Box 13, UNIA Papers; *Daily Worker,* Apr. 19, 1939, Apr. 22, 1939, May 28, 1939, June 10, 1939.

58. *Ibid.,* June 1, 1939.

59. New York City, Board of Elections, *Annual Report, 1938,* pp. 52–53. No systematic ethnic analysis of the Communist Party vote totals has ever been made. But the two assembly districts which gave Amter the highest vote totals,

the 23rd (2,071), and the 6th (2,143) were located in Washington Heights and the Lower East Side, both areas with heavy concentrations of Jewish population. This conforms with Waltzer's picture of the ALP's constituency, which he found concentrated largely in Jewish neighborhoods. However, the 17th and 18th AD's, which had a heavy Italian and Hispanic population, with some Finns, Slavs, and Jews, also gave Amter a respectable total (1,678 and 1,058 votes respectively).

60. *Daily Worker,* Mar. 15, 1939, Mar. 29, 1939, Apr. 5, 1939, Apr. 12, 1939, Apr. 28, 1939, May 3, 1939, June 11, 1939, June 18, 1939.

61. *New York Age,* Aug. 28, 1939; *New York Amsterdam News,* Aug. 26, 1939.

62. *New York Age,* Aug. 28, 1939, Sept. 30, 1939, Oct. 7, 1939, Oct. 14, 1939, Oct. 28, 1939; *New York Amsterdam News,* Aug. 26, 1939.

63. Waltzer, "The American Labor Party," 226–32; Carter, "Pressure From the Left," 115–21; *New York Times,* Oct. 5, 1939, Oct. 6, 1939, Oct. 7, 1939, Oct. 8, 1939; "For Immediate Release," Oct. 3, 1939, Negro Labor Committee Papers, Reel 5, B 124; Frank Crosswaith to Miss Marion Severn, Oct. 12, 1939, *ibid.*; *New York Age,* Oct. 14, 1939; *New York Amsterdam News,* Oct. 21, 1939, Oct. 28, 1939.

64. *Daily Worker,* Oct. 23, 1939; *New York Age,* Oct. 14, 1939; Frank R. Crosswaith to Rev. Adam Clayton Powell, Jr., Nov. 13, 1939, Negro Labor Committee Papers, Reel 9, D 19.

65. *Ibid.*; New York City, Board of Elections, *Annual Report, 1939,* pp. 30–31. The struggle for control of the ALP in Manhattan County was fought out in the board of elections and the courts, with the left winning a court-supervised election in March, 1940. In Harlem, the left wing controlled the 21st AD club, and the right wing the 19th AD club. Waltzer, "The American Labor Party," pp. 231–32; *New York Times,* Oct. 20, 1939; *Daily Worker,* Dec. 18, 1939.

66. For examples of Powell's denunciation of the CP following the Nazi-Soviet Pact, see *New York Amsterdam News,* Sept. 16, 1939, Nov. 11, 1939; *New York Age,* Nov. 18, 1939. For an analysis of Powell's ties to the Communist left during his various election campaigns, beginning in 1941, see Neil Hickey and Ed Edwin, *Adam Clayton Powell and the Politics of Race* (New York: Fleet Publishing, 1965), pp. 66–69; Ottley, *New World A-Coming,* pp. 231–35; Morsell, "The Political Behavior of Negroes in New York City," pp. 101–6; Kenneth Greenberg, "Benjamin Jefferson Davis, Jr., in the City Council: Harlem Reaction to Communism During the 1940's," (M.A. thesis, Columbia University, 1970), pp. 7, 16–17.

10

Communists in Harlem's Economy during the Popular Front

FOR BLACK LEADERS CONCERNED with Harlem's economic health, the late '30s began with great hopes and ended with profound despair. With the issue of physical survival settled by the provision of public relief, Harlem intellectuals and politicians increasingly turned their attention to the problem of black economic marginality. In 1936 and 1937, what they perceived gave them grounds for optimism: blacks had won jobs in many Harlem stores, civil service employment had expanded considerably, WPA programs had given Harlemites thousands of jobs, and a dynamic new labor organization had been formed — the CIO — which made unionization of blacks an important priority. But by the spring of 1939, much of this optimism had vanished. The WPA program, attacked by congressional conservatives, had lost much of its funding; the 1938 recession had increased black unemployment; and the CIO, though nondiscriminatory in its organizing, had proven an imperfect instrument for winning blacks access to new jobs. As a mood of fiscal austerity swept the nation, the gains blacks had made in government employment suddenly seemed of less significance than their weakness in the private sector — where blacks had suffered displacement from traditionally "Negro jobs." With black unemployment in New York more than double the white level, and the percentage of blacks on relief nearly three times the white total, Harlem leaders began to express fears that blacks were being pushed into a position of permanent economic dependence.[1] "Unemployment and relief agencies," the *Amsterdam News* warned, "have combined to make . . . droned mendicants and malcontents of the masses of New York's colored folks."[2]

This sharp deterioration of economic conditions, coming at a time of accelerating international tensions, presented difficult strategic dilemmas for Communist Party leaders. Throughout most of the '30s, Communists had won a reputation as militant advocates of the black unemployed, people who would risk arrest to stop an eviction or win people relief payments and who would take to the streets at a drop of the hat to protest reductions in relief funds. Seemingly untied to entrenched interests or elected officials, they had built up powerful organizations of relief recipients and WPA workers whose leaders were partisan Communists, but were otherwise courageous and honest. But the Popular Front strategy imposed responsibilities on Communists — and offered opportunities — which subtly undermined their role as exponents of popular militancy. In their efforts to cement "unity against reaction," and to protect the Party's position in the powerful CIO movement, Party leaders gradually shifted the center of gravity in Party organizing from the unemployed movement to the trade unions and began to deemphasize disruption in favor of lobbying and electoral action as a means of influencing public policy. Viewed from a national level, these policies coincided with a considerable growth in the Party's membership and political influence. At the time of the Nazi-Soviet Pact, Party membership stood at over 50,000, and the Party had a strong role in nearly one-third of the CIO unions.[3] But in Harlem, a community where the bulk of the population was *structurally incapable* of directly benefiting from the organizing drive of the CIO, whether because they were unemployed or had jobs which were difficult to unionize (especially domestic service), the new policies had ambivalent consequences. When the top Party leadership, in the spring of 1938, virtually suspended its critical posture toward the CIO and the New Deal, and sharply curtailed mass protests by its unemployed organizations, the Harlem Party suffered defections by key rank-and-file cadre and became the target of increasingly sharp criticism from both allies and enemies. "Many of us ex-Reds," Victor Vollmar wrote in October, 1938, "saw the Communist Party become a recognized political party. We saw backward leaders join and . . . turn the Party from a deep red, to a pale pink, and finally a bright yellow."[4]

This disillusionment with the Party, it should be emphasized, came only in the later phases of the Popular Front. During 1936 and most of 1937, Party organizing around economic issues in Harlem assumed an unprecedented militancy and breadth and touched the lives of Harlemites as intimately as it had at any time during the Depression. Moreover, the vision of change the Party invoked, defining the progressive wing of organized labor as the major force for black progress, excited the imagination of much of Harlem's intelligentsia. "Our future will be decided," Adam Clayton Powell, Jr., averred in July, 1937, "not by ourselves, but by a union of all working class forces, white and black."[5]

The loss of confidence in this vision, not only by Powell, but by some Communists as well, is a phenomenon that deserves explanation. Some commentators have suggested that conservative tendencies took hold in left-influenced popular movements when those movements decided to "press for legislation" and mobilize for elections. Arguing that disruption of institutions is the poor's best weapon, they criticize Party cadre for trying to build stable organizations of the unemployed that tried to bargain with relief officials and for diverting precious energy from mass protest to elections.[6]

This analysis does provide some cues to the Party's evolution. As we shall see, the Party's decision to participate in electoral coalitions with liberal politicians, and to make union recognition and stability preeminent goals, subjected Communists to pressures to conduct their activities in a more "responsible" manner. Communists, normally entering such alliances from a position of weakness, found that the atmosphere in trade unions, legislative coalitions, and government institutions (WPA projects or relief bureaus) sometimes made it difficult to aggressively promote black interests or to encourage Party constituencies to take their grievances "to the streets." But how much Communists *acceded* to such pressures represented a manner of conscious political choice, influenced by the Party leadership's (and the Comintern's) definition of political priorties. During the early years of the Popular Front, the manner in which Communists resolved the tension between the quest for institutional power and the stimulation of popular insurgency proved consistent with a wide range of Harlem activism and a dynamic relationship with black allies. Only in 1938, under the press of international events, did the Party leadership tilt the balance in a manner which allowed conservative tendencies to become dominant, suggesting that electoral activity, and an emphasis on stable organization, are not *in themselves* sufficient explanations for the loss of the Party's efficacy as an advocate of the downtrodden and an opponent of entrenched privilege.[7]

For a considerable period of time, the Popular Front strategy in Harlem seemed consistent with a high level of popular mobilization. During 1936 and 1937, Communists simultaneously participated in social welfare programs sponsored by the New Deal and maintained an insurgent posture toward them. Sending cadres into the WPA, they organized unions of project workers which protested reductions in project allocations by means of strikes, sit-ins, and marches. Though Communist strategy in the 1936 presidential campaign worked implicitly for Roosevelt's election, Party leaders, well into 1937, allowed local organizers to make the national administration the target of protest, even though they directed their main fire at congressional conservatives who opposed the WPA on principle.[8]

Party activity in the city relief apparatus proved even more effective. Here, Harlem Communists benefited from a remarkable symbiosis between unionized workers in the local relief system, and neighborhood organizers for the Workers Alliance (the Unemployed Councils merged with the Socialist-organized Workers Alliance in 1936, but Communists totally dominated the Harlem branch of the new coalition). From 1933 on, the city relief system had been the scene of the most effective Communist trade union work in Harlem, resulting in dramatic increases in black employment in the administration of relief and the emergence of a core of black left-wing union leaders—William Gaulden, Arnold Johnson, and Gladys Stone—who were bulwarks of the local chapter of the National Negro Congress and figures of considerable stature in the Harlem community. By 1936, the Party had functioning branches in every single relief bureau in Harlem. Devoting much of their attention to trade union issues—wages and working conditions of bureau employees, incidents of racial discrimination—they also participated in protests to win increased allocations for clients and used their position to give sympathetic, some argued preferential, treatment to Workers Alliance demands.[9]

With a core of veteran organizers and a virtual guarantee of sympathetic access to relief officials ("We have . . . authenticated information," a UNIA leader complained, "of people who sought membership in radical institutions in the definite belief that it would be possible for them to quicker obtain assistance,") the Workers Alliance won a reputation as the place where Harlemites went first when they wanted to get on relief or have a grievance adjudicated.[10] Mingling peaceful bargaining with sit-ins and mass demonstrations, the alliance emerged as the one Communist organization that touched the lives of Harlem's poor on a day-to-day basis. Harlem's ten alliance locals, claiming 2,800 members, were the recipients of an "endless stream of black people looking for help," Richard Wright observed.[11] Unstable in their membership, unable to make disciplined Communists (or even Communist voters) of most of those who used their services, alliance locals functioned as genuine popular institutions, giving Harlem's unemployed an enhanced sense of power and security. Richard Wright recounted the experience of a black woman who was "without food, and about to lose her flat," and who was referred to the Workers Alliance by a "Communist Woman" who lived in her building: "I went with her because I didn't have any other place to go. But in 24 hours, they got me food to eat and made sure that I would not be set outdoors. At first I was afraid. Whenever I went into the ERB station, I would try to tell the clerk I was hungry and I would break down and cry. But they soon got me out of that. They taught me to stand up and fight."[12] An article on Harlem in the *Saturday Evening Post* confirmed Wright's picture: "Anyone . . . who has difficulty in getting on relief, or being thrown off, or being on, desires a larger subsidy, can, and often does, take his case to the nearest Communist."[13]

Party agitation for better housing conditions also expanded in this period. Operating through the Consolidated Tenants League and the Workers Alliance, Communists helped organize parades against high rents, campaigned for the construction of public housing, and organized rent strikes to protest rent increases and inadequate building service. Some of this activity took place in elite sections of Harlem (Sugar Hill and Manhattan Avenue), where the Party, proportionately, drew its strongest support, but a good portion of it took place on blocks with tenement housing and large numbers of poor people—134th Street, 135th Street, 140th Street, 141st Street, and Upper Lenox Avenue. Organizers involved represented a cross-section of the Party, ranging from self-educated cadre like Louis Campbell and Audley Moore, to the Amherst-educated attorney Benjamin J. Davis, Jr. Their work affirmed the Party's penetration into the fabric of community life, as a service organization, if not as a focus of political loyalty.[14]

Party organizing around health-related issues also flourished during the Popular Front. Since the spring of 1933, Communists had agitated against discrimination against black nurses and doctors in Harlem Hospital, and had built up a strong core of members and sympathizers among both groups. In the fall of 1936, sparked by a rash of deaths in the infant ward of the hospital, Party members on the hospital staff joined with Communist neighborhood organizers in a picket line at the hospital. After several weeks of demonstrations, the hospital hired new infant nurses, began isolating sick infants, and issued new linen daily. From this point on, the Harlem Hospital branch became the largest and most dynamic Party "shop unit" in Harlem. Led by a nurse named Rose Gaulden, it grew to a membership of over fifty, composed of doctors, nurses, and nonprofessional workers, and agitated for the unionization of the hospital staff, the improvement of its facilities, and an end to discrimination in the city hospital system.[15] "We had all the doctors (only two or three who weren't)," Abner Berry recalled, "and two or three dentists. At Harlem Hospital, we had practically all the nurses. That was one of our biggest branches—a nurses' branch."[16]

Rose Gaulden's career symbolized the growing importance of black women in directing Party work in the human services area—health, housing, education, and relief. Like Bonita Williams and Frankie Duty of the Workers Alliance, and all-purpose organizer Audley Moore (who focused much of her attention on housing and conditions in Harlem schools), she gave the Party a voice that black working-class women could identify with. "She came out of rural Georgia," George Charney recalled, "and on occasion would take to the step ladder on Lenox Avenue and keep a crowd in stitches, describing in the idiom of the deep South a baseball game between her native small town team and the Tennessee Mudcats. The politics was interspersed with humor in a rollicking homespun fashion, though at party meetings she revealed a depth of thought beyond many of us."[17] "Strong-willed" women like Gaulden, Charney recalled,

faced difficult problems in their "efforts to make a new life in the movement." Victims of the social isolation women traditionally faced when
they assumed leadership positions, they encountered added difficulties in
a Party milieu where the strongest black men often formed relationships
with white women. But despite this pattern of cultural preferences, which
injected an undercurrent of tension into Party life, the Party did provide
black women with an outlet for the political skills, and its community organizing strongly benefited from their leadership.[18]
Communist activity in the labor movement had less effect on the day to
day lives of Harlemites than did its community organizing, but its political impact, and the expectations it generated may have been greater. In
the winter of 1936–37, trade union activity in Harlem's retail sector, on
the waterfront, and in the city relief system and the WPA, spearheaded
by the left, revived the alliance of Socialists, Communists, and Harlem
ministers that had arisen in support of the *Amsterdam News* strike and
rekindled hopes that labor would help blacks escape economic margînal-
ity. Two of these campaigns, by Harlem pharmacists, and by rank-and-
file seamen, became the focus of broad-based Harlem "citizen's committees," while organizing drives among Harlem butchers and grocery clerks
united Communists with their old antagonists on the Negro Labor Committee. Supporters hailed the trade union offensive as a turning point in
black life.[19] "The Negro worker can only raise his standard of living
through suffering and striking with his fellows," Adam Clayton Powell,
Jr., wrote. ". . . . Our only hope is no longer through a boss's office, but
through a picket line."[20]

Some unions, especially those in white-collar fields, seemed to act in a
manner consistent with these expectations. The Pharmacists Union, led
by Communists and Party sympathizers, made the hiring of unemployed
black pharmacists one of its major negotiating points, and forced stores
with whom it signed contracts to hire blacks when employees resigned, or
when they needed new personnel. The State, County, and Municipal
Workers Union, also leftist led, waged a bitter campaign against the imposition of civil service tests in the relief system (which ultimately removed
two-thirds of its black employees) and fought to have blacks who failed
the test retained by the system. WPA project workers unions fought
against across the board layoffs in Harlem WPA projects, arguing that a
higher black unemployment rate justified that black workers be retained
in disproportionate numbers. The willingness of such unions to make the
creation of job opportunities for blacks, and their protection from layoffs, an organic feature of their activities, almost coequal with the pre-
rogatives of union recognition and survival, reinforced the romantic image
of labor already well established among Harlem intellectuals, especially
since educated blacks most benefited from their activities.[21]

However, left-wing unions organizing "blue-collar workers"—e.g. butchers, grocery clerks, seamen—proved less innovative in their approach. Although they made use of black organizers and fought for equal treatment of black employees on the job, they did not try to open up jobs for blacks in stores (or ships) where they were not already employed, or force their promotion to higher job categories. Their appeal for support from black organizations rested on the argument that black workers— who were already employed in the three industries in question—would reap significant benefits in wages and working conditions from a struggle for union recognition, and from the elimination of racial differentials in wage scale for the same job.[22]

The diversity of approaches to racial issues taken by Communist-led unions dramatized the pressures Communists faced as they moved into the mainstream of organized labor. Though the Party strove for a consistent "line" on black employment and advancement, the imperatives of union leadership wrought havoc with such consistency. The Party's theoretical outlook, defining blacks an an "oppressed nation," justified special measures to improve the position of black labor, but once Communists abandoned "revolutionary unions" in favor of work with the established trade unions (whether AFL or CIO), they entered a milieu in which the exigencies of union recognition, and the protection of existing job rights, dominated all other priorities. Unless a strong party organization existed among the union rank and file, or white workers in the industry were sympathetic to blacks, Communist union leaders hesitated to use their position to try to reshape racial employment patterns in their industry. Among New York's seamen, grocery clerks, transit workers, and hotel and restaurant workers, Communists assumed leadership on the basis of their skills as organizers and administrators, not on support for their political views, and they departed from standard trade union practice chiefly in their willingness to appoint talented blacks to union staffs. Only in the fur industry, where Communists had conducted educational work since the early '20s, and in white-collar fields dominated by "Americanized" Jews of Eastern European background (who in the '30s seemed to be a particular bastion of racial liberalism) did Party union leaders feel they could fight for the special interests of black workers without jeopardizing their power.[23] "Many trade unions, including some progressive trade unions," admitted New York State Party Secretary Charles Krumbein, "do not fight for equal rights for the Negro people."[24]

During the formative years of the CIO (1936–37), few Harlem intellectuals perceived the conservative potential of the new unions. Excited by the emergence of dynamic black union leaders such as A. Philip Randolph of the Pullman Porters, Ferdinand Smith of the Seamen, Manning Johnson of the Restaurant Workers, and William Gaulden of the Municipal Workers, and by the proclaimed willingness of the CIO to organize blacks on the basis of equality, they enthusiastically supported organizing drives in multiracial settings and campaigned against the use of blacks as strikebreakers. "It is the duty of the church," Rev. David Licorish proclaimed, "to champion . . . all great movements that are demanding a decent living through collective bargaining."[25]

However, Garvey movement activists, commanding a sizable popular following, greeted the trade union offensive with greater skepticism. Committed to winning black control of Harlem's economy, they regarded unionization drives in Harlem's retail sector as a threat to their efforts to force Harlem storeowners to hire black workers and to make "race consciousness" the guiding principle in black economic life. In 1936, the most able of these leaders, Ira Kemp and Arthur Reid, developed an all-black "Harlem Labor Union" which simultaneously tried to place unemployed blacks in jobs in Harlem stores and to become the sole bargaining agent for Harlem's black workers. Because of Kemp and Reid's track record in finding jobs for their followers and their undeniable courage in espousing their political beliefs—both men had been arrested on numerous occasions—the HLU represented a formidable obstacle to AFL and CIO unions trying to organize in Harlem. In 1936 and 1937, organizers from the Meatcutters and Grocery Clerks Unions met with violent resistance from HLU leaders, who resented the prospect of interracial unions representing black workers employed largely through the HLU's agitation.[26]

The HLU's activities provoked considerable opposition among Harlem intellectuals, liberals as well as radicals. Committed to driving whites out of Harlem's economy, Kemp and Reid—and some of their less savory followers—supported boycotts of Italian-American merchants during the Ethiopian War and railed repeatedly in their speeches against Jewish storeowners and landlords. In addition, Kemp and Reid fought against interracial labor solidarity as a matter of principle, encouraging their followers to serve as strikebreakers in industrial disputes (they supplied shipowners with employees during the rank-and-file seamen's strike) and to win a position in the labor market by underbidding white workers. In dealing with Harlem employers, Kemp and Reid offered contracts providing considerably lower wages than traditional "union scale" and a firm guarantee of industrial peace (the HLU did not strike), stiffening employer resistance to the activities of established unions. Such "sweetheart contracts" followed logically from Kemp and Reid's economic philosophy, which defined black labor organizations largely as a stepping stone toward the development of black business. Rejecting wage labor as a permanent status, they paid little attention to adjudicating wages, working conditions, and fringe benefits, devoting the bulk of their attention to securing jobs for the unemployed and developing relationships with store-owners that assured them of a steady income from membership dues.[27]

Despite persistent efforts by the trade unions led by Frank Crosswaith of the Negro Labor Committee, to ban their activities, Kemp and Reid managed to carve out a niche for themselves in Harlem's retail sector and to command a sizable following among Harlem's unemployed and mar ginal workers. Their appeals to black solidarity, and their cynicism about interracial organizations, struck a responsive chord among Harlemites who had been left out of New Deal programs and remained divorced from organized labor, and their capacity to win jobs, however low paying, provided them with a valuable source of patronage. In addition, they maintained good relationships with black businessmen, who shared their entrepreneurial ideology and hostility to unions, and with black clubhouse politicians, who had learned to regard ethnic competition as a law of political life. But even some Harlem leaders who abhorred Kemp and Reid's philosophy—notably Adam Clayton Powell, Jr.,—believed they had a legitimate role to play in Harlem's efforts to end discrimination in employment, and that their activities, if kept limited in scope, put pressure on organized labor to give substance to its egalitarian rhetoric. At a time when interracial unionism had begun to reshape black economic life, the HLU emerged as an alternative center of black economic activism, a forum for unreconstructed Garveyites and for militants who became disillusioned with labor and the left.[28]

For most of 1937, enthusiasm for interracial unionism remained strong among Harlem intellectuals. The decision of the Committee for Industrial Organization to constitute itself as a separate labor federation was hailed by the Harlem press as a "new day" for black workers and it issued stiff warnings against leaders who tried to discourage blacks from participating. "If the Negro fails to enter the fight wholeheartedly for labor in general, and not so-called Negro labor only," the *Amsterdam News* editorialized, "the race faces a pauperized doom. . . . Decidedly, the Negro belongs in the vanguard of any group battling for the betterment of organized labor." Several CIO affiliates began organizing in Harlem stores, and one of them, Retail Grocery Clerks Local 338, won certification as official bargaining agent for large numbers of clerks previously represented by the HLU. Backed by the Negro Labor Committee, the Grocery Clerks Union drive, headed by veteran Communist Hammie Snipes, signed contracts that provided for substantial wage increases for the clerks, and a reduction in hours from 50 to 40 hours per week.[29]

The Communist Party, while supporting CIO activities, also concentrated its energies on defending federal and state welfare programs from conservative attacks. During the summer of 1937, the Party spearheaded protests against layoffs on Harlem WPA projects, mobilizing strikes and sit-ins among both middle-class blacks in the adult education and arts projects, and among working-class black women employed on the huge WPA sewing project. In addition, the Harlem Workers Alliance, led by Frances Duty (its first woman leader) conducted demonstrations at Harlem relief centers, mounted mass marches through Harlem aimed at forcing increased relief appropriations, and sent a twenty-five-person delegation to an alliance-sponsored jobs march on Washington. The Communist Party, though it now had "legislative representatives" in Washington and Albany, still saw strikes and demonstrations as a key way to exert pressure on legislatures, a view regularly echoed by non-Communist Harlem leaders.[30] "Practically all of the social and economic legislation passed during the Roosevelt Administration is the outcome of sustained agitation by Radicals and Liberals," the *Amsterdam News* averred. "The role of Negroes now is to join those groups which are agitating for social and economic justice in the United States."[31]

However, during the height of these protests, several incidents occurred which presaged a more complex and troubled relationship between the Party and black organizations and led some black intellectuals to question the Party's commitment to sustaining racial militancy.

The first of these took place on the National Job March to Washington in August, 1937. The atmosphere in the tent colony set up by the marchers, and indeed of the whole protest, shocked and embittered Frances Duty and Louis Campbell. Arriving at the camp three days late, the two Harlemites found that white leaders of the march (which included Communist and non-Communist alliance organizers) had failed to appoint black marchers, who were poorer and less educated than their white counterparts, to administrative positions in the camp or committees to visit Congress, and had not given them stipends for the camp commissary. When Duty and Campbell protested, the march leaders assigned blacks to policy positions in the camp and gave them free cigarettes and soap, but refused to appoint blacks to delegations lobbying Congress on the grounds that their presence might embarrass southern supporters of expanded relief. Upon his return to Washington, Campbell, a veteran of two previous Party "hunger marches" (1931 and 1932), joined Duty in bringing charges of white chauvinism against Sam Wiseman, the leading white Communist on the march, who directed the Workers Alliance in New York State. At a special session of Party leaders, Wiseman admitted that Party cadre on the march, concerned with extending the Alliance's influence, had made excessive concessions to the "backward prejudices" of new Alliance members, but Party leaders (noting the Alliance's rapid growth under his direction) let him off with a reprimand. Campbell, who bore the scars of numerous battles with Garveyites and police, regarded Wiseman's exoneration as a personal affront, and became openly hostile to Party and

Alliance leaders to whom he reported, though he stopped short, for the moment, of a public denunciation.[32]

The racial policies of the Transport Workers Union, one of the largest unions in the state headed by Communists and Party sympathizers, had a more direct negative impact on the Party's image in Harlem. The TWU organizing drive represented one of the Party's great success stories, a case where a handful of Irish radicals, helped by the Party apparatus, built a powerful union among Irish immigrant workers who were deeply religious and often politically conservative. Using Irish nationalism as a rallying point (even non-Irish Communists in the union affected a brogue and Irish names), and preaching bread-and-butter unionism, the leftist cadre in the union, concentrated *entirely* in the top leadership, managed to survive bitter opposition from employers and the Catholic hierarchy and win recognition from four important utility companies—the Fifth Avenue Coach Company, the New York Omnibus Company, the Brooklyn Manhattan Transit Company, and the Interborough Rapid Transit Company.[33] But in signing contracts, the TWU failed to eliminate discrimination against blacks practiced by these companies, which prevented blacks from finding jobs as bus drivers and mechanics, or subway conductors, motormen, and ticket agents. The TWU publicly opposed such discrimination and had initially proposed nondiscrimination clauses in contract negotiations, but had withdrawn them at the companies' insistence.[34]

Non-Communist Harlemites, as well as blacks who worked as porters and cleaners in these companies, found it profoundly disturbing that the TWU did not make the elimination of job barriers the first condition of its negotiations.[35] In the fall of 1937, Rupert Bath, a porter in the IRT and chairman of the TWU's organizing division for Negro workers, became so frustrated by his inability to persuade the Union's Executive Board to fight for the promotion of black workers (his own promotion to generator cleaner had been stalled for two years, and black workers had recently been denied consideration for seventy-five open positions as station agents) that he asked the NAACP and the Urban League to place additional pressure on TWU leaders.[36] NAACP officials Roy Wilkins, Charles Houston, and Walter White gave the issue their personal attention, but their communications to the TWU received no reply until they sent telegrams to CIO President John L. Lewis, and to sponsors of the city council race of TWU President Mike Quill, complaining of Quill's refusal to act on the grievances of his black members.[37] Finally, Quill and members of his staff met with NAACP and Urban League officials and worked out a strategy to secure Bath's promotion and get blacks access to some of the station agent jobs: Quill would work on the TWU's virulently racist white membership to try to win their approval of the promotions, while the black organizations would put pressure on the company to remove racial criteria from higher job categories.[38] This agreement temporarily eased tensions between the TWU and the NAACP (they would resurface a year later when promotions the two organizations had fought for were jeopardized by a white rank-and-file revolt, and the IRT's absorption of white station agents from the demolished Sixth Avenue El) but the timid, evasive behavior of the TWU leaders left a bitter taste in the mouth of NAACP officials and the TWU's black members. Given the racial attitudes of white subway workers, TWU leaders were understandably fearful of threatening the solidarity of their union by launching a frontal assault on racial hierarchy at the workplace, but they were insensitive to the needs of their black members to force an immediate resolution of the issue. That black members of a CIO union, and a Communist-led one at that, had to ask the NAACP's help in getting their union to fight job discrimination, exposed weaknesses in labor's role as a vehicle of racial uplift, and damaged the CP's credibility as an exponent of Negro rights.[39]

Recognizing that their support among blacks was in jeopardy, TWU leaders tried to improve their public image in Harlem by speaking at community meetings supporting the antilynching bill and protesting discrimination by Consolidated Edison and the New York Telephone Company, but their argument that discrimination was a company responsibility, coupled with their reluctance to challenge the prejudices of their white members, made many Harlem leaders adopt a more critical stance toward the CIO. In April, 1938, Adam Clayton Powell, Jr., reviewing the problem in transport, argued that henceforth blacks would have to conduct their struggle for equality on two fronts: "against the employer, and against the trade unions for admission, recognition, and advancement."[40]

The Harlem Party's position on the issue failed to still the union's critics. Instead of openly discussing the difficulties TWU officials faced in winning membership support for egalitarian measures, the Party echoed the union's complaint that discrimination was a company responsibility. In addition, it rejected the proposition that blacks needed to organize as an interest group to force unions to negotiate nondiscriminatory contracts. Arguing that "progressive forces" within the unions would ultimately end discrimination, Communists accused critics of the TWU of threatening the Negro-Labor alliance on which black progress depended and of dividing blacks from their "natural allies."[41]

The Harlem Party's arguments, unconvincing to most blacks, reflected important new developments in Party trade-union policy. Once the CIO emerged as a separate labor federation, with strong Communist participation, the Party leadership took the position that no domestic political concern should be allowed to jeopardize the success of the CIO's organizing drive or to interfere with smooth relations between Party trade-union functionaries and top CIO officials. In 1938, the Party dissolved its shop units, which had been the principal form of Party trade union activity for more than ten years, to counteract suspicions that Communists aimed to dominate the CIO, and to give Communist union leaders greater flexibility. But even earlier, Communists labor leaders had begun to avoid demands that might jeopardize their power or undermine their union's struggle for recognition. In unions like the Transport Workers, or the Hotel and Restaurant Workers, in which a left-wing leadership maintained an uneasy hegemony over a conservative and sometimes racist membership, the Party simply did not push the leadership hard to make antidiscrimination measures a primary focus, fearing that such a campaign might give conservative dissidents an opportunity to seize control of the union.[42]

Nevertheless, Harlem Party leaders knew that they could not avoid taking initiatives against job discrimination without severely damaging their credibility. Layoffs in the WPA, a late 1937 recession that sharply increased black unemployment, and hearings by a state legislative commission documenting widespread discrimination throughout the city's economy, all dramatized the marginality of Harlem's population. In addition, the presence of the Harlem Labor Union, ready to direct local discontent against trade unions and the left, helped convince Communists that they had to act forcefully to retain hegemony in Harlem protest. Early in 1938, Communists joined with Revs. Adam Clayton Powell, Jr., and William Lloyd Imes in forming a Greater New York Coordinating Committee on Employment which sought, with trade union support, to end discrimination against blacks throughout the city's economy. Choosing public utilities as their first target, the committee's founders welcomed support from all segments of the Harlem community, including nationalists. "Once you had the trade unionists from downtown," Abner Berry explained, "plus the social workers and middle class leaders from Harlem, there were only two nationalists, Kemp and Reid. So that their ideology would be subdued in there if they wanted to function at all."[43]

From the moment the coordinating committee was organized Adam Clayton Powell, Jr., became its dominant figure. A brilliant orator and a shrewd tactician, Powell had built a career as a protest leader by identifying with the militant interracialism of the Communists without neglecting his own base in the church or sacrificing his reputation as a man who couldn't be bought. Emotionally drawn to the causes of the Depression left — trade unionism and antifascism — Powell believed that blacks had to combine hardheaded ethnic bargaining with involvement in interracial movements and developed an alliance with Harlem Communists based on a limited number of shared values and a strong element of mutual manipulation. "My critics have often cited the names of many Communist-front organizations with which my name was associated," Powell later wrote. "Let it be said as a matter of record that no man ever used me, but in order to help my people, I used everyone that had any strength whatsoever, including the Communists." Powell's analysis of the relationship was substantially correct. Because Communists wanted access to his huge congregation and connections with the Harlem elite, Powell could periodically criticize Party policies—even on subjects like the Moscow trials—and still be courted by the Harlem left. Within the coordinating committee, Communists encouraged Powell to emerge as the group's "mass leader" and main political beneficiary, even though they couldn't control him. Fearful above all of rising nationalist sentiment, they needed a figure of Powell's stature to give the committee credibility and hoped that his own political ambitions would dictate that he maintain close ties with "progressive" unions that were becoming a force in city politics.[44]

Drawing upon the resources of Powell's church, of the Harlem CP, and of several left-wing unions, the coordinating committee launched a campaign to force Consolidated Edison and the New York Telephone Company to hire blacks as white-collar workers. Beginning with a "mass trial" of utility officials, the committee set up picket lines at local offices of the utilities and tried to disrupt their services by tying up phone lines and paying bills in a time consuming manner. After two months of protest, Con Edison agreed to open up jobs for blacks as cashiers and clerks in Harlem for the first time in its history, and New York Telephone made similar concessions shortly thereafter.[45]

The coordinating committee then turned its attention to 125th Street, where the Harlem Labor Union, stirred by an April, 1938, Supreme Court decision allowing organizations to employ picketing to protest the exclusion of minority racial groups from employment opportunities, had launched a new offensive. Appealing to popular disillusionment with trade unions, who had done little to break down hiring barriers in the private sector "downtown" or in Harlem, the HLU argued that blacks should gain control of all jobs in Harlem, where their numbers gave them leverage. Though most Harlem intellectuals vociferously opposed this tactic, enough unemployed blacks rallied to the group to create an intimidating presence on the street of Harlem, and a growing number of storeowners began to take HLU members on their payrolls, even if it meant discharging employees, black and white alike, who belonged to established unions.[46]

In response to this popular upheaval, leaders of the coordinating committee tried to develop a strategy that would open jobs in Harlem on a massive scale without jeopardizing the gains of "legitimate unions" or stirring up racial antagonism. After initiating its own picketing of stores on 125th Street, it entered negotiations with the Harlem Chamber of Commerce. In August, 1938, it signed an agreement with the chamber guaranteeing that one-third of all jobs in Harlem be given to blacks, with positions opening as white workers left or retired. Black employees would be referred to the chamber by the Urban League and the YMCA. In return, the coordinating committee would try to stop the picketing for jobs staged by the Harlem Labor Union.[47]

This agreement failed completely. Both Harlem newspapers criticized it for relinquishing the community's right to protest, and the HLU, a nominal affiliate of the coordinating committee, refused to stop its picketing. In addition, the agreement had little credibility among the unemployed and marginal workers to whom the HLU appealed, since it offered only hypothetical jobs in the future—through channels controlled by Harlem's "upper crust"—as an alternative to protests that were achieving results. Throughout the summer and fall of 1938, bitter controversy ensued between the HLU, the Coordinating Committee, and organized labor, with the HLU making considerable headway in small stores and black-owned concerns. In October, 1938, the principal groups on the coordinating committee conceded that the job question could not be settled by fiat, and worked out an agreement stipulating that the coordinating committee would focus on companies outside Harlem, the HLU on those inside, and that the HLU would refrain from organizing establishments where AFL or CIO unions had already signed contracts.[48]

The Communist Party's defensive posture in the 1938 jobs campaign, which saw it trying to suppress nationalist-led agitation for jobs on the grounds that it threatened interracial harmony and the gains of organized labor, aroused considerable controversy in Harlem. During the fall of 1938, several former Communists writing in black newspapers complained that the CP had become a "recognized political party" that had sacrificed much of its militancy to protect its ties to powerful politicians, and that its leadership was dominated by Harlem's "upper crust" rather than by "hogmaw, blackeye peas eating race men."[49]

Party actions in the Workers Alliance added fuel to these accusations. During the spring of 1938, national leaders of the CP ordered their cadre in the Workers Alliance to drastically deemphasize direct action tactics as a way of influencing relief policies and to concentrate instead on lobbying and campaigning for progressive candidates. Openly identifying the Party with New Deal reforms, Communists now insisted that the alliance not "direct the struggle of the unemployed against progressive officials supported by organized labor." In New York, where Communists considered Mayor Fiorello La Guardia and Governor Herbert Lehman progressive, and worked for their reelection, the new policy led to a drastic diminution in the use of the sit-ins and hunger marches that had once been an alliance trademark and evoked widespread discontent among non-Communist alliance leaders. Warning against "irresponsible" sit-down strikes and demonstrations, New York alliance head Sam Wiseman declared "the kind of militancy that was needed under Hoover is not needed today," and urged that the alliance work with organized labor to defend Roosevelt Administration programs.[50]

The Party's decision to discourage relief insurgency helped drive Frances Duty and Louis Campbell, heads of the alliance in Harlem, into open revolt. During October, 1938, they left the Communist Party and formed an all-black relief advocacy group called the United Afro-American Union. Long resentful of the financial and political privileges attained by more polished alliance leaders (especially Sam Wiseman, who made seven times Campbell's salary), Duty and Campbell saw little future in the organization for people like themselves whose strong suit was communicating with the Harlem poor and forcing action by city bureaucrats. The growth of the Harlem Labor Union had shown them that protest organizations built on nationalist lines could become self-supporting, and amass sufficient support to survive attacks from the left. Openly identifying with Harlem's nationalist subculture, which included UNIA chapters and black businessmen's groups as well as the HLU, Duty and Campbell issued public statements accusing the Communist Party of trying to subvert independent black organizations and discredit efforts of blacks to become "strong and self-reliant." Their actions led to massive membership losses in the Harlem Workers Alliance and a small exodus of black rank-and-file members from the Communist Party (no exact figures were provided in the Party press).[51]

Shortly after their departure, the Party suffered the loss of another black organizer who had helped establish it as a force among Harlem's poor—Hammie Snipes. Recruited out of the Garvey movement in 1931, Snipes had been the epitome of the Party street organizer, a fearless, combative man whom Party leaders assigned to the most dangerous situations. After working in the unemployed movement throughout the early '30s, Snipes had been assigned to labor organizing. Serving brief stints with the Pharmacists and Meatcutters Unions, Snipes had been hired by Grocery Clerks Local 338 to head its organizing drive in Harlem, and had helped enroll more than 200 clerks in the union in the face of fierce HLU opposition. But when the organizing drive was over, Snipes, who read and wrote with difficulty, found that white leaders of the union refused to appoint him to the executive board or pay him a decent salary, and made no efforts to place blacks in stores outside Harlem. After a year-long effort to change union policy, Snipes formed an all-black grocery clerks local, for which he won AFL affiliation, and installed himself as president. Opposed by the Negro Labor Committee and the Communist Party (which expelled him), Snipes could not sustain his organization more than a few months. But his efforts temporarily weakened Local 338 and added to the morale problems of the Harlem CP.[52]

The loss of Campbell, Duty, and Snipes significantly weakened the Party's efforts to sustain organizations among Harlem's unemployed and marginal workers. Not only did they draw people out of left-wing organizations, but their actions demoralized and confused many who remained and crystalized latent doubts about interracialism even among the converted. In February, 1939, Harlem Party leaders noted a significant loss of black membership due to the "expulsion of . . . enemy elements," and complained of a "Fifth Column" in Harlem working to undermine confidence in the Party. Though Communists absurdly denounced their opponents as "agents of Trotsky and Hitler," their concern was well grounded. By 1939, letters and articles by disillusioned ex-Communists, decrying the Party's declining militancy, had become regular features in the Harlem press and had given renewed intellectual respectability to nationalist ideas. Criticizing the Party and the trade unions for perpetuating black subordination, they urged blacks to organize ethnically in all fields of endeavor and approach interracial groups with great trepidation. Such arguments had little impact on the bulk of black intelligentsia (Claude McKay remained the only prominent Harlem writer to identify with them openly), but they had a considerable impact on self-educated militants active among Harlem's poor, who increasingly saw the Party as a defender of the privileges of unionized workers and a vehicle for the personal advancement of middle-class blacks.[53]

Nevertheless, the Harlem Party still maintained enough of a working-class cadre and membership to survive as an important force in Harlem's economic life. With the redoubtable Bonita Williams at its head, the Workers Alliance, though reduced in size, still served as an effective advocate at Welfare Department offices and coordinated protests against evictions and reduced-relief allotments. Party-organized tenants associations still remained active, trying to arouse support for the construction of public housing as well as working to improve conditions in individual buildings. And black Communist trade unionists remained influential in the WPA, the Welfare Department, and Harlem Hospital as well as private sector unions led by the left, especially the Fur Workers, Hotel and Restaurant Workers, Distributive Workers, and National Maritime Unions. Although left-wing unions continued to vary greatly in their willingness to promote black leaders and open jobs for blacks (with the Transport Workers proving laggard in both respects), enough of them did so to give the Party the reputation as a place blacks could gravitate to to pursue trade union careers.[54]

In addition, the Greater New York Coordinating Committee, in which the Party and left-wing unions remained influential, still survived as a viable entity. In the spring of 1939, it organized a movement to win jobs for blacks at the New York World's Fair featuring picket lines at the fair's Manhattan offices and at Flushing Meadow Park. The campaign did not achieve its intended breakthrough in white-collar employment— the more than 100 jobs it won were largely in menial categories—but it highlighted the charisma of Adam Clayton Powell, Jr., who served as the committee's spokesman and chief negotiator, and the organizational skills of Communists, who coordinated picketing and publicity and brought most of the white participants to the Committee's demonstrations.[55]

Still, the Party's role in Harlem had shifted markedly from the summer of 1937, when it had been the major catalyst for protest among Harlemites of all classes. Preoccupied with the international crisis, concerned with expanding their electoral influence and their power base in the CIO, Communists, in 1939, failed to give voice to the growing fears of blacks that they were being locked out of the mainstream of the economy. The late '30s recession brought home to blacks their extraordinary weakness in the private sector and their dependence on federal relief (the *Amsterdam News* spoke of "the most systematic exclusion policy affecting the Negro in jobs . . . in the history of the country"), but Communists lagged behind nationalists, activist ministers, and national leaders of the NAACP in directing popular indignation against companies that practiced discrimination and unions that condoned it.[56] "The horrors of Europe are still being shouted from the housetops and Columbus Circle," Adam Clayton Powell, Jr., observed in April, 1939, " . . . but nothing is being said about the plight of the Negro worker. Even my good friends down in Red Alley are strongly silent on this point, as they have been on lots of other points . . . concerning the Negro workers, such as the Transport Workers Union."[57]

The Party's response to massive WPA cuts in Harlem during the spring and summer of 1939 further dramatized its tactical conservatism. These reductions, implemented by a conservative Congress, inspired "terror and fear" in Harlem. Hundreds of Harlemites, particularly white-collar workers, lost their jobs, and were forced onto the relief rolls when they could not find employment in the private sector. Harlem newspapers complained that "unrest among relief clients was at the highest point in years," but neither the Workers Alliance nor the project workers unions sought to stimulate the kind of massive resistance—strikes, sit-ins and marches—that they had launched two years before in response to smaller cuts. The Workers Alliance put much of its dwindling energies into lobbying to rescind the cuts, but its efforts had no effect. The layoffs ensued unimpeded and Communist unemployed organizations suffered a loss of credibility because of their inability to protect the relief programs they had fought so hard to create.[58]

Even before the Nazi-Soviet Pact, therefore, Harlem Communists found themselves on the defensive in confronting Harlem's economic problems. Weakened by defections of rank-and-file organizers, challenged by nationalists for leadership of Harlem's poor, the Party experienced a narrowing of its local power base and growing skepticism of its political outlook. The Party's leadership of Harlem protest, from the mid-'30s on, had rested heavily on the expansion of federal employment programs and the rise of the CIO, but the dismantling of WPA, and the CIO's inaction against job discrimination, had shattered the confidence of many Harlemites in the power of interracial alliances to bring blacks into the economic mainstream. As Harlem leaders, fearful that blacks would become "permanent parasites," escalated their demands on trade unions and the government, Communists tempered their advocacy of direct-action tactics and tried to insulate the unions from popular wrath. Enmeshed in a set of alliances that eroded their aggressiveness, Communists lost touch with the spirit of popular militancy in Harlem that their own activities had helped to inspire, and rekindled deep-seated fears of white treachery and betrayal.[59]

NOTES

1. *New York Amsterdam News,* Dec. 31, 1938, Jan. 21, 1939, Feb. 4, 1939, Apr. 22, 1939; *New York Age,* Jan. 14, 1939, Apr. 1, 1939; "The WPA and After," *Opportunity,* 17 (Nov., 1939), 322.

2. *New York Amsterdam News,* Dec. 27, 1941.

3. On the Party's growth in influence during the Popular Front, see Nathan Glazer, *The Social Basis of American Communism* (New York: Harcourt, Brace, and World, 1961), pp. 109–16; Sidney Lens, *Radicalism in America* (New York: Thomas Y. Crowell, 1969), pp. 324–25. On the erosion of party militancy, see Bert Cochran, *Labor and Communism: The Conflict that Shaped American Unions* (Princeton: Princeton University Press, 1977), pp. 135–44; Kenneth Waltzer, "The Party and the Polling Place: American Communism and an American Labor Party During the 1930's," *Radical History Review,* 23 (Dec., 1980), 112–23.

4. *New York Amsterdam News,* Oct. 29, 1938.

5. *Ibid.,* July 14, 1937.

6. See especially, Richard Cloward and Frances Piven, *Poor People's Movements* (New York: Pantheon, 1977), pp. 1–180.

7. The periodization in the Popular Front that I am suggesting has not been emphasized in the historical literature, with the exception of Kenneth Waltzer's article, "The Party and the Polling Place: American Communism and an American Labor Party During the 1930's."

8. On protest activity in Harlem WPA projects, see *New York Times,* June 17, 1937, June 20, 1937, July 18, 1937; *New York Amsterdam News,* June 19, 1937, June 26, 1937, July 10, 1937, July 24, 1937; *New York Age,* July 17, 1937; *Daily Worker,* May 28, 1937, June 15, 1937. On Party strategy in 1937 WPA protests, see Herbert Benjamin, "Extending the Unity of the Unemployment Movement," *Communist,* 16 (Aug., 1937), 760–70.

9. Interview with Abner Berry, Nov. 20, 1973; Harry Dolimer and Allan Mackenzie, *The Negro Worker in the ERB* (New York: Association of Workers in Public Relief Agencies, 1937), pp. 1–11; Arnold P. Johnson to John P. Davis, May 4, 1937; "Union Statement on Johnson Dismissal," no date, 1937; William Gaulden to John P. Davis, Apr. 14, 1937, NNC Papers, Reel 5; James W. Ford, "Uniting the Negro People in the People's Front," *Communist,* 16 (Aug., 1937), 728; *New York Amsterdam News,* May 1, 1937; *New York Times,* Apr. 18, 1937; Ewart Guinier, "Careers for Negroes in Civil Service," *Opportunity,* 18 (Mar., 1940), 81, 94.

10. For complaints of preferential treatment of Workers Alliance members, see Capt. A. L. King to Hon. William Hobson, Jan. 15, 1937, UNIA Papers, Box 12, Reel 5; Better Harlem Welfare Committee to Department of Public Welfare, July 5, 1938, *ibid.*; *New York Times,* June 7, 1939; *New York Amsterdam News,* July 16, 1938, Oct. 22, 1938. The quote is from Capt. A. L. King to Joseph Strack, Feb. 11, 1937, UNIA Papers, Box 13, Reel 5.

11. The Wright quote is from *Daily Worker,* Aug. 4, 1937; the membership statistics from *ibid.,* Aug. 13, 1937.

12. *Ibid.,* Sept. 7, 1937.

13. Stanley High, "Black Omens," *Saturday Evening Post* (June 4, 1938), 38.

14. *New York Age,* Oct. 9, 1937; *New York Amsterdam News,* Oct. 17, 1936, July 16, 1937, Oct. 9, 1937, June 18, 1938, May 6, 1939; *Daily Worker,* Oct. 3, 1936, Oct. 9, 1936, Oct. 28, 1936, Sept. 16, 1937, Oct. 19, 1937, Nov. 23, 1937, Jan. 21, 1938.

15. "Some Shop Work Problems," *Party Organizer,* 11 (June, 1937), 12; R. G., "Hospital Workers on the March," *Party Organizer,* 12 (July, 1938), 21–22; Ford, "Uniting the Negro People in the People's Front," 731; *New York Amsterdam News,* Oct. 24, 1936; *Daily Worker,* Oct. 20, 1936, Oct. 21, 1936, Oct. 23, 1936, Dec. 31, 1936, Feb. 23, 1937; "Mass Meeting, To Stop Unfair Treatment in Harlem Hospital," no date, 1937, UNIA Papers, Box 11, Reel 4; interview with Abner Berry, July 5, 1977.

16. Interview with Abner Berry, Nov. 20, 1973.

17. George Charney, *A Long Journey* (New York: Quadrangle, 1968), p. 102.

18. On the problems faced by black women in the Party, see Charney, *A Long Journey,* pp. 102–3; *New York Amsterdam News,* Oct. 22, 1938, Oct. 29, 1938; Louise Thompson, "Negro Women in Our Party," *Party Organizer,* 11 (Aug., 1937), 25–27; Claude McKay, *Harlem, Negro Metropolis* (1940; rpt. New York: Harcourt, Brace, Jovanovich, 1968), pp. 233–35; interview with Audley Moore, Apr. 20, 1973; interview with Howard Johnson, July 23, 1977.

19. Lester B. Granger, "The AFL, the Negro and the Seamen's Strike," *Opportunity,* 14 (Dec., 1936), 378–80; *New York Age,* Nov. 28, 1936, Dec. 5, 1936, Jan.

23, 1937; *Daily Worker,* Oct. 13, 1936, Oct. 28, 1936, Nov. 10, 1936, Nov. 11, 1936, Nov. 15, 1936, Nov. 17, 1936, Nov. 23, 1936, Dec. 3, 1936, Dec. 10, 1936, Dec. 16, 1936, Dec. 23, 1936, Jan. 5, 1937, Jan. 13, 1937, Jan. 14, 1937, Feb. 4, 1937; *New York Amsterdam News,* Nov. 14, 1936, Nov. 21, 1936, Nov. 28, 1936, Jan. 9, 1937; George Blake, A. S. Berry, Manning Johnson, and Ben Davis to Frank Crosswaith, Feb. 1, 1937; minutes, conference between Frank Crosswaith and Communist Party representatives, Jan. 29, 1937, Negro Labor Committee Papers, Reel 2, B 25.

20. *New York Amsterdam News,* Nov. 14, 1936.

21. Interview with Leon Davis, Nov. 23, 1936; interview with Abner Berry, July 5, 1977; MacKenzie and Dolimer, *The Negro Worker in the ERB,* pp. 11–19; *New York Age,* Dec. 5, 1936, Aug. 14, 1937; *Daily Worker,* Nov. 14, 1936, Nov. 20, 1936, Dec. 10, 1936, Dec. 18, 1936, Jan. 29, 1937, Feb. 2, 1937; *New York Amsterdam News,* Dec. 5, 1936, Dec. 19, 1936, Dec. 26, 1936, Jan. 30, 1937, Mar. 6, 1937.

22. McKay, *Harlem, Negro Metropolis,* pp. 214–15; Ferdinand Smith, "Protecting the Negro Seamen," *Opportunity,* 18 (Apr., 1940), 112–14; *New York Amsterdam News,* Nov. 20, 1937; *Daily Worker,* Oct. 13, 1936, Nov. 10, 1936.

23. On pressure towards respectability experienced by Communist union leaders, see Len De Caux, *Labor Radical* (Boston: Beacon Press, 1970), pp. 239–41; Cochran, *Labor and Communism,* pp. 135–36. On the failure of many CIO unions to fight for expanded job rights for blacks, see New York State Temporary Commission on the Conditions of the Urban Colored Population, *Second Report,* p. 48; *Proceedings, 10 Convention, Communist Party, New York State,* pp. 105–51. Unions with a better record are described in Dolimer and MacKenzie, *The Negro Worker in the ERB,* pp. 1–19; Leon Strauss, "The Fur Floor Boys," *Young Communist Review,* 2 (Mar., 1937), 17, 19; Alice Citron, "An Answer to John Hatchett," *Jewish Currents* (Sept., 1968), 12–13

24. *Proceedings,' 10 Convention, Communist Party, New York State,* pp. 34–35.

25. *New York Amsterdam News,* Jan. 16, 1937.

26. Melville Weiss, "Don't Buy Where You Can't Work," (M.A. thesis, Columbia University, 1941), pp. 85–86; McKay, *Harlem, Negro Metropolis,* pp. 211–13; leaflet, Harlem Labor Union INC to Citizens of Harlem, undated, 1937, UNIA Papers, Reel 4, Box 11; *New York Amsterdam News,* Nov. 21, 1936; *Daily Worker,* Oct. 28, 1936.

27. Weiss, "Don't Buy Where You Can't Work," pp. 86–87, 89–91, 93–95; Claude McKay, "Labor Steps Out in Harlem," *Nation,* 145 (Oct. 16, 1937), 399–402; *New York Amsterdam News,* Aug. 21, 1937, Oct. 31, 1937.

28. Minutes of the Negro Labor Committee, Oct. 6, 1937, minutes of the Negro Labor Committee, Sept. 8, 1937, "For Immediate Release," Aug. 8, 1937, all in Negro Labor Committee Papers, Reel 1; McKay, *Harlem, Negro Metropolis,* pp. 128–31, 224–26; *New York Amsterdam News,* Oct. 30, 1937, Nov. 6, 1937; *Daily Worker,* Aug. 24, 1937.

29. *New York Amsterdam News,* Oct. 9, 1937; *New York Age,* Aug. 21, 1937; *Daily Worker,* Sept. 2, 1937; Weiss, "Don't Buy Where You Can't Work," pp. 88–89. The quote is from *New York Amsterdam News,* June 19, 1937.

30. James W. Ford, "Uniting the Negro People in the People's Front," 730–31; Benjamin, "Extending the Unity of the Unemployed Movement," 763, 769–70; *Proceedings, 10 Convention, Communist Party, New York State,* p. 193; *Daily Worker,* May 26, 1937, May 28, 1937, June 11, 1937, June 14, 1937, June 15, 1937, Aug. 13, 1937; *New York Times,* June 20, 1937, July 18, 1937.

31. *New York Amsterdam News,* Aug. 14, 1937.

32. *Proceedings, 10 Convention, Communist Party, New York State,* p. 195; *New York Amsterdam News,* Oct. 29, 1937, Nov. 12, 1938.

33. On the social composition of the Transport Workers Union, and the Party's role in building it, see James J. McGinley, S.J., *Labor Relations in the New York Rapid Transit System, 1901–1944* (New York: Kings Crown Press, 1949), p. 317; L. H. Whittemore, *The Man Who Ran the Subways* (New York: Holt, Reinhart, and Winston, 1968), pp. 16–30; Louis Sass, "Harlem Concentration on Transport," *Party Organizer,* 9 (Mar., 1935), 23–25.

34. New York State Temporary Commission on the Urban Colored Population, *Public Hearings,* vol. 8, pp. 1423–25.

35. On emerging Harlem discontent with the TWU, see *New York Amsterdam News,* Oct. 30, 1937; *New York Age,* Oct. 23, 1937.

36. Charles H. Houston to Rev. Adam Clayton Powell, Jr., June 4, 1938, NAACP Papers, C 414; [Charles H. Houston], "Memo from conference with Mr. Bath," July 3, 1938, *ibid.*; August Meier and Elliott Rudwick, "Communist Unions and the Black Community: The Case of the Transport Workers Union, 1934–1944," paper to be published in *Labor History,* p. 4. Meier and Rudwick directed me to material in the NAACP Archives on this issue.

37. *Ibid.,* p. 4; examples of NAACP officials' efforts to communicate with Quill and his supporters are telegram, Walter White to John L. Lewis, Oct. 4, 1937, NAACP Papers, C 414; Roy Wilkins to Michael J. Quill, Oct. 5, 1937, *ibid.*; Charles Houston to Michael J. Quill, Oct. 7, 1937, *ibid.*; Charles Houston to Committee of One Thousand for Michael J. Quill, American Labor Party, Oct. 27, 1937, *ibid.*

38. [Charles H. Houston], "Memorandum on meeting at Transport Workers' Union Headquarters, Saturday, Oct. 31, 1937, 11 a.m.," NAACP Papers, C 414; Charles H. Houston, "MEMORANDUM, Re: Interborough Rapid Transit Co. case," Aug. 1, 1938, *ibid.*

39. On resurgent tensions between the NAACP and TWU, see Meier and Rudwick, "Communist Unions and Racism: The Case of the Transport Workers Union, 1934–1944," pp. 6–8; *New York Age,* Nov. 5, 1938; Press Release, "SUBWAY UNION FAILED TO PROTECT COLORED MEMBERS, SAYS N.A.A.C.P.," Feb. 17, 1939, NAACP Papers, C 414; Roy Wilkins to Austin Hogan, Feb. 17, 1939, *ibid.* On difficulties the union leaders faced with the TWU rank and file, see Roy Wilkins to Father John La Farge, Aug. 18, 1938, *ibid.* Max Gordon, "The Party and the Polling Place: A Response," *Radical History Review,* 23 (Dec., 1980), 132.

40. *New York Amsterdam News,* Apr. 30, 1938.

41. *Daily Worker,* Mar. 23, 1938, Mar. 26, 1940.

42. On dissolution of shop units, see Cochran, *Labor and Communism,* pp. 135–36, and Starobin, *American Communism in Crisis,* p. 39. On failure of leftist

unions to push antidiscrimination measures see *Proceedings, 10 Convention, Communist Party, New York State,* pp. 23, 151; New York State Temporary Commission on Conditions of the Urban Colored Population, *Public Hearings,* vol. 8, pp. 1504, 1613–15; interview with Abner Berry, Feb. 4, 1978.

43. *Proceedings, 10 Convention, Communist Party, New York State,* pp. 103–5; James W. Ford, "Rally the Negro Masses for the Democratic Front," *Communist,* 18 (Mar., 1938), 270; Weiss, "Don't Buy Where You Can't Work," pp. 95–96; *New York Amsterdam News,* Feb. 26, 1938; *Daily Worker,* Feb. 17, 1938, Aug. 14, 1938; A. Clayton Powell, Jr., and Gladys Stoner to My Dear Friend, Feb. 1, 1938, UNIA Papers, Reel 5, Box 14; interview with Abner Berry, July 5, 1977.

44. Adam Clayton Powell, Jr., *Adam By Adam* (New York: Dial Press, 1971), pp. 32–67; Neil Hickey and Ed Edwin, *Adam Clayton Powell and the Politics of Race* (New York: Fleet Publishing, 1965), pp. 52–58; Ottley, *New World A-Coming,* pp. 220–35; interview with Abner Berry, Feb. 4, 1978. Powell's comments on his relations with Communists come from *Adam By Adam,* p. 67. Of all of Harlem's protests leaders, Powell was the most adept at maintaining working relations with the Communist Party without sacrificing his intellectual integrity or jeopardizing his image as a "man who couldn't be bought." Beginning with the Scottsboro protests in the spring of 1933, Powell, with rare exceptions, lined up with Harlem Communists in supporting mass interracial protest as the most effective means of challenging racial discrimination. He was an early supporter of the National Negro Congress, a strong advocate of interracial trade unions, and an "internationalist" who argued it was the black community's responsibility to challenge fascism wherever it appeared. At times, his rhetoric, especially in speeches, would seem to identify him as a Communist sympathizer. "He would announce that his church was open to the Communist Party, and that the first Soviet in Harlem would be organized from the Abyssinian Baptist Church," Abner Berry recalled (interview with Abner Berry, Dec. 2, 1973). "He would say, at another time, 'If the *New York Times* doesn't take it, and the *Daily News* doesn't take it, and won't write about these damnable conditions, we'll take it to the *Daily Worker* and the *New Masses* and we'll march!'" But Berry also said that "Powell never was, and probably never could be a Communist." He endorsed candidates the CP opposed (Lorenzo King's congressional bid in 1938), criticized left-wing unions in print if they failed to challenge discrimination (*New York Amsterdam News,* Jan. 21, 1939), and raised issues in his column which were "taboo" for Communists, such as loyalist atrocities in Spain (*New York Amsterdam News,* Sept. 19, 1936) and the absurdity of the Moscow trials (*New York Amsterdam News,* July 3, 1937). Powell's ability to use the Party to his own—and Harlem's—advantage, without becoming a prisoner of Party policies was one of the most impressive aspects of his rise to power.

45. Adam Clayton Powell, Jr., *Marching Blacks,* p. 103; interview with Abner Berry, July 5, 1977; *New York Amsterdam News,* Apr. 2, 1938, May 7, 1938; *Daily Worker,* Mar. 4, 1938, May 1, 1938, May 23, 1938; *New York Times,* Apr. 29, 1938, Aug. 10, 1938.

46. Weiss, "Don't Buy Where You Can't Work," pp. 91–95; Columbus A. Austin to Dear Sir, June 2, 1938, UNIA Papers, Box 11, Reel 4; Harlem Labor

INC. to Dear Rev., July 14, 1938, *ibid.*; *New York Age,* Apr. 9, 1938, Apr. 23, 1938, Apr. 30, 1938, Sept. 3, 1938.

47. *New York Times,* Aug. 8, 1938, Aug. 10, 1938; Weiss, "Don't Buy Where You Can't Work," pp. 96–102.

48. *Ibid.,* pp. 102–5; *New York Age,* Aug. 13, 1938, Nov. 5, 1938; *New York Amsterdam News,* Aug. 13, 1938, Oct. 22, 1938, Nov. 12, 1938.

49. *Ibid.,* Oct. 22, 1938, Oct. 29, 1938.

50. H.B., "Unemployment—An Old Struggle Under New Conditions," *Communist,* 17 (May, 1938), 425–27; *New York Times,* Sept. 25, 1938, Oct. 2, 1938, Feb. 12, 1939, Feb. 19, 1939; Cloward and Piven, *Poor People's Movements,* pp. 90–91.

51. *New York Age,* Dec. 31, 1938, Jan. 21, 1939; *New York Amsterdam News,* Oct. 22, 1938, Oct. 29, 1938, Nov. 12, 1938; Charney, *A Long Journey,* pp. 97–98; McKay, *Harlem, Negro Metropolis,* pp. 237–39; leaflet, "25,000 Persons Helped to keep their HOMES, hold their JOBS," undated, UNIA Papers, Reel 6, Box 14.

52. Weiss, "Don't Buy Where You Can't Work," p. 39; interview with Abner Berry, July 5, 1977; *New York Amsterdam News,* Feb. 18, 1939, May 6, 1939, Aug. 12, 1939, Aug. 19, 1939; *Daily Worker,* Jan. 26, 1939.

53. *Party Builder,* Apr., 1939, pp. 1–3; *Pittsburgh Courier,* Mar. 19, 1939; *New York Amsterdam News,* Apr. 15, 1939, May 13, 1939; *Daily Worker,* Apr. 10, 1939; McKay, *Harlem, Negro Metropolis,* pp. 218–19.

54. William H. Gaulden, Harold C. Green, Manning Johnson to Dear Sir, undated, 1939, UNIA Papers, Reel 5, Box 13; leaflet, "Save Your Homes, Schools, and Jobs," undated, 1939, *ibid.,* Reel 4, Box 12; *Daily Worker,* May 5, 1939, May 27, 1939, June 25, 1939, July 16, 1939; *New York Age,* Jan. 28, 1939, July 22, 1939, Sept. 9, 1939; *New York Amsterdam News,* May 30, 1939, Aug. 5, 1939.

55. Powell, *Adam By Adam,* p. 66; *New York Times,* Apr. 25, 1939; *New York Amsterdam News,* Apr. 8, 1939, Apr. 29, 1938, May 6, 1939; *Daily Worker,* Mar. 30, 1939, Apr. 4, 1939, Apr. 5, 1939, Apr. 13, 1939, Apr. 22, 1939, May 3, 1939.

56. *New York Amsterdam News,* Dec. 31, 1938, Jan. 21, 1939. The quote comes from the Jan. 21 issue of the paper.

57. *Ibid.,* Apr. 1, 1939.

58. *Ibid.,* Apr. 8, 1939, Apr. 22, 1939, Sept. 2, 1939; *New York Age,* Sept. 9, 1939, Sept. 23, 1939; *Daily Worker,* July 21, 1939. One commentator stated: "Communism made a bid for the Negro with promises of abundant home relief, but their promises failed, and since they could not offer Russia or Siberia, Garveyism has taken the lead again."

59. The warning that blacks might become "permanent parasites," is contained in an *Amsterdam News* article dated Jan. 21, 1939. Articles in black publications, written during that spring (1939) express a deep pessimism regarding the black community's economic prospects.

11

Communism and the Black Working Class during the Popular Front — The Limits of Radicalization

THE POPULAR FRONT era offers a sobering picture of obstacles Communists faced in trying to win the political allegiance of Harlem's population. To a degree greater than most commentators have imagined, Communists touched the lives of working-class Harlemites in a direct and intimate way. Through the Workers Alliance, through Party-sponsored tenants' organizations, through Party work in the school system and the WPA, through unionization drives and campaigns for employment opportunities, Party organizers came in contact with a large portion of Harlem's population and persuaded several thousand to join the Party and its affiliated organizations. According to Party membership statistics, over 2,000 blacks were members of the Harlem CP during the Popular Front years (1935 to 1939), with the highest total—1,000—being reached in the early spring of 1938. If one triples that total, one might get an appropriate estimate for the number of blacks involved in Party-affiliated groups like the Workers Alliance.[1]

But for most blacks involved in the Harlem Party, membership was short-lived and ambiguous in its political impact. There seems to be very little evidence of a massive conversion to Communism—whether reflected in voting patterns, folk culture, or political behavior. The Party's bread-and-butter organizing, especially around housing, relief, and education, commanded widespread respect among Harlem poor, but the movement as a whole did not kindle the kind of emotional enthusiasm among the masses excited by the Garvey movement in its prime. Very few Harlemites participated in the general social and cultural life of the Communist movement—its May Day marches, fraternal organizations, summer camps—except when those institutions emphasized racial themes, and the emancipatory vision of socialism seems to have touched black intellectuals far more than it did black workers. According to Communists I have interviewed, blacks comprised less than 5 percent of the visitors at Party summer camps and resorts, and participated only intermittently in demonstrations and cultural events held "downtown." Writing in the spring of 1939, Claude McKay commented on the "scanty number of Negro participants" in the Party's May Day parade, and saw this as a sign of the Party's failure to establish the kind of ethnic subculture among blacks that it had developed among Jews, Finns, and Eastern Europeans.[2]

The gap between the political culture of the Party, and that of the Harlem masses, remained a continuing source of concern to Party organizers. Throughout the Popular Front, Harlem Party leaders tried to "find ways to incorporate into . . . branch meetings the cultural forms of struggle of the Negro people," but never ended the enormous turnover in the Party's black membership. Between the spring of 1936 and the spring of 1938, the Communist Party in New York State recruited 2,320 blacks and lost 1,518. If we assume that Harlem accounted for two-thirds of the black Party members in the state (probably a conservative estimate), it meant that about a thousand blacks joined the Harlem Party and left it during those two years, a period when Party organizing displayed its greatest militancy and effectiveness.[3]

The Party's inability to hold blacks it attracted stemmed from many sources, some of them peculiar to Afro-American life, others typical of Party problems among *all* working-class constituencies. According to Abner Berry, the Party's leading black "troubleshooter" in Harlem during the period, the Party's artificially imposed interracialism contributed to the high rate of turnover. Working-class blacks, he felt, were so uncomfortable around whites that they found Party branch life a great strain. "The thing I came up against most often in Harlem" he recalled, "was that the blacks wanted to be together. They didn't mind on occasion being integrated, but in general, they wanted to be involved in something they could call their own, something they organized and led. This was not a 'hate whitey' thing. Rather, society had evolved in such a way that you had a separate people, and they had some things they wanted to discuss by themselves, for themselves. The Party was dead set against this." The Party's efforts to organize the total lives of its membership magnified the problem. Blacks who joined not only had to deal with interracial encounters in meetings and policital activities, but in social events as well.[4]

In addition, blacks and whites in the Party grappled with strong undercurrent of sexual tension and jealousy. For reasons which need to be further explored, black men and white women tended to gravitate toward one another in Party circles. Black women strongly resented this, and their discomfort, which they could not express politically within the Party's frame of values (or those of most mainstream black organizations) pervaded the Party and its surrounding organizations. Numerous jokes arose about interracial sex in the Party (some blacks spoke of the "ass struggle replacing the class struggle"), but the prevalence of such joking suggested a tension that hindered political commitment.[5]

In addition, the kind of demands the Party made on its membership, intellectually and emotionally, proved burdensome to the recent rural migrants that composed the bulk of Harlem's working class. Party life in Harlem, as everywhere, placed a premium on organizational skills and mastery of the Party's language and mode of reasoning; rewards went to those who were successful in both domains. Working-class Harlemites, having had limited exposure to trade unions and socialist politics, were often intimidated by the terms of political debate within the Party, and by the gruff, businesslike style of its leaders who had risen up through the ranks. Theodore Bassett, the Party's education director in Harlem, recalled having enormous problems in explaining the Party's goals and methods to its new members:

> I found that many people had no idea what the Party was like or how it functioned. We explained at the first session: "This is a Party of the working class, in the countryside, the Party of the poor and working farmers. It also supports the problems of the lower middle class. We are the Party of the black people and other oppressed people." We made it clear that the Party had nothing to give.
>
> Well, many of the black people in Harlem had come up from the South and were told by precinct leaders (Republican and Democrat), if you want favors done, join our political club. We had to make it clear that we had nothing to do with that. Many of the people who came into the Party through the unemployed movement were women, and we had to say to them: "The Party is not a sewing club."
>
> We told them: "This is not like any other organization. If you belong to the lodge, that's one thing, a church, that's another thing, but this is a Party of the working class."

Problems of the kind Bassett describes, it should be emphasized, occurred in many working-class districts where the Party was active. Fluctuation among working-class Communists was systematically higher than it was among white-collar groups, and was as high among Poles and Italians as it was among blacks. But Harlem represented a special area of difficulty because so much of its working class was composed of recent migrants and was located in marginal spheres of the economy—particularly domestic and personal service—which were difficult to unionize.[6]

In addition, the Party may have lost members because of its unwillingness to incorporate Afro-Christian imagery and symbolism into the life of Party branches. The church dominated the folk culture of working-class Harlemites, serving as a center of sociability and cultural expression as well as formal religious worship. By the time of the Popular Front,

Communists had come to recognize that church participation was essential in community struggles and had developed close working relationships with many Harlem ministers. Yet while Communists praised the black church as a repository of black traditions and a center of resistance, their official ideology, as expressed in publications, classes, and meetings, was militantly secular. Black Communists were encouraged to remain members of churches as a political tactic, but the Party did not adapt its inner life to make religious people feel comfortable in it.[7] "The black masses," Abner Berry recalled,

> came with an experience of church and church organizations, the typical organizations in the black community, where the meeting was opened with a prayer, the reading of the minutes of the last meeting, the agenda is read and adopted, then you have your doxology and closing prayer. Well, he comes in to the Communist Party and God is challenged right away. When he goes to a new member's class, he's instructed that "God has nothing to do with our business here."[8]

The unwillingness of the Party leadership to incorporate religious imagery into its branch life reflected its hope that religious beliefs would ultimately be "washed out" of new recruits and replaced by a secular vision. But the subtle—and not so subtle—pressures it exerted in that direction made religious blacks feel ashamed of customs and affiliations which were a source of great comfort and security, further reinforcing the sense that they didn't really belong.

These explanations, of course, all remain somewhat speculative. Until we have access to a large number of oral history interviews with Harlem residents who remember the 1930s, we will not have an accurate sense of what the Party looked like to a black domestic, longshoreman, transit worker, or elevator operator who joined it, or one of its surrounding organizations. From the available evidence, it does not appear that the Party penetrated the intimate social networks of many such people, as it did among French industrial workers, or small sections of the Jewish and Finnish working class in the United States. A Party-organized fraternal life did not flourish in Harlem: the International Workers Order (the Party's insurance and fraternal society) remained relatively small there and Party-sponsored sports clubs, singing clubs, and youth organizations assumed modest proportions. Black workers had a rich fraternal life, but it centered around the churches, the lodges, and the regional societies (South Carolinians, Barbadians, etc.), rather than the left. Communist fraternal organizations in Harlem, interracial as a matter of principle, exercised little appeal for working-class Harlemites, who preferred to organize their social and cultural lives on more familiar terrain.[9]

If the Popular Front failed to inspire a broad-based left-wing political culture among black workers, it had an impact on black intellectuals far exceeding that exerted by any previous wave of radicalism. Here, the movement *did* penetrate intimate social networks; among Harlem's doctors, nurses, and relief workers, as well as its writers and creative artists, Party membership was widespread and socially acceptable in the late 1930s. Moreover, Party membership had a strong cultural component. Left-wing theatre parties, benefit concerts, and dances were important centers of social life among Harlem's intellectual elite, and a valued source of contact with whites who possessed influence in the professions and the arts. In addition, the Party milieu in Harlem gave rise to study circles, book clubs, and discussion groups, sometimes interracial, sometimes all black, which presented a leftist perspective on domestic and international events. By the time of the Nazi-Soviet Pact, a good many of Harlem's teachers, writers, and professionals had been exposed to Marxism in a sympathetic (if somewhat dogmatic) context, and were more favorably disposed to the left than most of their white counterparts.[10]

However, given the configuration of Party affiliation in Harlem during the Popular Front—strong, if not always disciplined among the black intelligentsia; weak, and uneven, among Harlem's poor, one must conclude that "Americanization" fell far short of the Party's objectives. Although disagreement with Party policies accounts for some of the turnover in Party membership—especially its justification of Soviet actions during the Ethiopian War, and the increasingly conservative implications of its trade-union and unemployed strategies—the persistence of membership turnover, even in periods without major controversy, suggests that obstacles to the Party's success were deep-rooted and structural. Not only did the Party face formidable competition in the electoral arena from local black elites, but its whole mode of organization clashed with the cultural traditions of much of Harlem's population. Had the Party expressed its message in the language of black religion and incorporated religious rituals into its meetings, had it allowed all-black branches or cultural organizations to form when demography dictated it, or the membership requested it, then working-class blacks might have felt more comfortable in the Party. But in a Party forged in the image of the Russian Revolution, and distinguished, in its growth, by an interracial solidarity unparalleled in its time, the deepest convictions of its leading cadre, black as well as white, prevented them from suggesting such changes. For better or worse, Harlem Communists were defined by their interracialism, just as they were by their ties to the Soviet Union. If they paid a price for it, they did so with unbending consistency, and with open eyes.

NOTES

1. George Blake, "The Party in Harlem, New York," *Party Organizer*, 12

(June, 1939), 14–15; Max Steinberg, "Rooting the Party Among the Masses in New York," *Communist,* 17 (Sept., 1939), 829; *Party Builder,* Apr., 1939, 11; *Daily Worker,* July 10, 1936, Apr. 8, 1939. The Workers Alliance, at its peak strength in Harlem, claimed 2,800 members, although membership in it was even more unstable than it was in the Party.

2. Interview with Morris Schappes, Aug. 24, 1937; interview with Edith Segal, Apr. 16, 1977. The McKay article appeared in *New York Amsterdam News,* May 13, 1939.

3. *Proceedings, 10 Convention, Communist Party, New York State* (New York: New York State Committee, Communist Party, 1938), pp. 150, 298–99; Blake, "The Party in Harlem, New York," 17.

4. Interview with Abner Berry, Nov. 20, 1973.

5. Louise Thompson, "Negro Women in Our Party," *Party Organizer,* 11 (Aug., 1937), 25–27; interview with Howard Johnson, July 23, 1977; George Charney, *A Long Journey* (New York: Quadrangle, 1968), pp. 102–3; interview with Abe Shtob, Sept. 28, 1976. The following section of a Roi Ottley column was typical of Harlem humor about Communist interracialism: "But I believe a more profound reason has caused the breakdown of Communism among Mose. . . . The bait is beat. . . . The Ofay gals are very seedy, frowsy and sad-looking. . . . The Emancipated Mose, when he goes adventuring for a wife, is seeking a woman who has, along with other qualities, pulchritude" (*New York Amsterdam News,* Sept. 15, 1934).

6. Interview with Theodore Bassett, Dec. 15, 1973; Report on National Groups, Material for National Groups Commission, 10 Party Convention, May, 1938, Robert Minor Papers, Columbia University; Charney, *A Long Journey,* pp. 115–16.

7. On the role of the black church in Harlem, see "The Church in New York," unpublished manuscript, Federal Writers Project Papers, Reel 1; *New York City Guide: A Comprehensive Guide to Five Boroughs of New York* (New York: Random House, 1939), pp. 140–41; Claude McKay, *Harlem, Negro Metropolis* (1940; rpt. New York: Harcourt, Brace, Jovanovich, 1968), pp. 32–85; Roi Ottley, *New World A-Coming* (1943; rpt. New York: Arno, 1968), pp. 82–99. On the Party's approach to black religion, see *Daily Worker,* Sept. 15, 1936.

8. Interview with Abner Berry, July 5, 1977.

9. *Daily Worker,* Dec. 31, 1936, Feb. 3, 1937, Mar. 1, 1938. In 1938, the IWO claimed 140,000 members nationally, of which "hundreds were Negroes," an indication that the order had not posed itself as an effective alternative to the traditionally black lodges and insurance societies. On the problems of building Party youth organizations in Harlem, see Tony Morton "Two Conferences on Negro Youth Work," *Young Communist Review,* 1 (Dec., 1936), 4; Mike Martini, "A Lesson From New York," *Young Communist Review,* 1 (Dec., 1936), 6.

10. Interview with Ernest Rice McKinney, Nov. 1, 1973; *New York Age,* Nov. 18, 1939, May 25, 1940; George Streator, "Books," *Interracial Review,* 13 (Sept., 1941), 145; McKay, *Harlem, Negro Metropolis,* pp. 248–59; interview with Louise Thompson, Sept. 14, 1977; interview with Howard Johnson, July 23, 1977.

PART THREE

12

From the Nazi-Soviet Pact to Pearl Harbor— Isolation and Rebirth

THE COMMUNIST PARTY'S RESPONSE to the Nazi-Soviet Pact had a profound impact on its work in Harlem. Already weakened by controversies surrounding its trade-union work and its organizing of the unemployed, the Party's defense of Soviet actions, and its sudden shift of position on the New Deal and the fascist danger, deeply disillusioned most of its important Harlem allies and undermined the Party's ability to serve as a catalyst of community protest. With rare exceptions, leading Harlem ministers and social workers who had developed "united front" relationships with the Party stopped working with Communists in community coalitions and sought alternative means of developing alliances against discrimination. In addition, militant anti-Communism emerged as a powerful intellectual current in Harlem for the first time since the early Depression. A key group of black socialists—A. Philip Randolph, Frank Crosswaith, and Layle Lane—used their organizational influence and journalistic skills to press for the total exclusion of Communists from civil rights activity, and implemented this strategy effectively in the most important black protest movement of the period—the March on Washington Movement.

Attacked from every side, ambivalent themselves about some of the policies they were advocating, Harlem Party leaders failed to sustain morale in the neighborhood branches and suffered sizable membership losses. With the Workers Alliance split, WPA disintegrating, and unemployment remaining high despite war-inspired recovery, the Party's preoccupation with foreign policy dramatically increased its distance from the daily concerns of Harlem's poor. As Party neighborhood cadre, weakened by defections, lost the ability and will to consistently mount protests in defense of community needs, the Party lost much of the hold on the popular imagination that it had earned in the "heroic days" of the early and mid-'30s. "Communism made a bid for the Negro with promises of abundant home relief," one journalist noted, "but their promises failed, and since they could not offer Russia, or Siberia, Garveyism has taken the lead again."[1]

Nevertheless, the Pact did not mark the death knell of the Party's political influence. To an extraordinary degree, the Party's leading black cadre, including thirteen publicly identified Communist functionaries in Harlem (James Ford, Benjamin Davis, Abner Berry, Audley Moore, Bonita Williams, Rose Gaulden, Abner Berry, Theodore Bassett, Claudia Jones, Howard Johnson, Louise Thompson, James Burnham, Emmett May, and Richard Moore), remained loyal to the organization and struggled to salvage its reputation as an exponent of racial equality. Saddled with a line that invariably separated them from the main currents in American reform, they kept alive virtually intact the cultural struggles of the Popular Front—and in doing so maintained much of their influence among Harlem's creative artists and college-educated youth. Aided by the silence of the Comintern on matters of culture, the Party milieu continued to offer enthusiastic support for programs in black theatre and music, for the popularization of black history, and for criticism of the media's handling of the black experience, defining all of these as part of a struggle for the perfection of American democracy.

In addition, the Party maintained its following among unionized black workers and used its trade union base to reassert its claim to leadership in the struggle to end discrimination in employment. The left-wing unions, unlike Party unemployed organizations, expanded in influence and membership in the years following the Pact, and emerged as a major source of black leadership for the Harlem Party. By the spring of 1940, left-wing unions supplied much of the cadre and financial support for the local and national organization of the National Negro Congress and were dominant in the Manhattan and Harlem organization of the American Labor Party. Equally important, these unions, pressed by the Party leadership, began to act more aggressively to challenge discriminatory practices in their industries. By the spring of 1941, several unions in New York had initiated actions to break open white-only shops and the Transport Workers Union—long an embarrassment to Harlem organizers—had thrown its support behind a Harlem-wide movement to end discrimination in employment on city buses. Even before Hitler's invasion of the Soviet Union, these actions helped spark a revival of Party fortunes, bringing about a modest influx of black recruits (after a long period of stagnation) and impelling several former allies to resume communication with the Party. Though the Party's moral credibility had been permanently tarnished, and its enemies become more numerous and sophisticated, its base in the trade unions and the intelligentsia and the talents of its black cadre enabled it to survive as an effective instrument in important though limited spheres of Harlem's political and cultural life.[2]

The tenacity the Harlem Party displayed—under such demoralizing conditions—dramatized the peculiar mixture of courage and venality, opportunism and idealism, that the Party invoked among its leading functionaries. The Pact, and the Comintern's justification of it, forced Harlem Communists to repudiate many policies that had brought them into the mainstream of black life—it was an invitation to political suicide. Almost without exception, leading black Communists accepted the new Comintern guidelines, displaying their conviction that Soviet leadership constituted the essence of their movement, its ultimate energizing principle. But they came to this conclusion from an *American* political logic, a belief that only a Soviet-centered internationalism could give blacks the power and strategic insight to escape poverty and eliminate jim crow. Whether they were an Audley Moore, attracted by the Scottsboro movement in Harlem, an Abner Berry, drawn into unemployed councils in Houston, or a Ben Davis, involved in defending Angelo Herndon in Atlanta, their attachment to the movement flowed from a profound emotional response to the Party's egalitarian policies, reinforced by theory in the Party schools and cemented by ties of friendship and marriage with other Communists. To break with this life, which had given them recognition and power and a sense of political accomplishment, seemed like a forbidding prospect. Within the limited space provided by the Party's new line, they struggled to win back the popular support the Party once commanded.[3]

These efforts, as we shall see, were at once pathetic and impressive. On issues where the Comintern spoke specifically, Harlem Communists, like their comrades in other places, changed their analysis at the drop of a hat, attributed extravagant moral purpose to Soviet territorial designs, and generally showed a lack of intellectual integrity and moral balance. But on issues which the Comintern manifestos neglected to provide guidelines, they fought for racial and economic justice with a voice that still seemed powerful and authentic. The Party's persistent agitation against the poll tax and lynching, its efforts to insure black history was taught and respected, and its efforts to persuade white workers to fight for jobs for blacks all bespoke the continued power of the Party's vision of an egalitarian American future. In the Popular Front era, Communists had found a language and a set of symbols which linked Afro-American and American destiny in a forceful and persuasive way, and they fought to retain their credentials as authentic American radicals under circumstances which called into question both their patriotism and good sense.

As no other event in the Party's history, the Nazi-Soviet Pact left American Communists demoralized and confused. A Party of ethnic minorities, it had risen to political influence on the strength of a policy that defined Nazi Germany as the arch enemy of human progress and encouraged Communists to fight for reforms and defend liberal democracy against attacks from the right. When news of the Pact reached the United States, Party leaders tried to act as though little had changed. They described the Pact as a defeat for Hitler and issued slogans for the membership reminiscent of the Popular Front—"the defeat of fascist aggression," support for the New Deal, and the building of a "democratic front" against "tory reaction." But new Soviet actions soon undermined the Party's efforts to maintain continuity with prior policies. In the end of September, Party leaders received several communications from the Comintern demanding that the CPUSA abruptly drop antifascism as a political slogan and denounce both sides in the European conflict as equally guilty. It was now the responsibility of American Communists, the Comintern declared, to keep America out of the "imperialist war" and to direct their fire against "Social Democratic" leaders, including Roosevelt, who tried to mobilize American aid for Britain and France.[4]

Despite private reservations, and a sober awareness of the consequences, the Party leadership changed their strategy in line with Comintern specifications. Declaring that "the present war . . . has at one blow wiped out the division of the world between the camps of democracy and fascism," the Party's Politburo discarded the basic strategic precepts of the Popular Front years, including support for the New Deal and agitation against the fascist danger. The major priority for Communists, it now declared, was the organization of a "peace movement" to assure American neutrality, and a militant defense of Soviet actions, including its invasion and annexation of Eastern Poland and the Baltic states.[5]

In Harlem, the Party's response to Soviet actions served, as never before, to stamp it as a "Soviet agent" whose actions lacked integrity and whose commitment to its members and allies was fundamentally unstable. At the Party's first public meeting in Harlem following the Pact, Benjamin Davis, aided by Dr. Arnold Donowa, hailed the Pact as a proof of Nazi weakness, denounced Britain and France for opposing collective security and issued a long tirade against fascism and a statement praising the President.[6] One month later, following the partition of Poland, James Ford presented a completely different position, telling a Harlem audience that "this is not a war against fascism" and calling for a conference of black organizations "to discuss plans to keep the Negro people out of this imperialist war." From a public relations standpoint, both meetings were a dismal failure, drawing less than a hundred people. With or without antifascist slogans, Harlem Party leaders could not rally most of their black members, or any of their important allies, to defend a Soviet alli-

ance with the preeminent international symbol of race hatred and oppression.[7]

Party leaders compounded membership losses by pressing their branches
to give antiwar work preeminence. Not only was the political stance they
were asked to adopt difficult to defend but the task drained precious
energy from the economic concerns that troubled most Harlem residents.
During the fall of 1939, the *Amsterdam News* commented, Harlem's population "suffered greater unemployment and actual starvation . . . than at
any period since the beginning of the depression."[8] The liquidation of the
WPA—particularly the arts projects, the recreation project, and the adult
education project—left hundreds of Harlemites jobless and deprived tens
of thousands more of opportunities for recreation and self-improvement;
reductions in the city relief budget caused large numbers of Harlemites to
lose their benefits or be denied needed assistance; and persistent discrimination in employment prevented Harlemites from benefiting from a war-
inspired recovery.[9] Had the Party deemphasized international issues and
tried to mobilize community protest for increased home and work relief,
it might have retained much of its black membership. But in its anxiety to
defend the Soviet position, it devoted more attention to sponsoring meetings on the international crisis than to organizing marches, rallies, and
sit-ins to protest cuts in essential services, cutting deeply into its support
among Harlem's poor. "At the time of the Pact," Abner Berry concluded
in retrospect, "we should have said: 'That's the Soviet Union's business,
they have a country to run.' But we had to come down and defend it, to
make it the number one priority in the Party. Well this piece left, and
that piece left, and we were beginning to lose our base."[10]

While undermining membership morale, the Party's posture in the international crisis also inspired a bitter attack on Party policies in Harlem
newspapers and led to the gradual disintegration of Party alliances with
prominent community leaders. Beginning with the signing of the Pact
and continuing apace through the invasion of Poland and the "Winter
War" with Finland, a steady flow of letters, articles, editorials, and columns of opinion appeared in Harlem newspapers calling on blacks to reevaluate their friendly attitude toward Communism and the Soviet Union.

The denunciation of the Party came from a diverse set of perspectives.
First, there were letters from Harlem nationalists claiming that the Pact
exposed the treachery behind Communist internationalism and that the
"white race . . . is not to be trusted as far as black people are concerned."
"Negro students must cease to give their minds to Stalin and think for
themselves," one writer averred. " . . . every single nation today has been
built on nationalism and power politics."[11] Second, influential black liberals who had soft-pedaled their criticism of the Soviet Union during the

Popular Front, especially Roy Wilkins of the NAACP, argued that the Pact proved Soviet idealism was an elaborate sham and that it practiced power politics "in exactly the same manner as have Hitler, the Japanese, the Italians, the British and the French." Contemptuous of the arguments Communists used to justify Soviet actions, they asked blacks to look elsewhere for leadership "for the opportunism of the Stalinites is on a par with the opportunism of the Republic Party."[12] Third, the Party came under attack from longtime radical allies, such as Adam Clayton Powell, Jr., for betraying the antifascist principles it had espoused during the Popular Front, and for destroying the possibilities of an American radicalism that their own actions had helped to evoke. "American Communism is just about finished," Powell asserted. " . . . Fellow travellers must seek new companions and the united front must be born under new auspices."[13] Finally, Layle Lane and Frank Crosswaith, black socialist critics of the Popular Front, along with some black conservatives, argued that the Soviet alliance with Hitler revealed the Soviet regime's true essence and that Communism represented an evil that must be purged from black life. Pointing to the suppression of opposition in the Soviet Union and the "vilification, abuse and character assassination" employed against opponents of American Communism, they defined Communism as a "totalitarian" movement, akin to fascism, which was incompatible with the principles of a democratic society.[14]

The breadth of hostility to the Party's actions made it extremely difficult to sustain united-front relationships with Harlem churches, fraternal organizations, and NAACP and Urban League chapters. One by one, Harlem organizations which had been marked by close collaboration between Communists and non-Communists disintegrated or became inactive. During the fall of 1939, the Negro People's Committee for Spanish Refugees lost its two key Harlem officials, Lester Granger of the Urban League and Pauli Murray, a nonviolent activist affiliated with the Socialist Party, when its national organization refused to accept a proposed resolution by the Harlem group condemning the Nazi-Soviet Pact.[15] In the winter of 1939–40, the Coordinating Committee for Employment became paralyzed by inner turmoil when leading non-Communists in the group, including Adam Clayton Powell, Jr., launched a frontal attack on trade union discrimination that singled out the Transport Workers Union for criticism. Communists on the Committee temporarily withdrew rather than lend support to this policy.[16] And antiwar meetings called by the Harlem Party, in contrast to its Popular Front mobilizations for Spain and Ethiopia, failed to attract a single prominent Harlem minister, fraternal leader, or UNIA spokesman. Revs. Adam Clayton Powell, Jr., William Lloyd Imes, and Shelton Hale Bishop, all enthusiastic partisans of the Popular Front, carefully kept their distance from the Party's new perspective on international affairs, leaving it without a single important advocate in Harlem's religious community.[17]

Despite these setbacks, the Harlem Party refused to accept the inevitability of isolation. After fits and starts, it managed to develop a strategic outlook which defined mobilization for war as a threat to black rights and called for an escalation of black demands for citizenship and economic advancement. In addition, its international analysis resuscitated a critique of Western imperialism that had been central in the '20s and early '30s, but muted in the Popular Front, and a renewed call for colonial independence. Although the genesis of this analysis was the "changed international situation" rather than the Party's own consistent theorizing, the Party's most sophisticated black spokesmen and sympathizers, Ben Davis, Richard Moore, Dr. Max Yergan, and John P. Davis, managed to use it as the basis of a forceful critique of black subordination in the United States and the colonial world. Among limited segments of the Party's Harlem constituency—West Indian intellectuals and black college students—the Party's new analysis received a respectful hearing, among the former because of resentment of imperialism, among the latter because of fears of war.[18]

The emergence of Max Yergan as a leading Communist spokesman in Harlem (he functioned as an "influential" rather than a disciplined Party member) demonstrated the stubborn persistence of Party influence among sections of the black intelligentsia. A man of aristocratic manners who possessed a doctorate in education ("he had a maid, and liked formal dinners served at the same time every day," Abner Berry recalled), Yergan had been radicalized by his fifteen years as a director of YMCA work in South Africa, and returned to the United States in 1936 as a confirmed Communist sympathizer. "Ford and I met with him," Abner Berry remembered, "and he described the indignities he had to suffer in South Africa, how he couldn't teach the kids what he wanted. And he told us he wanted to put himself at the disposal of the Party. Ford and I looked at each other and thought: 'Look at the big fish we caught.' We took him down to Browder and talked to Browder. Well, he would have become anything we said, then."[19] Throughout the late '30s, Yergan divided his energies between the International Committee on African Affairs, an organization he directed aimed at disseminating information about Africa to liberal and left constituencies in Europe and the United States, and the Manhattan Council of the Negro Congress, where he devoted much of his attention to cultural issues. A sponsor of the Harlem Suitcase Theatre, and of several benefit concerts for left-wing causes, Yergan helped lead the NNC's campaign against cuts in the WPA arts and education projects.[20] But the role that brought him greatest prominence in Harlem was as the teacher of City College's first course in Afro-American history.

Created in 1937 in response to pressure from the college's Frederick Douglass Society (headed by Communist Louis Burnham), the position represented City's first formal recognition of the culture and history of the huge black community that adjoined it, and Yergan's accession to the post, which made him the first black instructor ever to teach at the school, endowed him with considerable personal prestige.[21] During the period following the Pact, Party leaders exploited this prestige for all it was worth, pushing Yergan to the forefront of its defense of Soviet actions.

With its prominent black cadre holding firm, the Harlem Party's base among black creative artists, and among black trade unionists, proved strong enough to survive its changing position with little apparent damage. Three leading black artists aligned with the Party, Paul Robeson, Richard Wright, and playwright Theodore Ward, took to the hustings to defend Soviet policies, claiming that its territorial acquisitions were buffers against "imperialist" aggression, and praising it as the only nation in the world with which blacks could identify. Although black journalists and political leaders criticized their statements, few black artists joined in the attack. Moved by tales, and sometimes experience of Soviet hospitality, attracted by the left's consistent support for black cultural expression, much of Harlem's creative community remained openly sympathetic to the Party, or conspicuously indifferent to efforts to uproot it.[22]

Black leaders of the left-wing unions also rallied to the Party's position. Grateful for Party support in their own trade union careers, they observed that the left's antiwar stance did not undermine its power in many of the unions it controlled, and in fact coincided at many points with the views of rank-and-file workers and top CIO leaders (especially John L. Lewis). Because of the relative security of their position, Party leaders increasingly relied on black trade union leaders—particularly Ferdinand Smith from the National Maritime Union, Manning Johnson, George Brown, and Charles Collins of the Hotel and Restaurant Employees International, Lyndon Henry of the Fur Dyers Union, and William Gaulden of the State, County, and Municipal Workers of America— to serve as general spokesmen in Harlem, appearing at antiwar meetings, youth congresses, and cultural programs as well as trade-union events.[23] "Today, it is more important than ever," top Harlem Party leaders asserted, "that Negro labor assert itself and place its stamp on the Negro movement."[24]

The solidity of the left's base among black trade unionists, and to a lesser degree among black youth, provided the basis for an ambitious attempt by Communists and Party sympathizers to revive the National Negro Congress. During the fall of 1939, John P. Davis, the congress's secretary, convened a meeting of its National Executive Committee and won their support for plans to hold a third national convention of the congress in the spring of 1940. Despite persistent attacks on the congress as a "Communist front" (one of them by the Dies Committee) and the refusal of most prominent black liberals to associate with the group, congress President A. Philip Randolph strongly supported Davis's plans. At planning meetings for the convention, he worked closely with Party sympathizers in the congress, declining to issue *any* public statements on Soviet foreign policy, or American Communist actions, which might make cooperation difficult. For their part, Party representatives in the congress, in an uncharacteristic display of tact, declined to press their foreign policy perspective in preconvention propaganda. The congress's press releases, and its preconvention calls, focused almost exclusively on domestic issues — passage of the antilynching bill, protection of black voting rights, defense of labor and civil liberties — containing only one minor reference to the dangers of American involvement in war. At a time when other important black leaders (Walter White, Adam Clayton Powell, Jr., Roy Wilkins) were denouncing the Party and being denounced in turn, Randolph's relations with the left had the appearance of a love feast. He vociferously defended the congress against charges of Communist domination, and was treated to a testimonial dinner by the congress's national office (staffed by Party sympathizers), who praised him extravagantly in all their announcements and mailings.[25]

However, as the convention approached, the congress's major organizer, John P. Davis, took a number of actions that offended Randolph deeply. A brilliant administrator who had kept the congress going on a shoestring budget since it was founded, Davis had never, even during the height of the Popular Front, been able to attract strong support for the congress from major black organizations other than the Urban League; the NAACP remained aloof (and in 1938 became downright hostile), while black church participation proved minimal. But in 1940, due to the sudden unpopularity of the congress's left-wing connections, Davis found himself facing a virtual quarantine from these groups. In desperation, Davis turned to the CIO unions and the Communist Party for the financial support and the delegate strength needed to put on the convention, and developed a convention program dominated by CIO leaders, featuring a keynote address by John L. Lewis. Worse yet, from Randolph's standpoint, Davis began to steer the convention toward an open endorsement of the Communist Party's position on foreign policy. At a meeting two weeks before the convention, the congress's resolutions committee drafted documents that, were they approved, would irrevocably have tied the congress to the CP and the CIO, one calling for affiliation of the congress with Labor's Non-Partisan League, the political action arm of the

CIO (which Lewis was using as a forum for his opposition to Franklin Roosevelt and his own presidential ambitions), and the other denouncing the President for supporting Britain in "an imperialist war."[26]

Randolph came to the convention prepared to take a strong stand against these policies, but he found himself facing a stacked deck. While the major black organizations had boycotted the meeting, the left had pulled out the stops to attract delegates from unions and student groups, including a sizable contingent of whites. The huge New York delegation, dominated by the left-wing unions, symbolized the political tone of the gathering. Of the 500-odd delegates, less than a score consistently voted against the recommendations of the Communist caucus. Though not all delegates came from left-wing organizations (some represented Y's and professional associations), very few came from the Urban League, the NAACP, or the city's largest churches, and the most prominent figures were Communists or Party sympathizers: Ben Davis, William Gaulden, Louis Burnham, and Claudia Jones. Young, intellectual, confident of their own futures (the *Amsterdam News* spoke of "socialites and celebrities . . . literally tripping over one another" at the Harlem send-off party for the convention), they found themselves at an event which was a model of administrative efficiency and at which no detail had been spared to give the left's perspective the aura of historic destiny.[27]

Randolph, alone among the major speakers, challenged the air of smug confidence that pervaded the convention. In a long speech, he argued that the congress had chosen a direction which rendered it incapable of accurately reflecting the perspective of Black America. Randolph criticized the congress for formally aligning itself with the CIO, for encouraging the participation and support of whites, and for endorsing the policies of the Communist Party and the Soviet Union. On the latter issue, Randolph spoke particularly sharply, equating the Soviet Union with Nazi Germany and denouncing the Communist Party as the agent of a foreign power. Though Randolph's speech coincided far more closely with the dominant political mood in black communities than Davis's denunciation of the "imperialist war," it provoked such hostility among convention delegates that Randolph resigned as president of the congress rather than submit his views to a vote. Max Yergan, the most important figure in the NNC's Manhattan Council, and a rising "star" in the Party milieu, succeeded Randolph as president.[28]

Randolph's departure did not destroy the congress, but it did sharply delimit the field of its operations. As Randolph correctly stated, the congress had taken positions on foreign policy and assumed organizational connections which prevented it from serving as a creditable exponent of black public opinion. Given the ambivalent record of CIO unions in fighting discrimination at the workplace, and the bitter opposition provoked by recent Communist policies, the congress could not depend exclusively for funds from these two sources and serve as a unifying element in black protest. But if the congress could no longer pretend to be credible as the "voice of the black masses" (a fact apparent to many long before this particular convention), its special relationship with the CIO made it a useful agency to increase black participation in unions and maximize the influence of black CIO leaders. Delegates to the third convention, over one-third of them representing unions, returned from the gathering with their enthusiasm intact, more impressed by Lewis's endorsement than by Randolph's predictions of doom.[29] "It would be . . . unfortunate . . . for Negro leadership openly to repudiate the Congress," Lester Granger warned. "It has a vitally important job to do in the field of labor's education. Until other organizations are ready to move into this field and show at least as much accomplishment as the Congress can point to, their criticism of the Congress effort is in some wise a criticism of themselves."[30]

In Harlem, the events at the third convention marked a decisive split in the prolabor coalition that Communists had helped to create in the Popular Front era. Not only did Randolph leave the congress, but he used his action as the occasion to call for the destruction of Communist influence in Afro-American life. After five years of public silence on the nature of the Soviet state, Randolph began denouncing Stalin as a totalitarian dictator akin to Hitler and asking blacks to eschew Communist propaganda "to save themselves from destruction." Although Randolph's arguments mirrored those of Frank Crosswaith and Layle Lane, his personal influence gave them far greater force. The most powerful black labor leader in America and arguably its most eloquent protest spokesman, Randolph alone among non-Communist Harlemites had the power to create a protest coalition that could simultaneously command substantial mass participation and attract labor and liberal support. His attack on the Communist Party—done in a manner which "burned his bridges behind him"—reflected both his personal political beliefs and his hardheaded judgment that blacks could now dispense with Communists in mounting an effective protest strategy. From this point on, Harlem Communists, for the first time in their history, faced competition from someone who could articulate the mass-protest tactics which had catapulted them to prominence and who had the organizational resources and the personal charisma to back up his words.[31]

The Harlem Party's initial response to Randolph's challenge did not bode well for its political future. Unwilling to answer Randolph's critique on a point-by-point basis, they accused Randolph, along with other prominent blacks, of giving way to antilabor policies "under pressure of the war drive of American imperialism" and of betraying the civil rights struggle by supporting FDR. In addition, they instructed their Harlem cadre to escalate the struggle to keep America out of war and to impress upon blacks that the "only bulwark for peace, the only country that offers any hope for the Negro people is the Soviet Union."[32] Affirming their allegiance to Soviet society with stubborn pride, they insisted that "the experience of the USSR shows beyond dispute that the victorious working class, pursuing the leninist-stalinist policy of national liberation . . . has solved every problem . . . which the Negro people face in the United States today."[33]

Had these expressions of "love and faith in the Soviet Union" (to use James Ford's words) represented the totality of Party policies, its Harlem organization might have suffered total collapse. But its leading cadre, determined to recapture some of the power they had wielded in the Popular Front, engineered a gradual renewal of the Party's practical work. Drawing upon the Party's base in the black intelligentsia, and its controlling influence in local CIO unions, they reasserted the Party's leadership in the struggle for black representation in cultural institutions and in efforts to mobilize the unions to end job discrimination. In doing so, they demonstrated that the Party, despite its hard-bitten public persona, could still inspire an idealistic commitment to racial reform among large sections of its cadre and sympathizers, and that predictions of its demise in Harlem were quite premature.[34]

More than any other aspect of Communist organizing in Harlem, Party cultural work survived the Nazi-Soviet Pact without losing its effectiveness. Despite a foreign-policy line that condemned "American imperialism" and bourgeois democracy generally, Communist artists, writers, and critics continued to use the "American democratic tradition," not the Soviet experience, as their reference point for black aspirations. The importance of black culture to a "progressive" American identity remained the keynote of the Party's approach and it sponsored a diverse array of programs to promote black artists and attack discrimination in cultural institutions.[35]

The exuberance displayed by Party cultural work reflected the deeprooted appeal of Popular Front cultural policies, particularly those relating to the black experience. Many of the major issues taken up by the Party press in that era—an affirmation of the black roots of American popular music, an identification with black athletes, and an interest in the reinterpretation of black history—flowed out of the personal experience and cultural tastes of American-born Communists and had a resonance and appeal extending far beyond the Party. In addition, key individuals in the Harlem Party leadership—Ben Davis, Abner Berry, and "Stretch" Johnson—came from literary and theatrical backgrounds and took a personal interest in using the Party to promote cultural programs. Sharing the literary and musical tastes of much of Harlem's middle class, they strove to prevent controversies surrounding the Pact from jeopardizing their ties with Harlem's creative community.[36] For their part, black artists and intellectuals showed little disposition to quarantine the left culturally, even when they did so politically. In October, 1939, blues composer W. C. Handy, hardly a radical, delivered a featured lecture at the Party's Workers School on the black contribution to American music.[37] One month later, Roy Wilkins, Lester Granger, and Rev. William Lloyd Imes, all of whom had attacked American Communists for their defense of the Pact, joined Richard Moore, Ben Davis, and Angelo Herndon in sponsoring a Frederick Douglass Historical and Cultural League that aimed to distribute Douglass's writings, popularize the "historical and cultural heritage of the Negro people" and "set forth the true role of the Negro in world history, ancient and modern."[38] Three months later, black and white Communists, including Richard Moore, Herbert Aptheker, and Doxey Wilkerson, played a major role in Negro History Week celebrations in Harlem, delivering many of the keynote speeches and sharing the platform comfortably with a large array of non-Communist participants.[39]

Designating the "battle for cultural development" as a part of the fight for "political expression," Communists launched a number of new initiatives to challenge the place of blacks in mass cultural institutions. Late in 1939, *Daily Worker* editor Ben Davis successfully pressed the Party to launch a boycott and educational campaign against "Gone With the Wind," the slickly produced Hollywood epic that romanticized the defeated Confederacy. In a display of personal power that impressed many Harlemites, Davis forced the resignation of a white *Daily Worker* critic who favorably reviewed the movie and commissioned a seven-part series by David Platt analyzing the "Negro in Hollywood films." Leading a picket line against "Gone With the Wind" when it appeared in Harlem, Davis used Du Bois's and James Allen's writings to show how the film distorted the role of blacks in fighting for their freedom and in working to establish democracy in the Reconstruction South. Arguing that the "fight of the Negro people for freedom has been identical with the struggle of the white common people to extend their liberties and raise their . . . standards," Davis excoriated the film as an attack on the traditions of "Lincoln and America," on the "democratic principles which the people have fought and died for."[40]

In a similar spirit, Communists continued agitating for the integration of organized sports. In the spring of 1940, the Young Communist League formed a committee to end jim crow in baseball that included left organizations, the Harlem Branch of the NAACP, and sportswriters from the *Amsterdam News* and college newspapers. Shortly thereafter, the Trade Union Athletic Association, organized by the left-wing unions, sponsored an "End Jim Crow in Sports" day at the World's Fair and collected 10,000 signatures on petitions demanding blacks in the major leagues.[41] An imagery of populist American nationalism dominated both campaigns. "If we are to preserve democracy," Richard Moore told the trade-union groups, "we must stand firm . . . against those forces who trample on the principles of sportsmanship."[42]

The Party's aggressive defense of black cultural opportunities was accompanied by a spirit of tolerance almost entirely lacking from its other activities. In their treatment of black artists, Party critics (and even Party functionaries) continued to display an appreciation of widely diverse styles and themes and declined to uphold a single standard of orthodoxy. Nowhere was this more apparent than in the Party's response to the publication of Richard Wright's *Native Son*. When the novel first appeared in the spring of 1940, it provoked a terrific furor within the Party because of its choice of a black criminal as a main character and its generally unflattering portrait of white Communists (the protagonist's lawyer was the only Communist favorably portrayed). Although the novel presented a chilling picture of the harshness of ghetto life, it failed to offer the approved "solution" of united action by black and white workers, offering instead a more ambiguous image of personal emancipation through violence. Many black and white Communists wanted to publicly attack the book, but Party cultural czar V. J. Jerome, anxious to bask in the novel's prestige, insisted that Communists claim the book as their own. The major review in the *Daily Worker,* written by Wright patron and protector Ben Davis, took Wright to task for presenting blacks as victims rather than political rebels, but offered extravagant praise for his portrayal of the effect of "capitalist oppression" on blacks. Following this, the *Worker* printed a rash of letters on the novel, some critical, some favorable, along with additional articles defending the book's greatness, and challenging, at least implicitly, the imposition of a narrow standard of socialist realism on left-wing writers.[43] "Richard Wright's book," Mike Gold wrote, "is a study in psychology that is worthy . . . of Dostoyevsky . . . It seems wrong to me to suggest to the author of such a book that he should have written a simple agitational novel instead. There is room in the great house of labor for all categories of art, from the strike leaflet to Dostoyevsky, not only room, but need."[44]

The Party's flexibility in dealing with black artists contributed powerfully to the survival of Harlem's left-wing cultural movement. Among Harlem's small community of professional artists and entertainers, especially those who aspired to a "downtown" clientele, Communists and party sympathizers maintained enough visibility and prestige to make a "muted" leftism an acceptable posture. Billie Holiday, by no means a political activist, sang "The Yanks Are Not Coming" (a Communist anti-war song) as part of her nightclub repertoire, provoking FBI intervention to remove it from her act, and left-sponsored concerts, including a second version of "From Spirituals to Swing" continued to attract topflight blues artists and jazz bands.[45] Towering over Harlem's leftist cultural scene, and giving it much of its energy, stood the figure of Paul Robeson, who returned to the United States in 1939. Robeson's luminous personality and immense talents gave an aura of legitimacy to his political posture, which differed little from the official Party line. But Robeson's relation to the Party never smacked of deference or appeared to compromise his personal dignity. So great was his prestige — internationally and domestically — that he defined, by virtue of his own artistic choices, much of the Party's approach to the black musical tradition and its relation to the music of other nations and cultures. Robeson's concerts and radio performances, whether of the populist "Ballad for Americans" or of spirituals and international folk songs, helped define the cultural tastes of a whole generation of American Communists and popularized a left-leaning cosmopolitanism among Harlem's cultural elite. Attracting large interracial audiences wherever he performed, Robeson projected an integrity and sincerity that no Communist *political* figure could match.[46] A writer in the Catholic journal *Interracial Review* criticized Robeson's political sympathies, but left one of his concerts deeply moved by the singer's persona and the "enthusiastic and united crowd" he attracted. "An intelligent man," she wrote, "a good man, a disinterested man — one can say all of those things of Paul Robeson on first acquaintance. And yet he had no place to go for leadership except to the CP. Where, in a Catholic circle, could you have duplicated such a group as were at that meeting? What Catholic group would have tolerated such a mixture of the two races as were there present on an equal footing?"[47]

Robeson featured prominently in the most ambitious cultural enterprise of the Harlem left following the Hitler-Stalin Pact — the formation of the Negro Playwrights' Company. During the fall of 1939, a group of black writers, playwrights, and actors who had come to prominence in the WPA theatre decided to found a permanent theatre that could provide employment for black actors and technicians and serve as "an outlet for the creative works of race dramatists." Choosing Theodore Ward's *Big White Fog,* an ambitious political drama, as their first production, the company's founders proclaimed their identification with historic black rebels (Frederick Douglass, Sojourner Truth, Nat Turner, etc.), denounced the "stereotyped distortions of Hollywood," and offered a somber, highly politicized, vision of the proper subject of the black writer.[48] "Only through portrayal of the deepest tragedy of the Negro people," the company proclaimed, "their oppression at the hands of American rulers, their struggle for equality and recognition, can a Negro culture be truthful and strong."[49]

Though this hardly represented a formula for a popular Harlem theatre, it struck a responsive chord among many black intellectuals. A benefit concert for the company, held at Harlem's Golden Gate Ballroom in September, 1940, dominated Harlem's society pages ("just about everybody was there, plus a few thousand more,") and drew the largest crowd ever to attend a cultural event in Harlem. Designed to attract "devotees of the concert stage, the literary world, and Cafe society," the program featured Richard Wright reading excerpts from "How Bigger Was Born," Paul Robeson singing a program of spirituals and international music, and Hazel Scott playing swing versions of classical compositions. The ability of the theatre's supporters to attract 5,000 "well paid admissions," three-quarters of them white, impressed Harlem promoters ("Damned if I see how they did it," one proclaimed) but dramatized the narrow social base of the left within Harlem itself. By emphasizing the social protest message inherent in black art and the black artist's mastery of Western cultural traditions (folk as well as classical), black left-wing artists found the "serious" mass audience that had escaped their predecessors in the 1920s, but they cut themselves off from the large portion of Harlem's population that wanted to be entertained and amused within an ethnic tradition inaccessible to whites.[50]

The play itself, premiering October, 1940, displayed many of the characteristic strengths and weaknesses of black "proletarian art." The first two acts of *Big White Fog,* dealing with a Chicago family of the '20s pulled between the hope of upward mobility and the Garveyite dream of Black Empire, projected great authenticity. Like Richard Wright did in his stories, Ward made serious political debate come alive amidst the personality conflicts and daily strivings of ordinary black families. But Ward's third act, projecting the conversion of one of his characters to Communism amidst the turmoil of the Depression, struck black critics as stilted and artificial. Like Langston Hughes before him, Ward could not successfully project his own political convictions onto black working-class characters; could not invoke words, gestures and attitutes which would make interracial harmony and revolt seem like creditable expressions flowing from their experience. Praised for its staging, acting, and confrontation with social issues, *Big White Fog* cut itself off emotionally from most black audiences with its undiluted affirmation of Communist convictions, made without the ambivalence, skepticism, and hostility such views commonly provoked. Like much of the explicitly political art created by black Communists, it failed to capture the imagination, or even the interest, of black common folk.[51]

Despite such problems, some black writers, artists, and entertainers continued to look to the Communist left for opportunities for expression. Though the dominant aesthetic values in the Party milieu weighed heavily on black artists, requiring the genius of a Wright or Robeson to transcend them, the Party did give black artists access to a large and enthusiastic (if not always knowledgeable) white audience capable of responding positively to symbols of black self-assertion. Given the primitive racial attitudes that pervaded much of the media and literary world, the Party's efforts to expose its white constituency to black culture and history commanded respectful attention. The International Workers Order, the Party's fraternal society, symbolized this commitment when it sponsored a pageant on "the Negro in American life," in the spring of 1941, to commemorate its eleventh anniversary. Composed of seventeen immigrant fraternal bodies, the IWO decided that the best way to dramatize the "unity of national groups" and their contribution to American culture was to highlight the black experience. Written by black playwright Carlton Moss and featuring songs by Paul Robeson, the pageant dramatized major events in Afro-American history, summarized the lives of black political and cultural figures, and used performances of spirituals and blues to explore the black contribution to American music. The political message of the pageant, sounded by Paul Robeson, was for all minorities to unite with the Negro to make "America a real land of freedom and democracy." The 6,000 people who came, almost all of them white, responded to this declaration with repeated cheers.[52]

Historians of black culture, pondering Robeson's continuing ties with the Communist left (and later those of Du Bois), need to explore the symbolism of this response to Robeson's speech. Whatever the Communist Party embodied as a political and social phenomenon—as an agent of Soviet diplomacy, an advocate of working-class power, a vehicle for the Americanization of ethnic minorities—it had become, by the late '30s, a major force in American society promoting systematic cultural interchange between whites and blacks and encouraging whites to recognize the black contribution to the nation's cultural heritage. That this effort touched only a minority within the black community (though a sizable portion of the black intelligentsia) and an equally small minority of whites does not negate its impact on those who experienced it. So long as Communists remained the most visible advocates of cultural and racial democracy, some black artists and intellectuals clung to the Party milieu with a stubborn loyalty, even when Communist mass-organizing in Harlem almost sputtered to a halt.

The odyssey of George Murphy, Jr., publicity director of the NAACP from 1938 to 1941, dramatizes the great effort extended by Communists to enroll influential blacks in its programs dealing with black history and culture. The only openly leftist sympathizer on an NAACP national staff dominated by people hostile to, or suspicious of the Communist Party, Murphy was in great demand as a speaker by Communist groups during the Popular Front, and served as a member of the board of the Harlem Suitcase Theatre and the Greater New York Committee for Better Negro Films, an organization founded by Emmett May and Paul Robeson.[53] After the Pact, Murphy, who declined to denounce Soviet actions, found himself literally bombarded with invitations from IWO lodges, and Communist-led youth groups, trade unions, and peace organizations to give lectures on black history, on discrimination in national defense, and on the status of the antilynching bill. Murphy accepted many of these invitations (his list of speaking engagements in 1940–41, preserved in the NAACP files, would serve as an excellent guide to the social geography of Communist influence in New York City), and became progressively more immersed in the Party subculture.[54] In July, 1940, Murphy became an associate member of the Negro Playwrights Company; in November, 1940, he joined the Negro Commission of the International Workers Order; in January, 1941, he agreed to chair a forum on black history at a Communist-run school in Harlem, and in February, 1941, he left the NAACP for a position in the national office of the National Negro Congress![55] That Murphy could pursue such a course right under the noses of Roy Wilkins and Walter White, with whom he interacted daily, suggests a high degree of tolerance for the cultural and educational activities of the left, even among blacks who emphatically rejected its political leadership.

In their economic organizing, Harlem Communists faced a far more severe challenge than they did in the cultural sphere. Not only had Party unemployed and WPA organizations become a shadow of their former selves, but Communists had become isolated from the Harlem movement to end job discrimination. By December, 1939, leaders of the Greater New York Coordinating Committee had begun to sharply criticize unions, especially the TWU, for tolerating discrimination in their industries and lobbying against bills in the state legislature banning trade union discrimination. With the Harlem Labor Union and the black press making similar arguments, labor's prestige in Harlem—and by association that of the Party—stood at its lowest point in years.[56] In addition, black leaders hostile to the Party, spearheaded by A. Philip Randolph and Walter White, had begun to mount steady pressure on the Roosevelt administration to desegregate the armed forces and to provide jobs for blacks in defense industries. Endorsing Roosevelt's interventionist stand, they put together a coalition for equality in national defense that included the largest black organizations—but pointedly excluded Communists—and won support for this effort from influential liberal leaders, including the governor and lieutenant governor of New York State and the mayor of New York City.[57]

In response to their growing isolation from the mainstream of black protest, party leaders began to call upon their cadre, even their prized trade union functionaries, to become far more aggressive in fighting for economic opportunities for black workers. Writing in July, 1940, James Ford admitted that there had been a "let down" in the struggle for Negro rights in "white territories," particularly around the "fight for jobs," and that Party branches in black neighborhoods had lost members as a result. "I must be sharp," Ford wrote; ". . . on the question of the fight for Negro rights in the trade unions. There are many trade unions where there are no Negroes. Why is this. Because there are no Negroes in the industry. And why is this. Because of the discrimination against the Negro people. . . . The white Communists must understand that and struggle for the right of Negroes to jobs in these industries."[58]

While shifting the onus for ending discrimination to Communists in the trade unions, a departure from Party policy during the last years of the Popular Front, Party leaders also tried to transform the National Negro Congress into an instrument which would open jobs for blacks "in utilities, in city, state, and federal services, and in the defense industries."[59] In November, 1940, the NNC sponsored an emergency statewide conference for Negro rights, attended largely by black leaders closely identified with the left, in which the main theme sounded was a "fight for jobs, jobs and more jobs for the Negro people." The program approved by the conference included "job-hunts" aimed at exposing discrimination in industry, pressure on government officials to open defense projects to black workers, and the formation of a committee to encourage trade unions in the state to organize black workers and "to cooperate with the . . . Congress in increasing the number of Negroes employed in the industries over which they have jurisdiction."[60]

Shortly after the conference, leaders of seven left-wing unions (including the Transport Workers Union, the National Maritime Union, and the State, County, and Municipal Workers Union) formed a trade union advisory committee of the congress and began meeting regularly with representatives of the Brooklyn and Manhattan Councils of the NNC.[61] By January, 1941, they had drafted a "Statement of Problems of Negro Workers in New York State," and an accompanying program of action, that called on unions, *for their own protection,* to seek unorganized blacks as members and "to win equal job and training opportunities for unemployed Negro workers." ". . . so long as the problem of employment of Negro workers remains thus acute," the statement warned, "the growing power and security of the entire labor movement is threatened." While reiterating labor's opposition to modifications in the State Labor Relations Act aimed at eliminating union bias, the statement called on unions to work for the passage of anti–poll tax and antilynching bills, expand educational work in black communities, and "campaign against the job-exclusion policies of government and industry against Negro workers." Phrased in terms of "cold" self-interest, it represented the first effort by left-led unions to jointly assume responsibility for ending discrimination in the city's economy.[62]

Assured, at least rhetorically, of support from key left-wing union leaders (including Joseph Curran, president of the National Maritime Union, Abram Flaxer, president of the State Council and Municipal Workers of America, and Saul Mills, secretary of the Industrial Union Council of New York), inspired by a new Party concern for the "economic struggles of the Negro people," Party activists initiated a series of actions aimed at opening jobs for blacks.[63] Between December, 1940, and March, 1941, Brooklyn and Manhattan councils of the NNC began sending delegations to local defense contractors which refused to hire blacks and pressing state authorities to act on their complaints. In Brooklyn, the NNC and the Transport Workers Union worked together to demand jobs for blacks on bus lines slated to replace the Brooklyn trolley system, while the United Electrical Workers Union signed an agreement with the congress to fight discrimination in shops under their jurisdiction. Operating largely in mid-town Manhattan, a new left-led trade union, Local 65 of the United Wholesale and Warehouse Employees Union, opened jobs for blacks in two shops from which they were excluded, claiming this was part of a "complete program" to break open their industry. These actions had the imprimatur of prominent left-wing blacks and the top leadership of the Party.[64] "We must educate the white workers, raise the issues among them, get them to fight for the rights of Negroes," Israel Amter wrote. "Wherever they are not brought forward and advanced to leadership, it is the job of the Communists and progressives to lead."[65]

In Harlem, the Party's new vigilance on questions of economic discrimination extended even to the transit industry, helping to defuse a potentially explosive conflict between the TWU and Harlem nationalists and setting the stage for a reconciliation between the Party and Adam Clayton Powell, Jr. In March, 1941, the TWU had captured the attention of Harlem activists by launching a strike for higher wages against the Fifth Avenue Coach Company and New York Omnibus Company. Shortly before the strike ended, members of the Harlem Labor Union began "picketing the pickets," demanding that blacks be given jobs as drivers and mechanics and accusing the union of blocking their employment.[66] In the past, Harlem Communists had responded to such initiatives by trying to exonerate the union from blame, but this time, they surprised Harlem nationalists by endorsing the demand for jobs and offering to work with other groups to see that they were won. In late March, 1941, leaders of the Party and the National Negro Congress joined with Revs. Adam Clayton Powell, Jr., and William Lloyd Imes, as well as some leaders of the HLU, in forming a United Negro Bus Committee which could coordinate mass meetings and picket lines in Harlem and send delegations to confer with the companies, the union, and city officials.[67] Just who initiated this committee remains unclear, but leftist input into it appears to have been strong. Two of the bus committee's key officials, Hope Stevens from the National Negro Congress, and Arnold Johnson, its executive secretary, were perceived by contemporaries as being Communist sympathizers (Johnson had been a Party member in 1937, but had been publicly reprimanded by James Ford for pursuing a grievance against James H. Baker, Johnson's supervisor in a Harlem relief bureau, and an official of the National Negro Congress), and the Party's Harlem organization featured prominently in all bus committee protests.[68]

In participating in such a coalition, Harlem Communists knew they could count on the support of TWU leaders, who, in the face of unprecedented community pressure (and private encouragement from the Party), pledged their "all out aid" to the job campaign. Long the objects of hostility and suspicion in Harlem, TWU leaders drew cheers at bus committee meetings with vociferous denunciations of company discrimination, and pledges to help bring it to an end. Equally important, the union's endorsement of a bus boycott to win jobs, coupled with the revived militancy of Harlem Communists, seems to have persuaded Adam Clayton Powell, Jr., to resume his "united front" with the left. In Bus Committee rallies, Powell cooperated with Communists in trying to isolate Harlem nationalists and to impart the community's protest with a prolabor tone. Drawing upon the resources of Harlem churches and left-wing organizations the movement grew to impressive proportions, attracting thousands to its protest rallies and generating an effective boycott of the bus lines in Harlem.[69]

Despite the size and militancy of the bus-boycott movement, the political alliances underlying it, especially between the TWU and Bus Committee leaders, remained extremely fragile. Always conscious of their own political base, TWU leaders had supported the boycott in the expectation that the bus companies would be hiring 200 new workers and that blacks could be hired without displacing any whites. But when the bus companies finally acceded to community pressures, they turned the tables on the union by insisting that the TWU give up seniority rights for its members in order to open up jobs "immediately" for competent blacks. Many participants in the boycott, especially nationalists, found the company's position eminently reasonable, and when negotiations began to work out an agreement, TWU leaders faced strong pressure to waive seniority rights for ninety-one of their white members who had been laid off by the companies. On this issue, the TWU would not yield, and their relations with much of the bus committee became tense and hostile. But after nearly two weeks of negotiations, the TWU leadership, pressed hard by the Party hierarchy (whose support it needed to manage the union) agreed to what, for the time, was an extraordinary set of racial hiring quotas, designed to go into effect after the ninety-one white TWU members were rehired. This gave the bus committee sufficient basis to conclude an agreement that they could "sell" to an aroused Harlem public. Written in the form of a contract between the TWU, the companies, and the bus committee, it provided that once the laid-off white workers were hired, a minimum of one hundred blacks be employed as drivers, and seventy as mechanics, before any whites were hired, and that additional blacks be hired on the basis of "one Negro to one white man" until the total number of black workers equalled 17 percent of the company's employees. This agreement, coming at a time when company business was expanding due to war-induced recovery, and when its need for workers was increasing because of a reduced work week won by the union, represented the most important single victory, in terms of number and quality of jobs, that the Harlem jobs movement had extracted from a major employer.[70]

The bus-strike settlement did not satisfy all participants in the boycott movement. In his column in the *New York Age,* Columbus Austin, speaking for nationalists who had initially launched the campaign, attacked leftists on the bus committee and Adam Clayton Powell, Jr., for monopolizing power on the bus committee and making unacceptable concessions to the union. Throughout the summer and fall of 1941, as the union's seniority list slowly expired, Austin continually questioned whether blacks would see the promised jobs, and denounced leaders of the bus committee as "Painted Horses" who sold out the interests of black workers to win trade union support for their personal careers (an accusation fueled by the accession of Hope Stevens, the NNC's representative on the bus committee, to the TWU's legal staff).[71]

Despite Austin's attacks, which represented a sizable section of Harlem opinion, the bus campaign marked a partial resurgence of Communist influence in Harlem. Not only did Party recruiting expand significantly for the first time in two years, but several important Harlem leaders who had kept Communists at arm's length since the Pact resumed participation in "united front" groups sponsored by the Party and began expressing a muted version of its antiwar position. During May, 1941, a Party-circulated statement attacking the impact of the war on civil rights and civil liberties (entitled "Negroes Speak Out—the Present Situation of the Negro People in America") attracted signatures from four Harlem ministers (Powell, Revs. John Robinson, Benjamin Robeson, David Lico-rish), James Egert Allen, the head of the New York State NAACP, Lawrence D. Reddick, curator of the Schomburg Library, and J. Finely Wilson, the national head of the black Elks. Though far less broadly based than Party initiatives during the Popular Front era, it nevertheless represented an important break from the virtual quarantine Harlem leaders had imposed on the Party when they sought to make their views heard on important national issues.[72]

The Party's revival, ironically, occurred in the midst of a concerted attack by city and state authorities on the Harlem left-wing's power base. During the fall of 1940, the Rapp-Coudert Committee of the New York State Legislature announced plans to "ferret out" Communist teachers in the Harlem schools, provoking a bitter interchange between editors of the *Amsterdam News,* who supported the investigation, and leaders of the Harlem Committee for Better Schools and some local PTA's. During 1941, four prominent blacks allegedly sympathetic to the Communist Party were forced out of their positions: Max Yergan as an instructor of Negro history at City College, Gwendolyn Bennett as head of the Harlem Art Center, and M. Moran Weston and Ewart Guinier as district supervisor and examiner in the Department of Public Welfare. These firings, affecting some of the most prominent and successful figures in Harlem's professional strata, bitterly polarized the black intelligentsia, eliciting opposition from some, support from others, but above all evoking concern whether the "witch hunt" against Communists would materially damage black prospects.[73] "What we fear most," the *New York Age* editorialized, "is that in the swing away from the socially conscious and class conscious attitude of the past few years, the conservatives will not stop at putting the reds in their place, but will make a stronger effort to keep the Negro and all minority groups in such a state of subjection that advances made in recent years will be wiped out."[74]

Although many Harlemites felt ambivalent about these attacks on the Party's power base, especially because they coincided with a revival of Party agitation in behalf of economic equality, Harlem's black socialists, Layle Lane, Frank Crosswaith, and A. Philip Randolph, stuck firmly to the position that Communism represented a "Fifth Column" in American life that had to be destroyed at all costs. Not only did they refuse to defend blacks accused of Communist sympathies, but they supported the expulsion of Communists from the trade unions and urged liberals to lead the way in initiating such measures. When Thurgood Marshall of the NAACP wrote a letter protesting the expulsion of three left-wing locals from the American Federation of Teachers, Layle Lane (an AFT vice-president) defended the union for protecting "democratic education" from subversive elements, even though the locals in question had been most forceful in fighting to improve schools in Harlem and had supported NAACP efforts to equalize teacher salaries in the South.[75]

Unfortunately for Harlem Communists, these leaders had a political influence far exceeding their numbers. Here, as before, A. Philip Randolph proved to be the critical figure. Since his resignation from the National Negro Congress, Randolph had made militant anti-Communism a central part of his political credo, persuading the Brotherhood of Sleeping Car Porters to pass a resolution barring Communists from union office. At the same time, he had moved to the forefront of the national lobbying campaign to force equality in national defense. Attuned to white liberal attitudes and the frustration of the black masses, Randolph had become convinced that drastic action was required to force the federal government to incorporate blacks into the military-related industries that were reshaping the economic life of the nation. In January, 1941, following National Defense Day rallies sponsored by the NAACP, he called upon 10,000 blacks to march on Washington to "demand jobs in national defense and placement as soldiers and officers . . . in all ranks of the armed forces." "If the Negroes are going to get anything out of this National Defense," he proclaimed, "we must fight for it and fight for it with gloves off."[76]

When Randolph issued this proclamation, he seemed to lack the organizational resources to make such a march happen. But so eloquently did he voice the danger of black exclusion from the defense establishment ("If the Negro is shut out . . . the race will be set back over fifty years"), and manipulate the symbols of popular protest that he rapidly became a rallying point for a broad spectrum of black opinion. By calling for an all-black march, Randolph invoked the still vital tradition of Garveyite militancy, and by calling for mass protest and disruption, he identified with strategies pioneered by Communists, but his chosen constituency was the mainstream black organizations—the churches, fraternal organizations, the Urban League, and the NAACP. When Randolph formed a committee in Harlem to help plan for the march, it consisted of leaders who, with one important exception (Rev. William Lloyd Imes), were better known for their political and intellectual stature than for their expeience as leaders of mass-protest activity—Frank Crosswaith and Layle Lane, Walter White, Henry Craft of the YMCA, and Lester Granger. Although Randolph's press releases consistently pointed to "organized mass pressure" as the most effective method to achieve social change, he excluded from his inner circle the two groups in Harlem who had done the most to bring the black masses "into the streets," the nationalists and the Communists.[77]

For nearly five months following Randolph's first call, Communists declined comment on the march. Opposed to the foreign-policy stand

Randolph espoused (all-out aid to Britain), his equation of Nazism and Communism, and his exclusion of whites from the march, they hoped that Randolph would discredit himself by failing to amass a following. But so quickly did black organizations rally to the action (the *Amsterdam News* spoke of "the NAACP, the Urban League, the YMCA, the Elks, the Clergy, College Clubs, labor groups ... cooperating in the pilgrimage"), and so effectively did Randolph articulate popular frustrations, that Communists felt they had to identify with the march in order to maintain their credibility. Three weeks before the date set for the march (July 1), black Party leaders issued a series of convoluted statements hailing the march as a reflection of growing black militancy, but attacking the motives, methods, and outlook of those who initiated it. Accusing Randolph of launching the march as a "counter move against effective leadership," aimed at "delivering the Negro people to the imperialist war program," they called upon their followers to open up the march to white participation and turn it into a demonstration "against the Administration's entire war program."[78] "Even though the March is being prepared by A. Philip Randolph," one Party leader asserted in justification of this strategy, " ... the idea for it grew out of the nationwide movement to end discrimination, especially in defense industries ... mainly led by the National Negro Congress."[79]

The Party's eleventh-hour effort to enter into the movement — and to claim credit for its occurrence — brought a stinging response from Randolph. Denouncing Communists as a "definite menace, pestilence, and nuisance, as well as a danger to the Negro people," he insisted that "Communists and their fellow-travelers and allies" would be excluded from local March on Washington Committees and from the march itself.[80] Whether Randolph could have accomplished this objective, and indeed whether he could have brought 100,000 blacks to Washington, remains open to question, but changes in federal policy soon rendered these issues academic. Following intensive negotiations with the march's sponsors, President Roosevelt issued a proclamation banning discrimination in defense industries and announced that a federal commission would be established to enforce his order. Having achieved much of what he wanted, Randolph called off the march and redirected the movement's attention toward monitoring the commission's performance.[81]

The success of the March on Washington movement boded ill for Harlem Communists. Not only had an arch-enemy of the Party achieved the most far-reaching civil rights victory in recent memory, but he had stolen the mantle of protest leadership from the Party's hand and invested it with an elan and aura of effectiveness that Communists could not match. Based on an astute reading of the political climate in the nation, Randolph had showed that it was possible to unite black organizations behind a program that was at once militantly anti-Communist and committed to direct action, and he stuck to this formula for the remainder of his career. Keeping the march committees alive after the presidential proclamation, Randolph rebuffed all Communist efforts to participate in their work, even when the Party adopted a prowar position following Hitler's invasion of the Soviet Union. The rallies that Randolph sponsored during the early years of war, attracting a cross-section of black leadership, added to the legitimacy of Randolph's stance, showing that a powerful tradition of black protest had emerged independent of Communist influence and that "mass pressure" techniques, once the trademark of the left, had become acceptable to the most powerful and well-established black organizations[82]

The March on Washington movement, in the short run, did not undermine the power base of the Harlem Communist Party. The major sources of Party vitality in Harlem during the Pact years—its commitment to the popularization of black history and culture, and its use of the power of the left-wing unions as a lever for racial change (and a source of political patronage)—remained untouched by Randolph's triumph or by the change in the Party's line following Hitler's invasion of the Soviet Union. With the exception of Richard Wright, important black cadre and sympathizers who had stuck with the Party through the difficult Pact years retained their loyalty, expecting that the "new world situation" would spark a revival in the Party's fortunes. Their expectations proved well founded. As the Party shifted gears to the promotion of national unity and the concentration of political energies toward "the defeat of Hitlerism," its membership began growing substantially and the attacks directed against it—by government agencies and political enemies—diminished considerably.[83]

In Harlem, the Party's rapid movement toward the political center helped pave the way to an electoral alliance with Adam Clayton Powell, Jr. Having worked closely with Harlem Communists in the bus-boycott movement and emerging from the experience with his prestige enhanced—and with powerful trade union allies—Powell sought left-wing support for his camaign to become the first black to win election to New York's City Council. Powell's appeal drew a warm response from the Party, which had defined its election goals in 1941 as the defeat of Tammany candidates and the election of "anti-Hitler" leaders. Not only did the Party withdraw Max Yergan's name from the American Labor Party slate to make room for Powell, but it put its resources—and those of left-wing unions—at Powell's disposal in both Harlem and white Manhattan neighborhoods. Welcoming white support, Powell gave his campaign a distinctly left-wing tone, presenting himself as a militant anti-fascist as well as a partisan of black solidarity. Building a huge "People's Committee" in Harlem to advance his candidacy (based on his church, sympathetic unions, and the left), Powell outpolled his only black opponent, Herman Stoute of Tammany, by a huge margin, winning election to the council with the third highest vote total in the entire city.[84]

Having contributed significantly to the election of the city's first black city councilman, Harlem Communists now functioned as political insiders to an unprecedented degree. Prominent within Powell's "People's Committee," where their organizational skills were valued, they also helped Powell acquire funds for his own newspaper, the *People's Voice,* which emerged as a full scale rival of Harlem's other black weeklies. Powell, as always, carefully maintained his independence, participating in March on Washington rallies from which Communists were excluded and supporting the "Double V" campaign of the *Pittsburgh Courier,* which Communists opposed. But when Powell resigned from the city council in 1943 to seek election to Congress, he designated Ben Davis, Jr., a prominent Harlem Communist, as his chosen successor, virtually guaranteeing Davis's election to the post. This step represented hardheaded political bargaining as well as respect for Davis's considerable abilities. To win election to Congress, even more than to the city council, Powell needed white votes; alone among political groups, Communists, acting through the Manhattan ALP, had the power and the will to supply them.[85]

With Davis's accession to the city council (in 1944), the Harlem Party seemed to have fully recovered from the disintegration that had beset it following the Nazi-Soviet Pact. Linked to powerful forces in the city's trade union movement and intelligentsia, and to Harlem's most popular politician, the Harlem CP built up its black membership to Popular Front levels and restored working relationships with influential Harlem ministers, fraternal leaders, and politicians.[86]

Nevertheless, the Party stood in substantially different relation to black protest activity than it had during the Popular Front. In New York City politics, in the trade union movement, in the school system, and in the intellectual world, Communists remained an important force fighting to open opportunities for blacks, but they had lost their ability to shape the goals and tactics of the civil rights movement as a whole. The Party's wartime obsession with national unity partially accounted for this, particularly their opposition to mass protests against racism in the armed forces, but their actions following the Pact also had an effect. Observing Communists discard some of their most effective programs and strategies in response to changes in Soviet diplomacy, many Harlemites, especially those in positions of leadership, came to doubt whether Communists could provide leadership or inspiration to major movements for social change. On local issues, they still would respond to Communist initiatives, but on national issues, they looked to the March on Washington movement, the

Urban League, and the NAACP, organizations whose activities carried more weight with federal officials and which did not have the taint of "unreliability." Respected for their trade union and political connections and willingness to practice racial equality, Harlem Communists no longer stood on the cutting edge of black protest or possessed a monopoly on direct action techniques. When the postwar repression arrived, their vulnerability would become painfully apparent.[87]

NOTES

1. *New York Amsterdam News,* Feb. 27, 1940.

2. *Daily Worker,* May 22, 1941, June 23, 1941. On the role of left-led unions in providing funding, see John P. Davis to Mike Obermeir, Mar. 4, 1940, NNC Papers, Reel 9; John P. Davis to Ferdinand Smith, Mar. 4, 1940, *ibid.*

3. Interview with Audley Moore, May 3, 1974; interview with Abner Berry, July 29, 1974; Benjamin J. Davis, *Communist Councilman from Harlem* (New York: International Publishers, 1969), pp. 53–81.

4. Peggy Dennis, *The Autobiography of an American Communist* (Westport: Laurence Hill, 1977), pp. 133–35. Al Richmond, *A Long View From the Left* (Boston: Houghton Mifflin, 1973), pp. 283–86; Philip J. Jaffe, *The Rise and Fall of American Communism* (New York: Horizon Press, 1975), pp. 38–48; *Daily Worker,* Sept. 5, 1939, Nov. 5, 1939; Gene Dennis, "The Bolshevization of the Communist Party of the United States in the Struggle Against the Imperialist War," *Communist,* 19 (May, 1940), 406–7.

5. Dennis, *The Autobiography of an American Communist,* pp. 135–40; "America and the International Situation," *Communist,* 18 (Nov., 1939), 995–1001; "Peace to the People," *ibid.* (Dec., 1940), 1091–96. The quote beginning "the present war" comes from "America and the International Situation," 997.

6. *New York Amsterdam News,* Sept. 23, 1939; *Daily Worker,* Sept. 12, 1939.

7. *New York Amsterdam News,* Oct. 21, 1939; *Daily Worker,* Oct. 10, 1939; interview with Howard Johnson, July 23, 1977.

8. *New York Amsterdam News,* Dec. 20, 1939.

9. *Ibid.,* Sept. 2, 1939, Sept. 23, 1939; *New York Age,* Dec. 9, 1939.

10. Interview with Abner Berry, Nov. 20, 1973.

11. *New York Amsterdam News,* Sept. 23, 1939, Sept. 20, 1939.

12. *Ibid.,* Sept. 9, 1939, Sept. 30, 1939, Dec. 9, 1939, Mar. 2, 1940.

13. *Ibid.,* Sept. 16, 1939, Nov. 11, 1939; *New York Age,* Nov. 18, 1939. The quote about American Communism being "finished" comes from *New York Amsterdam News,* Nov. 11, 1939.

14. *New York Age,* Oct. 14, 1939, Nov. 18, 1939; *New York Amsterdam News,* Oct. 21, 1939, Oct. 28, 1939.

15. *Ibid.,* Nov. 18, 1939.

16. *Ibid.,* Dec. 16, 1939, Dec. 23, 1939; "Statement on Problems of Negro Workers in the State of New York," undated, 1941, NNC Papers, Reel 10.

17. *New York Amsterdam News,* Nov. 18, 1939, Jan. 20, 1940.

18. *Daily Worker,* Dec. 15, 1939, Mar. 19, 1940; *New York Amsterdam News,*

Nov. 4, 1939, Jan. 6, 1940, Jan. 13, 1940, Mar. 2, 1940; *New York Age,* Oct. 28, 1939, Mar. 16, 1940; Henry Winston, "Negro Youth Federation to be Organized," *Young Communist Review,* 5 (Mar. 14, 1940), 14.

19. Interview with Abner Berry, July 5, 1977.

20. On Yergan's work in the International Committee on African Affairs, see *Daily Worker,* June 11, 1937; on his work with the Manhattan Council of the National Negro Congress, see Max Yergan, Rex Ingram, Gwendolyn Bennett, Langston Hughes, and Louise M. Johnson to Dear Friend, Oct. 15, 1938, NAACP Papers C 383; Vivienne France to John P. Davis, June 24, 1938, NNC Papers, Reel 7; Max Yergan and Vivienne France to Dear Friend, June 29, 1938, *ibid.*

21. On the creation of the first black history course at City College, see *Daily Worker,* June 14, 1937; *New York Amsterdam News,* Apr. 7, 1937, May 3, 1941, June 7, 1941.

22. *New York Age,* Feb. 10, 1940; *New York Amsterdam News,* Nov. 4, 1939, Dec. 30, 1939; *Daily Worker,* Oct. 25, 1939, Dec. 12, 1939, Feb. 2, 1940, Feb. 11, 1940.

23. Bert Cochran, *Labor and Communism: The Conflict That Shaped American Unions* (Princeton: Princeton University Press, 1977), pp. 144-46; *Daily Worker,* Jan. 5, 1940, Mar. 10, 1940, Mar. 14, 1940, Mar. 25, 1940; Louis Burnham to Thomas Jasper, July 26, 1940, NNC Papers, Reel 11.

24. Theodore R. Bassett and A. W. Berry, "The Negro People and the Struggle for Peace," *Communist,* 19 (Apr., 1940), 334.

25. Max Yergan to John P. Davis, Oct. 18, 1939, NNC Papers, Reel 9; A. Philip Randolph to John P. Davis, Jan. 2, 1940, *ibid.*; minutes, National Negro Congress Executive Board, Jan. 14, 1940, *ibid.*, Reel 10; Proposed Plan for Third National Negro Congress, Feb. 23, 1940; John P. Davis to Louisa V. Jones, Mar. 12, 1940, *ibid.*; *Daily Worker,* Feb. 2, 1940, Feb. 20, 1940, Feb. 21, 1940; *New York Age,* Feb. 3, 1940, Mar. 9, 1940.

26. Lawrence S. Wittner, "The National Negro Congress: A Reassessment," *American Quarterly,* 22 (Winter, 1970), 898-901; Jervis Anderson, *A. Philip Randolph, A Biographical Portrait* (New York: Harcourt, Brace, Jovanovich, 1973), p. 339; *New York Age,* May 18, 1940; *Daily Worker,* Apr. 16, 1940; "Report of the Resolutions Committee," no date, 1940 NNC Papers, Reel 11; John P. Davis to Abram Flaxer, Mar. 13, 1940, *ibid.*, Reel 9.

27. "Delegates' Credentials to Date," Apr. 12, 1940, *ibid.*; John P. Davis to James H. Baker, Apr. 16, 1940, *Ibid.*, Reel 10; Max Yergan to John P. Davis, Apr. 24, 1940, *ibid.*, Reel 11; *New York Age,* May 18, 1940; *Daily Worker,* Apr. 20, 1940, Apr. 26, 1940. The quote about "socialites and celebrities" comes from *New York Amsterdam News,* Apr. 20, 1940.

28. Anderson, *A. Philip Randolph,* pp. 234-38; Wittner, "The National Negro Congress: A Reassessment," 898-99; *New York Amsterdam News,* May 4, 1940.

29. *New York Age,* May 25, 1940; *Daily Worker,* Apr. 28, 1940, Apr. 29, 1940, May 13, 1940; Theodore R. Bassett, "The Third National Negro Congress," *Communist,* 19 (June, 1940), 544.

30. Lester Granger, "The National Negro Congress—Its Future," *Opportunity,* 18 (May 1940), 166.

31. Randolph's attack on the Party first reached Harlemites in the form of long

statements in the *New York Age* and the *Amsterdam News.* See *New York Age,* May 11, 1940, May 18, 1940; *New York Amsterdam News,* May 11, 1940.

32. *Daily Worker,* May 19, 1940.

33. Bassett, "The Third National Negro Congress," 550.

34. The Ford quote comes from James W. Ford, "The Negro People and the New World Situation," *Communist,* 20 (Aug., 1941), 700.

35. On the Comintern's growing denunciations of "bourgeois democracy" following the Pact, see Fernando Claudin, *The Communist Movement: From Comintern to Cominform* (Hammondsworth, England: Penguin Books, 1975), pp. 295–302.

36. Interview with Howard Johnson, July 23, 1940; interview with Abner Berry, July 5, 1977.

37. *Daily Worker,* Oct. 1, 1939.

38. Angelo Herndon to John P. Davis, Nov. 30, 1939, NNC Papers, Reel 9.

39. *New York Amsterdam News,* Feb. 17, 1940; *Daily Worker,* Feb. 11, 1940, Feb. 12, 1940, Feb. 18, 1940.

40. *New York Age,* Jan. 6, 1940, Jan. 13, 1940, Apr. 6, 1940; *New York Amsterdam News,* Dec. 30, 1940; *Daily Worker,* Oct. 29, 1939, Dec. 7, 1939, Jan. 6, 1940, Jan. 9, 1940. Davis's comments come from articles in the *Daily Worker,* Dec. 24, 1939, Feb. 11, 1940.

41. "To Ask Ban Off Negro in Baseball," Apr. 26, 1940, NNC Papers, Reel 10; *Daily Worker,* Mar. 6, 1940, May 16, 1940, July 9, 1940, July 25, 1940; Steve Bernard, "Sports," *YCL Review,* 5 (Mar. 14, 1940), 15.

42. *Daily Worker,* July 8, 1940.

43. Interview with Abner Berry, July 5, 1977; Claudia Jones, "The Story of Bigger Thomas," *YCL Review,* 5 (Apr. 11, 1940), 4; *Daily Worker,* Apr. 14, 1940, May 4, 1940, June 23, 1940.

44. *Ibid.,* Apr. 17, 1940.

45. Interview with John Hammond, Sept. 26, 1978; interview with Howard Johnson, July 23, 1977. The incident with Billie Holiday is recounted in *New York Amsterdam News,* Aug. 31, 1940.

46. *New York Age,* Feb. 10, 1940; *Daily Worker,* Nov. 4, 1939, Nov. 12, 1939, Oct. 9, 1940, Dec. 29, 1940; Virginia Hamilton, *Paul Robeson: The Life and Times of a Free Black Man* (New York: Harper and Row, 1974), pp. 82–89.

47. Marie Conti, "Catholics Should Be Radical," *Interracial Review,* 14 (July, 1941), 109.

48. James H. Baker to John P. Davis, Mar. 27, 1940, NNC Papers, Reel 10; *Daily Worker,* July 27, 1940; *New York Amsterdam News,* July 20, 1940, Aug. 10, 1940; *New York Age,* July 29, 1940.

49. *Daily Worker,* Oct. 27, 1940.

50. *New York Amsterdam News,* Aug. 31, 1940, Sept. 14, 1940; *Daily Worker,* Sept. 15, 1941.

51. *Ibid.,* Oct. 27, 1940; *New York Amsterdam News,* Nov. 2, 1940; Theophilus Lewis, "Plays and a Point of View," *Interracial Review,* 13 (Nov. 1940), 174–75.

52. *New York Amsterdam News,* Mar. 1, 1941, Mar. 15, 1941, Mar. 29, 1941; *Daily Worker,* Feb. 6, 1941, Feb. 27, 1941.

53. For evidence of Murphy's ties with the Communist left during the Popular Front, see Ernie Mason to George Murphy, July 20, 1939, NAACP Papers, C 179; Esther Weissman to George Murphy, June 13, 1939, *ibid.*; George B. Murphy, Jr., to Clinton Oliver, Feb. 20, 1939, *ibid.*, George B. Murphy, Jr., to Abraham Markoff, July 18, 1939, *ibid.*; George B. Murphy, Jr., to Emmett May, Oct. 20, 1939, *ibid.*

54. Some examples of invitations received by Murphy after the Pact are Audley B. Moore to George B. Murphy, Nov. 4, 1939, NAACP Papers, C 179; Grace Johnson to Geo B. Murphy, Jr., Jan. 8, 1940, *ibid.*, II A 527; Edith Jones to George Murphy, Mar. 13, 1940, *ibid.*; William H. Gaulden to George B. Murphy, Jan. 18, 1940, *ibid.* Some examples of Murphy itinerary are "Mr. Murphy's Engagements in November," Dec. 5, 1940, *ibid.*; and "Memo to Miss Black From Mr. Murphy," Jan. 29, 1941, *ibid.*, II A 528.

55. On Murphy's participation in the Negro Playwrights Company, see *New York Amsterdam News,* July 20, 1940; on his participation in the International Workers Order, see George B. Murphy, Jr., to Edith M. Benjamin, Nov. 4, 1940, NAACP Papers, II A 527; on his involvement in the black history forum, see Alison Burroughs to George B. Murphy, Jr., Jan. 6, 1941, *ibid.*, II A 528; and on Murphy's leaving the NAACP for the NNC, see George B. Murphy, Jr., to Roy Wilkins, Mar. 26, 1941, *ibid.*, II A 418.

56. *New York Amsterdam News,* Dec. 23, 1939, Mar. 16, 1940, Mar. 23, 1940, Aug. 31, 1940; *New York Age,* Dec. 2, 1939.

57. Lester Granger, "The President, the Negro and Defense," *Opportunity,* 19 (July, 1940), 204–7; Herbert Garfinkel, *When Negroes March: The March on Washington Movement in the Organizational Politics for FEPC* (Glencoe: Free Press, 1959), pp. 33–39; Anderson, *A. Philip Randolph,* pp. 241–47.

58. James W. Ford, "Win the Negro People: The Fight for Negro Rights is the Responsibility of the Entire Party," *Party News,* (July, 1940).

59. Memorandum, from William Gaulden and John P. Davis to Abram Flaxer, July 14, 1940, NNC Papers, Reel 10; minutes, Administrative Committee of the National Executive Board, July 14, 1940, *ibid.*, Reel 11. The quote comes from *Daily Worker,* Nov. 18, 1940.

60. *Ibid.*, Nov. 6, 1940, Nov. 11, 1940, Nov. 17, 1940, Nov. 18, 1940; *New York Age,* Nov. 9, 1940, Nov. 30, 1940; "Welcome to Delegates," Nov. 16 and 17, 1940, NNC Papers, Reel 10. The final quote comes from "Program of Action, Statewide Confere," no date, 1940, *ibid.*

61. John P. Davis to Dear Friend, Mar. 18, 1940, *ibid.*, Reel 14; memorandum, Max Yergan, William H. Gaulden, Hope Stevens, Malcolm Martin, Jan. 24, 1941, *ibid.*, Reel 11.

62. Statement on Problems of Negro Workers in the State of New York, undated, 1941, *ibid.*, Reel 10.

63. *Ibid.* The above-listed union leaders signed the statement. The quote about the party's concern for the "economic struggles of the Negro People" appeared in James W. Ford, "Organize the Struggles of the Negro People," *Party News* (Mar.–Apr., 1941).

64. Al Sloan, "Boss Jim Crow Cracked By Union," *YCL Review,* 5 (Feb. 3,

1941), 13; Nat Shapiro to John P. Davis, July 30, 1941, NNC Papers, Reel 15; George Kleinman to John P. Davis, Mar. 18, 1941, *ibid.*, Reel 12; *New York Age,* Jan. 11, 1941, Jan. 25, 1941; *Daily Worker,* Dec. 5, 1940, Jan. 10, 1941, Jan. 13, 1941, Feb. 27, 1941, Mar. 10, 1941.

65. *Ibid.*, Jan. 7, 1941.

66. On the TWU strike, see John P. Davis to Michael Quill, Mar. 18, 1941, NNC Papers, Reel 12; *Daily Worker,* Mar. 14, 1941; *New York Amsterdam News,* Mar. 15, 1941. On the Harlem Labor Union's Action, see *ibid.*, Mar. 22, 1941 and Meier and Rudwick, "Communist Unions and the Black Community: The Case of the Transport Workers Union, 1935–1944," 9.

67. *New York Amsterdam News,* Mar. 22, 1941, Mar. 29, 1941; *Daily Worker,* Mar. 26, 1941; *New York Age,* May 17, 1941; interview with Abner Berry, July 29, 1974.

68. Meier and Rudwick, who have made the most thorough investigation of the bus boycott to date, found it difficult to clarify which individual or group took the first step in founding the United Negro Bus Committee (Meier and Rudwick, "Communist Unions and Racism," 10, 32, 33). On the role of the left in the United Negro Bus Committee, see Columbus Austin's columns in the *New York Age,* May 17, 1941, Sept. 6, 1941. Austin's accusations about Communist "domination" of the committee, via the National Negro Congress, were repeated by Frank Crosswaith in *New York Age,* May 31, 1941. Ben Davis boasted of strong Communist presence in the campaign in *Daily Worker,* Apr. 27, 1941. James W. Ford referred to the Johnson-Baker controversy, without actually naming the two protagonists, and referred to Johnson as a Communist in "Uniting the Negro People in the People's Front," *Communist,* 16 (Aug., 1937), 728. There is an extensive file on the Johnson-Baker controversy in the National Negro Congress Papers, Reel 5. Abner Berry confirmed that Johnson was a Communist at one time in the 1930s but did not indicate whether he was a Party member during the bus boycott. My own view is that Johnson was close to the Party, and had access to Harlem Party leaders, but was not a disciplined member.

69. *New York Amsterdam News,* Mar. 29, 1941; *Daily Worker,* Mar. 26, 1941, Apr. 2, 1941, Apr. 7, 1941; interview with Abner Berry, July 29, 1974.

70. On the complex maneuvers between company, union, and community that produced the bus agreement, see Meier and Rudwick, "Communist Unions and the Black Community," 10–13; *New York Amsterdam News,* Apr. 5, 1941, Apr. 12, 1941, Apr. 26, 1941, May 24, 1941; *New York Age,* Apr. 12, 1941, Apr. 25, 1941, July 26, 1941; *Daily Worker,* Apr. 20, 1941, Apr. 27, 1941; Howard Johnson, "Harlem Kayoes Jim Crow," *YCL Review,* 5 (May 12, 1941), 14–15; "A Victory for the Negro People," undated, 1941, NNC Papers, Reel 14. Abner Berry recalled that the bus boycott was discussed in the Party Politburo and that the Politburo urged the TWU leadership to make concessions. "It took a lot of persuading. . . . But at the time Quill was so dependent on the Party apparatus. These fellows had little training so each one — more or less — had a commissar who could evaluate what needed to be done. They depended on the Communists, who were crackerjack administrators, who were well trained, even from a bourgeois point of view, many had been in insurance and other things. And they knew ex-

actly how to administer all the things that the union would have to do now for itself. Quill had no alternative, he had to depend on the Party, and the Party could make certain demands."

71. *New York Age,* May 17, 1941, May 24, 1941, May 31, 1941, July 26, 1941, Aug. 16, 1941, Aug. 30, 1941, Sept. 6, 1941, Dec. 13, 1941.

72. *New York Amsterdam News,* May 31, 1941; *Daily Worker,* May 22, 1941, May 27, 1941, June 23, 1941.

73. *New York Amsterdam News,* Dec. 7, 1940, Dec. 14, 1940, Dec. 21, 1940, Dec. 28, 1940, Jan. 4, 1941, Jan. 11, 1941, Jan. 18, 1941, Feb. 22, 1941, May 3, 1941, June 7, 1941; *New York Age,* Mar. 1, 1941, Apr. 12, 1941, May 10, 1941; *Daily Worker,* Apr. 28, 1941, July 23, 1941; Ewart Guinier to John P. Davis, Nov. 27, 1941, NNC Papers, Reel 12.

74. *New York Age,* Feb. 22, 1941.

75. *Ibid.,* Aug. 31, 1940, Sept. 21, 1940, Nov. 30, 1940, Mar. 1, 1941, May 10, 1941.

76. Garfinkel, *When Negroes March,* pp. 37–41; Anderson, *A. Philip Randolph,* pp. 47–49; *New York Amsterdam News,* Sept. 21, 1940. The quotes are from a Randolph statement printed in *New York Age,* Jan. 25, 1941.

77. Garfinkel, *When Negroes March,* pp. 40–42; Anderson, *A. Philip Randolph,* pp. 249–51; *New York Age,* Mar. 14, 1941, Mar. 22, 1941, Apr. 12, 1941, May 17, 1941, June 14, 1941; *New York Amsterdam News,* May 24, 1941. Randolph's quote about the "race being set back fifty years" comes from *New York Amsterdam News,* Apr. 12, 1941.

78. Interview with Abner Berry, July 5, 1977; Garfinkel, *When Negroes March,* pp. 52–53; *New York Amsterdam News,* May 31, 1941; *Daily Worker,* June 11, 1941, June 12, 1941, June 23, 1941. The quotes from Party statements come from *Daily Worker,* June 16, 1941.

79. *Ibid.,* June 17, 1941.

80. *New York Amsterdam News,* June 21, 1941.

81. *New York Age,* June 21, 1941, June 28, 1941, July 5, 1941; Anderson, *A. Philip Randolph,* pp. 255–61; Garfinkel, *When Negroes March,* pp. 60–71.

82. *Ibid.,* pp. 72–96; Anderson, *A. Philip Randolph,* pp. 262–67; *New York Age,* Aug. 16, 1941; *New York Amsterdam News,* Aug. 3, 1941.

83. Adam Clayton Powell, Jr., *Marching Blacks* (New York: Dial Press, 1945), pp. 67–69; interview with Howard Johnson, July 23, 1977; interview with Abner Berry, July 5, 1977; Joseph Starobin, *American Communism in Crisis, 1943-1957* (Cambridge: Harvard University Press, 1972), pp. 24–25. The Party's commitment to mobilize its membership in the unions seems to have survived both Hitler's invasion of the Soviet Union and the American entry into the war. See Theodore Bassett, "The Negro People and the Fight for Jobs," *Communist,* 20 (Sept., 1941), 805–17; Cochran, *Labor and Communism,* pp. 226–28; *New York Age,* Jan. 24, 1942; minutes, Citizens Committee to End Discrimination at Horn and Hardart Co., Aug. 15, 1942, NNC Papers, Reel 12.

84. Ralph Lord Roy, *Communism and the Churches* (New York: Harcourt, Brace, 1959), p. 169; Neil Hickey and Ed Edwin, *Adam Clayton Powell and the Politics of Race* (New York: Fleet Publishing, 1965), pp. 67–69; Roi Ottley, *New*

World A-Coming (1943; rpt. New York: Arno, 1968), pp. 234–35; *Daily Worker,* Oct. 18, 1941, Oct. 24, 1941, Nov. 2, 1941, Nov. 13, 1941, Nov. 22, 1941.

85. Roy, *Communism and the Churches,* p. 169; John A. Morsell, "The Political Behavior of Negroes in New York City," (Ph.D. dissertation, Columbia University, 1950), pp. 101–6; Ottley, *New World A-Coming,* pp. 234–35; Kenneth Greenberg, "Anti-Communism in Harlem During the 1940's: Reactions to Benjamin Jefferson Davis Jr., in the City Council," (unpublished paper in possession of author), 6–20; Davis, *Communist Councilman from Harlem,* pp. 101–14.

86. Powell, *Marching Blacks,* pp. 67–69; Davis, *Communist Councilman from Harlem,* pp. 115–28; Greenberg, "Benjamin Jefferson Davis in the City Council," 2–6; interview with Audley Moore, May 3, 1974.

87. Wilson Record, *Race and Radicalism: The NAACP and the Communist Party in Conflict* (Ithaca: Cornell University Press, 1964), pp. 120–31; Henry Lee Moon, *Balance of Power: The Negro Vote* (Garden City: Doubleday, 1949), pp. 119–31; Ottley, *New World A-Coming,* pp. 236–52.

APPENDIX

Black-Jewish Relations in the Harlem
Communist Party

THE QUESTION OF JEWISH PARTICIPATION in the
Harlem Communist Party during the 1930s, and of black-Jewish relations within the Party's organizations, is extremely difficult to discuss
with rigor and precision. There is no hard statistical evidence, either from
Communist or black sources, which establishes Jewish predominance
among whites in the Harlem Section. Not only did the Party fail to provide an ethnic breakdown of its cadres in Harlem (it *did* provide a racial
one), but the black press, during the Depression years, described the influx of Communist white to Harlem as a racial rather than an ethnic phenomenon. Moreover, articles or letters in black newspapers discussing
the role of Jews in Harlem, during the Depression years at least, never
mentioned the Communist Party. Rather, they focused attention, when
negative, on the activities of Jewish landlords, small businessmen, and
employers of domestic labor, and when positive, on the role of Jewish phi-
lanthropists in supporting black education, and on the support extended
by Jewish leaders for civil rights causes.[1]

Despite this silence, comments from my interview subjects, black and
white alike, suggest that a majority of whites active in the black neighborhoods of Harlem may have been of Jewish ancestry (in the Harlem Section as a whole, extending from Yorkville to Washington Heights, there
were many Communist Finns, Italians, Hungarians, Germans, and Latin
Americans as well as blacks and Jews). According to Richard B. Moore,
Jewish-Americans provided many of the shock troops for Harlem protests around the Scottsboro issue and constituted the bulk of the white administrators and education directors sent in to the Harlem section after
James Ford's accession to leadership. Alice Citron and Morris Schappes,
whites active in the Harlem section, recall that almost all of the white
Communist teachers and relief workers in Harlem were of Jewish ancestry. And interviews and published sources alike confirm that the two

white "org-secs" who worked under James Ford from 1933 to 1939, Louis Sass and George Blake (Charney), were of Jewish ancestry.[2]

Given the current polarized state of black-Jewish relations in the United States, it may seem odd that the preponderance of Jews among the Harlem CP's white membership provoked so little controversy or systematic discussion. But it nevertheless seems true that while black-Jewish relations in Harlem were a subject that aroused great passions—especially during the heyday of the "Don't Buy Where You Can't Work" campaign —black-Jewish relations in the Harlem Communist Party, and in the left in general, remained almost invisible as a public issue until the tail-end of the Depression, and it was brought up first by black Communists rather than black critics of the Party.

Why was there so little of a "Jewish issue" surrounding the Harlem Communist Party in the 1930s? Any answer must be highly speculative because of the absence of hard evidence, but a good place to start might be to look at the chosen "persona" of Jewish Communists in Harlem and guess how their behavior affected their black comrades and Harlem residents in general. During the early Depression years, most Jews in the Harlem CP probably did not try to call attention to their Jewishness, either in their personal behavior, or in the articulation of a specific ethnic ideology or outlook. During this period of its history, the Communist Party, still fresh from its attack on the power of the foreign language federations, was not conducive to ethnic consciousness among its Jewish cadre, or among the cadre of any white ethnic group. As a result, quite a few Jewish Communists (in Harlem and elsewhere) adopted anglicized names, but even those who did not emphasized their class background or political beliefs as the major motivation of their actions, not their Jewishness. Although many were products of the self-contained Jewish radical subculture, the bulk of the Jews who volunteered for work in Harlem were American born, English speaking, and enmeshed in a Communist version of an assimilationist dream. Participation in the affairs of the Party in a black community not only represented a highly valued political duty, but constituted an adventure in learning about American culture and values, albeit from a group whose experience was highly ambivalent. Though their Jewish ancestry may have endowed them with cultural reflexes that dictated a strong emotional response to black oppression, and though as individuals they may have been aware of this, the assimilationist atmosphere in the Party, as well as their own political ambitions, probably discouraged them from calling attention to it in any systematic way.[3]

What did black Harlemites make of their behavior? For most blacks, the salient feature of Party life was the prospect of daily, intimate contact with *whites,* an experience so unfamiliar that they initially felt little need to draw ethnic distinctions. In the Harlem Party of the early '30s, it is possible that few individuals, black or white, could confidently separate the Jewish cadre from the gentile; with anglicization, names were not a guide, and American-born Jews presented too great a variety of physical types to be identified on appearance alone. Unless Jewish Communists called attention to themselves as Jews, which they did not, their presence did not immediately trigger the range of stereotypes and feelings that the term "Jew" evoked in Harlem.

With time and familiarity, blacks in the Party perhaps began to recognize certain cultural and genotypical patterns among the white cadre that they could define as "distinctively Jewish." And perhaps they began to perceive that Jews constituted an extraordinarily large element of the Party's constituency in New York. If they traveled outside Harlem — to Party summer camps, or to educational forums or rallies sponsored by Communist organizations in white neighborhoods — they would have seen the Jewish presence in the Party in a far more palpable form than in Harlem.[4]

But such familiarity did not, in the '30s at least, generate a great deal of antisemitism. It is striking that not one prominent black person who defected from the Harlem Communist Party in the 1930s and issued public statements denouncing the Party (Herman Mackawain, Louis Campbell, Frankie Duty, Harold Williams, Hammie Snipes) mentioned Jewish domination of the Harlem Party as an issue in their departure.[5] Moreover, the most bitter and sophisticated critic of the Harlem Party during the period, Claude McKay, never mentioned Jewish influence as a force distorting Party activity.[6]

Antisemitism existed in Depression-era Harlem, but its symbolic targets, unlike those of the Coughlin movement or the German-American Bund, were not the Jewish Communist and plutocrat. Anti-Jewish hostility in Harlem centered almost exclusively around the image of the Jew as neighborhood exploiter — the small businessman or landlord who grew rich on black labor or patronage while protesting his "friendship for Negroes." In the early '30s, white Jewish Communists in Harlem, insofar as they were identifiable as such, contravened this negative image rather than reinforced it — most were young, poor, and willing to take substantial physical risks in behalf of black neighborhood residents or black victims of injustice. In addition, some courted social ostracism by marrying and dating blacks. Such individuals sometimes could be — and were — condemned for arrogance and insensitivity, but they did not make convincing exploiters, since they appeared to gain very little in a material sense from their participation in the movement.[7]

In the late 1930s, however, changes took place in the atmosphere of the Party, and in international and American politics, that made the Jewish presence in the Harlem CP more visible, and ultimately more controversial. First of all, the rise of Nazism, and of mass antisemitic movements in the United States (the most visible of which, in New York, was the Coughlin movement), made all Jews—including assimilated Jewish Communists—more aware of their vulnerability and distinctive problems. As Jews of all backgrounds and political persuasions began to mobilize against antisemitism, the Jewish cadre in the Party, though by no means unified, began to press its concerns on the Party leadership. But equally important, the logic of the Popular Front policy impelled the Party to give partial encouragement to the resurgence of Jewish identity among its cadre and to try to draw the Jewish American community as a whole into the "united front against fascism." This had two immediate consequences: first, the Party as an organization began to devote an important part of its efforts to combating antisemitism in the United States, and secondly, it encouraged the Jewish subculture attached to the Party, which had been in semihibernation since the assault on the foreign language federations, to promote a "progressive Jewish identity" as a positive good.[8]

These developments had a subtle but important impact on the Party in Harlem. In the last two years of the Popular Front, black Communists, when challenging antisemitism in Harlem, began to speak of a distinctive Jewish contribution to labor and civil rights, and to call for "unity of the Negro people and the Jewish people in the struggle against fascism." In a speech before the National Council of Jewish Communists in December, 1938, James Ford declared: "... in the long struggle to build a progressive movement in America, which is today flowering, which has brought more than 500,000 Negroes into the ranks of organized labor ... who more than the Jews have been instrumental in aiding this development. Or take Herndon-Scottsboro-Ethiopia-Spain. ... To their eternal credit, the Jewish people have played a prominent role in every progressive movement, in every struggle for Negro rights."[9] This is the first time, to my knowledge, that such rhetoric was ever used by a black Party leader, but it would not be the last. From this point on, the "Negro-Jewish alliance" would become a theme of increasing importance for Communists in black and Jewish neighborhoods, reaching full fruition during World War II when the "struggle against Hitlerism" became the Party's overarching political priority. Although the impact of this new line on Jewish cadre in Harlem must be the subject of conjecture, it is likely that it gave them an incentive to assign greater prominence to their own ethnic concerns, which were profound and traumatic, and to define their ethnic background as being central to their Communist beliefs and their support for racial equality.[10]

Within Harlem, the Party's open espousal of a "Negro-Jewish alliance," and its increasing vigilance against manifestations of antisemitism, served to highlight the prominence of Jews in the Communist left and in protests against racial discrimination. In some instances, this heightened positive feelings toward Jews. Adam Clayton Powell, Jr., writing in 1945, claimed that the participation of Jews in radical causes affecting blacks had been an effective counterweight to the antisemitic agitation of some black nationalists: "The Scottsboro case was the first successful refutation of the anti-semitic propaganda with which the Negro had been bombarded. The recent fight of Jews in the trade union movement for Negro rights has been the crowning touch."[11] Benjamin J. Davis, Jr., in his autobiography, also spoke of a special affinity of Jews for progressive causes, and claimed that the Jewish vote had been central to his election to the city council.[12] And Paul Robeson, the left's premier black artist, spoke often of his "especially close bond with the Jewish people," (his son recalled that the "Jewish cultural tradition" had "always been a part of my family's cultural heritage") and prominently featured Yiddish songs in his concert repertoire.[13]

But among some blacks who locked horns with the Communist Party, or had bad experience with it—and this was particularly true among black nationalists—the Party's increasing emphasis on the Jewish presence in the left helped encourage a reformulation of existing antisemitic ideology in a manner that made "Communism" part of the litany of grievances that blacks held against Jews. This phenomenon remained an undercurrent during the late '30s—indeed, it is hard to get evidence from the black press that it existed at all. But occasionally, in a manuscript collection, one comes across a letter, or a leaflet, which directly or indirectly invokes the images of the Jewish Communist as an "exploiter,"[14] Within the NAACP files, for example, I found a memorandum of an interview between George Murphy, Jr., and Greta Steward (dated November 16, 1939), in which she complains about persecution by Jewish Communists on the Federal Theatre Project: "She claims that the entire labor set up is controlled by Jews who are for the most part communistic, keeps Negroes out of white collar jobs. She says she has been told that unless she joined the Communistic party and cooperated with those seemingly in control of the union that they would see to it that she would get no home relief. She claims that . . . the communistic-Jews saw to it that she was kept off Home Relief from the 1st of August . . . until two weeks ago. . . . A Miss Alberta Heneley . . . has asked her to go to a meeting of the United Afro-American Union . . . at which time the Union is to discuss ways and means of combatting the control of union labor by Jews and particularly communistic Jews."[15]

Such a letter probably could not have been produced five years before. What gave its views resonance—albeit with a small segment of the Harlem community—was not only the heightened consciousness of Harlemites about the Jewish role in the Communist Party, but a substantial growth in the Party's political and economic power. During the Popular Front years, the Party, for the first time, began to assume leadership of important trade unions, and exert power in some city agencies, in a manner that involved control over jobs and resources. In addition, some Communist union leaders began to command decent, though not ostentatious salaries, and college-educated Communist teachers, technicians, and social workers began to find employment at an income commensurate with their education (a phenomenon which accelerated with wartime recovery). In New York especially, the proportion of middle-class whites in the Party increased steadily, rising to over 50 percent by the end of the war. As a result of these changes in the Party's power and social composition, white Communists in Harlem no longer appeared to be an undifferentiated mass of impassioned street agitators and youthful idealists; some were hard-nosed, pragmatic reformers who were confident in the exercise of power and commanded a visibly higher standard of living than the average Harlemite. That these individuals were often "Jewish" as well as white, and that they increasingly emphasized their Jewish identity in response to the horrors of the Nazi epoch, touched a sore nerve among some blacks who were alienated from the Party. Regarding the CP as a new kind of establishment, they perceived the involvement of Jewish Communists in black life as yet another example of Jews preying on the weakness of blacks to their economic advantage.[16]

This viewpoint, it should be emphasized, only began to surface in the late '30s, and it remained extremely marginal within the overall pattern of Harlem life: not one important black intellectual gave it systematic expression, not one black newspaper articulated it editorially. On the whole, Jewish Communists in Harlem were probably regarded more favorably than not, and some of them, especially those who taught in the Harlem schools, were viewed with great respect and affection.[17]

But with the advantage of hindsight, one can see patterns emerging which would eventually produce explicit black-Jewish tension within the Harlem Party in the late 1940s and impart a problematic quality to black-Jewish relations within the American left. Bluntly put, the more Jews in the Communist Party became preoccupied with their own ethnic survival and identity (although for the most compelling historical reasons), and the more their economic status and political power became visibly greater than the mass of blacks, the more their presence in Harlem would become a source of controversy. Rising nationalist feeling among Jews, coming at a time of rising nationalist feeling among blacks, inevitably evoked a drama of conflicting claims which Communists had avoided in the 1930s, exacerbated by perceived (and real) differences in status.[18] Appalled by Nazism and the Holocaust, inspired and rendered anxious by the creation of the state of Israel in the midst of hostile Arab peoples, Jewish radicals could hardly be blamed for becoming preoccupied with their own "burden of history." But blacks had their own burden to work out, and the "Negro-Jewish alliance," though it would remain visible in numerous nooks and crannies of movements for social change, would henceforth be subject to considerable strain.

NOTES

1. Articles discussing Jewish influence in black life can be found in *New York Age,* Oct. 20, 1934; *New York Amsterdam News,* July 16, 1939, Aug. 27, 1938, Dec. 3, 1938.

2. Interview with Richard B. Moore, Nov. 14, 1973; interview with Alice Citron, Aug. 20, 1979; interview with Morris Schappes, Aug. 24, 1979; interview with Abner Berry, Nov. 20, 1973; George Charney, *A Long Journey* (New York: Quadrangle, 1968), p. 56.

3. On the assimilationist pressures experienced by Jewish Communists in the late '20s and early '30s, see Paul Buhle, "Jews and American Communism: The Cultural Question," *Radical History Review,* 23 (Dec., 1980), 21-22; Arthur Leibman, *Jews and the Left* (New York: John Wiley and Sons, 1978), pp. 493–505; "Readers' Forum on Jews in the International Brigades," *Jewish Currents,* 35 (May, 1931), 31-34; "Ethnic Chauvinism vs. Ethnic Progressivism," *Jewish Currents,* 35 (Oct., 1981), 29.

4. On the size and breadth of the Jewish subculture surrounding the Communist Party in New York City, see Leibman, *Jews and the Left,* pp. 305-8; "The Utopia We Knew: The Coops," *Cultural Correspondence,* 6-7 (Spring, 1978), 95-97.

5. Public denunciations of the Party by these important individuals are found in *New York Amsterdam News,* Aug. 17, 1935, Oct. 22, 1938, Oct. 29, 1938, Feb. 18, 1939; *New York Age,* Jan. 21, 1939; *Pittsburgh Courier,* Mar. 18, 1939.

6. McKay in fact holds up Jews as a model for blacks in developing an effective ethnic strategy in the United States. See *New York Amsterdam News,* June 5, 1938, and McKay, *Harlem Negro Metropolis* (1940; rpt. New York: Harcourt, Brace, Jovanovich, 1968), pp. 217–18.

7. On the ideology of the Coughlin movement, and the German-American Bund, see Geoffrey S. Smith, *To Save a Nation: American Counter Subversives, the New Deal, and the Coming of World War II* (New York: Basic Books, 1973), pp. 87–100, 122–38. For two classic statements of Harlem's "grievances against Jews," one by Adam Clayton Powell, Jr., and one by Arnold Demille, see *New York Amsterdam News,* July 16, 1938, Dec. 3, 1938.

8. On the influence of the Coughlin movement in New York City, and its impact on Jewish sensibilities, see Ronald H. Bayor, *Neighbors in Conflict: The Irish, Germans, Jews and Italians of New York, 1929—1941* (Baltimore: Johns Hopkins University Press, 1978), pp. 94–107. On the resurgence of Jewish consciousness among Jews in the Communist Party, and the leadership's partial encouragement of it, see Leibman, *Jews and the Left,* pp. 317, 350–51; Nathan Glazer, *The Social Basis of American Communism* (New York: Harcourt, Brace,

& World, 1961), pp. 160–61; Buhle, "Jews and American Communism," 22–26; Harold Cruse, *Crisis of the Negro Intellectual* (New York: William Morrow, 1967), pp. 148, 165–68.

9. James W. Ford, *Anti-Semitism and the Struggle for Democracy* (New York: Council of Jewish Communists, 1939), p. 19.

10. For a typical invocation of the "Negro-Jewish alliance" as a counterweight to anti-Jewish feeling in Harlem, see *Daily Worker,* May 5, 1940. George Charney also mentions this as a feature of Party strategy in *A Long Journey,* p. 56.

11. Adam Clayton Powell, Jr., *Marching Blacks* (New York: Dial Press, 1945), p. 66.

12. Benjamin J. Davis, Jr., *Communist Councilman from Harlem* (New York: International Publishers, 1969), pp. 106–7.

13. The Robeson quote, and an elaboration of his grounds for identification with Jewish culture comes from "Bonds of Brotherhood," *Jewish Life* (Nov., 1954) as quoted in Philip S. Foner, ed., *Paul Robeson Speaks: Writings, Speeches, Interviews, 1918–1974* (New York: Brunner/Mazel, 1978), p. 392. His son's recollections come from Paul Robeson, Jr., "How My Father Last Met Itzik Feffer," *Jewish Currents,* 35 (Nov., 1981), 4.

14. Leaflet, "Racketeers At Work," no date, UNIA Papers, Reel 6, Box 14; leaflet, "Are You Entitled to Relief?" no date, *ibid.*

15. Memorandum, from Mr. Murphy to Mr. Marshall, Nov. 16, 1939, NAACP Papers, C 298.

16. On the changing social composition of the Communist Party in New York, and the concentration of American-born Jewish Communists in white-collar professions, see Glazer, *The Social Basis of American Communism,* pp. 116–17, 138, 140–51; Leibman, *Jews and the Left,* pp. 368–75, 433, 463–65; Irving Howe and Lewis Coser, *The American Communist Party: A Critical History* (New York, Praeger, 1962), p. 421. Antipathy to "Communist Jews" in Harlem is at the moment hard to document. Yet the few leaflets that I have seen from nationalist organizations in the late '30s or early '40s, and the letter I previously quoted from the NAACP files suggest that such feelings did have some currency. A full analysis of this issue, however, must await a careful examination of leaflets, pamphlets, and newspapers produced by nationalist organizations during the war years and after, since the major black newspapers simply did not give much space to nationalist arguments and viewpoints.

17. Interview with Rev. David Licorish, May 11, 1978.

18. On the intensification of Jewish consciousness among the Party's Jewish cadre and following after World War II, see Leibman, *Jews and the Left,* pp. 507–14. On emerging black-Jewish tension with the Party, in Harlem and elsewhere, after World War II, see Charney, *A Long Journey,* p. 56, and Cruse, *Crisis of the Negro Intellectual,* pp. 158–59, 163, 169–70.

Bibliographical Essay

WRITING THE HISTORY of the American Communist Party, or any section of it, is a complex task. Because the Party did not keep written records of its deliberations and preserve them for posterity, there is no one collection of documents that the scholar can turn to to shed light on its decision-making process, or the rationale for changes in its leadership. As a result, the historian must reconstruct the inner workings of Party life from a large combination of sources, among them articles from the Party press, government documents, manuscript collections of organizations the Party controlled, manuscript collections of organizations the Party competed against, articles from newspapers in communities where the Party was active, and in-depth interviews with former party organizers and leaders.

Fortunately, the activities of the Party's Harlem section generated a great deal of information in most of these domains. Because the Harlem Communist Party was a "national concentration point" of the CPUSA, its activities were extensively discussed in the Party press. Because it was an important political force in Harlem, its role was debated in both Harlem-based newspapers and black periodicals with a national audience. And because the Party competed so openly—and at times so effectively—with major black organizations, its activities are sometimes discussed quite extensively in their manuscript collections. Interview data was also readily available. I was fortunate enough to begin my research at a time—the late '60s and the early '70s—when many of the leading figures from the Harlem CP of the 1930s were alive, and willing to talk. Had I begun my research ten years earlier, when the McCarthy Era was just passing and the Cold War was at its height, most of my informants would have refused to talk with me for fear of jeopardizing their careers and/or their families. Had I begun my research ten years later, I would have found that many of informants were dead, or too ill to be interviewed. But I started at a time when many of the key people I contacted were anxious to tell their side of the story, and their cooperation has added incomparably to the richness of this account.

The following is a brief assessment of the sources that made this book possible.

Manuscripts and Primary Documents

Several manuscript collections in the Schomburg Collection in Harlem were essential to this study. The papers of the International Labor Defense, which are now on microfilm, provided extensive documentation of the Party's conflict with the NAACP over the Scottsboro case, and of the activities of protest organizations that the Party sponsored in Harlem in behalf of the Scottsboro defendants. It also contains a huge clipping file on the Scottsboro case, and some publications of Communist organizations not directly related to Scottsboro, including the only copies I have ever seen of *Hunger Fighter,* the newspaper of the Unemployed Councils of New York City.

The papers of the National Negro Congress, an organization in which the Party was quite influential, contain an extensive correspondence file which rarely touches on Party policy directly, but reveals the threads of political influence that linked the Party, and Party-affiliated trade unions, to the leadership of the Congress. Letters from Harlem Party activists, as well as flyers produced by Party organizations in Harlem, appear extensively in the collection.

The papers of the New York Division of the Universal Negro Improvement Association not only contain important documents produced by nationalist organizations with which the Party competed, but also document the Party's efforts to form a "united front" with the UNIA during the middle and late 1930s. There is an especially good collection of leaflets, pamphlets, and clippings from Ethiopian defense coalitions in which the Party participated.

The papers of the Negro Labor Committee, headed by Frank Crosswaith, contain good documentation of the often tense relationship between Socialist and Communist trade unionists in Harlem during the Depression. The Federal Writers Project Papers, largely consisting of unpublished essays and memoranda on Harlem life, contain useful background information on Harlem churches, fraternal organizations, and nationalist groups.

Two manuscript collections outside the Schomburg Collection also proved essential to this research. The papers of the National Association for the Advancement of Colored People, located in the Library of Congress, not only provide useful documentation of the impact of Communist Scottsboro agitation on the NAACP's Harlem "constituency," but shed light on Communist activities in a number of other spheres, among them the work of the National Negro Congress, the campaign for the anti-lynching bill, and efforts to improve conditions 'for blacks in the New York City school system. The Fiorello La Guardia Papers, located in the Municipal Archives of New York City, contain several boxes of leaflets, pamphlets, and shop papers produced by Communist organizations in Harlem, collected following the Harlem Riot of 1935. They also contain transcripts of some of the hearings of the Mayor's Commission on Conditions in Harlem, formed after the riot, as well as several documents relating to the 1934 "Scottsboro Riot" in Harlem.

Less important, but still useful, were the personal papers of Robert Minor, at Columbia University, and Earl Browder, at Syracuse University. Browder's collection seems to have been stripped of controversial items, but Minor's contained some scattered documents shedding light on the evolution of the Party's position on the Negro Question, particularly in the late '20s and early '30s.

In addition, some mention should be made of the collection of Communist Party pamphlets at three libraries in New York: the Schomburg Collection, the New York Public Library (main branch), and the Tamiment Library at New York University. The Schomburg Collection also has a full collection of the government reports produced following the Harlem Riot of 1935, including the report of the Mayor's Commission on Conditions in Harlem (never officially released, but reprinted by the *Amsterdam News*) and the two reports, and public hearings, of the New York State Temporary Commission on Conditions of the Urban Colored Population.

Finally, I would like to thank two individuals, Martin Glaberman and Harry Haywood, for allowing me to xerox items from their extensive collections of pamphlets and documents relating to the Communist position on the Negro Question.

Newspapers and Periodicals

A good portion of the information in this book derived from a careful reading of Communist publications and the black press. Among Communist publications, by far the most useful source was the *Daily Worker*. I read through every single issue of it from January, 1928, through February, 1942, and found it to be filled with information about Communist Party "Negro work" and Communist activities in Harlem. Of equal importance for the years 1927 to 1936 was the publication variously titled the *Negro Champion,* the *Liberator,* the *Harlem Liberator,* and the *Negro Liberator,* which contained articles on the theoretical issues which affected Party Negro work and accounts of day-to-day Party organizing in Harlem. Several other Party publications provided essential information: *Communist,* the Party theoretical journal; *Party Organizer,* a publication discussing problems faced by Party cadre in workplace and neighborhood organizing; *Young Worker,* the weekly newspaper of the Young Communist League; *Young Communist Review,* a monthly magazine published by the same organization; *International Press Correspondence,* a Comintern publication that reproduced speeches and resolutions from the Sixth and Seventh World Congresses; *Negro Worker,* a publication of the International Trade Union Committee of Negro Workers; and *Labor Defender,* a publication of the International Labor Defense. All of these publications are on microfilm or in bound versions reprinted by Greenwood Press. The most important source on Party literary and cultural policy was the *New Masses,* which is preserved on microfiche.

Among black newspapers, the most useful were the *New York Amsterdam News* and the *New York Age,* both of which are available on microfilm for the entire length of this study. Also helpful was the *Negro World,* the weekly publication of the Garvey movement, available on microfilm from the early '20s through 1933; the *Interstate Tatler,* a Harlem "gossip sheet" that contained some political discussion; and the *Spoken Word,* a publication of the Father Divine movement. I consulted the *Pittsburgh Courier* and the *Baltimore Afro-American* for information on important events such as the Scottsboro case, the Harlem Riot, and the Ethiopian defense protest, since both papers had Harlem columnists and covered events in that community.

The black periodicals most helpful to me were *Crisis* and *Opportunity,* publications of the NAACP and the Urban League respectively, each of which contains a good summary of the main currents of Afro-American social thought during the Depression years, as well as a careful evaluation of the Communist challenge. Also useful, for the years 1935 to 1941, was *Interracial Review,* a publication of the Catholic Interracial Society.

Among "white," non-Communist publications, the only one which proved consistently useful was the *New York Times,* which contained extensive coverage of important events in Harlem. Other New York newspapers such as the *New York Herald Tribune* and the *New York Post* were consulted intermittently, usually when articles appeared in the clipping file of the International Labor Defense or other organizations whose manuscript collections I examined.

Interviews and Oral History

Interviews with Communists active in Harlem during the Depression, or with people who closely observed Communist activities in Harlem, have been central to this project from its inception. Not only did they provide me with important information that was not "in the public record," but they helped sensitize me to nuances of Party life that made the documentary record read in an entirely different way.

Three people deserve particular mention for helping me get a firm grounding in this project: Abner Berry, Theodore Bassett, and Harry Haywood. Leading black figures in the Communist Party during the '30s (Berry was a section organizer in Harlem, Bassett was the educational director in Harlem, and Haywood was the Party's leading black theoretician), they spent long hours with answering questions I raised, evaluating materials I had written, and engaging in a dialogue with me about the theoretical issues my research raised. Their taped comments are amply cited in the text, but their collective persona—marked by intelligence, sophistication, and humor—did much to destroy, in my mind at least, the oft propagated image of the black Communist as a "dupe," a "frontman," or a naive victim of white manipulation.

The following are the individuals who allowed me to interview them during the course of this project:

James Allen	James Jackson
Herbert Aptheker	Howard Johnson
Theodore Bassett (four interviews)	Rev. David Licorish
Abner Berry (seven interviews)	Ernest Rice McKinney
George Charney	Richard B. Moore
Alice Citron	Henry Lee Moon
Edna Coleman	William Patterson
Samuel Coleman	Louise Thompson Patterson
Leon Davis	Jibby Needleman
Theodore Draper	Sam Neuberger
Philip Foner	Morris Schappes
Max Gordon	Edith Segal
Solomon Harper	Abe Shtob
Harry Haywood (four interviews)	William Weinstone
John Hammond	

General Studies and Firsthand Accounts

Prior to this work, there were two systematic attempts to evaluate the work of the Communist Party in Harlem: Claude McKay, *Harlem: Negro Metropolis* (1940; rpt. New York: Harcourt, Brace, Jovanovich, 1968), and Harold Cruse, *Crisis of the Negro Intellectual* (New York: William Morrow, 1967). Both works are provocative and theoretically suggestive, but have a polemical tone and are based upon a rather superficial reading of primary sources. Wilson Record's general study, *The Negro and the Communist Party* (Chapel Hill: University of North Carolina Press,

1951), is more exhaustively documented, but offers a conspiratorial picture of Communist "Negro work" that misses some of the ambiguities of the black-Communist encounter. Mark Solomon, "Red and Black: Negroes and Communism, 1929–1932," (Ph.D. dissertation, Harvard University, 1972), is far more carefully researched and subtly argued, but it covers only a relatively brief time period.

Several important Communists active in Harlem have written autobiographies, but they are of uneven quality. William Patterson, *The Man Who Cried Genocide* (New York: International Publishers, 1971) contains an excellent description of Patterson's life in Harlem during the 1920s, but loses its subtlety when he begins to discuss his activities as a Party leader during the Depression. Benjamin Davis, Jr., *Communist Councilman from Harlem* (New York: International Publishers, 1969) is even weaker, touching on no inner Party controversies and presenting Davis's Party career as a mixture of unbroken triumphs and relentless persecution. George Charney, *A Long Journey* (New York: Quadrangle, 1968) is a far more thoughtful work, containing one excellent chapter on his activities as an "org. sec." in Harlem from 1936 to 1939. Charney evaluates his own and the Party's weaknesses with considerable sensitivity. Harry Haywood, *Black Bolshevik: Autobiography of an Afro-American Communist* (Chicago: Liberator Press, 1978) is also a valuable book, containing a fascinating account of Haywood's years in the Soviet Union and of the evolution of Party policy on the Negro Question. One need not agree with Haywood's conclusions (he is something of an unreconstructed Stalinist) to learn from Haywood's portrait of inner Party life, key theoretical debates, and important Party personalities.

To date, there is still no general work dealing with Harlem in the 1930s. For texture and background, McKay, *Harlem: Negro Metropolis,* and Roi Ottley, *New World A-Coming* (1943; rpt. New York: Arno, 1968) are helpful, but both are more journalistic than scholarly. Four works on Harlem in the 1920s were quite useful to me: Nathan Huggins, *Harlem Renaissance* (New York: Oxford University Press, 1971); Gilbert Osofsky, *Harlem, The Making of a Ghetto* (New York: Harper and Row, 1968); David Levering Lewis, *When Harlem Was in Vogue* (New York: Alfred A. Knopf, 1981); and Theodore Kornweibel, Jr., *No Crystal Stair: Black Life and the Messenger, 1917–1928* (Westport: Greenwood Press, 1976).

On black protest in the 1930s, several works were helpful: Jervis Anderson, *A. Philip Randolph: A Biographical Portrait* (New York: Harcourt, Brace, Jovanovich, 1973); Raymond Wolters, *Negroes and the Great Depression: The Problem of Economic Recovery* (Westport: Greenwood Press, 1970); and August Meier and Elliott Rudwick, "The Origins of Nonviolent Direct Action in Afro-American Protest: A Note on Historical Discontinuities," in *Along the Color Line: Explorations in the Black Experience* (Urbana: University of Illinois Press, 1976). Melville Weiss, "Don't Buy Where You Can't Work," (M.A. thesis, Columbia University, 1941) is still the best discussion of nationalist boycott movements in Harlem. Harvard Sitkoff, *New Deal for Blacks, The Emergence of Civil Rights as a National Issue: The Depression Decade* (New York: Oxford University Press, 1978) provides an excellent discussion of the larger policy issues that affected black Americans throughout the Depression period.

On the history of the Communist Party of the United States, the books I found most useful were: Theodore Draper, *American Communism and Soviet Russia* (New York: Viking Press, 1960), which contains a section dealing with the origins of Party policy on the Negro Question; Bert Cochran, *Labor and Communism: The Conflict that Shaped American Unions* (Princeton: Princeton University Press, 1977); and two books which deal most suggestively with the Popular Front, Joseph Starobin, *American Communism in Crisis, 1943–1957* (Cambridge: Harvard University Press, 1972), and Al Richmond, *A Long View From the Left* (Boston: Houghton Mifflin, 1973).

On the ethnic dimensions of Communist Party participation, Nathan Glazer, *The Social Basis of American Communism* (New York: Harcourt, Brace, and World, 1961), and Arthur Leibman, *Jews and the Left* (New York: John Wiley and Sons, 1978), proved to be extremely helpful.

On the history of the Communist International, one book is unparalleled: Fernando Claudin, *The Communist Movement: From Comintern to Cominform* (Hammondsworth, England: Penguin Books, 1975). My interpretation of events in the international Communist movement rests heavily on Claudin's work.

Index

Abbott, Robert, 182

Abraham Lincoln Brigade, 197

Abyssinian Baptist Church, 21–22, 76, 79, 84, 123, 139, 147

African Blood Brotherhood for African Liberation and Redemption, 3, 17–18; attitude toward UNIA, 7–8; demise of, 10; founding of, 5–6, 7; recruitment to CP from, 5

African Patriotic League, 118, 138

Afro-American history. See Black history

Alabama State Supreme Court, Scottsboro case and, 64, 66, 70

Alexander, Charles, 36

Allen, Gerald, 242

Allen, James Egert, 96, 123, 146, 176, 299, 309

All People's Party, 227; in elections of 1936, 233, 234; and formation of ALP, 232–33; founding of, 231–32

Alpha Phi Alpha fraternity, National Negro Congress and, 179

Amalgamated Clothing Workers Union: and formation of ALP, 232; and National Negro Congress, 181

American Federation of Labor (AFL): and American Negro Labor Congress, 13; and CP united front policy, 80

American Federation of Teachers, 195; and ALP, 233; expulsion of left-wing locals from, 309–10; and Harlem schools, 214–16

American Labor Party (ALP), 172; attitude toward black leadership and candidates, 236, 237; and black music, 212; CP and, 227, 234–38, 240–42, 245–47; in elections of 1936, 233, 234; in elections of 1937, 237–38; in elections of 1938, 240–42; in elections of 1939, 245; formation of, 232–33; after Nazi-Soviet Pact, 288; and Powell's election of City Council, 312;

split in, 246–47; and Tammany machine, 244; trade union support for, 232–33

American League Against War and Fascism, 129, 155, 174–75, 196, 197–98

American Legion, 121

American Negro Labor Congress, 13–14

American Newspaper Guild, and boycott of *Amsterdam News*, 176–77

American Scottsboro Committee, conflict with ILD, 132–34

Amsterdam News, 5, 38, 196; on agitation for reforms, 264; on ALP in 1938 elections, 241; on antidiscrimination bill, 243; attacks on CP in 1934, 131–32; on black WPA employment, 194; boycott of, 176–77; on boycott movement, 122; on causes of Harlem Riot, 144–45; on CP anti-eviction strategies, 41; on CP defense work, 75; on CP influence in WPA projects, 205; on CP involvement in Scottsboro case, 61, 64–65, 66, 71, 74; on CP organization of unemployed, 205; on CP speeches at founding convention of National Negro Congress, 183; on Crosswaith candidacy, 246; on delegates to Third Convention of National Negro Congress, 296; on demonstration including CPers and Father Divine supporters, 129–30; on economic conditions in Harlem in 1939, 291; on Engdahl, 74–75; on Ethiopia defense movement march, 157–58; on Ford, 99; and formation of American Scottsboro Committee, 132–34; on Gonzales funeral demonstration, 40; Harlem CP relations with, 96; on Harlem Riot, 143; on Harlem unemployed and relief recipients, 255; on interracial unionism, 263; and March on Washington movement, 311; on Moscow trials, 198; on NAACP criticism of ILD, 82–83; and National Negro Congress, 180, 199; on

A Note on the Author

MARK NAISON received a Ph.D. degree in history from Columbia University in 1976. He is currently associate professor of Afro-American studies at Fordham University and director of its urban studies program. A corresponding editor of *Radical America* and the *Journal of Ethnic Studies,* Dr. Naison has written numerous articles on Afro-American radicalism, ethnic relations, and the history of sports. In addition to his scholarly activities, he has worked as a community organizer in Harlem, the Upper West Side, and the Bronx. He currently serves as chairman of the board of Sports for the People, a sports advocacy group based in the South Bronx.

Selected Grove Press Paperbacks

17106-3 BRECHT, BERTOLT / Mother Courage and Her Children / $1.95
17472-0 BRECHT, BERTOLT / Threepenny Opera / $2.45
17393-7 BRETON, ANDRE / Nadja / $3.95
17439-9 BULGAKOV, MIKHAIL / The Master and Margarita / $3.95
17108-X BURROUGHS, WILLIAM S. / Naked Lunch / $2.95
17749-5 BURROUGHS, WILLIAM S. / The Soft Machine, Nova Express, The Wild Boys: Three Novels / $5.95
62488-2 CLARK, AL, ed. / The Film Year Book 1984 / $12.95
17038-5 CLEARY, THOMAS / The Original Face: An Anthology of Rinzai Zen / $4.95
17735-5 CLEVE, JOHN / The Crusader: Books I and II / $4.95
17411-9 CLURMAN, HAROLD, ed. / Nine Plays of the Modern Theatre (Waiting for Godot by Samuel Beckett, The Visit by Friedrich Durrenmatt, Tango by Slawomlr Mrozek, The Caucasian Chalk Circle by Bertolt Brecht, The Balcony by Jean Genet, Rhinoceros by Eugene Ionesco, American Buffalo by David Mamet, The Birthday Party by Harold Pinter, and Rosencrantz and Guildenstern Are Dead by Tom Stoppard) / $11.95
62024-0 Coe, Sue and Metz, Holly / How to Commit Suicide in South Africa / $5.00
17962-5 COHN, RUBY / New American Dramatists: 1960-1980 / $7.95
17971-4 COOVER, ROBERT / Spanking the Maid / $4.95
17535-2 COWARD, NOEL / Three Plays by Noel Coward (Private Lives, Hay Fever, Blithe Spirit) / $4.50
17740-1 CRAFTS, KATHY & HAUTHER, BRENDA / How to Beat the System: The Student's Guide to Good Grades / $3.95
17219-1 CUMMINGS, E. E. / 100 Selected Poems / $1.95
17329-5 DOOLITTLE, HILDA / The Selected Poems of H.D. / $8.95
17863-7 DOSS, MARGARET PATTERSON / San Francisco at Your Feet (Second Revised Edition) / $4.95
17398-8 DOYLE, RODGER & REDDING, JAMES / The Complete Food Handbook. Revised and Updated ed. / $2.95
17987-0 DURAS, MARGUERITE / Four Novels (The Afternoon of Mr. Andesmas, 10:30 on a Summer Night, Moderato Cantabile, The Square) / $9.95
17246-9 DURRENMATT, FRIEDRICH / The Physicists / $3.95
17239-6 DURRENMATT, FRIEDRICH / The Visit / $4.95
1799-0 FANON, FRANTZ / Black Skin, White Masks / $6.95
17327-9 FANON, FRANTZ / The Wretched of the Earth / $4.95
17754-1 FAWCETT, ANTHONY / John Lennon: One Day at a Time, A Personal Biography (Revised Edition) / $8.95
17902-1 FEUERSTEIN, GEORG / The Essence of Yoga / $3.95
62455-6 FRIED, GETTLEMAN, LEVENSON & PECKENHAM, eds. / Guatemala in Rebellion: Unfinished History / $8.95
17483-6 FROMM, ERICH / The Forgotten Language / $3.95
62114-X GARWOOD, DARRELL / Under Cover: Thirty-five Years of CIA Deception / $8.95

17222-1   GELBER, JACK / The Connection / $3.95
17390-2   GENET, JEAN / The Maids and Deathwatch, Two Plays / $3.95
17470-4   GENET, JEAN / The Miracle of the Rose / $3.95
17903-X   GENET, JEAN / Our Lady of the Flowers / $2.45
17956-0   GETTLEMAN, LACEFIELD, MENASHE, MERMELSTEIN, &
          RADOSH (eds.) / El Salvador: Central America in the New Cold
          War / $8.95
17994-3   GIBBS, LOIS MARIE / Love Canal: My Story / $6.95
17648-0   GIRODIAS, MAURICE, ed. / The Olympia Reader / $4.50
17067-9   GOMBROWICZ, WITOLD / Three Novels: Ferdydurke,
          Pornografia, and Cosmos / $9.95
17764-9   GOVER, BOB / One Hundred Dollar Misunderstanding / $2.95
17832-7   GREENE, GERALD & CAROLINE / SM: The Last Taboo / $2.95
62490-4   GUITAR PLAYER MAGAZINE / The Guitar Player Book (Revised
          and Updated Edition) / $11.95
17124-1   HARRIS, FRANK / My Life and Loves / $4.95
17936-6   HARWOOD, RONALD / The Dresser / $5.95
17653-7   HAVEL, VACLAV / The Memorandum / $5.95
17022-9   HAYMAN, RONALD / How to Read a Play / $2.95
17125-X   HOCHHUTH, ROLF / The Deputy / $3.95
62115-8   HOLMES, BURTON / The Olympian Games in Athens: The First
          Modern Olympics, 1896 / $6.95
17241-8   HUMPHREY, DORIS / The Art of Making Dances / $9.95
17075-X   INGE, WILLIAM / Four Plays (Come Back, Little Sheba, Picnic,
          Bus Stop, The Dark at the Top of the Stairs) / $5.95
17267-1   IONESCO, EUGENE / Exit the King / $2.95
17209-4   IONESCO, EUGENE / Four Plays (The Bald Soprano, The Lesson,
          The Chairs, Jack or The Submission) / $4.95
17805-X   IONESCO, EUGENE / Macbett / $5.95
17226-4   IONESCO, EUGENE / Rhinoceros & Other Plays / $4.95
17081-4   JAMES, HENRY / The Sacred Fount / $2.95
17077-6   JAMES, HENRY / Italian Hours / $2.95
17485-2   JARRY, ALFRED / The Ubu Plays (Ubu Rex, Ubu Cuckolded,
          Ubu Enchained) / $7.95
62123-9   JOHNSON, CHARLES / Oxherding Tale / $6.95
62124-7   JORGENSEN, ELIZABETH WATKINS & HENRY IRVIN / Eric
          Berne, Master Gamesman: A Transactional Biography / $9.95
17200-0   KEENE, DONALD / Japanese Literature: An Introduction for
          Western Readers / $2.25
17221-3   KEENE, DONALD, ed. / Anthology of Japanese Literature:
          Earliest Era to Mid-19th Century / $7.95
17278-7   KEROUAC, JACK / Dr. Sax / $3.95
17171-3   KEROUAC, JACK / Lonesome Traveler / $2.95
17287-6   KEROUAC, JACK / Mexico City Blues / $5.95
17437-2   KEROUAC, JACK / Satori in Paris / $2.25
17035-0   KERR, CARMEN / Sex for Women Who Want to Have Fun and
          Loving Relationships With Equals / $7.95

17981-1   KINGSLEY, PHILIP / The Complete Hair Book: The Ultimate Guide to Your Hair's Health and Beauty / $8.95
62424-6   LAWRENCE, D.H. / Lady Chatterley's Lover / $3.50
17600-6   LESSER, MICHAEL, M.D. / Nutrition and Vitamin Therapy / $7.95
17178-0   LESTER, JULIUS / Black Folktales / $4.95
17481-X   LEWIS, MATTHEW / The Monk / $5.95
17391-0   LINSSEN, ROBERT / Living Zen / $8.95
62413-0   LORCA, FEDERICO / Poet in New York / $6.95
62429-7   MALCOLM X (Breitman, ed.) / Malcolm X Speaks / $3.95
17023-7   MALRAUX, ANDRE / The Conquerors / $3.95
17068-7   MALRAUX, ANDRE / Lazarus / $2.95
17093-8   MALRAUX, ANDRE / Man's Hope / $6.95
17016-4   MAMET, DAVID / American Buffalo / $3.95
62049-6   MAMET, DAVID / Glengarry, Glen Ross / $6.95
17040-7   MAMET, DAVID / A Life in the Theatre / $6.95
17043-1   MAMET, DAVID / Sexual Perversity in Chicago & The Duck Variations / $5.95
17471-2   MILLER, HENRY / Black Spring / $4.95
17760-6   MILLER, HENRY / Tropic of Cancer / $3.95
17295-7   MILLER, HENRY / Tropic of Capricorn / $3.95
17765-7   MISHIMA, YUKIO / Sun and Steel / $4.95
17933-1   MROZEK, SLAWOMIR / Three Plays: Striptease, Tango, Vatzlav / $12.50
17869-6   NERUDA, PABLO / Five Decades: Poems 1925–1970, Bilingual ed. / $8.95
52270-2   NICOSIA, GERALD / Memory Babe: A Critical Biography of Jack Kerouac / $22.50
17092-X   ODETS, CLIFFORD / Six Plays (Waiting for Lefty; Awake and Sing; Golden Boy; Rocket to the Moon; Till the Day I Die; Paradise Lost) / $7.95
17650-2   OE, KENZABURO / A Personal Matter / $6.95
17002-4   OE, KENZABURO / Teach Us to Outgrow Our Madness (The Day He Himself Shall Wipe My Tears Away; Prize Stock; Teach Us to Outgrow Our Madness; Aghwee The Sky Monster) / $4.95
17242-6   PAZ, OCTAVIO / The Labyrinth of Solitude / $7.95
17084-9   PINTER, HAROLD / Betrayal / $3.95
17232-9   PINTER, HAROLD / The Birthday Party & The Room / $6.95
17251-5   PINTER, HAROLD / The Homecoming / $4.95
17539-5   POMERANCE / The Elephant Man / $4.25
62013-5   PORTWOOD, DORIS / Common Sense Suicide: The Final Right / $8.00
17658-8   REAGE, PAULINE / Story of O, Part II; Return to the Chateau / $2.25
17147-0   RECHY, JOHN / City of Night / $2.95
17130-6   RECHY, JOHN / Numbers / $3.95
17983-8   ROBBE-GRILLET, ALAIN / Djinn / $4.95

62423-8   ROBBE-GRILLET, ALAIN / For a New Novel: Essays on Fiction / $9.95

17117-9   ROBBE-GRILLET, ALAIN / The Voyeur / $2.95

17490-9   ROSSET, BARNEY, ed. / Evergreen Review Reader: 1962-1967 / $12.50

62498-X   ROSSET, PETER and VANDERMEER, JOHN / The Nicaragua Reader: Documents of a Revolution under Fire / $8.95

17446-1   RULFO, JUAN / Pedro Paramo / $2.45

17123-3   SADE, MARQUIS DE / Justine, Philosophy in the Bedroom, Eugenie de Franval, and Other Writings / $12.50

17979-X   SANTINI, ROSEMARIE / The Secret Fire: How Women Live Their Sexual Fantasies / $3.50

62495-5   SCHEFFLER, LINDA / Help Thy Neighbor: How Counseling Works and When It Doesn't / $7.95

62438-6   SCHNEEBAUM, TOBIAS / Keep The River on Your Right / $9.95

17255-8   SCHUTZ, WILLIAM C. / Joy: Expanding Human Awareness / $1.95

17467-4   SELBY, HUBERT, JR. / Last Exit to Brooklyn / $2.95

17948-X   SHAWN, WALLACE & GREGORY, ANDRE / My Dinner with Andre / $5.95

62496-3   SIEGAL AND SIEGAL / Aids: The Medical Mystery / $7.95

17887-4   SINGH, KHUSHWANT / Train to Pakistan / $3.25

17797-5   SNOW, EDGAR / Red Star Over China / $8.95

17905-6   SOPA, GESHE LHUNDUP & HOPKINS, JEFFREY / The Practice and Theory of Tibetan Buddhism / $4.95

17939-0   SRI, NISARGADATTA MAHARAJ / Seeds of Consciousness / $9.95

17923-4   STEINER, CLAUDE / Healing Alcoholism / $4.95

17926-9   STEINER, CLAUDE / The Other Side of Power / $6.95

17866-1   STOPPARD, TOM / Jumpers / $2.95

17260-4   STOPPARD, TOM / Rosencrantz and Guildenstern Are Dead / $2.25

17884-X   STOPPARD, TOM / Travesties / $3.95

17912-9   STRYK, LUCIEN, ed. / The Crane's Bill: Zen Poems of China and Japan / $4.95

17474-7   SUZUKI, D. T. / Introduction to Zen Buddhism / $2.95

17224-8   SUZUKI, D.T. / Manual of Zen Buddhism / $5.95

17599-9   THELWELL, MICHAEL / The Harder They Come: A Novel of Jamaica / $7.95

17969-2   TOOLE, JOHN KENNEDY / A Confederacy of Dunces / $3.95

17403-8   TROCCHI, ALEXANDER / Cain's Book / $3.50

62168-9   TUTUOLA, AMOS / The Palm-Wine Drinkard / $4.50

62189-1   UNGERER, TOMI / Far Out Isn't Far Enough (Illus.) / $12.95

17560-3   VITHOULKAS, GEORGE / The Science of Homeopathy / $9.50

17331-7   WALEY, ARTHUR, JR. / The Book of Songs / $9.95

17211-6   WALEY, ARTHUR, JR. / Monkey / $6.95

Black Studies Books
Published by Grove Press

GROVE PRESS, INC., 196 West Houston St., New York, N.Y. 10014

At your bookstore, or order below.

Grove Press, Inc., 196 West Houston St., New York, N.Y. 10014.

Please mail me the books checked above. I am enclosing $ _____
(No COD. Add $1.00 per book for postage and handling.)

Name _____

Address _____

City_____ State _____ Zip _____